38.50p
R
m87

Papers on Psychoanalysis

PAPERS
ON
PSYCHOANALYSIS

HANS W. LOEWALD, M.D.

New Haven and London, Yale University Press

Printed in the United States of America by Murray Printing Co., Westford, Mass.

The author gratefully acknowledges the following for permission to reprint previously published material:

The Annual of Psychoanalysis, for "Comments on Some Instinctual Manifestations of Superego Formation," vol. 1, 1973, copyright © 1973 by The Institute for Psychoanalysis of Chicago.

International Journal of Psycho-Analysis for papers first published on the dates indicated—"Ego and Reality," vol. 32, 1951; "The Problem of Defense and the Neurotic Interpretation of Reality," vol. 33, 1952; "On the Therapeutic Action of Psychoanalysis," vol. 41, 1960; "Superego and Time," vol. 43, 1962; "Some Considerations on Repetition and Repetition Compulsion," vol. 52, 1971; "On Internalization," vol. 54, 1973. All copyright © by The Institute of Psycho-Analysis, London.

International Universities Press, Inc. for "Discussion: 'The Id and the Regulatory Principles of Mental Functioning,' by Max Schur," in The Unconscious Today: Essays in Honor of Max Schur, edited by Mark Kanzer, 1971; "Perspectives on Memory," in Psychology versus Metapsychology: Psychoanalytic Essays in Memory of George Klein, Psychological Issues, vol. 9, no. 4, monograph 36, 1976; "Psychoanalytic Theory and the Psychoanalytic Process," in The Psychoanalytic Study of the Child, vol. 25, 1970, copyright © 1970 by International Universities Press, Inc.

Journal of The American Psychoanalytic Association (published by International Universities Press, Inc.) for papers first published on the dates indicated—"Hypnoid State, Repression, Abreaction, and Recollection," vol. 3, 1955; "The Transference Neurosis: Comments on the Concept and the Phenomenon," vol. 19, 1971; "Freud's Conception of the Negative Therapeutic Reaction, with Comments on Instinct Theory," vol. 20, 1972; "Psychoanalysis as an Art and the Fantasy Character of the Psychoanalytic Situation," vol. 23, 1975; "Instinct Theory, Object Relations, and Psychic-Structure Formation," vol. 26, 1978; "The Waning of the Oedipus Complex," vol. 27, 1979.

The Psychoanalytic Quarterly for papers first published on the dates indicated—"Internalization, Separation, Mourning, and the Superego," vol. 31, 1962; "Book Review: 'Psychoanalytic Concepts and the Structural Theory,' by Jacob A. Arlow and Charles Brenner," vol. 35, 1966; "Book Review: Heinz Kohut, 'The Analysis of the Self,'" vol. 42, 1973; "Book Review Essay on The Freud/Jung Letters," vol. 46, 1977; all copyright © by The Psychoanalytic Quarterly, Inc.

Yale University Press for "Primary Process, Secondary Process, and Language," in Psychoanalysis and Language, edited by Joseph H. Smith, Psychiatry and the Humanities, vol. 3, 1978, copyright © 1978 by the Forum on Psychiatry and the Humanities of the Washington School of Psychiatry; "On Motivation and Instinct Theory," in The Psychoanalytic Study of the Child, vol. 26, 1971, copyright © 1972 by Ruth Eissler, Anna Freud, Marianne Kris, Seymour Lustman; "The Experience of Time," in The Psychoanalytic Study of the Child, vol. 27, 1972, copyright © 1973 by Ruth Eissler, Anna Freud, Marianne Kris, Albert Solnit; and "Reflections on the Psychoanalytic Process and its Therapeutic Potential," in The Psychoanalytic Study of the Child, vol. 34, 1979, copyright © 1979 by Albert J. Solnit, Ruth Eissler, Anna Freud, Marianne Kris, Peter B. Neubauer.

Library of Congress Cataloging in Publication Data

Loewald, Hans W   1906–
    Papers on psychoanalysis.

    Includes bibliographical references and index.
    1. Psychoanalysis—Addresses, essays, lectures.
I. Title. [DNLM: 1. Psychoanalysis—Collected
works. WM460 L8265p]
BF173.L566   150.19'5   80–12012
ISBN 0–300–02406–1

10   9   8   7   6   5   4   3   2   1

CONTENTS

PREFACE

The papers collected here were written over a period of thirty years. They appeared in various psychoanalytic periodicals between 1951 and 1979; only a few textual and bibliographical corrections have been made. The decision to publish them in book form owes its main impetus to the urgings of a number of respected colleagues. It gives me pleasure and a sense of accomplishment to see them assembled in one volume, and I hope it will be useful to interested readers to have them available in this compact form.

Where it seemed to me indicated, I have written a few brief introductory comments on particular papers. They do not discuss or summarize content but give some information about chronology or the context in which an article was written or published. The division of the book into two sections, Concepts and Theory and The Psychoanalytic Process, corresponds to a bifurcation of my interest. At the same time, a sharp and lasting dichotomy between these two emphases is neither intended by me nor, to my mind, possible or fruitful. Therefore, assigning a given paper to one section rather than the other is more or less arbitrary; I believe it will be apparent that the main theme of most of the papers cannot be that neatly defined.

Theory and concepts, and the material of experience to which they pertain, are inextricably intertwined. In psychoanalysis it becomes increasingly clear that *interactional* processes — those that are intra-psychic and inter-psychic ones, and these two in their interactions — are the material of investigation, epitomized and highlighted in the psychoanalytic process. It is for that reason that this interactional situation itself is the subject matter par excellence. It provides the best experiential basis and testing ground for our theories.

Saying that interactional psychic processes are now more and more seen as the material of psychoanalytic investigation ("object relations theory" being one of the more obvious indications of this development) implies, of course, that our theories and concepts are changing. Such changes are not exclusively determined by the material of investigation; nor are changes in the latter exclusively determined by our changing theories. Nevertheless, there exists a reciprocal responsiveness that is quite decisive. More purely theoretical discussions attempt to organize and articulate what is obscurely inherent, as proto-theory, in changing modes and emphases of psychoanalytic observations and interventions.

Much of what may still be sufficiently significant in these papers to justify their republication I owe to others: members of my family, friends, patients, teachers, students, colleagues, authors in our and related fields. Interaction, influence, collaboration, education, identifications as well as separations and emancipations, play their roles here as anywhere else in psychic life. To this must be added the impact of fateful vicissitudes of historical life circumstances. Apart from psychiatric and psychoanalytic training, I owe a great deal to my education in philosophy and to my general medical education. The latter I mention specifically because nowadays it is so often maligned as contributing next to nothing to the development of a psychoanalyst. That has not been my experience. To the contrary, medical education has given me a sound and, for me, necessary foundation: in the basic sciences and their self-discipline; in biology and the developmental-reconstructive approach to life sciences; in the acquisition of diagnostic-prognostic criteria and of skilled therapeutic interventions; in the sense of responsibility and concern for patients, the close familiarity with others' pain, suffering, death, and joys; in the appreciation of the destructive and healing forces of nature. It gave me a glimpse into the obscurities of psychosomatic illness. Last but not least, medical training helped me to appreciate the need for pragmatic level-headedness in dealing with patients and the varieties and vagaries of human affairs, so essential for any therapist.

Philosophy has been my first love. I gladly affirm its influence on my way of thinking while being wary of the peculiar excesses a philosophical bent tends to entail. My teacher in this field was Martin Heidegger, and I am deeply grateful for what I learned from him, despite his most hurtful betrayal in the Nazi era, which alienated me from him permanently.

Freud is close enough to my generation to have been a commanding living force as I grew up and became a psychiatrist, although I never met him in person. He has remained for me, through his writings, that living presence.

I thankfully acknowledge financial support for my research and writing I received from the Robert P. Knight Fund and the Wood Kalb Foundation, and the help given me by the editorial staff of Yale University Press in preparing this volume.

PART I.

CONCEPTS AND THEORY

1

EGO AND REALITY

In psychoanalytic theory we are accustomed to think of the relationship between ego and reality as one of adjustment or adaptation. The so-called mature ego has renounced the pleasure principle and has substituted for it the reality principle. It does not follow the direct path of instinctual gratification, without regard to consequences, to the demands of reality, does not indulge in hallucinatory wish fulfilment, but tests external reality and thinks and acts accordingly, adapting its thoughts and actions to the demands of reality. This conception of the relationship between ego and reality presupposes a fundamental antagonism that has to be bridged or overcome otherwise in order to make life in this reality possible.

And indeed we see that Freud, in *The Ego and the Id,* calls the ego "a frontier-creature," trying to "mediate between the world and the id, to make the id pliable to the world and . . . to make the world fall in with the wishes of the id" (S.E. 19:56). We know that Freud's first conception of the ego was that it represents the repressive, defensive agency within the psychic apparatus. Only later did he stress the synthetic function of the ego. He speaks then of the ego as "an organization characterized by a very remarkable trend towards unification, towards synthesis" (S.E. 20:196). Yet he tends to see this synthetic function itself as a defense. In *The Ego and the Id* he describes vividly the unfortunate role of the ego, sandwiched between id and outer world (and superego), trying to compromise between and to satisfy these masters and to defend itself against their different demands. Freud's recognition of the defensive function of the ego has never ceased to play a predominant role in his conception of the ego, and has again and again overshadowed other aspects of the ego in psychoanalytic thinking. Correspondingly, external reality

Based on a paper read before the Baltimore Psychoanalytic Society, June, 1949.

has predominantly been seen in the aspect of a hostile, threatening power.

Freud also characterizes the ego as "a kind of façade of the id, as a frontage, like an external, cortical, layer of it." "We know that cortical layers owe their peculiar characteristics to the modifying influence of the external medium on which they abut. Thus we suppose that the ego is the layer of the mental apparatus (of the id) which has been modified by the external world (of reality)" (S.E. 20:195). (*The Problem of Lay Analysis*)

We have then, so far, the following picture of the ego: it is a mediator between the outer and inner world (between external reality and id), an organizing agency, tending toward synthesis and unification (as against the id which is "scattered" and individualistic). Genetically speaking, it is differentiated from the id through the modifying influence of external reality; in biologistic terms, it is the outer, cortical layer of the id and has as such become different from the inner stratum. The influence of external reality, which has brought forth the ego, is seen as essentially threatening and hostile. Correspondingly, the predominant function of the ego is a defensive one, not only against reality but also against the inner world of the id, which disregards reality. It is this threatened position of the ego, threatened from three sides (external reality, id, and superego), which makes it so susceptible to inner conflicts and disturbances.[1]

The only statement we have heard so far about the genesis of the ego is that it becomes differentiated from the id through the modifying influence of the medium bordering on the id, the external world. How did this modification come to pass? How did the ego develop?

I shall condense a passage from *Civilization and its Discontents* which throws some light on this question. Freud states in the first chapter that the ego feeling of the adult must have had a

---

1. "Reality," in this paper, is meant in the sense of the "external world," the world of "external objects." In *The Ego and the Id* Freud says "the id, however, is its [the ego's] second external world" (S.E. 19:55). In this sense, the ego is in between two realities or outer worlds, the id and the external world, and thus by implication not real itself, since Reality and Outer World are synonymous terms for Freud. The problems raised by this implication of the ego as unreal (due to certain philosophical preconceptions) and its far-reaching consequences for psychoanalytic theory and practice cannot be discussed in this paper.

development which we can try to reconstruct. The neonate does not as yet distinguish an ego from an outer world. Some sources of stimulation, in which later on he will recognize his body organs, can send him sensations at any time, while others do so at times and at other times are not available. The most important of these latter sources of stimulation is the mother's breast. It is not always available. In this way for the first time something like an "object" becomes constituted, an outside against an inside, and therewith a border between the two. It is important to realize that when we speak of object and ego at this stage of development, these terms characterize the most primitive beginnings of the later structures thus designated. Ego, id, and external reality become distinguishable in their most primitive, germinal stages. This state of affairs can be expressed either by saying that "the ego detaches itself from the external world," or, more correctly: the ego detaches from itself an outer world. Originally the ego contains everything. Our adult ego feeling, Freud says, is only a shrunken vestige of an all-embracing feeling of intimate connection, or, we might say, unity with the environment.[2]

In other words, the psychological constitution of ego and outer world go hand in hand. Nothing can be an object, something that stands against something else, as long as everything is contained in the unitary feeling of the primary, unlimited narcissism of the newborn, where mouth and mother's breast are still one and the same. On the other hand, we cannot, in the strict sense, speak of an ego, a mediator between an id and an external world, where there is as yet nothing to mediate. The infant's repeated experience that something, in his original feeling a part of him, is not always available, this repeated experience of separateness leads to the development of an ego which has to organize, mediate, unify. Freud in his essay on narcissism[3] already expresses this clearly, saying "The development of the ego consists in a departure [*Entfernung*] from primary narcissism and gives rise to a vigorous attempt to recover that state" (S.E. 14: 100).

2. S. Freud, S.E. 21:66–68. Freud refers in this connection to the contributions to this subject by Ferenczi and Federn, which clearly have influenced his thinking.
3. S. Freud (1914) "On Narcissism: An Introduction."

It should be clear, then, that in correspondence to a primary ego, a pre-ego so to speak, of the primary narcissistic stage, we have to conceive of primary objects and primary reality; and further, that this primary reality, and its subsequent stages of development, are very different from "reality" as a finished product that is related to the "mature" ego.

The trend of thought in the theory of the development of the ego, so far, appears to be as follows: The ego is pictured as a cortical layer of the psychic apparatus. This layer comes into being through increasing tension between the psychic apparatus of the organism and what later is experienced as the external world. This is an image borrowed from biology, in analogy to a biochemical system consisting of two phases, separated by a membrane, which membrane is the structural expression, or crystallization, of the dynamic interrelationship between forces in the two media bordering on each other. In psychological terms, in successive stages, the growing infant and child moves away from primary narcissism in which there were as yet no boundaries separating him from an "outside world." The development of the relationship with the mother is representative of this growth process, even though this does not for long remain the only "outside" the child is related to. There is, biologically and psychologically, an increasing emancipation from the mother that leads to an ever-growing tension. The less mother and child are one, the more they become separate entities, the more will there be a dynamic interplay of forces between these two "systems." As the mother becomes outside, and hand in hand with this, the child an inside, there arises a tension system between the two. Expressed in different terms, libidinal forces arise between infant and mother. As infant (mouth) and mother (breast) are not identical, or better, not one whole, any longer, a libidinal flow between infant and mother originates, in an urge towards re-establishing the original unity. It is this process in which consists the beginning constitution of a libidinal object. The emancipation from the mother, which entails the tension system between child and mother and the constitution of libidinal forces directed towards her, as well as of libidinal forces on the part of the mother toward the child—this emancipation and tension culminate in the phallic phase of the psychosexual development, lead to the Oedipus situation, and to the emergence of the super-ego.

The development away from primary narcissism, that is, the development of the ego, culminates in the resolution of the Oedipus conflict through the castration complex. The castration threat, directed against the gratification of libidinal urges toward the mother so that she is given up as a libidinal object, is seen as the representative of the demands of reality, and the submission to the castration threat as the decisive step in the establishment of the ego as based on the reality principle.

This schematic outline of the psychosexual development is sufficient for our present purpose. It must be recognized, however, that what is condensed in the terms Oedipus conflict, castration complex, etc., takes place as a process over a long period of time, is not one event or one conflict. The time dimension contained in such concepts as Oedipus conflict, castration complex, as well as in the concepts of ego and reality, not being adequately verbalized, is all too easily omitted from our thinking. The investigations of the British School, especially of Melanie Klein, have shown that Oedipus, castration complex, superego, have all forerunners or developmental stages going back to much earlier ages than those originally postulated by Freud. This was already recognized by Ferenczi in his concept of the sphincter morality. When I speak here of Oedipus and castration complexes, etc., I understand them as processes, not as anything like circumscribed events, while their names derive originally from "traumatic events," which at best may be called representative of the processes in question.

If we understand the Oedipus conflict and the castration threat as the prototype of the demands of reality, it should be clear how strongly for Freud the concept of reality is bound up with the father. Fundamentally, for Freud the father is a hostile figure who has to be fought or submitted to. This is the basic tenet in *Totem and Taboo*, as well as in his later writings dealing with the origins of religion (*The Future of an Illusion, Civilization and its Discontents*).

Reality, then, is represented by the father who as an alien, hostile, jealous force interferes with the intimate ties between mother and child, forces the child into submission, so that he seeks the father's protection. The threat of the hostile reality is met by unavoidable, if temporary, submission to its demands, namely to renounce the mother as a libidinal object, and to acknowledge and submit to paternal authority. It is of no impor-

tance for the purposes of this presentation that actually roles
may be less well defined, or even reversed, that the mother may
to a large extent represent authority and reality demands rather
than the father.

The significant point in this discussion is that reality is seen
as an outside force, for Freud most typically and decisively
represented by the paternal figure, which actively interferes
with the development of the child in such a way that the ego
essentially is on the defensive, and in fact becomes the defensive
agency within the psychic apparatus. The interference is directed
against the strivings for gratification of the libidinal urges toward
the mother, and under the assault of reality (father) the psychic
apparatus undergoes a series of modifications, repressions, deflections of its original tendencies, the structural representative
of which is the ego.

On the other hand, we know from considering the development of the ego as a development away from primary narcissism,
that to start with, reality is not outside, but is contained in the
pre-ego of primary narcissism, and becomes, as Freud says, detached from the ego. So that reality, understood genetically, is
not primarily outside and hostile, alien to the ego, but intimately
connected with and originally not even distinguished from it.

I believe that in Freud's thinking these two concepts of reality
have never come to terms with each other, and without doubt the
former concept of reality as an essentially hostile (paternal)
power, has remained the predominant one for him.

In his discussions of the origin of religious feelings, which he
sees as an attempt to cope with the threatening reality, the conflict with the father and the need and longing for his protection
are entirely in the foreground. "The derivation of religious needs
from the infant's helplessness and the longing for the father
aroused by it seems to me incontrovertible, especially since the
feeling is not simply prolonged from childhood days, but is permanently sustained by fear of the superior power of Fate. I cannot think of any need in childhood as strong as the need for a
father's protection" (S.E. 21:72). This harks back to *Totem and
Taboo* where the longing for the father is described as "the root
of every form of religion" (S.E. 13:148). And in this same connection Freud writes: "I cannot suggest at what point in this process
of development a place is to be found for the great mother-

goddesses, who may perhaps in general have preceded the father-gods" (S.E. 13:149). And again, in *Civilization and its Discontents*: "Thus the part played by the oceanic feeling, which might seek something like the restoration of limitless narcissism, is ousted from a place in the foreground. The origin of the religious attitude can be traced back in clear outlines as far as the feeling of infantile helplessness. There may be something further behind that, but for the present it is wrapped in obscurity" (S.E. 21:72).

Religious feelings, thus, are understood as originating in an attempt to cope with hostile reality forces. The creation of father-gods is an expression of the need for help and protection from the father, in order to avoid the castrating reality that the father represents. The longing for the father, seeking his help and protection, is a defensive compromise in order to come to terms with his superior, hostile power. The idea that religious feelings may contain elements having to do with the primary narcissistic position in which reality is comprised in the primary ego, and therefore with the mother—this idea is, if not rejected, declared to be obscure, at best of secondary importance, and objectionable.

In a significant passage in *Civilization and its Discontents* that has been commented upon by several authors,[4] Freud confesses his unwillingness to plunge into the depths of primordial, buried psychological levels of the primary narcissistic or related stages, and investigate them. Much in contrast to the proud and rebellious motto of *The Interpretation of Dreams—Flectere si nequeo superos, Acheronta movebo*—here he exclaims "Let him rejoice who breathes in the rosy light of day,"[5] as against the

---

4. Paul Federn (1931) "Die Wirklichkeit des Todestriebes," *Almanach der Psychoanalyse,* Vienna. Internationaler Psychoanalytischer Verlag (translated: *Psychoanalytic Review* 19:129–51 [1932]). Fritz Wittels (1949) "A Neglected Boundary of Psychoanalysis," *Psychoanal. Quart.* 18:47.

5. Ibid., p. 73. This verse is from Schiller's poem "The Diver" (translation modified), which, understood analytically, clearly symbolizes primary anxiety about a return to the womb. The assembled knights are challenged by the king to recover a cup from the depths of the ocean. He who returns the cup may keep it. A young squire accepts the challenge and dives in, returns the cup, and informs the king of the horrors of the depths and of the fact that there are further depths still unexplored. The king promises the squire his daughter if he will plunge in again to explore these dreadful regions. The squire does not return from his second dive. The greater part of the poem is given to a vivid description of the horrors and dangers of the depths.

diver who has to plunge into the depth and darkness of the ocean. Yet he touches on this problem in the same book, speaking of "the more general problem of preservation in the sphere of the mind. The subject has hardly been studied as yet" (SE 21:69) — the subject, that is, of psychological survival of original stages beside the later stages of development. And further: "If we may assume that there are many people in whose mental life this primary ego-feeling has persisted to a greater or less extent, it would exist in them side by side with the narrower and more sharply demarcated ego-feeling of maturity, like a kind of counterpart to it. In that case, the ideational contents appropriate to it would be precisely those of limitlessness and of a bond with the universe. . ." (S.E. 21:68).

Let us try to take some steps towards the clarification of the problem of reality, to see whether we can bring the two contrasting concepts closer to each other.

In the primary narcissistic stage, as we have seen, there is as yet no ego confronted with objects. It is the undifferentiated stage in which the infant and its world are still one, are only beginning to differentiate from one another, which means also that the differentiation of the psychic apparatus itself into its structural elements still is dormant. In his paper on narcissism, Freud asks the question, "what makes it necessary at all for our mental life to pass beyond the limits of narcissism and to attach the libido to objects." His tentative answer is "that this necessity arises when the cathexis of the ego with libido exceeds a certain amount" (S.E. 14:85). But, we have to say now, in the primary narcissistic position there are as yet no objects as such. We should speak, therefore, not of a passing beyond the limits of narcissism to objects, but of a differentiation into id–ego and objects out of the primary stage of unity or identity. As Freud expressed it himself: the (primitive) ego detaches an external world from itself.

The two types of libido, ego libido and object libido, derive genetically from the same source, the primary narcissistic stage of libido in which ego and object are not as yet distinguishable as such. Freud frequently calls this primary narcissistic libido the ego–libido. This is confusing since he uses the same term, ego, for the fully developed ego of the post-oedipal stage as well as for the psychic apparatus in its original, unstructured, narcissistic stage.[6]

The following formulation, at this point, seems justified: The relationship of ego to reality is not primarily one of defense against an outer force thrust upon the ego, originally unrelated to it. The relatedness between ego and reality, or objects, does not develop from an originally unrelated coexistence of two separate entities that come into contact with each other, but on the contrary from a unitary whole that differentiates into distinct parts. Mother and baby do not get together and develop a relationship, but the baby is born, becomes detached from the mother, and thus a relatedness between two parts that originally were one becomes possible.

This does not imply, of course, that the emergence of an ego and of reality is unassociated with pain and anxiety, and, as it were, unresisted; or that there is, for the observer, no world, no environment that sends stimuli to the organism. We are concerned here merely with the question how this world becomes psychologically constituted. And we want to stress the point that the boundaries between ego and external reality develop out of an original state where, psychologically, there are no boundaries and therefore there is no distinction between the two.

It is from here that the synthetic, integrative function of the ego can be understood. The ego mediates, unifies, integrates because it is of its essence to maintain, on more and more complex levels of differentiation and objectivation of reality, the original unity. To maintain or constantly re-establish this unity, in the face of a growing separation from what becomes the outside world for the growing human being, by integrating and synthe-

---

6. Freud, it should be called to mind here, introduces primary narcissism as a new concept in an attempt "to subsume what we know of . . . schizophrenia . . . under the hypothesis of the libido theory" (S.E. 14:74), to explain the withdrawal of libido from objects, as well as the megalomania (omnipotence) of psychotics, primitives, and children. He says: "Thus we form the idea of there being an original libidinal cathexis of the ego, from which some is later given off to objects, but which fundamentally persists and is related to the object-cathexes much as the body of an amoeba is related to the pseudopodia which it puts out" (S.E. 14:75). In the discussion referred to here, Freud struggles with the problems involved in the assumed dualism of ego- and object-libido (ego instincts and sexual instincts) without coming to a satisfactory conclusion ("On Narcissism: An Introduction").

sizing what seems to move further and further away from it and fall into more and more unconnected parts—this is part of the activity of the ego which constitutes it as an organization, in the sense of an agency that organizes.

The Oedipus conflict would be one very decisive step in this growing separation of the individual from its environment. The tension system between child and mother, seen from this angle, through the paternal castration threat, is forced on to, is transposed to a new level of integration.

It would be justified to look at the defensive function of the ego, seen in the light of the above considerations, from an entirely different point of view. What the ego defends itself, or the psychic apparatus, against is not reality but the loss of reality, that is, the loss of an integration with the world such as it exists in the libidinal relationship with the mother, and with which the father seems to interfere in the Oedipus situation (castration threat).

Do we then advocate swinging from a paternal concept of reality to a maternal one? Here we have to make a fresh start and consider again the relationship between child and mother. We have taken into account only the positive libidinal tension between them, with which various factors, such as especially the paternal castration threat, interfere. We have maintained that this castration threat cannot be considered as the prototype of "reality." We have to add now that, while it is not reality, it is one factor in the constitution of reality. The question is, in which way, and further, is this factor adequately described if it is seen merely as a hostile, castrating factor that calls for defense on the part of the ego, and nothing else?

We have seen that ego and reality evolve gradually in conjunction with each other; the psychic apparatus undergoes a series of modifications, repressions, deflections of its original tendencies towards re-establishment of the primary narcissistic unity or identity with the environment (mother), under the interfering influence of the (paternal) castration threat. The resultants of this development are the structures which we call ego and reality.

Obviously, without any "interference" (of which the paternal castration threat is only one representative, but which starts in extrauterine life with the first instance of withdrawal or unavail-

ability of the breast, and continues in such occurrences as wean-
ing, toilet training, etc.), there would be no development of either
ego or reality.

The paternal castration threat (in its broadest sense), would
then represent the interference with the primary narcissistic
position in which ego and reality have as yet not evolved into
distinct structures, and as such would be the stimulus necessary
for their development. Thus it is one factor in the constitution of
reality (and ego). But is it merely a "hostile" factor?

It was assumed throughout this paper, and this assumption
is explicit or implicit in the whole psychoanalytic literature, that
the castration threat is essentially paternal. Even where the
maternal aspects of the castration threat and the fear of it as the
dread of the womb are discussed, these are generally understood
as in the last analysis deriving from the fear of the paternal penis
fantasied inside the vagina or womb.[7] Jones quotes "the exceptional opinion" of Karen Horney "that this dread of the vulva is
not only earlier than that of the father's penis—whether external
or concealed in the vagina—but deeper and more important than
it; in fact, much of the dread of the father's penis is artificially put
forward to hide the intense dread of the vulva."[8]

It seems to me that there is clinical material to support the
thesis of a "dread of the vulva" earlier than and independent of
the dread of the father's penis, whether or not we agree with
Karen Horney's idea that this dread of the vulva is derived "from
the boy's fear of his self-esteem being wounded by knowing that
his penis is not large enough to satisfy the mother"[9] (an explanation that strikes me as touching just the surface of the problem).
This fear of the woman is expressed by patients in terms such as
being drowned, sucked in, overpowered, and this in regard to
intercourse as well as in regard to the relationship to mother, in
particular in cases where there is no father or where the father
has remained an insignificant and weak figure.[10]

7. See Ernest Jones, "The Phallic Phase" in *Papers on Psychoanalysis,* 5th ed. (1948),
pp. 452 ff.

8. Ernest Jones, loc. cit. (1932), pp. 458–59, quoting Karen Horney, "The Dread of
Women," *Int. J. Psycho-Anal.* 13 (1932).

9. Ibid.

10. It is impossible, within the limits of this paper, to enter into a discussion of these
problems. I feel sure, on clinical grounds, however, that a clear distinction has to be made
between the castrating mother as a masculine figure on the one hand, and the mother who

If we assume that one component of the castration threat is maternal in origin, in the sense stated above, this component could not be described as interfering with the primary narcissistic position. On the contrary, it would be the threat to perpetuate or re-establish this position, to engulf the emerging ego into the original unity.

We meet here with a "castration threat" diametrically opposed to the "paternal" threat of interference with the mother–child unity, and later, mother–child libidinal relationship. Against the threat of the engulfing, overpowering womb, stands the paternal veto against the libidinal relationship with the mother. Against this threat of the maternal engulfment, the paternal position is not another threat or danger, but a support of powerful force.

The ego, it is true, is for ever in an embattled position where it has to defend itself against powerful forces. But the danger is not all on the side of frustration of and threat to the primary narcissistic position and its genetic derivatives, the libidinal urges towards the mother. The danger is as much on the other side, on the side of the overpowering, annihilating mother. To express it in broader terms: the original unity and identity, undifferentiated and unstructured, of psychic apparatus and environment is as much of a danger for the ego as the demand of the "paternal castration threat" to give it up altogether. Against the threatening possibility of remaining in or sinking back into the structureless unity from which the ego emerged, stands the powerful paternal force. With this force an early identification is attempted, an identification that precedes and prepares the Oedipus complex. It would seem that Freud has in mind this positive, non-hostile aspect of the father figure (preceding the later passive identification due to the castration threat) when he speaks of an identification that "plays a part in the early history of the Oedipus complex. A little boy will exhibit a special interest in his father; he would like to grow like him and be like him. . . . This behavior has nothing to do with a passive or feminine attitude towards his father (and towards males in general); it is on the contrary typi-

---

is feared as an all-engulfing womb, even though these two aspects may very well be fused together in the patient's unconscious.

cally masculine. It fits in very well with the Oedipus complex, for which it helps to prepare the way" (S.E. 18: 105). And further: the boy then "exhibits, therefore, two psychologically distinct ties: a straightforward sexual object-cathexis towards his mother and an identification with his father which takes him as his model" (S.E. 18: 105). These two currents meet and, in mutual modification, help to form the Oedipus complex.

The father figure, then—and we are supported in this view by the above-quoted passage from Freud—is not *primarily* hostile, representing the threat of castration with which the boy copes by passive submission and/or rebellion. Earlier, and in my opinion more essential for the development of the ego (and reality), is his positive stature with whom an active, nonpassive, identification is made; an identification that lies before and beyond submission as well as rebellion.

It seems that in the development of psychoanalysis, notwithstanding other observations, the predominant emphasis was laid on the secondary, threatening character of the father imago. And further, this threatening character of the father imago was understood as the personal representative, so to speak, of reality. The ego, then, was seen as developing partly in submission to and partly in protest against such a reality.

The foregoing analysis leads us to the assumption of two pairs of relationships to the parent figures: (1) in regard to the mother, a positive libidinal relationship, growing out of the primary narcissistic position, and a defensive, negative one of dread of the womb, dread of sinking back into the original unstructured state of identity with her; (2) in regard to the father, a positive, "typically masculine" identification with him, which lends powerful support against the danger of the womb; and a defensive relationship concerning the paternal castration threat.

The early positive identification with the father, as well as the early dread of the engulfing mother, both enter into the Oedipus complex, form components of it, as much as the positive libidinal relation to the mother and the castration fear of the father. What, on the level of the Oedipus complex, has been called the paternal castration threat, is now understood as consisting of two components, a genetically later, hostile (castration) threat, and an early positive identification "with an ideal." Equally, what on the level of the Oedipus complex has been described as the positive libidinal relation to the mother, is understood as consisting of the two components: need for union with her and dread of this union. It is claimed here that, as the dread of the womb cannot be explained primarily by the fear of the father's penis, so the positive identification with the father cannot be reduced to the fearful submission to his castration threat.[11]

We have said earlier that the ego mediates, unifies, integrates because it is of its essence to maintain, on more and more complex levels of differentiation and objectivation, the original unity stemming from the primary narcissistic position. Reality on the post-oedipal level, however, is constituted by just these characteristics, differentiation and objectivity, which the post-oedipal ego evolves in its integrative, organizing activity. In terms of parental relationships (representing the experiential basis for this development), the original identity differentiates into the libidinal tension system child–mother. Primary identification with father and "dread of the womb" in mutual reinforcement drive toward further structuralization of this tension system, which is held together as a system, as it were, by the continuing libidinal urge towards the mother. The paternal castration threat operates as a further stimulus for differentiation, that is, toward the constitution of libidinal objects *as such.*

In this view, the unstructured nothingness of identity of "ego" and "reality" represents a threat as deep and frightening as the paternal castration threat. It is the threat of the all-engulfing womb. Dread of the womb and castration fear, both, may be powerful motives for defense, but not just defense against reality. They threaten loss of reality. Reality is lost if the ego is cut off from objects (castration threat); reality is lost as well if the boundaries of ego and reality are lost (the threat of the womb). Loss of reality always means also loss of ego. Loss of reality, in

11. In the analysis of male homosexuals it can frequently be shown that their homosexuality is fed from two sources: the fear of women and the lack of opportunity for masculine identification. The fear of the woman is, if not predominantly a fear of being engulfed by her, a mixture of this and the fear of her as the woman with a penis. In such cases the homosexual partner is sought not only in feminine identification with the mother, but also representing the ever-recurring attempt at the pre-oedipal, masculine identification with the father that could not be achieved in early childhood. It is my impression that this masculine identification can become impossible also if the father is not weak, but so overwhelming that there seems to be no hope of being like him, a constellation that easily becomes fused with and overlaid by the later castration threat.

the sense here intended, does not mean that a "part" of reality gets lost (while another part is preserved). It means that the ego–reality integration sinks back, regresses to an earlier level of organization. What we observe in clinical or experimental states of regression is not that objects get lost, but that they become less objective, as it were. Ego and reality, in a compulsion neurosis, regress to a magical level of integration, as they regress further in a schizophrenic reaction.[12] Upon a threat to the existing ego–reality integration, in the organizing activity of the ego they become reintegrated on a different level.

Between the danger of a loss of object-relationships and the danger of a loss of ego–reality boundaries the ego pursues its course of integrating reality. While the primary narcissistic identity with the mother forever constitutes the deepest unconscious origin and structural layer of ego and reality, and the motive force for the ego's "remarkable striving toward unification, synthesis"—this primary identity is also the source of the deepest dread, which promotes, in identification with the father, the ego's progressive differentiation and structuralization of reality.

There is, then, a profoundly ambivalent relationship with the parent figures at work in the constitution of ego and reality. In psychoanalytic theoretical constructions concerning ego development and structure, the positive libidinal relationship to the mother and the hostile–submissive relationship to the father had overshadowed, if not led to a neglect of, the role of the dread of the womb and of the primary positive identification with father, in the constitution of the ego. The concept of reality had been dominated by the emphasis on the paternal castration threat, notwithstanding the introduction of the concept of primary narcissism and the investigation of early ego development. We have tried to show that for a deeper understanding of ego and reality it is necessary to elaborate the implications of early ego development. Ego and reality cannot be considered separately as they

12. In an obsessive character disorder, the difficult therapeutic task is to bring about ego–reality organization on a higher level, against the patient's "intellectual" adjustment to what he is told is reality, but remains unreal to him. This adjustment, to him, therefore, is at best a successful trick by which the hostile world is controlled. It is this misconception of reality that lurks behind the notion of the ego as a defense agency against a hostile reality.

evolve together in successive stages of ego-reality integration.

A few implications of this approach to the ego–reality problem will be indicated in the following remarks.

It should be clearly understood that the conception of ego–reality development discussed above does by no means deny or disregard the essential role played by infantile aggression, anxieties, guilt feelings, etc., in ego formation and reality formation. It should, on the contrary, further the understanding of these phenomena if they are seen on the background given above. The various processes of infantile aggression, the various stages of incorporation and projection are considered as early stages of the activity of the primitive ego, whose synthesizing and differentiating is still much more concrete action than the comparatively abstract activity of the fully developed ego.[13] Introjection and projection are such early stages of ego activity. In the beginning phases, as in some psychotic disturbances, it is hardly possible to distinguish between introjection and projection, as the boundaries between "inside" and "outside" are still so rudimentary and fluid that the two terms signify different directions of the same process rather than two different processes.

This leads to the problem of psychotic phenomena. Paul Federn, who made such important contributions to our understanding of ego psychology and psychology of schizophrenia, has pointed out the loss of ego boundaries which occurs in schizophrenic disorders.[14] He considers this loss of ego boundaries, rather than any loss of or withdrawal from reality, as the primary process in schizophrenia. The schizophrenic does not primarily defend himself against reality by withdrawing from it, but reality regressively changes its character in such a way that the boundaries between ego and reality (and that means also the boundaries of ego and of reality) become fluid and to various degrees get lost. It is a regression to more primitive stages of ego–reality integration. This should throw some light on the question of transference in schizophrenia. Freud claimed that schizophrenics were inaccessible to psychoanalysis because they do not develop trans-

13. Ferenczi spoke of an "omnipotence of movements" that would precede omnipotence of thought. See O. Fenichel (1937), "Early Stages of Ego Development" in *The Collected Papers of Otto Fenichel*, second series, W. W. Norton & Co., New York, 1954, p. 34.

14. See especially "Psychoanalysis of Psychoses" in *Ego Psychology and the Psychoses*, Basic Books, New York, 1952.

ference. This is true if transference is understood as an object relationship. The often precipitous and extremely intimate transference, of hatred as well as of love, which is so frequently experienced with schizophrenics — a relationship to the therapist that seems to leap over and disregard conditions and considerations of the reality situation (as experienced by the therapist) — this transference is not an object relationship. It is an earlier stage of relatedness to others, closer to the primary narcissistic and magical feelings of identity and mutual influence. The extreme sensitivity, the "sixth sense" many schizoid people have concerning other persons and the empathic quality of their relationships is due to a more fluid and less differentiating ego–reality integration, similar to earlier stages.

It is impossible to grasp the full significance of such different ego–reality integration unless it is seen that the magical quality exists not only on the side of the ego, but also on the side of reality. Not only the ego, at such a stage, has magical powers or is a magical power, but also reality is a magical power. The empathic relationship between baby and mother is a mutual one; not only is the baby in empathic communication with the mother, but also the mother is in empathic communication with the baby. The magical quality of this relationship may be experienced by the child not only as magical identity or communication of a positive nature, but also as a threatening, overpowering force. Omnipotence is not something that the ego experiences as within itself only, but reality is also omnipotent (whether it be so for the "objective" observer or not), and against this the ego may experience itself as completely impotent. For a deeper understanding of the regressive phenomena in neurotic and psychotic disorders these considerations have to be taken into account.

In the formation of the ego, the libido does not turn to objects that, so to speak, lie ready for it, waiting to be turned to. In the developmental process, reality, at first without boundaries against an ego, later in magical communication with it, becomes objective at last. As the ego goes through its transformations from primitive beginnings, so libido and reality go through stages of transformation, until the ego, to the extent to which it is "fully developed," has an objective reality, detached from itself, before it, not in it, yet holding this reality to itself in the ego's synthetic activity. Then the ego's libido has become object relationship.

Only then does the ego live in what we call an objective reality. In earlier stages of ego formation the ego does not experience reality as objective, but lives in and experiences the various stages of narcissistic and magical reality.

I mentioned earlier that Freud has raised the problem of psychological survival of earlier ego stages side by side with later stages of ego development, a problem that he says has as yet hardly been investigated. If we look closely at people we can see that it is not merely a question of survival of former stages of ego–reality integration, but that people shift considerably, from day to day, at different periods in their lives, in different moods and situations, from one such level to other levels. In fact, it would seem that the more alive people are (though not necessarily more stable), the broader their range of ego–reality levels is. Perhaps the so-called fully developed, mature ego is not one that has become fixated at the presumably highest or latest stage of development, having left the others behind it, but is an ego that integrates its reality in such a way that the earlier and deeper levels of ego–reality integration remain alive as dynamic sources of higher organization.

2

THE PROBLEM OF DEFENSE AND THE
NEUROTIC INTERPRETATION OF REALITY

Experience gained in analytic work with psychotics already during early stages of psychoanalysis, notably through the influence of the Zürich school, had led Freud to pay greater attention than previously to early ego development and to formulate his concept of primary narcissism. Further analytic investigation of psychotic states, and the more and more frequent observations of certain character disorders, have made it obvious that the deficiencies and deformations in the organization of ego structure, over and above the neurotic defense systems and mechanisms, are of prime importance for the understanding of such disorders. Freud's distinction between narcissistic and transference neuroses is a sign of this recognition.

Nevertheless, it has been the predominant tendency in psychoanalytic thinking to keep the phenomena of conflict and of defense mechanisms in the forefront of clinical investigation, to make them the basis of theoretical constructions concerning the psychic apparatus and its dynamics and economics, and to understand developmental processes as such in terms of defense. Interest was centered on the structure and functions of neurotic symptom formation and other phenomena in the series of psychological manifestations of anxiety, conflict, and the defensive reactions against them.

The central importance of conflict, anxiety, and defense for any concrete understanding of normal and pathological psychological processes is based on very specific constellations in the growth period of human beings. The infant and child, equipped at birth only with certain automatic mechanisms for maintaining himself in equilibrium with the environment, increasingly be-

Paper read at the 17th International Psychoanalytic Congress, Amsterdam, 1951. It has been slightly revised for publication, and a few references have been added.

comes confronted with external conditions of an extremely complex nature. These complex external conditions, external from the point of view of the observer, are not merely sets of "biological" events, but events of different orders of integration which we call psychological, cultural, social. These events and processes are of a degree of integration and differentiation utterly incongruous with and superior to the level of integrative functioning of the infant and child. Thus, special efforts have to be made by the environment, and over a prolonged period of time, to create approximately appropriate psychological conditions for his development. The fact of human civilization, in its broadest sense, and its state of complexity renders a problem of how the human being can become an integral part of it, that is, integrated into its texture and participating in its further evolution. Neurotic and psychotic developments are the expression of a failure of the human being to achieve or maintain this integration on the level of integrative behavior that we call psychological.

It is the discrepancy between the state of integration of "external reality" into which the infant is born and his integrative mechanisms and capacity at birth and for a long time to come that brings about multiple occasions for deviation, deficiency of organization, arrest of development, and pathogenic defenses. The environment in our culture is first represented by the parents, the family, who thus are in the position of having to create and maintain conditions for psychological survival and development.

The parental, and in the early stages especially the maternal, supply of satisfaction of needs and of support and channelling of maturation processes constitute a regressive movement on the part of the parents that minimizes the objective discrepancy and allows the infant to remain in integrative interaction with the environment. Active support and channelling consist of creating a regressive, primitively structured environment with which the child is able to integrate; this, ideally, should continue in a sliding balance between the maturing biopsychological structures, functions, and needs, and parental support.[1] In actuality, however, the opportunities and conditions of practical necessity for

1. A view consonant with the theoretical formulations attempted here is developed, for instance, by Margaret E. Fries, "The Child's Ego Development and the Training of Adults in his Environment," in *The Psychoanalytic Study of the Child*, vol. 2 (1946).

an imbalance in this relationship, especially in our culture, are legion. Too little or too much, too early or too late support and channelling, and the varieties of conflict between the two parents in their capacity as supporting agents to the child represent a multitude of possibilities for such imbalance. With the increasing complexity of a culture other agents, in addition to parents, gain in importance, and the period of maturation lengthens.

For a discussion of the specific constellations obtaining in the growth period of human beings, and of their crucial importance in the causation of neurosis, I refer to Freud's description of the situation in the last chapter of *Inhibitions, Symptoms, and Anxiety*. He distinguishes three factors in the causation of neurosis: the one just mentioned of the prolonged dependency; the factor, which he calls phylogenetic, of the diphasic psychosexual development; and, third, the "psychological" factor. This latter is connected with the differentiation of the psychic apparatus into ego and id and consists in the fact that by virtue of the dangers of external reality certain instinctual impulses become dangers. The ego cannot flee from the id, but has to defend itself against the instinctual danger by restricting its own organization and by symptom formation.[2]

Discrepancy, then, between the individual's needs and the support of the environment, discrepancy between maturation level and environmental channelling of maturation processes, constitute basic threats. To the extent to which the growing individual develops under the sway of such discrepancy, anxiety and the possibilities for conflict situations arise. I wish to emphasize that the discrepancies referred to cannot be assumed to be due to specifically hostile forces of the environment impinging on the individual. Such hostile forces may exist too. But what is meant here is the difference between the integrative level of the individual and the integrative level of the environment. To the extent to which this difference is being bridged by the regressive supportive channelling of the environment, development can proceed without this threat, as the progressive integration of reality on the part of the child is undisturbed by this factor.

Defense, in the sense in which we speak of it when dealing with neurotic mechanisms, is based on the development of the

2. S. Freud, *Inhibitions, Symptoms, and Anxiety*. S.E. 20:154–56.

ego as a specialized structure within the psychic apparatus, and, correspondingly, on the formation of and interaction with libidinal objects. A certain degree of ego structuralization and of object structuralization has to have occurred to make defense processes and operations possible. Ego structuralization and object formation occur to the extent to which synthetic-integrative processes can proceed relatively undisturbed by the above-formulated discrepancy. This, under ordinary circumstances, takes place to a degree sufficient for the gradual formation of an ego and of a reality of some cohesive organization.

It is only on the basis of the work accomplished by early integrative processes, such as projection, introjection, and identification, through which an ego and objects come into being, that defense processes become possible, and that neurosis becomes possible. In psychosis, and to certain degrees in character disorders, defenses are not available or break down because of the weakness and deficiencies of the ego structure and the lack of reality organization.[3]

Defense is intimately related to *regression*. But regression is not one of the defense mechanisms. In the defense process, representing a failure in integration and an attempt at re-integration on a regressive level, the ego falls back on older methods, on more primitive processes of integration that serve as substitutes. They serve to establish and maintain a restricted level of "adjustment" to a piece or an aspect of reality that cannot be integrated adequately. Defense mechanisms, seen from this angle, are regressive attempts to come to terms with experiences that cannot be integrated on the level of development reached by the ego in other areas of its integration with reality. They may, in

3. Ives Hendrick, notably in his paper "Early Development of the Ego: Identification in Infancy," *Psychoanal. Quart.* 20 (1951), expresses a similar view. He states: ". . . the pathology of psychoses, and also that of many character problems, was primarily the result of defects in functions usually considered components of the ego. These personalities differ in their essential dynamics from what is characteristic of the psychoneuroses. The symptoms are not primarily the result of a healthy ego's defense against an unresolved infantile conflict; they result from a fundamental inadequacy of some essential function of the ego itself. These studies suggested, therefore, that such defective functions are end results of failures in ego development, failures, however, at much more immature stages of ego development than those already extensively appraised by analysis." Hendrick speaks in this connection of grouping "such personality problems together as different varieties of ego defect neuroses." (p. 44).

certain instances, however, at the same time serve the function of furthering the progress of integration in other areas.

The Oedipus complex, the "core of neurosis," is the prototype of a conflict that takes place, in one form or another, in every human being in our type of culture, a struggle that ends in a temporary defeat and, for a time, in the kind of restricted adjustment of which I spoke. The repression of the Oedipus complex is the outstanding example also of a defense process where the regression helps to further development in other areas.

Since by the time the Oedipus conflict has fully developed, the ego has gained considerable strength, and since in fact oedipal development can take place in full realization only under circumstances that permit sufficient solidification of the ego and a differentiated configuration of mutually related libidinal objects, defense structures typical for neurosis can largely be understood in terms of oedipal and post-oedipal development. For the understanding of psychotic and related phenomena we have to have recourse to pre-oedipal phases where neither ego nor reality are as yet sufficiently organized and differentiated from one another to make defense processes possible.

To reformulate: Defense, in the sense in which we speak of it in neurosis, and therefore to a certain degree in normal development,[4] is based on that stage in the development of individual–environment configuration, of ego–reality integration, in which an organized ego and organized reality have been differentiated from each other. What I mean here by organized reality may be indicated by saying that it implies (among other things) the establishment of distinct, libidinally invested (parental) figures mutually related to each other and the ego, such as they come into being in the development of the Oedipus situation. Only then is a stage in the constitution of ego and of reality reached in which a defense struggle between an ego and an "external" object world, and the resulting defense against id impulses can occur. Psychotic and related processes are located in pre-oedipal levels of development where the relatedness to the environment is of a more primitive cast than the relationship of an individual, structured into id, ego, and superego, with an external world. On pre-

---

4. It should be kept in mind that neurotic processes, the Oedipus conflict being the prototype as the infantile neurosis, form part of "normal" development.

oedipal levels the integrative processes are still those introjective, projective, and identificatory interactions of a narcissistic and magical nature that lead to the above-mentioned definitive structures. In the analysis of psychotic states, and of many character disorders, it is these early, predefensive processes of integration, of relatedness to the environment, that represent the main subject and the main problem of our therapeutic endeavor.

The regressive element in the defense process lies in the fact that pre-oedipal integrative mechanisms of a narcissistic-magical nature, in which no external reality in the full sense is yet constituted, are substituted for a more mature relationship to "objects" that fails to materialize to the extent to which a conflict cannot be mastered. This implies that in the defense process reality regresses, that is, becomes less objective, just as the ego regresses. In a neurotic symptom as well as in neurotic adjustment the *organization* of reality itself is affected.[5] The clinical and theoretical importance of this fact has not been recognized, to my knowledge, by psychoanalysts, even though the clinical evidence of it, particularly in character neuroses, is overwhelming.

In psychosis and character disorders the regression is more complete, and, as it were, unopposed by a more mature part of the ego, which in neurosis opposes the regression. Freud, in discussing the obsessive character and obsessional neurosis, formulates the difference between the two as follows: "In both cases the work of regression is apparent. But whereas in the former we find complete regression . . . , in the neurosis there are conflict, an effort to prevent regression from occurring, reaction-formations against it and symptom-formations produced by compromises between the two opposing sides. . . ." (S.E. 12:324).

I have discussed the difference between integrative processes as such, and defense processes that are possible only on the basis of a certain level of integration on which an ego and an external reality have already been differentiated to a sufficient degree. And I wish to emphasize that interaction as such, between individual and environment, cannot be understood as defense. Defense mechanisms, such as they occur in neurosis and normal

5. The situation becomes complicated by the fact that elements of later stages of integration with the environment are drawn into the regressive process and and reintegrated on the more primitive level, thus simulating more mature integration. This simulation of mature living is perhaps one of the most outstanding features in many character neuroses seen in analysis.

adjustment, are specific and comparatively late processes, operations of faulty, regressive integration, in reaction to discrepancies between the integrative capacity of the individual and the level of integration of the external world, *once the individual has reached the (oedipal) stage in which what it interacts with has become for him an external world.* The central importance of defense operations in human life is due to the fact that active support and channelling of maturation processes play such a predominant role still *after* the organization of an ego structure and the corresponding reality organization, and more so in our culture. This fact creates and constantly maintains occasions for discrepancy and accounts for the ubiquity of neurotic adjustment. Support and channelling have to have been reasonably adequate in early childhood to make it possible for the child to reach the Oedipus level, to develop defenses, which implies being able to fall back on earlier integrative mechanisms. If these early integrative processes are already decisively interfered with through lack of sufficient support and channelling, the result is ego deficiency and deformation, not defense.

Since dynamics of neurotic symptom formation were largely understandable in terms of defensive dealing with conflict between the different psychic structures, there has been the tendency to interpret in terms of defense, intrapsychic dynamics as such, and *any* interplay of forces in the organism–environment field, any interaction of psychic apparatus with "reality," and specifically also the dynamics of early, pre-oedipal stages and their clinical derivatives.

This all-inclusive use of the concept of defense obscures and confuses the understanding of concrete defense mechanisms and operations with which we deal in neurosis and in the psychoanalytic treatment of neurosis. And it misleads and falsifies the understanding of early development and psychotic and ego-defective states. Psychoanalytic theory, from its inception, has tended to understand the very organization of the psychic apparatus in terms of defense. The reality principle is seen as a defensive modification of the pleasure principle, and ultimately of the Nirvana principle.[6] Thus, the neurotogenic conflict situations,

---

6. Already in his early theoretical formulations, concerned with "neurological" psychology, Freud speaks of "a trend that may perhaps govern the construction (*Aufbau*) of the nervous system out of several systems: an ever-increasing keeping-off (*Abhaltung*)

as the sources for the genesis of defense mechanisms, arising on the oedipal level and later, lose their distinctive character.[7]

The relationship between organism and environment, between individual and reality, in general has been understood in psychoanalytic theory as basically antagonistic. It is Freud's "biological assumption" that a stimulus is something hostile to the organism and to the nervous system. Ultimately, instinct itself is understood as a need or compulsion to abolish stimuli.[8] Any stimulus, as stimulus, represents a threat, a disturbance. On the psychological level, Freud comes to the conclusion that at the stage of the original reality ego, "at the very beginning, it seems, the external world, objects, and what is hated are identical" (S.E. 14:136).

This whole conception is neither in accord with modern biological thinking, nor with Freud's own insights concerning the differentiation of ego and external reality out of an original identity in the early stage of primary narcissism.

But just as instincts have been seen as opposed to external stimulation imposed upon the organism and the nervous system, so the individual has been understood as essentially opposed to and imposed upon by the external world and cultural development. In experiential terms this is personified in the all-important hostile role of the father in the Oedipus situation and in the castration threat.

This biological and cultural, theoretical framework itself has been shaped to a large extent by historical experience. Freud as

---

of quantity of energy from the neurones. Thus the structure (*Aufbau*) of the nervous system would serve the purpose of *keeping off* quantity from the neurones, and its function would serve the purpose of *discharging* it" (*Project for a Scientific Psychology*, S.E. 1: 306). In other words: defense against stimuli is the cause for, and the abolition of stimuli the function of, the neurone system.

7. The view expressed here should not be confused with Heinz Hartmann's concept of the conflict-free sphere. This, if I understand him correctly, is meant as a functional area in ego development that is, in the main, not promoted and not complicated by conflict, but by other factors. The present discussion deals, in contradistinction, with genetic problems of conflict and defense, and attempts to point out when, in ego–reality development, we can begin to speak of such phenomena as conflict and defense in the sense in which they are commonly understood in the psychoanalytic theory of neurosis.

8. "It seems, then, that an instinct is an urge inherent in organic life to restore an earlier state of things that the living entity has been obliged to abandon under the pressure of external disturbing forces" (S.E. 18:36).

well as many others before and after him have been profoundly
influenced in their way of experiencing life, and therefore in their
thinking, by the overwhelming and increasing impact of social,
political, economical, and cultural changes on the individual.
The high degree of differentiation and complexity of our civilization, which seems to have run away from its human sources and
foundations and to have taken a course all its own, seldom mastered and understood, has led to the view that culture and reality
as a whole is basically and by definition inimical to the individual. The estrangement of man from his culture (from moral
and religious norms that nevertheless continue to determine his
conduct and thus are experienced as hostile impositions) and the
fear and suppression of controlled but nondefensive regression
is the emotional and intellectual climate in which Freud conceived his ideas of the psychological structure of the individual
and the individual's relationship to reality. It is also the climate
in which neurosis grows — and here we hark back to our exposition of the neurotogenic conflict situation. The hostile, submissive-
rebellious manipulation of the environment and the repressive-
reactive manipulation of inner needs, so characteristic and necessary for man who cannot keep pace with the complexity of his
culture and for a culture that loses contact with its human origins, is the domain of neurotic development. It is the above-
described discrepancy situation, repeated and re-enacted on a
different level.

This historical experience is perhaps the main reason for the
overextension of the concept of defense in dynamic psychology —
as well as for the rise of dynamic psychology itself. The discrepancy between the integrative capacity of the individual and the
level on which the cultural environment and development has to
be integrated by the individual in order still to be experienced as
his own, and not as a hostile imposition, has constantly increased.
But it is discrepancy, tension, and conflict that make us aware of
dynamics, of the interplay of forces that otherwise remains
hidden. And we may understand psychoanalysis and psychoanalytic treatment itself as an expression and utilization of the
need to rediscover and reactivate the submerged communication
channels leading from the origins of our lives to the solidified,
alienated structures of behavior, automatic attitudes and responses, cultural institutions, conventions and beliefs, neurotic

symptom formations, and defense systems and operations, which seem to have taken over and run their own inhuman course.

On three levels, then, the biological, psychological and cultural, psychoanalysis has taken for granted the neurotically distorted experience of reality. It has taken for granted the concept of a reality as it is experienced in a predominantly defensive integration of it. Stimulus, external world, and culture, all three, on different levels of scientific approach, representative of what is called reality, have been understood unquestioningly as they are thought, felt, experienced within the framework of a hostile-defensive (that is regressive-reactive) ego–reality integration. It is a concept of reality as it is most typically encountered in the obsessive character neurosis, a neurosis so common in our culture that it has been called the normal neurosis.

Psychoanalysis has most searchingly analyzed and shown us the neurotic structure and the defensive function of obsessive symptoms and of the obsessional character formation. But it has not recognized, in its dominant current, that psychoanalytic theory has unwittingly taken over much of the obsessive neurotic's experience and conception of reality and has taken it for granted as "the objective reality." While in this paper I cannot attempt to show in detail the parallels and similarities that, I believe, exist between the reality experienced by the obsessive character and the concept of reality implicit in psychoanalytic theory, I would like to point out a parallel, Freud's understanding of religion. He takes, as we know, the view that essentially religion is the equivalent of an obsessional neurosis in all its intricacies of a system of magical security operations. From our present perspective, it can be said that Freud took into consideration only certain, and not the most essential, aspects of religion, aspects, to be sure, that are elucidated to a considerable degree by his treatment of the problem. These aspects show a great deal of similarity with obsessive-compulsive symptoms in their structure, function, and genesis. The significant point, as a parallel to our thesis, is that Freud, living in a culture in which, for the majority of people, the meaning and function of religion is narrowed down to these magical-compulsive aspects, took this to be what religion "objectively" is.

In regard to the lack of a clear distinction between defense and integration as such, some further remarks may be indicated.

Repression concerns the forward-moving tendencies of libidinal integration of and with reality. A distinction should be made between repression and what might be called canalization of libidinal forces. Not only the understanding of early, pre-oedipal integrative processes has remained confused by the tendency to interpret integration in terms of defense, but also that of later phases of development. The problems of transformation of primary into secondary processes; the "translation" from unconscious to preconscious language of which Freud speaks in his early letters,[9] in *The Interpretation of Dreams,* and again in his paper on "The Unconscious"; and especially the nature of the processes indicated under the title sublimation, have thus remained obscure.[10]

The conception of organism–environment, ego–reality, as an antagonistically related pair of opposites or isolated systems, lets the reality principle appear as a defensive-adaptive principle by virtue of which the pleasure principle becomes repressively modified, and fantasy becomes an isolated remnant of this earlier principle. In the process of reality testing and the establishment of the reality principle, fantasy is seen as split off. To the extent to which this happens as a defensive-reactive process, fantasy stays behind or has to be repressed in company with pregenital strivings. But this also indicates something about the fate of the ego and of reality. To the extent to which fantasy is split off, ego and reality in their mutual integration become restricted and impoverished, as can be seen in hysterical and obsessional symptom formation and in the corresponding character disorders.

Projective-introjective processes, which are elements of the still rather obscure complex of integrative activities we call fantasy, continue in more highly differentiated forms to operate in the development and elaboration of reality during man's lifetime. Otherwise reality would be static (as indeed it has been con-

---

9. S.E. 1:230.

10. Fenichel speaks of channelling and canalization in his discussion of sublimation. Yet he subsumes sublimation under the general heading of defenses and calls it a successful defense, as against the pathogenic defenses that are unsuccessful defenses. The terminological and conceptual confusion concerning sublimation, the deficient understanding of what he calls the successful defenses, comes out very clearly in his discussion of the subject, and is frankly admitted by him (Otto Fenichel, *The Psychoanalytic Theory of Neurosis,* New York, 1945, pp. 141–67).

ceived as being in psychoanalytic theory). It becomes static and hostile, visible in each individual patient, to the extent to which his life has become merely a defensive-reactive struggle. It is this neurotically impoverished reality, a form of reality that is exercising its great destructive power on all of us, in whose image the psychoanalytic concept of reality has been formed.

The psychoanalytic investigation and understanding of ego development and ego structure, as it progresses, will also lay the foundations for an understanding of the *dynamic* nature of reality. The clearer the distinction between integration as such and defensive types of integration becomes, the more apparent also will be the difference between the idea of an alien, hostile reality (a finished product imposed on the unsuspecting infant, from there on and forever after) and the integrated, dynamic reality (forever unfinished) on the elaboration and organization of which we spend our lives.[11]

11. In a paper entitled, "The Superego and the Theory of Social Systems" read at the Psychoanalytic Section of the American Psychiatric Association Meeting in Cincinnati, Ohio, 7 May, 1951 (*Psychiatry,* vol. 15, 1952), Talcott Parsons expresses similar ideas concerning the dynamic structure of reality and reality integration. While he is mainly concerned with problems of the superego, he brings out very clearly the conception of the relationship between reality and the individual as an interaction system. He stresses particularly that not only the emotional and moral integration with reality, but also what he calls the "cognitive frame of reference" is based on introjective-projective and identificatory interactions.

3

HYPNOID STATE, REPRESSION, ABREACTION, AND RECOLLECTION

It was the investigation of hysteria which led Freud toward the fundamental discoveries of psychoanalysis. In the following remarks I propose to re-examine some of Freud's early ideas concerning the mechanisms of hysterical phenomena, in an attempt to make explicit certain insights, implied in his earlier writings, which seem to have been blurred subsequently. In particular, I wish to re-examine the early conception of the hypnoid state and its relation to repression.

It appears that Freud, under the impact of his discovery of the basic phenomenon of defense, abandoned the concept of hypnoid hysteria, formulated in accordance with Breuer's ideas about hysteria. In the paper "On the Psychical Mechanism of Hysterical Phenomena" (1893) Freud says, concerning the hypnoid state: "For we find, under hypnosis, among the causes of hysterical symptoms ideas which are not in themselves significant, but whose persistence is due to the fact that they originated during the prevalence of severely paralysing affects, such as fright, or during positively abnormal psychical states, such as the semi-hypnotic twilight state of day-dreaming, autohypnoses, and so on. In such cases it is the nature of the states which makes a reaction to the event impossible" (S.E. 2:11). In other words, this "group of conditions are determined not by the content of the memories, but by the psychical states in which the patient received the experiences in question" (S.E. 2:11). And somewhat later in the same paper: ". . . the associative working-over fails to occur because there is no extensive associative connection between the normal state of consciousness and the pathological ones in which the ideas made their appearance." It will be recalled that Freud in this paper points out the importance, for the normal process of reaction to experiences, of (1) a direct discharge of feeling at the time of an affective experience (abreaction), and (2) associative absorption "in the great complex of associations" that has the experience "ranged alongside of other experiences." In his paper on "The Aetiology of Hysteria" (1896) Freud has all but abandoned the concept of hypnoid hysteria and concentrates his attention completely on defense mechanisms and the etiological factor of sexual trauma.

It seems, however, that concomitantly with his rejection of hypnoid hysteria and his postulation of the sexual etiology, the hypnoid state re-enters the stage by the backdoor, and for good reasons, without Freud's being aware of it. In "The Aetiology of Hysteria" he writes: "In this way we obtain an indication that a certain *infantile* state of the psychical functions, as well as of the sexual system, is required in order that a sexual experience occurring during this period shall later on, in the form of a memory, produce a pathogenic effect" (S.E. 3:213, Freud's italics). And in an important footnote, in "Further Remarks on the Neuro-Psychoses of Defence" (1896), he elaborates on this necessity and its relation to the psychological theory of repression. Before discussing this footnote in some detail I wish to point out that the psychological character of the "hypnoid state" is intimately related to the "infantile state of the psychical functions."

Defense presupposes the possibility of a psychological response to a traumatic experience. In the hypnoid state, a psychological reaction to a traumatic event is impossible. The same obtains concerning a sexual trauma occurring "at a time of sexual immaturity." If a sexual stimulation occurs during the period of sexual immaturity, of an "infantile state of the psychical functions as well as of the sexual system," no psychic elaboration or associative absorption of the event is possible. However, a memory trace remains that can be reactivated later when both the psychic functions and the sexual system have attained greater maturity and permit a psychological response to sexual stimulation. At that later time, the old memory trace, without becoming conscious, exercises its influence on the way the new stimulation is experienced, namely as though the new stimulation were still something the psychic functions and the sexual system cannot cope with—and this is what we call repression.

It has been argued (Jones, 1953) that Freud at this time still had not recognized the fact of infantile sexuality, that with this recognition the notion of sexual immaturity could not stand up.

Once it became clear to Freud—so the argument runs—that in many cases such sexual traumata in early childhood have not occurred, but that we deal with fantasies stemming from the activity of infantile sexuality, the importance of sexual immaturity for repression is no longer tenable. This argumentation, however, does not take into account that the problem of infantile sexuality, which leads with such inevitable force to the infantile neurosis, lies in the fact that it is doomed to failure because of the immaturity of the sexual system and of the psychic functions related to it. The new observation, that sexual stimulation in early childhood is instinctual and not merely dependent on external factors such as seduction, does not alter the fact of sexual immaturity at that period. In *Inhibitions, Symptoms and Anxiety* (S.E. 20) Freud stresses again as one of three main factors in neurotic development in humans the diphasic development of sexuality. Without it the problem of sexual repression would not arise.

In the above-mentioned footnote to "Further Remarks on the Neuro-Psychoses of Defence" Freud says that "an inverted relation . . . between real experience and memory seems to contain the psychological precondition for the occurrence of repression" (S.E. 3:167). What is meant by this inverted relation between real experience and memory? ". . . if the sexual experience during the period of sexual immaturity and the memory of it is aroused during or after maturity, then the memory will have a far stronger excitatory effect than the experience did at the time it happened" (S.E. 3:167). Ordinarily, excitation processes in the genital organs are stronger when brought about by actual sexual stimulation of some kind than when aroused by a recollection of such experience. During the period of sexual immaturity, or, as we may say now, of infantile sexuality, the actual experience has incomparably less effect on the sexual system and on the psychical sphere than the recollection of this experience has at the time of sexual maturity. "The traumas of childhood operate in a deferred fashion as though they were fresh experiences; but they do so unconsciously" (ibid.).[1] We deal here, then, with unconscious

---

1. German text: "*Die Kindertraumen wirken nachträglich wie frische Erlebnisse, dann aber unbewusst.*" The German word *nachträglich* is translated as "in a deferred fashion." In the original publication of my article I translated *nachträglich* as "belatedly." For a discussion of the concept of deferred action see: J. Laplanche and J.-B. Pontalis, *The Language of Psychoanalysis*, New York: W. W. Norton, 1973, pp. 111ff.

memories that act like fresh experiences once they are aroused later, during maturity, when they can be dealt with by the psychic functions, the arousal being due to the now mature sexual system. If, for the sake of clarity, we reserve the term "recollection" for conscious memory function, it is unconscious memory ("reminiscences") that is operative in repression, while it is conscious (or preconscious) recollection that is involved in de-repression. "'Repression' of the memory of a distressing sexual experience in maturer years is only possible for those in whom that experience can activate the memory-trace of trauma in childhood" (S.E. 3:166). The recognition of infantile sexuality would lead to a modification of this sentence only in so far as such repression is now understood as occurring universally rather than merely in certain people who happen to have had experiences of sexual seduction in childhood.[2]

Repression, we conclude, occurs on the basis of the reactivation of unconscious memory traces. The original unconscious nature of the memory trace, however, is not in itself already due to "repression" but to the infantile condition of the psychic functions and of the sexual system.

In the description of the hypnoid state we may recognize now, not so much an "abnormal mental condition" as such, but, genetically, the "mental condition" of early childhood, or, as we would say today, a regressive equivalent of an early ego state. We may reformulate the essence of our discussion so far as follows: Freud, after initial agreement with Breuer on the importance of the hypnoid state as a factor in the production of hysteria, later rejects this notion in favor of his defense theory. His observations also lead him to the assumption of the early sexual trauma as an indispensable factor in hysteria. Later he modifies this view, concluding that no actual external sexual seduction is necessary but that there exists an infantile stage of sexuality that implies instinctual stimulations and fantasies irrespective of external stimulation. The hypnoid state, freed of its naive implications of an obscure abnormal mental condition, reveals itself as the equivalent of the ego state corresponding to the

2. It is noteworthy that Freud, in a footnote added in 1924, points out that, despite his revision of his views on infantile sexuality, "seduction retains a certain etiological importance," and that some of the psychological discussions given in this part of the paper he considers as accurate even today (ibid., p. 168).

period of infantile sexuality. This state has two characteristics that are important here: (1) no associative absorption or "working-over" of sexual instinctual experiences is as yet possible because of the immature condition of the psychological functions, and (2) "traumatic" experiences at that period of development are laid down as "unconscious memories," in predominantly somatic "memory traces."

When Freud says that hysterics suffer principally from reminiscences, he does not mean recollections, but rather the unconscious memory traces that are reactivated as such in later life at the time of the outbreak of the illness. The analytic task is to transform these unconscious memory traces into recollections, to take them out of the realm of somatic response based on somatic, unconscious memory, and to integrate them into "the great complex of associations . . . ranged alongside of other experiences." Other experiences during this stage of ego development, experiences for the associative absorption of which this ego is already mature enough, will not simply be laid down as unconscious memory traces but will be "abreacted" or "merged in the great complex of associations." "Traumatic," then, is any experience with which the immature ego is yet unable to cope by abreaction or associative absorption (I shall later try to clarify these terms used by Freud in his early formulations) and an experience that would need such an ego response for an adequate discharge of the amount of excitation involved. Traumatic experiences are merely laid down as unconscious memory traces. Repression, as a defense, is a regressive repetition of this nonarrival at consciousness. But while the original nonarrival at consciousness was due to the immature state of the ego, the later edition of such nonarrival is to be considered as an action of the more mature ego that can make defensive use of early, primitive mechanisms. The ego repeats, as a more integrated and differentiated unit of functioning, an early process. It is as though the early lack of associative absorption of an experience, the unmediated force of the unconscious memory trace, exercises a powerful influence on the more mature ego in the sense of tending to pull it back to its earlier state of immaturity, a temptation to which the ego partially succumbs: it represses the new experience because the new experience conjures up the infantile mechanism by way of the unconscious memory trace of the early experience.

If we are correct in recognizing in the "hypnoid state" a disguised version of what psychoanalysis has come to understand as an early ego state, the conclusion presents itself that it is not a question of defense hysteria against hypnoid hysteria but that both repression and "hypnoid state" are essential elements of hysterical mechanisms; furthermore, the phenomenon of repression cannot be fully understood without recognizing that it represents a more integrated version, on the part of the more mature ego, of a primitive mode of functioning of the psychophysical apparatus. The relation between "hypnoid state" and repression appears to be analogous to the relation between instinctual, id anxiety, and anxiety as a signal appropriated and used by the ego.

Freud's later concept of the repetition compulsion, I believe, reflects his growing insight into the power of the unconscious to pull back into its realm later life experiences, operating in conjunction with the defensive-rejecting tendencies of the ego. The repetition compulsion, which he comes to consider as such an important element in the phenomenon of transference, represents a recognition of the enormous power of the unconscious memory traces before and beyond the rejecting power of ego defenses. It would seem that Freud, when he first became aware of repression as a defense, postulated the Unconscious and Consciousness simply as opposing forces. Gradually it dawned on him to what extent what he comes to call the ego in his later writings is a translation into another language of the Unconscious (transformation of primary into secondary processes). In his most important theoretical paper after the seventh chapter of *The Interpretation of Dreams,* in the paper "The Unconscious" (1915), he discusses this problem in terms of the relations between the systems Ucs and Pcs.

In each and every analysis we are confronted with two problems that are at the same time two fundamental problems of psychological dynamics: The ego resists "insight," it defends itself against admitting unconscious processes and "contents" into its presence that would imply their transformation into secondary processes (anticathexis in the Pcs); and it attempts in many circumstances to reject what had already been so transformed and to repress it into the unconscious. But on the other hand—and this is still less clearly recognized and understood—the unconscious resists this transformation into secondary processes and tends to draw back into its realm what had already been so transformed (Ucs cathexis). This is not defense but repetition compulsion. In terms of the analytic work this means that, inextricably interwoven with the analysis of defenses, is the task of working through. In a section entitled "Modifications of Earlier Views" in *Inhibitions, Symptoms and Anxiety*, Freud says: "But we have to ask ourselves whether it [i.e., ego resistance] covers the whole state of affairs in analysis. For we find that even after the ego has decided to relinquish its resistances it still has difficulty in undoing the repression; and we have called the period of strenuous effort which follows after its praiseworthy decision, the phase of 'working-through.' The dynamic factor which makes a working through of this kind necessary and comprehensible is not far to seek. It must be that after the ego resistance has been removed the power of the compulsion to repeat—the attraction exerted by the unconscious prototypes upon the repressed instinctual process—has still to be overcome. There is nothing to be said against describing this factor as the *resistance of the unconscious*" (S.E. 20:159–60, Freud's italics).

Working through is understood here as a process in which the resistance of the unconscious, the repetition compulsion, is being overcome. Working through is not primarily conceived of here as the undoing of repressions or other defenses, but is seen as the strenuous task of helping to lift unconscious processes onto a new level of integration, the level of secondary processes. This task is difficult enough in and of itself, as anyone can attest to who tries to "bring up" children—hard, and rewarding, for both child and parent. It is very much harder if these unconscious processes or experiences, because of the time at which and the environment in which they took place, were not capable of being lifted onto a level of higher integration—if they took place in a period of an "infantile condition of the psychic functions and of the sexual system," or, in Freud's earliest language, in a "hypnoid state."[3]

---

3. The problems of introjection and identification and their all-important role in the mechanisms of ego integration and of the transformation of primary into secondary processes, cannot be discussed in this paper. I am also aware that the term "repetition compulsion" covers a multitude of phenomena, and that resistance of the unconscious is only one of them.

At this point, it will be useful to return to the paper "On the Psychical Mechanism of Hysterical Phenomena" for further clarification of Freud's early and later writings. I had mentioned that Freud points out as important mechanisms in the normal process of dealing with experiences: (1) a discharge of feeling at the time of an affective experience (abreaction), and (2) associative absorption.[4] It appears that neither one of them takes place under the conditions that lead to hysterical phenomena (in a hysterical attack, for instance, there is involuntary motor discharge, but no discharge of feeling). Freud also distinguishes between a discharge of feeling through action, and discharge through the "substitute for action," language (S.E. 2:8). "Catharsis" through "abreaction" has fallen into disrepute as the handling and interpretation of defenses moved into the foreground of attention in analysis. A careful study of Freud's discussion of the cathartic method and of the normal mechanisms of dealing with affective experiences can show, however, that abreaction and associative absorption are essential elements of the analytic process. They are supplemented and often made possible, but by no means superseded, by the interpretation of defenses and instinctual derivatives.

According to the description in this early paper, a cure occurred if the exciting event was brought to clear recollection, the accompanying affect aroused with the recollection, and if the patient related the event in as detailed a manner as possible and expressed his accompanying affects in words. It is somewhat later in this paper that Freud uses the expression: "*Hysterics suffer mainly from reminiscences*" (S.E. 2:7, Freud's italics). The description of the therapeutic method given above is that of the cathartic method, by "abreaction." Abreaction may come about by direct expression of affect, by an "energetic reaction." "By 'reaction' we here understand the whole class of voluntary and involuntary reflexes—from tears to acts of revenge—in which, as experience shows us, the affects are discharged" (ibid.: 8). But

4. The words "associative absorption" are the translation in the Collected Papers (vol. 1:21–41) of the German *assoziative Verarbeitung* (Gesammelte Werke 1:90), translated in S.E. as "associative working-over," a more literal translation. "*Verarbeitung*" contains the same verb "*arbeiten*" that is used in the expression "working through," "*durcharbeiten*." For Freud—and this is manifest in his using the same verb—associative working-over and his later expression "working through" are closely related.

abreaction may also occur by way of "a substitute for action," namely speech. The above description of the cathartic method mentions both the arousal of the affect and the expression of feelings in words. At the same time, it mentions the bringing of the exciting event to clear recollection.

In the light of our previous discussion, abreaction through recollection, affective discharge, and verbalization is beyond and deeper than the undoing of repression, a lifting of unconscious processes (unconscious memory traces) onto a higher level of integration, a transformation of primary into secondary process. "Reminiscences" become "recollections." This goes hand in hand with the associative absorption of the event, now recollected, into the "great complex of associations" that allows it to be "ranged alongside of other experiences." This is an important element in the process we now call working through. In analysis we can see again and again that the true recovery of a childhood memory (which, of course, is never the recollection of an "objective event" but of a "subjective experience") is not a copy, a re-recording, but a new version of something old. We frequently see, in the course of an analysis, various versions of the same old experience, on more and more mature levels of integration and insight. It is often clear that in a so-called recovery of a childhood memory we are confronted, not with the recall of something forgotten, but with a creative event in which something for the first time can be put into words. The definite impression is that it never had been put into words, and more, that it never had been capable of being put into words because the original experience had taken place on a level of integration which did not render it available for preconscious or conscious integration. Recollection, as against reminiscence as used by Freud in this paper, is not a re-recording, but the creation of something new. While originating in something old, inscribed into the organism as an unconscious memory trace (body memory), it had not existed in this form before.

Very much interwoven with abreaction is what Freud calls associative absorption or working-over and associative correction (S.E. 2:17). These expressions appear to be the earliest versions of what he later refers to as the synthetic function of the ego. A traumatic event is one that cannot as yet be associatively worked-over or absorbed, due to the immature state of the psychological functions, i.e. it cannot be integrated by the immature ego. Working through in analysis consists of the process of "abreaction," especially at the symbolic level of language, and of the "associative correction" founded on it.

REFERENCES

Freud, S. (1893): On the psychical mechanism of hysterical phenomena. S.E. 2:3–17.
_____. (1896): The aetiology of hysteria. S.E. 3:191–221.
_____. (1896): Further remarks on the neuro-psychoses of defence. S.E. 3:162–85.
_____. (1915): The unconscious. S.E. 14:166–204.
_____. (1926): Inhibitions, Symptoms, and Anxiety. S.E. 20:87–172.
Jones, E. The Life and Work of Sigmund Freud, vol. 1. New York: Basic Books, 1953.

4

SUPEREGO AND TIME

I am going to present a particular point of view from which I intend to consider the superego here. My approach to the problem will thus be one-sided. It is an experiment in thinking and should be taken as such. As I began to concern myself with the theory of the superego, it soon became apparent that this led, among other things, to the problem of psychic structure. What is psychic structure? Physical structures are arrangements in space or, perhaps more accurately, arrangements characterized by spatial relations. What is the principle of arrangement, what is the nature of the relations obtaining in and between psychic structures? We cannot conceive of them as spatial. If we do, we leave psychology and the psychic realm and consider possible physical substrata of psychic structures, not psychic structure as such. The relations between ego and superego, for example, or the relations between various elements within the ego, are not spatial relations. Yet they must, insofar as we think in terms of structure and structural relations at all, conform to some principle of arrangement which allows us to conceive of them as structural relations. I suggest that this principle is time, that psychic structures are temporal in nature.

Psychic structures exist in time and develop in time. But I do not speak of time here as a linear continuum of duration or of the sequence of events in physical time-space as observed in objective, external reality. The time concept involved here, psychic time, implies an active relation between the temporal modes

This paper develops some thoughts on the futurity of the superego and on a psychoanalytic conceptualization of time that were first adumbrated in my paper "Internalization, Separation, Mourning, and the Superego" (chapter 15 of this volume). While the two papers were published the same year (1962), "Superego and Time" was written some two years later than the original version of the other one as a contribution to a panel on "The Superego and the Ego-Ideal" held at the 22nd International Psychoanalytic Congress in Edinburgh in 1961.

past, present, and future. Dynamic mutual relations between psychic past and psychic present are familiar to us in psychoanalysis. From the point of view of objective time, what we call the psychic past, as in transference phenomena, is not "in the past" but in the present; it is active now, yet active as psychic past, it is the actuality of past experiences. The same is true for unconscious memory traces and their relationship to day residues. Both here and in clinical transference phenomena, the psychic past acts on and in the present, it acts on the psychic present and in the objective present. But the psychic present also has an impact on the psychic past; it activates the psychic past. Memory, as recollection for instance, manifests psychic time as activity; it makes the past present. Anticipation makes the future present. When we speak of object representation, object presentation, drive representation, a concept of time is implied in which "present" is understood as an active process—to present something. To represent or present means to make or keep present, to present, maintain, or re-create presence. Reminiscences, in the sense in which Freud speaks of them when he says that hysterics suffer from reminiscences, pull the psychic present back into some psychic past, although this takes place in the objective present.

Speaking of time in an active sense can be compared to speaking of organization in an active sense. When we call the ego an organization we do not only mean that the ego is a structural unit whose elements are mutually interdependent and interdependent with the whole, not only that it is a system of interdependent functions, but we also have specifically in mind the integrative and differentiating functions of the ego. In other words, the ego is an agency which organizes. It is useful to think of the ego's function of presentation and representation, of creating and recreating presence, as the temporal aspect of its synthetic or organizing function.

That time plays a prominent part in the structure of the mind as explored by psychoanalysis, is, of course, an implicit and explicit tenet of psychoanalytic theory and practice. The study of dreams and neurosis, the importance of infantile development, the phenomena and concepts of regression, fixation, transference, repetition compulsion—to name just these few—make this evident. The temporal modes involved here are past and present.

The remarkable fact is that in mental life the past, that is psychic past, is not in the (objective) past but is active now as past, and that the psychic present acts on the psychic past. The psychic past and the psychic present are represented in psychic systems, agencies, or structures, as Freud has variously called them, which are actual and active in the objective present of mental life. I think it is clear that the system unconscious and, in the later conceptualization, the id are prominently related to what we call the psychic past, although it is by no means clear what the nature of this relation is. It seems to me equally obvious that the system Preconscious–Conscious and, in the later formulation, the ego show prominent relations to the temporal mode psychic present; we need only think, apart from the representational function of the ego, of the connections between the system Pcs–Cs and perception and motility, and of the closeness to the external world and of the reality-oriented functions of the ego. Here again, the nature of such relations to psychic present is obscure. In passing it is worth mentioning that Freud thought there was no need to assume a spatial arrangement of the psychic systems, even though he speaks, by analogy, of the idea of psychic locality, but that it would be sufficient to assume, as he puts it, "that in a given psychical process the excitation passes through the systems in a particular temporal sequence" (S.E. 5:537). The concept of time involved here is that of objective time, not of psychic, active time; nevertheless, some kind of temporal principle of arrangement is hypothesized.

As I said in the beginning, it was my concern with the superego as a psychic structure that led me to such considerations. More specifically, my attention was drawn to the significance of the future, as a temporal mode, for a deeper understanding of the superego, and it was this idea that stimulated the considerations outlined above.

Insofar as the superego is the agency of inner standards, demands, ideals, hopes, and concerns in regard to the ego, the agency of inner rewards and punishments in respect to which the ego experiences contentment or guilt, the superego functions from the viewpoint of a future ego, from the standpoint of the ego's future that is to be reached, is being reached, is being failed or abandoned by the ego. Parental and other authorities, as internalized in the agency of the superego, are related to the child as representatives of a future and of demands, hopes, misgivings, or despair, which pertain to an envisaged future of the child. The superego watches, commands, threatens, punishes, forewarns, admonishes, and rewards the ego, it loves and hates the ego. All this we can do with ourselves only insofar as we are ahead of ourselves, looking back at ourselves from a point of reference that is provided by the potentialities we envisage for ourselves or of which we despair. Conscience speaks to us from the viewpoint of an inner future, whether it tells us what we should do or how we should behave in the future, or whether it judges past and present deeds, thoughts, and feelings. Past deeds and thoughts we condemn inasmuch as we have expected more from ourselves, or we approve of them inasmuch as we have lived up to our expectations. Only insofar as we are in advance of ourselves— conceive of ourselves as potentially more, stronger, better, or as less, weaker, worse than we are at present—can we be said to have a superego. That our expectations may be unrealistic, that we may mistake and misjudge our potentialities, is another matter. Conscience, the mouthpiece of the superego, speaks to us, one might say, in the name of the inner future that envisages us as capable or incapable, as willing or unwilling to move toward it and encompass it, just as parents envisaged us in our potentialities and readiness for growth and development. It is possible that the psychoanalytic concept of self as superordinate to the categories id, ego, and superego, when further developed and clarified, may help us to conceptualize these internal relations more precisely.

Freud has used, more or less successively, at times interchangeably, three different terms: ideal ego, ego-ideal, superego. At the risk of doing violence to the fluidity of these terms as used by him, I am going to consider them insofar as they can serve as terms for successive stages in the development toward superego structure. Briefly, the ideal ego represents a recapturing of the original primary-narcissistic, omnipotent perfection of the child by a primitive identification with the omnipotent parental figures. It is an identification representing the re-establishment of an original identity or unity with the environment and would seem to have connotations akin to hallucinatory wish fulfilment. (Just as the early deprivations and disillusionments are undifferentiated antecedents of the later separations and relinquishments, so the early wish-hallucinations are antecedents of the later internalizations and so-called "restitutions of the object in the ego.") This ideal ego represents a return to an original state of perfection, not to be reached in the future but fantasied in the present. This state of perfection of the ego—perhaps the ideal undifferentiated phase where neither id nor ego nor environment are differentiated from one another—gradually becomes something to be wished and reached for: it becomes an ego-ideal, an ideal for the ego, seen in a much more differentiated and elaborated form than previously in parental figures. Perfection now is to be attained by participation in their perfection and omnipotence on the basis of an as yet incomplete distinction between inside and outside, between ego and parental object; it is magical participation. Here a future is envisaged for the ego, but not yet a future *of* the ego. The future state of the ego is to be attained by merging with the magical object. No stable internal structure representative of the ego's self-transcending exists as yet; the self-transcending is dependent on a magical communion with an ideal authority and model taking an intermediate position between external and internal. The ego's future needs to be still embodied externally in order to have any claim on the ego.

We speak of superego, of an inner future of, not merely for, the ego once a share of the oedipal objects is relinquished, once the libidinal-aggressional relationship with the oedipal figures (having gradually developed during the oedipal phase into a relationship with external objects) has been partially given up as an external relationship and has been set up in the ego as an internal relationship; then the ego envisages an inner future of itself, the superego being the representative of the ego's futurity. We know that many people never reach the stage of a reasonably stable superego structure, that the superego as a late structure is peculiarly prone to regressive tendencies in the direction of re-externalization, or on the other hand to a brittle rigidity that permits no further enrichment and growth. For many of us our inner development depends to a large extent on those with whom we surround ourselves to support the weak superego, or we confine ourselves within narrow self-limitations without wider horizons; it is then as though time stands still. The superego as a late structure in mental development shows great variations and fluctuations from individual to individual, as well as in any given individual during his life. As the latest differentiating grade in mental organization it is not only fragile, tending toward de-differentiation and regression, but also indicating, we may assume, the direction of future human evolution.

Earlier I alluded to the assumption that the temporal mode of the ego, understood as organizing agency, is the present—the present not as a state but as activity, the ego as presence-creating. Similarly, the temporal mode of the superego, the future, is not to be understood as a state but as activity. We cannot do justice, conceptually, to psychic structures unless we conceive of them as systems of action-patterns. The relationship between ego and superego, in terms of psychic time, would be a relation between psychic present and psychic future. I shall come back to these relations.

Speaking genetically, the superego is not only a representative of external authorities and models with their demands and expectations, their prohibitions and allurements, but it is also a representative of the id. It is not possible for me to go into the complex connections that seem to exist between the two structural concepts, id and superego. I will emphasize only one aspect: the oedipal introjects, constituting the superego, do not represent strictly realistic external prototypes, but their character is co-determined by the quality and strength of the libidinal and aggressive drives of the Oedipus complex, so that the introjects represent the drives as much as the drive objects. Freud can say, therefore, that "the superego takes up a kind of intermediate position between the id and the external world" (S.E. 23:207). This implies the recognition that the superego is a system, not of introjected "objects," but a system of introjections of interactions between id–ego and external world, with the emphasis here on the id aspects of such interactions. In earlier interactions between psychic apparatus and external world objects and ego become differentiated one from the other; these earlier interactions are the introjections and projections contributing to the formation of the ego (seen from the vantage point of achieved superego formation, they can be recognized as being antecedents or prototypes of superego formation). They do not represent as yet interactions between id–ego and objects but interactions between less differentiated, more fluid systems. The superego, considered as a psychic structure, is, as Freud had clearly seen, a further differentiation of the ego. This further differentiation is brought about by interactions between psychic apparatus and external world that are of a higher order than was possible prior to the relative completion of the organization of the ego and of objects. But it remains a system of internalizations of interactions and not of objects. The interactions that are internalized as superego elements take place between a psychic apparatus definitively differentiated into ego and id, and an external world definitively differentiated into distinct objects.

It is clearly the passionate nature of the oedipal object relationships that lets the id loom so large in the nature of the superego. Later modifications of the superego temper this picture if a workable resolution of the Oedipus complex has occurred.

I will only allude here to the relations that must exist between the id and the temporal mode Past. Freud says that one might see the id, "with its inherited trends," as representing the organic past, and the superego as representing "more than anything the cultural past." But since the superego "takes up a kind of intermediate position between the id and the external world, it unites in itself the influences of the present and of the past" (S.E. 23: 206). Freud, however, speaks here of time not as psychic time in the sense in which I tried to delineate it. He speaks, in this same passage, of the external world as representing "the power of the present," meaning "the external world in which the individual finds himself exposed after being detached from his parents" (ibid). The ego is not mentioned in this connection; nor is the future, except by implication in his quotation from Goethe's *Faust* which throws some light on the superego: "What thou hast inherited from thy fathers, acquire it to make it thine" (S.E. 23: 207). The id, if it can be said to represent the inherited past, the degree and quality of organization with which we are born, has a future insofar as we make it ours by acquiring it, by imprinting on it the stamp of ego organization. Insofar as this is an unfinished task, and to the extent to which we experience it as an unfinished, never-finished task, our superego is developed. The superego then would represent the past as seen from a future, the id as it is *to be organized*, whereas the ego proper represents the id as organized at present. The three organizational levels—while representing the three temporal modes in a being who has memory, creates presence, and anticipates—co-exist as embodied in the three psychic structures, and at the same time are successive. And co-existing they communicate with each other, define, delimit, and modify each other. A more refined concept of self, as well as a deeper understanding of the phenomenon of consciousness, may help us here.

Considering psychic past and psychic future from a different angle, we can say that the future state of perfection, which is the viewpoint of the superego by which we measure, love and hate, judge ourselves and deal with ourselves, recaptures the past state of perfection that we are said to remember dimly or carry in us as our heritage and of which we think we see signs and traces in the child's innocence when he is at one with himself and his environment.

I shall now very briefly discuss some aspects of the superego as a psychic structure representing internalizations of oedipal and post-oedipal relationships. The superego as a later structure, is more fluid, less stable than the ego, although its elements, the superego introjects (owing to the more structured relationship of ego and objects that is the material of these introjections) are more structured than the ego-introjects and therefore more easily visible. I suggest viewing the superego as an enduring structure–pattern of introjections whose elements may move in the direction of the ego or in the direction of external objects; they may thus lose their character as superego elements and either merge into the ego or regain a measure of object quality; new elements may become part of this structure–pattern. This conception implies the notion of degrees of internalization and externalization. Patients re-externalize aspects of their superego by projecting them on to the analyst and internalize aspects of the analyst's personality or, more precisely, of the analyst's relationship with the patient. We frequently hear patients describe the analyst's watchful "presence" in some vague form as the patient engages in given activities in his daily life, showing a certain degree of internalization that does not yet have the quality of being part of the patient's superego. It has more the quality of a fantasy object. In certain hallucinatory experiences of this kind, as most often described by borderline or psychotic patients, externalization has gone a step further, or, seen from the other direction, internalization has not gone as far. A complete relinquishment of the external object relationship has not taken place in these instances. While the superego as a structure–pattern is established through the resolution of the Oedipus complex and to the extent to which this resolution has occurred, new elements enter, are assimilated into this structure–pattern at various later stages in life, most clearly in adolescence. But they, too, become part of a structure–pattern that represents the ego's futurity, and they are selected insofar as they might fit, might be capable of assimilation into this pattern. Superego elements may be given up, expelled; persons in the external world representative of such abandoned elements may be repulsive to the superego, which shows that these elements have left residues in the superego.

Superego elements may merge into the ego as certain goals set for the ego's development have been reached; but the ego, under conditions of stress and ego conflict, may lose hold of them so that they return into the superego structure. Lest the impression arise that I visualize something like peripatetic particles wandering back and forth between ego, superego, and external world, let me emphasize that internalization and externalization are not manipulations perpetrated on passive and static entities, nor movements performed by such entities. The process of internalization or introjection involves a change in the internal organization of the elements; this, while hard to conceptualize, is of the utmost importance. The more clearly the aspects of an object relationship, for instance between father and son, are internalized, become part of the son's inner world, the more they lose their object-relation character. Another way of attempting to formulate this is to say that internalization involves the process of neutralization. The relationship, being internalized, becomes (relatively) desexualized and deaggressivized. The changing of superego elements into ego elements involves a further desexualization and de-aggressivation. The degree of modification and reorganization of material for introjection that is brought about by internalization varies with the degree of internalization. In insufficient or in pathological, distorted superego development the sexual-aggressive character of the internalized element is usually pronounced. Mourning, inasmuch as it involves the relinquishment and internalization of aspects of the lost object relationship, leads to an enrichment of the superego. Such internalization, if observed over long periods of time, may be progressive so that eventually this superego element merges into the ego, becomes an ego element, becomes realized as an ego trait rather than being an inner ideal or command.

In terms of psychic time, the relation between ego and super-ego can be seen as a mutual relation between psychic present and psychic future. In the structure of the superego the ego con-fronts itself in the light of its own future. The establishment of the superego completes the constitution of an inner world whose dimensions may be said to be the temporal modes past, present, and future. They have to be conceived, like anything in the mental realm, as active modes, not as observed attributes. If we conceive of the superego as a psychic structure representing the ego's future from the standpoint of which the ego is judged, loved, and hated, the degrees of internalization, measured by the distance from the ego, would be steps in the movement from psychic future to psychic present, as organized in these two structures.

I am aware of the fragmentary and partly speculative nature of this presentation and of the fact that it raises rather than solves problems. However, the whole orientation of psychoanalysis as a genetic approach to mental life, as an attempt to understand mental disease in terms of the history of mental development and to cure it by promoting a resumption of this history—using the faculty of remembering as a main tool—points to the importance of time as being somehow the inner fiber of what we call psychical. It seems to me also that, together with the awareness of differentiation of inner and outer and their relatedness, the awareness of differentiation of past, present, and future stands at the threshold of higher mental organization.

REFERENCES

Freud, S. The Interpretation of Dreams. S.E. 5.
_____. An Outline of Psychoanalysis. S.E. 23.

5

BOOK REVIEW AND DISCUSSION

Psychoanalytic Concepts and the Structural Theory,
BY JACOB A. ARLOW AND CHARLES BRENNER

This book attempts to demonstrate the superiority of the structural theory of the mind over the so-called topographic theory as outlined by Freud in *The Interpretation of Dreams.* The authors make a strong plea for giving up the earlier theory and for not using terms of the early and later theories interchangeably. They describe and compare the two theories—to the extent to which they have been consistently and precisely formulated by Freud— and reformulate such issues as the theory of regression, the concepts of primary and secondary process, unconscious and preconscious, as well as dream theory and the theory of psychosis, in terms of the structural theory. They come to the conclusion that the two theories, while showing many similarities, are incompatible with each other, and that the structural theory is superior in regard to its explanatory value and logical consistency.

Many aspects of psychoanalytic investigation and theoretical formulation, undertaken within the framework of the mental apparatus as divided into the systems Ucs and Pcs–Cs, have not been integrated, or not sufficiently integrated, into the structural theory and reformulated in terms of the division of the mind into the structures id, ego, and superego. This book is a step in that direction, as is Merton Gill's monograph.[1] It would be tempting to put the two monographs in juxtaposition; but the scope of a

Jacob A. Arlow and Charles Brenner, *Psychoanalytic Concepts and the Structural Theory,* New York: International Universities Press, 1964, 201 pp.

1. Merton M. Gill, *Topography and Systems in Psychoanalytic Theory. Psychological Issues,* vol. 3, no. 2, monograph 10. New York: International Universities Press, 1963.

brief review is far too narrow to allow for a more comprehensive and detailed discussion of this kind.

In fact, I have been in somewhat of a quandary about just how to discuss Arlow and Brenner's book. I am in agreement with their aim to clarify and make psychoanalytic theory more consistent, to reformulate or redefine important and familiar concepts and issues in terms of the structural theory. But I have misgivings about the way they go about it and in regard to the neatness of some of their conclusions. They state in the Preface that "the views which we present in this monograph we do not consider to be fixed, permanent, complete, official, or dogmatic. They represent our understanding of the relationship among the fundamental concepts of psychoanalysis at the present stage of its development" (p. xi). This, of course, is as it should be. And they do present their views clearly and concisely and leave no doubt as to where they stand. But the reader is left with the impression that in their view issues are settled, concepts well defined and precise, problems well understood and in no need of further inquiry, many of which are neither as clear-cut nor as simple and one-dimensional as they are represented to be by the authors. The discussions of primary and secondary process, of the concept of the preconscious, of the superego, the chapter on psychosis, are examples of this general stance.

In the course of studying the monograph, I often asked myself to whom it is addressed. Since it discusses and attempts to further the understanding and theoretical penetration of some of the most basic and complex issues in psychoanalysis, it seems to be intended for the community of experienced, theoretically sophisticated analysts who struggle with these problems and who are equal to the task of comparing the topographic and structural theories in their theoretical and practical import. For them, I think, the authors' approach is too elementary, not to say simplistic. Thus in many ways the book seems to be addressed to the beginner who is supposed to have little background information of theory and scanty clinical experience. But should the beginner in the study of psychoanalysis be expected simply to absorb and learn facts and concepts as known and understood by the experts, in a fashion similar to the conventional learning of anatomy; or should he, too, be asked to learn by seeing problems, raising questions, considering issues as open and in need of further understanding, looking at the observable material with fresh eyes, although increasingly informed by the knowledge and understanding which a teacher's greater experience and more penetrating study can convey? In this book, I am afraid, more issues are closed than opened, more answers given than questions raised and discussed in the spirit of scientific inquiry. The book gives an air of finality, both by its manner of discourse and argumentation, which appears to foreclose different avenues of approach and understanding, and by its frequent oversimplification of the views its authors oppose at the same time that it makes their own views and arguments sound deceptively simple and clear.

To my mind, Freud's earlier way of conceptualizing and ordering his observations, deductions, and ideas, comprised under "the topographic theory," is reduced by the authors to a scheme more rigid and final than it actually was. What might conceivably be justified for purposes of didactic exposition is not justified in a considered discussion and comparison of the two theories. By the same token, their own exposition of the structural theory, which they consider superior, is equally rigid, oversimplified, and final in tone and quality. There seem to be no open ends, debatable issues, genuinely obscure phenomena and meanings. But most psychoanalytic concepts, and above all the more basic ones, are subject to a continuous process of re-examination and redefinition, of expansion and deeper or new understanding; new meanings of old concepts become apparent and unexpected connections between early and later formulations move into sight.

I am convinced, with the authors, that the structural theory in many ways represents an advance over the topographic theory, but I believe that many problems in psychoanalysis so far cannot be dealt with without the distinction between unconscious and preconscious mental processes. This distinction indicates an essential psychological difference between two categories of mental processes, a difference in many respects more fundamental than that between unconscious and conscious; and it indicates a difference between mental processes, as contrasted with mental structures between and within which such processes take place. If we were to abandon the term preconscious, we should be left with a purely economic characterization of primary and secondary process. It is in the light of theory prior to the structural theory that the main investigations into the interplay between primary and secondary processes and of the transformations of primary into secondary processes have been carried out. These issues have an important, but so far not well-understood, bearing on the question of the interconnections between the three structures of the mind. K. R. Eissler called attention to this when he stated: "The present . . . division of ego, superego, and id to a certain extent leaves unaccounted for a fundamental question, namely, what the pathways of communication are among the three provinces of the personality."[2] This whole problem has so far not been sufficiently considered within the new orientation of the structural theory, with its increasing concentration on problems of psychic functions, to the detriment of consideration of the nature of psychic or mental processes— with the exception of economic considerations. Arlow and Brenner, in agreement with other authors such as Beres, wish to define psychic structures as groups of functions, which leaves the question of mental processes and their role in the formation and maintenance of psychic structure out of account. Are we to understand functions as something to be carried out without structures (of whatever nature) that perform them; that structure is constituted not by the nature of the grouping but rather by the mere fact of a set of functions? Such issues and questions may indicate how many unresolved and obscure problems are hidden behind the façade of seemingly simple and clear, common-sense formulations.

In so far as Freud attempted to use the difference between unconscious and preconscious processes as a criterion for dividing the psychic apparatus into systems or agencies (a structural division, although it was not so termed), his theory came to grief, since this distinction, as Arlow and Brenner lucidly explain, does not furnish an adequate basis for a division of this kind and does not account for many aspects of mental conflict. The two different types of psychic processes taking place in the mind cannot be located in or conceived as residing in different substructures of the mind. The different substructures are likely to be

2. K. R. Eissler, "On the Metapyschology of the Preconscious" in *The Psychoanalytic Study of the Child*, vol. 17. New York: International Universities Press, 1962, p. 13.

constituted by different kinds or levels of organization and integration of these two types of mental processes with each other.

In an important sense the two theories represent two different general theoretical constructions regarding the subject matter of psychoanalysis. Whereas the topographic theory conceives of the mind as an apparatus or instrument, analogous to a reflex arc or to a microscope, the structural theory conceives of the mind as an organization, analogous to an organism. Many of the advantages the authors rightly ascribe to the structural theory (see, for instance, their important chapter on regression) derive, I believe, from this difference. Perhaps the most far-reaching change was brought about by Freud's increasing understanding of the role of identification in mental life, identification not as one of the defense mechanisms, but as a crucial factor in the formation of ego and superego. This changes the role of object relations from mere need gratification to a constituent in the formation of psychic structure. Intimately connected with the theory of identification is the developing concept of narcissism and the whole problem of what Arlow and Brenner call the self-directed drives. They allude to the importance of this in regard to the new instinct theory with its duality of sexual and aggressive drives and emphasize the parallel development of the theory of aggression and of the concept of superego. I agree with them, yet I believe it equally important to stress and to elaborate the relationship between the formulation of the structural point of view and the theory of narcissism, the libidinal component of self-directed drives in its relevance for both superego and ego formation. It is the "self-directedness" of drives that is involved in formation of psychic structure (as distinguished from repression where cathexis remains object-oriented) and in its pathogenic vicissitudes and pathological developments that are most clearly visible in psychosis. And it is in this connection that the theory of narcissism is of utmost relevance to the development of the structural theory.

Since the authors pay much attention to the impact the structural theory has had on clinical problems of psychoanalysis, it is regrettable that so little is said about the importance the issue of identification has come to assume in clinical analysis. The role of defense and conflict is justifiably a center of attention in any psychoanalytic consideration, theoretical as well as clinical. But the more we advance in our understanding of psychoanalytic problems, the more, I believe, we become impressed with the importance of the deeper problems of deficiency and deformation of the psychic structures themselves, over and above the problems of conflict between the structures and defenses against it. If the authors had taken these issues more fully into consideration—and the structural theory in good part is both the result of and a guide to a clearer understanding of just these issues—they would have done more justice to the "superiority" of the structural theory; and they probably would have written a vastly different chapter on the psychopathology of the psychoses in that case.

To sum up: *Psychoanalytic Concepts and the Structural Theory* aims to establish the superiority of the structural over the topographic theory as a more valid and internally consistent conceptualization of the material of observation, as well as in its practical applications. It does so efficiently and expeditiously in a series of detailed and closely reasoned discussions of a number of issues and concepts basic in psychoanalytic theory and practice. But it does so at the cost of leaving many of the most important and difficult aspects of this theoretical shift and of its partly unrealized implications untouched, or barely touched. The mode of presentation and argumentation strikes me as dogmatic and often too elementary and didactic for this kind of material. Many unsolved and obscure questions of psychoanalytic theory look as though they were now taken care of and cleared up. This approach simplifies theory at too high a price, for the gain of a smooth, neat surface.

"The Regulatory Principles of Mental Functioning,"
BY MAX SCHUR

Schur's paper, wide-ranging, searching, closely reasoned, and dealing with some of the most abstract theoretical issues in

This section is, with a few additions, the text of my prepared discussion of a paper presented by Max Schur, entitled "The Regulatory Principles of Mental Functioning," to a scientific meeting of the Western New England Psychoanalytic Society in New Haven on February 12, 1966. A few months later his book *The Id and the Regulatory Principles of Mental Functioning* was published. His paper was a condensed version of Part 2 of that book.

psychoanalysis, requires concentrated attention and is not easy to discuss. I had the opportunity to read the manuscript of his forthcoming book, of which today's presentation is only one part, and an abbreviated part, because of time limitations. So much work and mature thought have gone into this study that it would be presumptuous to assume one could do justice to it in a brief discussion. What I will try to do is highlight and comment on some of the issues that have been of particular interest to me, as well as consider briefly aspects of some problems that he has not stressed, although I have good reason to think that he is well aware of them.

The work, of which this is the second section, is concerned with a reconsideration of the concept, id. The regulatory principles, pleasure–unpleasure principle and repetition compulsion, which Schur has chosen as subjects of today's paper, have particular relevance to the id and the instinctual drives, just as the reality principle has specific relevance to the ego. This is not to say that there is a one-to-one correlation between the pleasure–unpleasure principle or the repetition compulsion and the id, and between the reality principle and the ego. The regulatory principles, insofar as they are conceived as broad principles regulating mental functioning, mental life in its totality, would have to apply to all aspects or layers of it. Only the reality principle appears to be less inclusive, insofar as it is understood as a modification of the pleasure principle brought about by the exigencies of life, and insofar as the ego is seen as the agency shaped by these exigencies and specifically designed to deal with them.

One might speculate that it was Freud's idea of a *hierarchy* of principles that led him ultimately to postulate the repetition compulsion beyond and overriding the pleasure–unpleasure principle—as though he wished to enunciate three principles, the last two of which are modifications of the first, most comprehensive, and elementary principle: repetition compulsion; modifications imposed by the evolution from inanimate matter to biological and finally to mental life. The reality principle would apply to the highest forms of psychic life, but still be only a modification of the pleasure–unpleasure principle which, in its turn, would be but a modification of the repetition compulsion brought about by the development of life. In phenomena of human life that appear not to conform to the pleasure–unpleasure principle, one might then see evidence of deficient modification of the repetition compulsion; in behavior not conforming to the reality principle one might see evidence of deficient modification of the pleasure–unpleasure principle. I wish to make it clear that I am not committed to such a view, nor can it be said that Freud was. I mention it as a possible way of understanding Freud's hierarchy of regulatory principles.

Schur begins with an examination of the pleasure–unpleasure principle. Before doing so, he stresses an important distinction that he re-emphasizes a number of times in the course of his paper, the distinction between pleasure and unpleasure as used in the concept of a regulatory principle, and pleasure–unpleasure as affects or "experiences." It is in fact impossible to deal with the various aspects and implications of the pleasure–unpleasure principle, if these terms are understood as signifying solely the feeling of pleasure or unpleasure as conscious affective states. Confusion results, even in Freud's writings, when the applicability or nonapplicability of the principle is examined in terms of whether pleasure or unpleasure is felt. Further confusion may result when the question is raised whether it is the id or the ego that "experiences" the pleasure at issue, or whether it is the id or the ego whose wish is fulfilled or thwarted.

Freud in his earlier writings frequently used the term unpleasure principle, or the term pleasure–unpleasure principle. This is significant because of his basic theoretical assumption— from which he departed only in his last instinct theory (life–death instincts)—by which stimulation and unpleasure are equated. To be more precise: stimulation, insofar as it implies accumulation of excitation in the system that is stimulated, the psychic system, leads to unpleasure, to a state of tension or unrest within the system, which as soon as possible is reduced to zero or at least to a minimum. On the level of such a system as a psychic apparatus, stimulation, the accumulation of excitation, manifests itself as unpleasure; and any diminution of excitation manifests itself as pleasure. Unpleasure thus regulates the work of the apparatus, is the motive force of the apparatus. While it is true, therefore, that unpleasure and pleasure are not meant in this context as affects or feelings in the ordinary sense, I believe that, insofar as we are dealing with a *psychic* apparatus, unpleasure and pleasure are nevertheless to be understood as the psychic or mental representatives of accumulation and decrease of excitation, to be distinguished from the phenomena obtaining in purely biological systems (plants, for instance, or lower animals).

What is involved here is the problem of whether and in what sense one can speak of unconscious affects, in other words, the uncertain status of affects in psychoanalytic theory. And it is not clear why the notion of unconscious affective states (which are not "experienced" as such) should give greater concern than the notion of unconscious thought processes or ideas (which also are not "experienced" as such). Thus pleasure–unpleasure, as used in the concept of the pleasure–unpleasure principle, to my understanding cannot be reduced to purely biological or purely economic terms, nor should they be taken as applying to conscious-preconscious affective states except secondarily. But the very term for the model situation for the development of a wish (Schur, especially p. 68), namely the *experience* of satisfaction, indicates that something experiential, albeit unconscious, is denoted by these terms.

I believe it is justifiable to say that the repetition compulsion as a regulatory principle, tied as it is for Freud to the death instinct concept, does not go as far beyond the pleasure–unpleasure principle as one might think, except insofar as it enunciates the basic regulatory principle in more generally applicable terms, that is, in terms that apply to biological systems and to inanimate matter as well. It needs to be stressed at this point—and I fully agree here with Schur—that the concept "instinct" as used by Freud in the terms life and death instinct is a far cry from the concept "instinct"—*Trieb*—as used in the term instinctual drive prior to his last instinct theory. Instinct in his last formulation—Eros/Thanatos, life (or love) and death instinct—has connotations of primary polar forces universally applicable along the scale of cosmic evolution, connotations that were not implied in Freud's earlier instinct theories. Instinct, or instinctual drive, as used in the terms life and death instinct, is no longer a stimulus impinging on the psychic apparatus, which latter seeks to extinguish the results of a stimulation coming from outside the apparatus. In fact, what, in "Instincts and Their Vicissitudes" (Freud, 1915), was defined as the task of the psychic apparatus in its dealings with instincts (as stimuli impinging on it), has now, in

the formulation in "Beyond the Pleasure Principle" (Freud, 1920),
quoted by Schur (1966, p. 161), become the definition of an instinct. And insofar as Freud, in the same sentence, calls an
instinct "the expression of the inertia inherent in organic life,"
the constancy or inertia principle, the basis of the pleasure–
unpleasure principle, is now called instinct.[3] It looks as though
instinct now means regulatory principle. This, I believe, has
implications for the whole conception of what a psychic apparatus is and does, and these implications have to do with the
formulation of the structural theory—a theory conceptualizing
the interplay of forces and the conflicts within an organization,
constituting and structuring this organization, in contrast to a
theory of an apparatus designed to reduce or eliminate forces or
stimuli impinging on it from outside. It remained an insoluble
problem for Freud to fit his life instinct into this new definition of
instinct. While as a definition of instinct the formulation is new,
it still contains his basic theoretical assumption, mentioned before. The inertia or constancy or unpleasure or Nirvana principle,
of which the repetition compulsion is merely a broader, all-
inclusive version with an emphasis on repeating or returning to
an original state of things, fits in perfectly with the death instinct,
insofar as the latter is "the expression of the inertia inherent in
organic life." In this sense, the death instinct is really nothing
new, not a conception that should have taken psychoanalysts by
surprise. It seems to imply a conception of evolution as a circular,
or spiral, rather than a straight line, movement. What is new, and
does not seem to fit with the inertia principle (as Freud, 1940,
chapter 2, clearly acknowledges), is the concept of Eros, the life
or love instinct.

I am in essential agreement with Schur (1966), therefore,
when he says: "In *The Ego and the Id* (Freud, 1923), the role of
Eros emerged more distinctly as the disturber of the pleasure

3. The relevant passages are as follows: "[T]he nervous system is an apparatus
which has the function of getting rid of the stimuli that reach it, or of reducing them to the
lowest possible level; or which, if it were feasible, would maintain itself in an altogether
unstimulated condition" (Freud, 1915, p. 120). "*It seems, then, that an instinct is an urge
inherent in organic life to restore an earlier state of things* which the living entity has
been obliged to abandon under the pressure of external disturbing forces; that is, it is a
kind of organic elasticity or, to put it another way, the expression of the inertia inherent
in organic life" (Freud, 1920, p. 36).

principle (which Freud at this juncture equated alternately with the constancy and the Nirvana principles, under the dominance of the death instinct)" (p. 147). Schur calls attention to formulations in *The Ego and the Id* and in "The Economic Problem of Masochism" (Freud, 1924) that clearly show the emergence of Eros as distinct and different from the constancy principle and the Nirvana principle, which are "entirely in the service of the death instincts." And in the latter paper Freud gives a new meaning, conforming to his conception of Eros, to the term pleasure principle, and to the term libido. I therefore believe it is useful to make a distinction between a pleasure principle and an unpleasure principle, as Schur proposes, and that such a distinction is in accordance with some of Freud's most significant later formulations.

I have difficulty, however, in following Schur when he claims that Freud, in his earlier writings, meant withdrawal from *too intense* stimulation, in stipulating the unpleasure principle as the regulatory principle. I maintain that it was Freud's basic premise that *any* stimulation gives rise to unpleasure, that he defined unpleasure not as *excessive* excitation but as any degree of excitation, and that this view was essential to his theory of the workings of the psychic apparatus as then conceived by him. His life instinct, Eros or libido, and pleasure principle as reformulated in "The Economic Problem of Masochism" (1924), is a breach in this theory—a breach that Freud rather desperately tried to mend, for instance, in some of his speculations in *Beyond the Pleasure Principle* (1920). To my understanding, according to Freud's theory as formulated in *The Interpretation of Dreams* (1900), the memory of the experience of satisfaction is cathected insofar as it leads to the extinction of instinctual stimulation, and not because the stimuli inherent in this memory are sought for themselves. True: if life instinct has any meaning it must mean that excitation, tension inherent in life processes, is sought and not simply abolished or fended off, that stimuli are sought. This, I assume, is also Schur's understanding of the "approach response." But such a conception (with which I agree) is incompatible with Freud's models, "utilized both implicitly and explicitly in describing the development, functioning, and protection of the mental apparatus, and its 'regulating principles,'" as listed by Schur (1966, pp. 142–143), including the fifth model (experience of satisfaction, wish, and instinctual drives). Any wish to recathect a memory including certain stimuli was based for Freud on the unpleasure inherent in stimulation (in this context, stimulation by instinctual stimuli). The experience of satisfaction, as far as his model goes, consists in the diminution or extinction of excitation. To quote from chapter 7: ". . . the accumulation of excitation . . . is felt as unpleasure and . . . sets the apparatus in action with a view to repeating the *experience of satisfaction, which involved a diminution of excitation and was felt as pleasure.* A current of this kind in the apparatus, starting from unpleasure and aiming at pleasure, we have termed a 'wish'" (Freud, 1900, p. 598, italics added). Pleasure, the experience of satisfaction, means diminution of excitation. The experience of external fright, which Freud discusses in the same context (ibid., p. 600), is adduced by Schur to show that Freud, in speaking of the unpleasure principle, had excessive stimulation in mind (Schur, 1966, pp. 133–34), and not stimulation per se. But it seems to me that Freud's discussion of this issue is concerned with the crucial alternative to the experience of satisfaction (as defined by him two pages earlier), in the absence of the possibility of its realization: if the excitation cannot be diminished by an experience of satisfaction or its recathected memory trace, if unpleasure cannot be diminished or extinguished in this way, then another mechanism comes into play, namely turning away from or the avoidance of the painful memory, i.e., the prototype of repression (Freud, 1900, p. 600). Freud's discussion of the experience of external fright does deal with too intense stimulation, but it does no more than explain the regulation by the unpleasure principle in this particular and crucial case; it does not deny or revoke the notion that stimulation that can be diminished by the experience of satisfaction is also unpleasurable and that this sequence of events, too, is "regulated" by the unpleasure principle.

My insistence on this issue does not prevent me from recognizing that Freud, even at this stage of his research, was keenly aware of the *phenomena* that have been subsumed under such terms as stimulus seeking, stimulus hunger, approach response, and that they significantly entered into his considerations of the experience of satisfaction. But his explanatory concepts, at this time, were firmly based on the constancy principle and reflex arc physiology, and predicated on the postulate that the psychic apparatus is a system whose function and purpose it is to reduce or, if feasible, abolish stimulation. As late as 1915 this is clearly stated in the introductory pages of "Instincts and Their Vicissitudes" (Freud, 1915, pp. 118–20). Some doubts are expressed, without being elaborated, pointing in the direction his thought is going to take him in *Beyond the Pleasure Principle* and especially in "The Economic Problem of Masochism," toward the end of this introduction (ibid., p. 121, see also footnote by Strachey). But I thoroughly agree with Schur that with the emergence of the structural theory and the life instinct, pleasure, libido, and thus a pleasure principle take on different connotations. This has to do, I believe, with the important change of Freud's views on the significance of object relations in the broadest sense (environmental "stimuli") and the emergence of identification and internalization as crucial psychological processes.

I will have to abstain from a more detailed discussion of Schur's consideration of the repetition compulsion. Difficult, ambiguous, and controversial as the concepts of a repetition compulsion and a death instinct are, I feel that they cannot be easily discarded and deserve further consideration. This is true particularly if, as Schur so convincingly shows in his chapters on the id, the id concept deserves much fuller understanding and elaboration than it has been accorded under the impact of ego psychology. In this spirit, let me say a few words about the daemonic.

I don't think that Freud, when speaking of the daemonic, is primarily concerned, as Schur states, "with the consequences and not with the forces at work" (Schur, 1966, pp. 168–69). For instance, in his discussion of repetition in "The Uncanny" (Freud, 1919), published a year before *Beyond the Pleasure Principle,* he clearly is concerned with the daemonic in the sense of the power of early, primal forces and experiences (whether for good or evil as to consequences) that dominate life and that, insofar as they are recognized or intimated, convey the sense of the uncanny. According to Webster (1947), daemon (in Greek religion) is "a deity regarded as a supernatural power rather than as a person; hence, some being never definitely personified, but recognized as exerting power, especially over the lives and fortunes of men." I believe the concern with the daemonic is a reflection of Freud's working up to the concept of the id as something we are lived by. The id concept has connotations implying that we are lived by forces we never fully control or master, forces that thus have an impersonal or not quite personal character; forces that are earlier in time than what we might call the forces or strength of the ego and in a sense override all later developments and acquisitions of personal will and control, as though the latter were new-comers, superficial layers of the personality, not the kernel and essence of our motivations and actions. Schur, in his extensive discussion of the id concept (1966, pp. 11–122) points out the fallacy of current tendencies to reduce the concept id to a purely economic one, although Freud in some ways has contributed to this tendency. It is also implied in a more comprehensive id concept that these forces, in pure culture so to speak, represent both the most creative and most destructive potentialities of the personality. The words "daemonic," Eros, death instinct, must be heard in that sense, too. Such potentialities, this daemonic core, the id (the psychoanalytic concept of omnipotence is related to this), need limitations and discipline to allow the conduct of a human life. But human life ends through illness or self-exhaustion, and in this sense it can be said that it destroys itself, compelled by forces beyond its control to repeat the cycle of life and death. If we look at the death instinct and the repetition compulsion in that light, perhaps the last word has not been said about these concepts and their range and validity. I am convinced that Freud struggled with such ideas, attempting to force them into the rather uncongenial channels of somewhat antiquated scientific-economic concepts and formulations.

When it comes to the examples Freud gives of phenomena and processes, which in his view tend to demonstrate the rule of the repetition compulsion as an all-embracing and "impersonal" principle, it is my impression that he was not so much regarding them as "scientific proofs" for his new theory, but that he felt these phenomena contain a residuum of inexplicability in terms of his old theories, which made him grope for different explanations. As suggestive as Schur's explanation of the repetition of traumatic events in dreams is, for me such a residuum remains; and this generally applies, in my opinion, to the "resistance of the id," so closely related to Freud's conception of the repetition compulsion. This does not deny or in any way minimize the ego aspects of post-traumatic dream repetition, which Schur so convincingly describes.

The repetition compulsion as manifested, for Freud, in the resistance of the id, leads me to the last point I wish to comment on, namely the relations between id resistance and working through. Working through is an activity in which the ego, but not necessarily or exclusively the conscious ego, works over the old conflictful experiences and their "compulsive" repetitions in current life and particularly in the transference situation. As I have stated elsewhere (1955), I believe that the term working through does not primarily apply to that sector of the analytic work that has to do with the lifting of repressions and the analysis of ego defenses, but most specifically to the work concerned with id resistances, the compulsion to repeat in the clinical sense, with "the attraction exerted by the unconscious prototypes upon the repressed instinctual process" (Freud, 1926, p. 159). There undoubtedly is, in this compulsion to repeat painful affects and conflicts, in the compulsion to re-enact traumatic events in dreams and in the transference neurosis and the "fate neuroses," a more or less prominent component of a "wish to undo the past" (Schur, 1966, p. 189). But there is likely to be also—and I believe I am here in essential agreement with Schur—a wish for re-doing the past—not exclusively a wish to do away with what happened to the patient by dint of unfeeling parents or evil fates, but also a wish to experience, to deal with whatever happened in a different way. This wish tends to be thwarted by "the attraction exerted by the unconscious prototypes upon the repressed instinctual process." This wish would also be an ego aspect of the compulsion to repeat, not of the primitive ego and its magical operations, but of the more mature part, which tends to repeat on higher levels of organization. Repetition is a term that requires further clarification; it should not be restricted to the meaning of mere duplication.

One also gains the impression that frequently there is a tendency in patients to stick to and repeat the traumatic experience just *because* of its age, so to speak, just because of its intensity and primordial quality; one might say: just because of its daemonic quality. If one wishes to speak of masochism here, it could be characterized loosely as a masochistic surrender of the ego to the id. One can sense such things particularly in some young patients: a resistance to having to give up something that is precious, whether painful or blissful, in its intensity and uniqueness—a uniqueness that also has to do with the fact that the event was experienced for the first time, something that tends to give experiences a poignancy never to be attained again, but forever longed for. Working through has to contend with such resistances, among others. If you say that I am talking here not so much of a death instinct in Freud's sense, but more of an urge toward the bliss and pain of consuming oneself in the intensity of being lived by the id, you may be right. Ecstatic states, whether induced by drugs or religious and erotic ecstasies, may have this lure where love and self-destruction, Eros and Thanatos are merged into one. Yet, with regard to Freud's death instinct and repetition compulsion, such things were likely to be in his mind, too, when he brooded over the death instinct and the fusions and defusions of libido and aggression, over primary narcissism and primary masochism and the repetition compulsion.

Working through seems to be the work of the ego to repeat "actively" what was experienced "passively," to repeat on a higher level—a level of more dimensions and further differentiated and integrated experience and functioning. Working through has decidedly to do with redoing, not with undoing, the past. The repetition involved here is not duplication or reiteration, but re-creation, to be distinguished from reproduction. To speak of such re-creative repetition as a "compulsion" means speaking from a point of view that is outside the self, beyond the ego and the id and the superego, overreaching the pleasure and reality principles.

REFERENCES

Freud, S. (1900): *The Interpretation of Dreams*. S.E. 5.
———. (1915): S.E. 14.
———. (1919): S.E. 17.
———. (1920): S.E. 18.
———. (1923): S.E. 19.
———. (1926): S.E. 20.
———. (1940): S.E. 23.
Loewald, H. W. (1955): Hypnoid State, Repression, Abreaction and Recollection. *J. Amer. Psychoanal. Assn.* 3:201–10. Reprinted in this volume.
Schur, M. (1966): *The Id and the Regulatory Principles of Mental Functioning*. New York: International Universities Press.

6

ON INTERNALIZATION

When we speak of psychic life everything depends on the standpoint we take. If we take the standpoint of the sexual and aggressive drives, of id psychology, anything short of direct achievements of their aims, anything short of immediate gratification of the needs they bespeak, represents at best a detour, at worst a failure. Seen from this point of view, the whole of man's psychic life is a detour and a failure, and man may be called the sick animal. From the viewpoint of object relations as the manifestation of these needs, narcissism, psychic structure formation, internalization appear to be a second-best born of frustration, disappointment and fear, a defensive flight from reality or adaptational devices of dubious merit.

Seen from the standpoint of the inner life of man, of his inner world that appears to have come about in the ways just alluded to, the reality from which it was supposed to be an escape or to whose exigencies it was supposed to be an adaptation—this reality tends to seem an illusion. The objects, whose loss or the withdrawal from which were supposed to make such an inner world of substitutes necessary, from the standpoint of that mental world seem themselves like substitutes, fleeting, ephemeral, insubstantial in comparison with the enduring inner reality.

This paper, first published in 1973, was presented in a shorter version to the San Francisco Psychoanalytic Society in 1965. During the academic year 1965–66, under the auspices of the Western New England Institute for Psychoanalysis, a series of postgraduate seminars on the subject of Internalization was held in New Haven. The topic was proposed by me; Roy Schafer and I were the discussion leaders. A number of invited guest speakers—Edith Jacobson, Heinz Kohut, Heinz Lichtenstein, Samuel Novey, Talcott Parsons, and Max Schur—presented their views at different sessions. The first session was devoted to discussions of some of my pertinent papers, including the early version of the present article. These discussions and presentations contributed to clarifications and expansions of some of the issues involved.

A more ambitious writing project of mine was to encompass the material of this paper, but it grew in the process and is still unfinished. I therefore decided in 1972 to publish the paper in its present form.

If we adopt the point of view of psychic structure and of the life of the mind under a somewhat different perspective, we may see the instinctual drives as elements, rudiments, as primitive manifestations of man's psychic life, rather than as manifestations of biological processes that have degenerated in the course of time to defensive and unhealthy forms of life, which we have come to call psychic processes. Likewise, early object ties may be viewed then as necessary antecedents, as foreshadowings and portents of intrapsychic relations and structures, of the character of a man, and of his interactions with the world of external reality.

Much can be said for an oscillation between such various standpoints, as perhaps in their juxtaposition and combination lies the secret of success in understanding more about the conflicted and ambiguous creatures that we are. The richness and imprecision of psychoanalytic psychology are, to an extent, due to such oscillations, implicit as they have for the most part remained. It also is one of its characteristics that psychoanalytic psychology does not view the psychic life of the individual in isolation, but in its manifold relations and intertwinings with other spheres and aspects of life, such as social-cultural life and the somatic-biological sphere. It tends to see these as reflected in and as reflections of the individual psyche; and in these respects they are within the realm of psychoanalytic investigation. Nevertheless, the ultimate commitment of psychoanalysis as a science is to human psychic structure and functioning and their development and vicissitudes. If the physical nature of the universe is the topic of the physical sciences, and the nature of life the topic of biology, it is the nature of the individual psyche that is the topic of psychoanalysis. In this sense psychoanalysis is a far more limited science than physics or biology, and more limited than psychology viewed as a general science of psychic phenomena.

The concept of internalization allows us to approach the question of how psychic structure and psychic functioning in the individual come about and how they are maintained and developed. Our question here is not primarily what functions and purposes psychic structures serve; we are not asking about ego and superego *functions,* what ego and superego do once they are there. But we ask how they are formed, maintained, and develop, *how they function,* by virtue of what genetic and dynamic principles—granted that their functions and purposes may throw light on these matters. Internalization, to anticipate, is conceived as the basic way of functioning of the psyche, not as one of its functions.

The terms *internalization, internalize, inner world,* and *internal world* have been used in a number of different ways. Nietzsche, whose direct and indirect influence on Freud and his early followers has been generally underrated, discusses internalization in his book *The Genealogy of Morals* in the context of an evolutionary consideration of the genesis of guilt and conscience (Nietzsche, 1887). He writes:

> All instincts [*Instinkte* in the original] that do not discharge outwardly turn inward. This is what I call man's internalization; with it begins to grow in man what later is called his "soul" (p. 217; translation modified).

Compare with this formulation Freud's "vicissitude" of "an instinct's turning round upon one's own person" (1915). Nietzsche maintains here that internalization (*Verinnerlichung*), speaking phylogenetically, developed under the pressure of novel biological and socializing conditions. However, the turning inward of instincts, according to him, is not so much a direct consequence of external pressures, but an indirect one: changed environmental conditions and new cultural-societal developments tended to render outward drive discharge pointless and unprofitable in certain respects, rather than that it was simply suppressed by external forces. It is not so much pressure from external, overpowering and hostile forces, leading ultimately to what today would be called repression, but pressure from inner, instinctual forces, deprived of their interaction with external forces, which leads to internalization according to Nietzsche. We might say that he does not conceive of instincts as internal stimuli impinging on a psychic apparatus, but as psychic forces that when turned inward and deployed in the interior of the psychic force-field, bring about the formation of a soul, of a "psychic apparatus." In psychoanalytic terms, what Nietzsche describes is the transformation of libidinal and aggressive cathexis into narcissistic and masochistic cathexis, with a one-sided emphasis in the passage quoted on aggression. His discussion also demonstrates an abrupt and conscious change of viewpoint, at first vividly describing the unhappy fate of an animal whose instincts become unhinged, then switching to a description of the novel and fascinating "spectacle" of the genesis of a soul, of man as human. Hartmann's (1939) "change of function," a concept discussed and much emphasized by Nietzsche in this chapter of his book, is related to this change of viewpoint.

Freud rarely uses the word "internalization," but he does speak of the internalization of aggressive tendencies in the process of development from primitive to civilized man (1933b, 1937) and tentatively brings it into connection with a predilection for internal conflict and with the death instinct (1937). In "Group Psychology and the Analysis of the Ego" (1921) he speaks of "external obstacles becoming internal," in the "New Introductory Lectures" (1933a) of internalization of external restraints, and in "Inhibition, Symptoms and Anxiety" (1926) of the internalization of danger. In the latter work he implies degrees of internalization from castration anxiety to social anxiety and to fear of conscience. The term "inner" or "internal world" (Innenwelt) is used by him in reference to thought processes (ideational representation) as well as to identification.

Hartmann (1939) and Hartmann & Loewenstein (1962), while defining internalization more precisely, use it and the term inner or internal world, in a global sense similar to Freud's, with adaptation as the commanding point of view. They attempt to differentiate internalization from identification, incorporation and introjection, but their discussion remains admittedly inconclusive. Basically, Freud and Hartmann & Loewenstein speak of internalization as a process by which "regulations . . . in interaction with the outside world" (Hartmann & Loewenstein, 1962) become intrapsychic, regardless of the processes involved and of the kind of internality created. Schur (1966), even more than Hartmann, conceives of internalization in broad evolutionary-biological terms, a view that does not run counter to my use of the term but is far broader and not specifically psychoanalytic.

Rapaport (1957) and Sandler (1960), each in a different way and using different terminology, specifically discriminate between the construction of inner models or schemata (Sandler) or an inner map (Rapaport) of the external world, and "taking in" processes subsumed under such terms as identification, introjection, etc. Rapaport makes a distinction between "the inner world, which regulates the orientation in the external world," an "inner map," and the internal world of "the major structures, the identifications, defense structures, ego, id., etc." He criticizes Hartmann, I believe correctly, for lumping these two different processes together in his definition of internalization, but states that "man's inner map of his world is . . . in the force-field of the organization of the internal world" (1957). I believe it to be crucial to make such a distinction. My own use of internalization refers to the processes involved in the creation of such an internal world and to its structural resultants, and not to the construction of inner models, schemata, or maps, which are representations of the external world of objects and of their relations. The latter I will tentatively consider as mental functions made possible by the creation of that internal world.

Important as it is, I will not discuss in this paper the Kleinian concept of internalization and internal objects. Nor can I consider here Roy Schafer's important contribution to the subject (1968) and his critique of my conceptions referring to an earlier version of the present paper.[1]

INTERNALIZATION AND REPRESSION-DEFENSE

For the moment, I will subsume under the term "internalization" a variety of differently named processes, such as psychic incorporation, introjection, identification, and an instinct's turning round upon one's own person ("self-directed drives," Arlow & Brenner, 1964).

I have stressed the importance of the standpoint one takes in considering psychic development. Taking the standpoint of the constancy principle, processes of living matter, and *a fortiori* psychic processes, are deviations, detours on the road to a state of rest, and must ultimately be understood as defenses against influences that disturb the original state of rest. Defense, then, is the essential function and purpose of psychic processes, and their higher, more complex organization in the course of develop-

1. W. W. Meissner, in a series of papers, significantly contributed to the clarification of the concepts of internalization and identification (1970, 1971, 1972, 1974). These papers were not available when I wrote my article.

ment is only further evidence of the continuing defensive battle, comparable to Freud's description of the development and organization of phobic constructions. Repression, insofar as it misfires in what is called the return of the repressed, is unsuccessful as a defense, and that share of the repressed which tends to return in neurotic manifestations should be included in the ego organization rather than be excluded by the ego. Instead of defending against the troublesome material by repressing it, the ego, especially in analysis, may accept and include the material in its own organization. This acceptance may take various forms. But here we must halt and ask ourselves what has happened to our concept of defense. Has the ego, whose function and purpose as a psychic formation it was to ward off or abolish influences that disturb the return to an original state of rest, albeit by complex detours—has this ego not in fact given up its function of defense, if we can say that defense is replaced by acceptance?

What has happened is that our standpoint has shifted. When we started to speak of repression as defense and of the ego's organization that should include rather than exclude the repressed material, our standpoint became that of the ego. The ego's acceptance and inclusion of the repressed may, from the point of view of the constancy or Nirvana principle, be seen as nothing but a defensive operation of a higher order than repression. But from the point of view of the ego, defense has been replaced by acceptance, the ego has been enriched. For the ego it is a gain in its organization and functioning. What from the viewpoint of psychic life is higher and richer organization, from the viewpoint of the constancy principle is a further complication and delay on the return road to the state of rest. One might indeed maintain that repression, to the extent to which it is successful, deadens and restricts psychic life, thus being a more direct route to the state of rest and preferable from this standpoint. With further and higher ego organization, far from getting closer to a state of rest, there is more life.

Once we adopt the point of view of the ego, of psychic organization, we operate with a concept of defense where defense is understood as being in the interest of the ego and as being useful only insofar as it is in the interest of the ego. The ego defends itself against forces that would disrupt it, but in so doing it runs the risk of limiting its domain, while unsuccessful defense tends

to be more disruptive. Internalization, in the sense of identification as used by Freud most explicitly in the third chapter of *The
Ego and the Id,* is a process radically different from repression as
a defense mechanism of the ego by which the ego protects its
own current organization. In internalization, in contrast, the ego
opens itself up, loosens its current organization to allow for its
own further growth. Similarly, I submit that the formation of the
superego, from the viewpoint of the ego, cannot be understood as
a defense, successful or unsuccessful, against the Oedipus complex, or as a repression of it, but as something quite different.
Freud suggested this without going further into the problem. The
impulses involved in the Oedipus complex are not repressed, to
the extent to which a genuine superego structure is formed, but,
as Freud puts it, the complex is destroyed, dissolved. In its stead
and out of its elements psychic structure is formed by the process
I call internalization. In "The Dissolution of the Oedipus Complex" (1924*b*) Freud writes: "the process ... is more than a repression"; if it is not, the Oedipus complex "persists in the id and will
later manifest its pathogenic effects," granted that normally,
fluid and fragile as the superego is as a psychic structure, both
processes are involved in the "resolution" of the Oedipus complex.

I wish to make it clear that, while superego formation is a
particularly accessible instance of internalization, internalization comprises much more than the formation of the superego; it
is crucially involved in the formation of the ego itself. In this
paper, however, I shall predominantly have reference to the
superego as a clear example of internalization.

What is the nature of the process called destruction of the
Oedipus complex? Insofar as the complex reappears, although
on a different level, after the latency period, at the beginning of
puberty, Freud can speak of "the ego's turning away" from it
(*ibid.*). But if there is something like a destruction of the complex
taking place, which "ushers in the latency period" (*ibid.*), can that
be termed as a turning away? To the extent to which the complex
is destroyed, the ego does not turn away from it, does not turn the
complex away from itself, repress it, but turns to it and "demol-
ishes" it or assimilates it to itself. Such assimilation involves,
using the analogy of biological metabolic processes, a destruction of relationships and structures into their elements and an
internal restructuring of these elements within a different organ-

izational setting, so that novel but in some ways related structures evolve.

I believe it is of the utmost importance, both theoretically and
clinically, to distinguish much more sharply and consistently
than Freud ever did between processes of repression and processes of internalization. The latter are involved in creating and
increasing coherent integration and organization of the psyche
as a whole, whereas repression works against such coherent
psychic organization by maintaining a share of psychic processes
in a less organized, more primitive state or returning them to
such a state, the state of the id. The libidinal-aggressive object
cathexes of the Oedipus complex, by repression, are kept in a
deficient mode of discharge processes with objects; they are not
"destroyed" and assimilated by the coherent ego but are, instead,
repressed, maintained in a state of lower psychic organization,
and interactions with objects continue to take place on lower
levels of psychic organization. Repression tends to keep object
representations and object relations on an infantile level. Internalization, on the other hand, is a process by which, in the
example of superego formation, oedipal object relations are renounced as such, destroyed, and the resulting elements enter
into the formation of higher psychic structure, leading in turn to
the development of object relations of a higher order of organization. Whether and to what extent repression or internalization
predominates in a given case depends, as far as we know, to a
considerable degree on environmental conditions, i.e., in the
oedipal situation, on the parental figures since they are vitally
involved in the interaction process. It seems safe to say that renunciation and destruction of the Oedipus complex, and its
internal reconstruction in the form of the superego, is most likely
to occur where the oedipal relationships have been adequate,
neither overwhelming nor excessively frustrating and prohibi-
tory.

While in defensive organization (repression) object cathexis
is maintained on an infantile level, internalization implies a
transformation of object cathexis into narcissistic cathexis, that
is, more complex ego organization. The destruction of the Oedipus complex consists in the relinquishment of oedipal object
relations, the dissolution of oedipal object cathexes and their
transformation out of the ruins, so to speak, into narcissistic

cathexes, cathexes that establish and maintain psychic structure (I use narcissistic here in a metapsychological, not in a clinical-descriptive sense.) The process is akin to the work of mourning as I have attempted to describe it in a previous paper (1962).

In repression the oedipal object cathexes, while detached from the parental persons, persist in unconscious fantasies of such object relations, whereas in genuine superego formation we are confronted not with unconscious fantasies—portrayals, as it were, of object relations—but with intrapsychic reconstructions, non-objective, if I may use this term here in a sense similar to what we mean when speaking of non-objective art. There, too, a destruction of the object and of the ordinary relations with the object takes place, and a reconstruction, following new principles of structuring. We may say that non-objective art, by communicating such novel structuralization, opens up new dimensions of reality organization. The same holds true for internalization insofar as object relations, based on higher or novel psychic structure achieved by the process of internalization, are thus raised to a new level; the objects with which these relations are entertained have thus gained a new degree and quality of integration. In our superego example, the relinquishment and internalization of oedipal object relations leads to object relations of a new, more mature cast. The primitive, archaic modes in which the child sees and relates to his parents give way to a more mature relationship to them as well as to non-incestuous objects. For the child the reality of parents and other objects changes as he matures, he does not simply relate in a different way to fixed, given objects.

Under certain circumstances the formation of psychic structure by internalization is reversible to a certain degree, just as repression under certain circumstances is reversible. Such reversions may take place in analysis, and what may be termed a return from internalization is familiar to us from the vicissitudes of superego changes during the psychoanalytic process. The reversibility of internalizations plays a prominent role in psychosis due to the lability of psychic structure in psychotic disorders; space does not permit me to go into this important area here.

We return to the "destruction of the Oedipus complex" as an instance of psychic structure formation through internalization. The destruction of the complex in itself, of course, is but a step in psychic structure building. I emphasize the destruction phase at this point in order to make it clear that the factor involved in superego formation is not repression; or, to be cautious, that repression is not enough. Something that is repressed is not destroyed, insofar as it stays repressed and is not crushed. Its structure is preserved, although its "location" is changed and its structure may be loosened or under strain. What is radically changed is the relation of the repressed to the coherent ego; the coherent ego has turned it away from itself, or has turned away from the repressed. Freud, in *Beyond the Pleasure Principle* (1920), at the beginning of the third chapter, and in *The Ego and the Id* (1923), end of the first chapter, corrects his view of the dynamics of neurotic conflict: from a structural point of view the antithesis is not between the conscious and the unconscious, but "between the coherent ego and the repressed." The point in this new formulation is that it is not the fact of its being unconscious that characterizes the repressed (although it *is* unconscious), but the fact of its being split off from the coherent ego. What is internalized, in the sense in which I use the term, is not split off from the coherent ego but becomes or has become an integral part of the coherent ego. While what is internalized and what is repressed are both unconscious (in the dynamic sense), the former is a structural element of the coherent ego, the latter, the repressed, is not. The superego, as a "differentiating grade in the ego," is not split off from the coherent ego but a further differentiation of it, a further organization of ego structure made possible by the dissolution of the Oedipus complex. We might say that such terms as desexualization and neutralization denote destructive (catabolic) phases of the process involved in internalization, while such terms as identification and sublimation indicate constructive (anabolic) phases of the process.

We may ask whether repression, under given circumstances, could be a way-station on the road to internalization. It is conceivable that repressed material may ultimately be dealt with by the coherent ego, not by "making the unconscious conscious," but by unconscious ego processes which undo the splitting off. But insofar and as long as repression is an active process, characterized by the ego's defensive activity of protecting its current organization against disruptive influences, repression is in opposition to internalization and prevents it, as much as it prevents or inhibits adequate interaction with the external world.

In the course of the development of his last instinct theory Freud began to shift his position in regard to the constancy principle and its elaborations in the form of the pleasure–unpleasure principle, the Nirvana principle, and the death instinct. The subject is far too complex to discuss here in any detail. Max Schur, in his book *The Id and the Regulatory Principles of Mental Functioning* (1966), has materially contributed to its clarification. Suffice it to say, in our present context, that the proposition of a duality of Eros and Thanatos, the life instinct and the death instinct, as a metapsychological assumption, for the first time establishes, although only tentatively, an independent psychic force that does not follow the constancy or Nirvana principle. The metapsychological (economic) meaning of pleasure, in the old pleasure principle, was the abolition or diminution of unpleasure or "stimulus tension," in pursuit of the return to a state of absolute rest or "death." This tendency in psychic processes is now called the death instinct. In this sense the death instinct is nothing new, but merely a new conceptualization of the constancy principle. What *is* new in Freud's last instinct theory is the life instinct as a force or tendency *sui generis,* not reducible to the old pleasure–unpleasure principle (I follow here Freud's brief exposition in "The Economic Problem of Masochism," 1924a). The pleasure principle is newly defined as owing its reign to the power of Eros, while the old pleasure–unpleasure principle or Nirvana or constancy principle owes its power to Thanatos, the death instinct. This change of viewpoint is, at least in part, due to Freud's finally capitulating before the fact that stimulus tension is, in and of itself, not necessarily unpleasurable and a state that tends to be avoided, no matter how much the constancy principle demands this conclusion. Tension is no longer seen exclusively from the standpoint of inanimate matter, as a disturbance—to be abolished—of the state of absolute rest, i.e., as something to be defended against. Life and psychic life are no longer seen simply as circuitous processes ultimately ruled exclusively by the Nirvana principle and motivated by the death instinct. According to this new development in Freud's theory formation, a force must be assumed to operate in mental processes that favors the tensions of mental life, works in opposition to as well as in fusion with the motivating power of the death instinct, and which promotes higher or more complex organization of the psychic structures resulting from, and transforming in their turn, psychic processes.

Seen in this perspective, we might attempt the formulation that repression, insofar as it maintains psychic processes and structures on lower organizational levels, is under the sway of the death instinct or of the constancy–Nirvana principle. While internalization, insofar as it leads to higher organization and an enriched psychic life, is under the sway of Eros or of the newly defined pleasure principle and its modification, the reality principle. Such a formulation allows for a share of the other polar force in both processes. This is necessary in order not to do violence to the fact that repression–defense has a protective function, and that internalization, if unchecked by the lure of objects external to the psyche's own structures, and if these structures are unprotected against overload by defensive barriers, leads to inner sterility and diffusion. To complete the picture of the change in his fundamental standpoint, it should be stated that Freud's old sexual and ego instincts were both conceived as following the unpleasure or Nirvana principle: the sexual instincts inasmuch as their aim was satisfaction (understood as the elimination of stimulus tension); the ego instincts inasmuch as their ultimate aim was defense against stimulation, although by circuitous routes.

The role of object ties and object relations—and this is most important for the understanding of internalization—is no longer that of being merely means for the achievement of satisfaction, that is, for discharge of stimulus tension (the definition of the object of an instinct in "Instincts and Their Vicissitudes"). Object ties in the form of identifications and introjections become constitutive elements in psychic structure formation, in the formation of ego and superego seen not as defense structures against instinctual and environmental stimuli, but as more developed and more structured organizations of instinctual-interactive forces.

INTERNALIZATION AND IDENTIFICATION

Internalization takes place on different levels of development. Object relations in the strict sense become constituted only on the level of the Oedipus situation; prior to this stage in development, reality is pre-objective. Boundaries between subject and object, distinctions between them, on pre-oedipal levels are either nonexistent or only fleetingly present, fluid, blurred, so that at least no clear or constant distinction between self and object world, between inside and outside, is maintained. If this is so, speaking of internalization on such early levels of development means speaking of processes by which inner and outer are being differentiated by recurrent sortings and resortings. As I have formulated it in my paper "Internalization, Separation, Mourning, and the Superego" (1962), internality as well as externality is being established by such early, primary internalizations and externalizations. These are to be considered as the first steps in ego organization. Only on the basis of this relatively firmly established psychic structure do the later, secondary internalizations and externalizations take place, such as those leading to superego formation. I cannot in this paper discuss the assumption of primary ego autonomy (Hartmann), which is not in keeping with the ideas on ego formation advanced here. In my opinion Hartmann's hypothesis raises metapsychological problems, which render its unquestioned acceptance premature, to say the least.

The usage of the terms "object" and "object relations," when referring to pre-oedipal stages of ego development, can be justified only by the fact that such distinctions exist for the nonpsychoanalytic observer. The naive observer sees a baby relate to his mother, one individual to another; but this clearly is not the psychological situation for the baby. Nor is it the psychological situation for the mother at all times, at any rate during early infancy. There are other situations and phenomena in adult life in which the subject–object distinction tends to become blurred or temporarily to vanish, as for instance in a passionate love relationship and other "ecstatic" states, which, while rare and exceptional, cannot be called pathological.

We are dealing here with the fact that early levels of psychic development are not simply outgrown and left behind but continue to be active, at least intermittently, during later life including adulthood. They coexist, although overshadowed by later developmental stages, with later stages and continue to have their impact on them. Ernst Kris has discussed these and related problems under the title "regression in the service of the ego," and Freud referred to them as the "general problem of preservation in the sphere of the mind" or of the survival of earlier ego states. Perhaps it is significant that Freud in this connection again considers the question of the destruction of "what is past in mental life," discussing the possibility that "some of what is old is effaced or absorbed . . . to such an extent that it cannot be restored or revivified by any means" (1930). I believe that he touches here on the question, raised earlier in my paper, of the reversibility of internalizations. In the present context this question is relevant insofar as primary internalizations may and do continue to play a role in post-oedipal and adult life. That is to say, the distinction between inside and outside—the basis for what we call object relations and objective reality—may become blurred or vanish for certain aspects and during more or less brief periods of reality organization; a dedifferentiation may take place by which the two become re-merged and subsequently re-differentiate from one another in novel ways—psychic events that are most important for the understanding of creative processes.

But even where the subject–object distinction seems firmly established, where there seems to be no question of a weakening or loss of ego boundaries as we may observe it in exceptional or pathological states, the situation is less clear than we often assume. Any close, intimate object relationship has narcissistic features, identifications are involved. We become aware of this most acutely at a time of separation from such an object, or when we lose it. We may feel then that we have received a wound, as though a part of ourself has been torn off, a part that was strongly cathected with a kind of cathexis similar to the investment in our own body parts, of which we become aware when such a part is injured. What many people experience when their car is damaged is of a similar nature.

The psychological phenomena mentioned suggest that object relations contain elements of libidinal-aggressive cathexes as well as identification elements in varying proportions, frequently one aspect more or less completely overshadowing or predominating over the other. Internalization involves a giving up of both, the libidinal-aggressive as well as the identification elements in object relations. Here I will be concerned with the difference between identification and internalization, considered as end states or resultants of mental processes. Identification as such leads to an identity of subject and object or of parts or aspects of them. Insofar as, in identification, they become identical, one and the same, there is a merging or confusion of subject and object. Identification tends to erase a difference: subject becomes object and object becomes subject. Identification is a way-station to internalization, but in internalization, if carried to completion, a redifferentiation has taken place by which both subject and object have been reconstituted, each on a new level of organization. When we speak of the internalization of object relations, such as in the resolution of the Oedipus complex and in the work of mourning, it is not, if the processes are brought to completion, a matter of maintaining identifications with the objects to be relinquished; the latter is the case in melancholia where the object and the identifications with the object cannot be given up. In internalization it is a matter of transforming these relations into an internal, intrapsychic, depersonified relationship, thus increasing and enriching psychic structure: the identity with the object is renounced. Internalization as a completed process implies an emancipation from the object. To the extent—always limited in the vicissitudes of human life—to which internalization comes to completion, the individual is enriched by the relationship he has had with the beloved object, not burdened by identification and fantasy relations with the object. We are most familiar with the transformation I am trying to describe from the development of the child's love attachments to his parents into the adult's mature heterosexual love relationships, a development that includes oedipal object relinquishment and internalization, freeing the individual for non-incestuous object relations. This freedom is not simply freedom from old object ties that have been cast off, but an inner freedom we call maturity, achieved by internalization of old ties.

By internalization, then, the libidinal-aggressive relations between subject and object, as well as identity of subject and object, are given up, destroyed, and separate "identities" are formed or reconstituted. The identity of the individual as well as the identity of his objects becomes defined or redefined. In this sense, identity does not mean identity between subject and object, but self-sameness, individuality. In this sense Erikson and others speak of ego identity, and correlative to this ego identity is the objective and clearly delimited identity of objects as objects. Mental life is so constituted that it oscillates between the two poles: internal identity, which makes object relations in the true sense possible, and identification that dissolves the differences between subject and object. I hardly need mention that I do not mean that object relations such as between children and parents come to an end by internalization. But through the successful preliminary resolution of the Oedipus complex, ushering in the latency period, the character of the relationship changes, becomes more objective, less colored by identifications and less passionate.

It seems that there are life phases in which internalization as a process is more active or predominant than in others. One such phase, under normal circumstances, is the latency period of childhood when the fires and passions of the oedipal period give way to a restructuring of psychic life in many areas. The moratorium of which Erikson speaks, so often required in one form or another in young adults after the renewed melting-down of inner structure and passionate external involvement of adolescence, corresponds to the need for another such latency period, during which internalization processes may have a chance to predominate or exert their influence. Therapeutic analysis, of course, represents or should represent such an internalizing phase in life, the patient's need for which so often is brought about by upheavals of the nature of emotional disappointments, frustrations in work and love and of ambitions, calling for de-repressions, renunciations, and internal readjustments. Thus it is an inner necessity, not an arbitrary requirement for the sake of frustration *per se*, that an analysis, to be successful, be carried out in relative "abstinence," allowing for a period of respite from too much external involvement, to the extent to which this is possible in people's lives.

In order to clarify the difference between identification and internalization I have somewhat overstated my case. There are degrees of internalization, as I have suggested in my previous paper on the subject, and identifications may be and often are way-stations on the road to internal, psychic structure. The ideal outcome of internalization is identity in the sense of self-sameness as an individual, and not identification and identity with objects. Identifications, though necessary as preliminary phases, to the extent to which the unending process of internalization succeeds, are dissolved, destroyed internally and something novel, psychic structure, comes into being.

I will end by quoting from a poem by Andrew Marvell which, I believe, speaks of the metamorphosis on which I have tried to throw some light:

> The mind, that ocean where each kind
> Does straight its own resemblance find;
> Yet it creates, transcending these,
> Far other worlds, and other seas;
> Annihilating all that's made
> To a green thought in a green shade.

REFERENCES

Arlow, J. A., and Brenner, C. (1964): *Psychoanalytic Concepts and the Structural Theory.* New York: International Universities Press.

Freud, S. (1915): Instincts and their vicissitudes. S.E. 14.

_____. (1920): Beyond the pleasure principle. S.E. 18.

_____. (1921): Group psychology and the analysis of the ego. S.E. 18.

_____. (1923): The ego and the id. S.E. 19.

_____. (1924a): The economic problem of masochism. S.E. 19.

_____. (1924b): The dissolution of the Oedipus complex. S.E. 19.

_____. (1926): Inhibitions, symptoms and anxiety. S.E. 20.

_____. (1930): Civilization and its discontents. S.E. 21.

_____. (1933a): New introductory lectures on psychoanalysis. S.E. 22.

_____. (1933b): Why war? S.E. 22.

_____. (1937): Analysis terminable and interminable. S.E. 23.

Hartmann, H. (1939): *Ego Psychology and the Problem of Adaptation.* New York: International Universities Press, 1958.

Hartmann, H., and Loewenstein, R. M. (1962): Notes on the superego. *The Psychoanalytic Study of the Child,* vol. 17.

Loewald, H. W. (1962): Internalization, separation, mourning, and the superego. *Psychoanal. Quart.* 31:483–504.

Meissner, W. W. (1970): Notes on Identification. I. Origins in Freud. *Psychoanal. Quart.* 39:563–89.

_____. (1971): Notes on Identification. II. Clarification of related concepts. *Psychoanal. Quart.* 40:277–302.

_____. (1972): Notes on Identification. III. The Concept of Identification. *Psychoanal. Quart.* 41:224–60.

_____. (1974): Identification and Learning. *J. Am. Psychoanal. Assn.* 21:788–816.

Nietzsche, F. (1887): The genealogy of morals. In *The Birth of Tragedy and The Genealogy of Morals.* Garden City, N.Y.: Doubleday Anchor Books, 1956.

Rapaport, D. (1957): A theoretical analysis of the superego concept. In *Collected Papers,* New York and London: Basic Books, 1967.

Sandler, J. (1960): On the concept of superego. *The Psychoanalytic Study of the Child,* vol. 15.

Schafer, R. (1968): *Aspects of Internalization.* New York: International Universities Press.

Schur, M. (1966): *The Id and the Regulatory Principles of Mental Functioning.* New York: International Universities Press.

7

SOME CONSIDERATIONS ON REPETITION AND REPETITION COMPULSION

It is difficult to speak of repetition without becoming involved in a vast area of phenomena and problems. Freud's treatment of the subject, limited as it is in some respects, is proof of this. Repetition is a concept of such generality that one quickly gains the impression that it is, in one way or another, applicable to most if not all phenomena and processes of life, biological and psychological. My fragmentary and programmatic remarks will deal with only a few issues of repetition as a psychological phenomenon and will attempt to show that the concept of repetition is implied in some key psychoanalytic conceptualizations. In the course of this discussion some more general, but to my mind crucial, ideas concerning the meaning and import of repetition in human life will be considered.

Repetition on the psychological level cannot be defined simply in terms of reiteration or replica in a mechanical sense, although more or less stereotyped and automatic repetitions of prior experiences, prior behavior, thoughts, feelings and actions play an important role in normal and pathological processes. It is, in fact, one of the most important issues confronting us in a psychoanalytic consideration of repetition to make the distinction between such relatively passive or automatic repetitions and active repeating, and to study the conditions under which transitions from one to the other take place, although little will be said here about the latter point. Any consideration of the relations between id, ego, and superego has to deal with the passivity–activity issue in terms of repetition, and so does any consideration of psychoanalysis as a therapeutic process.

A shorter version of this paper was presented at the International Psychoanalytic Congress in Amsterdam in 1965.

Nor can we cling to a distinction of repeating and remembering such as is implied in the notion that repetitions in the transference are to be substituted by memories. Repeating and remembering are narrowly defined in that context, in order to
make clear an important contrast and relationship between two
different modes of psychic functioning. But simple reflection
shows that precisely such transference repetitions, as well as
similar kinds of repetition in the form of behavior or symptoms,
have been described by Freud as reminiscences, i.e., as manifestations of unconscious memories. On the other hand, conscious
remembering is a kind of repetition, a repetition in the mind.
Repetition in the form of action or behavior and affect is a kind of
remembering, albeit unconscious, and remembering as a conscious mental act is a kind of repetition. If one adheres, as psychoanalysis does, to the concept of unconscious memory, repetition
and recollection can be understood in terms of each other, depending on whether we focus on the present act, in which case
we speak of repeating, or on the past prototype, in which case we
see recollection.

Indeed it can be claimed that to understand repetitions ("reproduction as an action"—Freud) as a form of remembering, and
to understand remembering as an act of repeating, as a "reproduction in the psychical field" (Freud), is one of the cornerstones
of psychoanalytic psychology. It ties together past and present,
the id and the ego, the biological and the psychological. Insofar
as remembering is a form of repeating, we may distinguish two
forms of repetition in human life, namely repeating by action,
"acting out," and repeating in the psychical field. Freud has discussed this in his paper "Remembering, Repeating and Working-
Through" (1914). It is important to keep in mind that acting out is
a concept that is strictly related to the concept of reproduction in
the psychical field, i.e., acting out is an alternative to remembering in the narrow sense; to designate an action as acting out
makes sense only insofar as action is seen under the perspective
of an alternative to "reproduction in the psychical field." In the
context of psychoanalytic treatment, this alternative outside of
the analytic situation is undesirable (though this statement needs
qualifications that I cannot elaborate here); within the analytic
situation, as a transference manifestation, it is a vehicle of the
therapeutic process.

Freud discovered and stressed repeatedly the diphasic nature of psychosexual development, and particularly the importance of this fact for the aetiology of neurosis. Owing to this fact, according to Freud's description (1926, ch. 10), there is the danger that in puberty the re-efflorescence of sexuality is drawn into the process of repression, which had been the fate of at least a share of infantile sexuality, the danger that sexuality will succumb to the attraction exerted by the infantile prototypes and their fate of being repressed. In puberty the drama of the oedipal situation is repeated, and the danger Freud describes is that it will be repeated—not on a new level of organization due to further ego development taking place during the latency period if things proceed normally, but on approximately the same level on which the original conflict took place and temporarily resolved itself. Schematically speaking, in analysis the conflict is reactivated, is made to be repeated and, through the work of interpretation, to be repeated in an active way, that is actively taken up by the ego's organizing capacity an important element of which is remembering. The diphasic nature of psychosexual development and the vicissitudes the oedipal conflict may undergo are a prime example of repetition in human life. And I indicated the two possibilities of repeating in this process, namely the relatively passive reproduction of infantile unconscious prototypical experiences in neurosis, and the active repetition of them in non-neurotic development (normal adolescence), or in the induced revival of the infantile neurosis in analysis in which organizing ego activity is mediated by the analyst and his interpretations. In the latter cases repetition means reactivation on a higher level of organizing potential, which makes possible novel configurations and novel resolutions of the conflict.

The understanding of the difference between a healthy life development and one blocked or stunted by excessive repression and ego restriction may be furthered by applying the concepts of passive and active repetition. Psychoanalysis has always maintained that the life of the individual is determined by his infantile history, his early experiences and conflicts; but everything depends on *how* these early experiences are repeated in the course of life, to what extent they are repeated passively—suffered again even if "arranged" by the individual that undergoes them (Freud, 1920, p. 21)—and to what extent they can be taken over in the ego's organizing activity and made over into something new—a re-creation of something old as against a duplication of it. In such re-creation the old is mastered, where mastery does not mean elimination of it but dissolution, and reconstruction out of the elements of destruction. We may thus distinguish between repetition as reproduction and repetition as re-creation, the passive and the active form. This distinction is akin to, although not the same as, the one made by Bibring (1943) between the reproductive and restitutive aspects of repetition. Rapaport (1953) has stressed the crucial importance for psychoanalytic theory of the passivity–activity problem and discussed various aspects of it.

I have implied that the Oedipus complex—itself already a repetition of pre-oedipal experiences on a new organizational level—is repeated not just in puberty but throughout life, in varying mixtures and combinations of more or less passive reproductions ("neurotic" repetitions) and of active re-creations. This takes place in the guise of personal relationships in its various developments during life, and in the evolution of the inner world. The two go hand in hand, and we encounter repetition here again, in a different perspective. It is the repetition in the inner world of what has taken place in interaction with the outer world. The dissolution (not repression) of the oedipal conflict, the extent to which it succeeds in its aspects of mourning and internalization of abandoned object relations, with the erection of the superego as a new differentiation in the ego, is a prime example of re-creative repetition in the psychic field—in contrast to passive reproduction in the psychic field represented by the perpetuation of oedipal fantasies or pathological introjections. Internal re-creative repetitions of external involvement and its dissolution enable the individual to progress to repetitive mastery of the Oedipus complex in the external arena of personal ("heterosexual" and "homosexual") involvements in later life.

I mentioned earlier that action in the outer world can be understood as acting out only insofar as it is seen as taking place instead of repetition in the psychic field. If such action occurs as the external manifestation of or as the result of psychic re-creation, then it is not acting out but re-creative repetition in the external arena. As we have become more sophisticated in our analytic work, we have come to discriminate between a patient's acting out and his re-creative repetition in action, although both elements may be blended in a given action. And we hope for his increased capacity, as an outcome of analysis, for re-creative repetition in external action on the basis of his re-creative repetitions in the psychic field carried out in the analytic work.

Reproduction and re-creation as defined here ("passive" and "active" repetition) are not merely in an oppositional relationship; they are also complementary. At this point it should be made explicit that reproduction and re-creation as forms of repetition both take place in the psychic field as well as in the field of external action. In both fields the passive reproduction of experiences does present the opportunity for arriving at re-creative repetition, depending on a variety of internal and external conditions that cannot be gone into here. Transference repetitions in analysis as a vehicle of the therapeutic process are an example of this. If they are not present or go unrecognized, there is no adversary to be dealt with, as Freud has put it, there is no tangible reproduction lending itself to the internalizing work of re-creation in the psychic field, which leads to higher levels of organization. This work of the patient is stimulated and fostered by the analyst's interpreting activity, which is needed because conditions for the accomplishment of this psychic task in the early, formative period were not favorable. Analysis tends to remain shallow, although not necessarily altogether ineffective, where internalization of the formative experiences of life is not based, to a considerable extent, on the destruction and internal re-creation of current transference repetitions (resolution of the transference neurosis).

Let us consider the passivity–activity issue from a different angle. The psychoanalytic understanding of the destiny of a person, for instance in the extreme form of the so-called fate neurosis, is an example of understanding the vicissitudes of human life as manifesting a great deal more personal "activity" than heretofore had been recognized. I speak here of those happenings that seem to befall the person, and not of what we call proudly our actions and deeds, which we think we as conscious rational beings determine and will. It is a curious fact that psychoanalysis takes the view that these apparently purposeful voluntary acts are, much more than previously realized, determined by forces in us that we do not control, while it considers

the slings and arrows of outrageous fortune as less outside of our
control than we thought. The point in both cases is the role of
inner, unconscious forces. But while in the first case the emphasis
is on the *power* of unconscious motivations, in the second case
the emphasis is on their *potential for coming under the ego's
organizing control.* Psychoanalysis has discovered psychic determinism, which implies that behavior that either had been considered as chance occurrence, or as a matter of conscious choice
and in that sense not predetermined, or as caused by biological
processes, could be demonstrated as being determined by unconscious memories, fantasies, conflicts. What has been mainly
emphasized about psychic determinism is the fact of cause–effect
relations between psychic events, the causes being unconscious,
the effects frequently being conscious psychic events or processes. But the main impact of psychic determinism resides in its
being *psychic* determinism: the causes are conceived not as
purely external or physical and biological, but as potentially
personal, unconscious processes having a psychological effect
on overt behavior. And secondly, these causes thus are susceptible to being influenced and modified in their turn by psychological processes. If this were not so, the whole idea that the
reactivation of unconscious conflicts and their re-creation and
working through in analysis could lead to change in present behavior would fall to the ground.

The compulsion to repeat unconscious conflicts, wishes, experiences passively is due primarily to their having remained
under repression, that is, not exposed to the influence of the
organizing activity of the ego, which would lead to what we have
identified as re-creative repetition. When we speak of repetition
compulsion in psychoanalysis as a psychological phenomenon,
and not as an ultimate principle inherent in cosmic processes in
general, it is primarily the passive, reproductive repetition that
we have in mind, at least in the context of clinical psychoanalysis.
Once the distinction is made between passive, reproductive and
active, re-creative repetition, it may be feasible to postulate a
"compulsion" to repeat, on general theoretical grounds, which
would include re-creative repetition. Here, however, compulsion
then is understood—as Bibring also has pointed out in his paper
—as a general tendency of life, including psychological processes. Compulsion in the specific psychoanalytic-clinical sense

in which the term is used in the word "compulsion neurosis" applies only to reproductive repetition, a repetition compelled by unconscious forces which have remained outside, removed from, the ego organization.

The patient is compelled to repeat in the transference unconscious infantile experiences; bringing these to consciousness is a step toward the removal of such compulsion since it opens up the possibility of the ego's organizing activity exerting itself. The actual implication of such transference interpretations goes further than simply revealing unconscious infantile contents. They convey the message that the infantile processes are personal experiences that reveal psychic activity of some kind, granted that this psychic activity had been or long since had become—not merely unconscious—but automatic, removed from intra- and extra-psychic influence, and thus a process passively reproduced. The patient is not merely to be made aware of the existence of such contents in his psyche, but he is asked, implicitly if not explicitly, to own up to them as *his* wishes and conflicts and defenses, to re-experience them as psychic activity of a nonautomatic nature. The analyst, in other words, tends to evoke in the patient a sense of personal psychic involvement as compared with purely unconscious automatic process. We try to make the patient see, or rather feel, that he as an actor is or can be involved, that he was compelled by his unconscious because it had been automatic and autonomous. The difference between automatic process and personal activity we convey to the patient when we point out to him that the unconscious he becomes aware of is *his* unconscious, or that *he dreamed* the dream he had. Undoubtedly there is suggestion at work here, an appeal is made to the patient; it is similar in nature to the suggestion we make to a child that he is able to take a step by himself. (He may or may not follow the appeal at the time, but it is justified by our knowledge that the child has the wherewithal to walk.) Reliving infantile experiences in the transference starts out as passive, reproductive repetition. Through the analyst's interpretations, revealing and articulating the infantile connections and thus evoking the sense of personal, nonautomatic activity both in the present *and* in the infantile past, transference repetitions may take on the character of re-creative repetition.

The distinction of reproductive and re-creative repetition can be applied to the concepts of primary and secondary process and can help to elucidate the relations between id, ego, and superego. I must confine myself here to what amounts to allusions as the following ideas require careful and detailed discussion and elaboration for which I am not prepared at this point. The ego repeats, on a new level of organization which in our subjective experience and to our observation appears as heightened psychic activity as compared with the antecedent level, the processes which we conceptualize as id; the ego, insofar as it does not defend against them, repeats them in reorganizing them, i.e., re-creatively. This new level of organization, *in the act of re-creation*, of reorganization, seems to have the quality of (more or less acute) consciousness, while later it tends to lose this quality without necessarily retrogressing to a lower or earlier organizational level, although this may occur if defensive forces are brought to bear on what had been so reorganized. When we say that a great part of the ego is unconscious too, it would seem that we have reference to earlier ego levels and to this later stage—as if consciousness were connected in some way with the act and *moment of generating new organization.*[1] Freud's notion that consciousness and memory traces exclude each other, that consciousness arises instead, in the place of, memory traces, may be related to this. Insofar as memory (in the sense of memory traces) as a record is passive repetition, conscious remembering can be described as active repetition that, while founded on it, replaces and reorganizes the record in the act of remembering. Conscious recollection, in the sense in which in analysis we attempt to have the patient substitute it for reproductive repeating, would be an act of re-creating, the moment of generating new organization of something old. We know from analytic and postanalytic observation that such new organization of experiences can persist while losing its character of consciousness: a new element of the unconscious ego has been added. The sense of loss which may be felt when such creative remembering and reorganizing in analysis recedes from consciousness while the gain from such conscious experience is not lost, is evidence of this course. And there can be another sense of loss of the opposite kind, when some

---

1. "Unconscious ego" is used here descriptively, comprising both dynamically unconscious and preconscious elements.

memory, some unconscious id wish becomes conscious, because the new organization achieved in this conscious moment of re-creation hinders retrogression to an earlier organizational level: something of the poignant intensity and immediacy, of the youth of living on that level is to be given up. The unconscious id wants to reproduce on its own level and resists organization. It is here that there are connections between remembering, working through and the work of mourning that deserve close study.

I may add here that it is not justified to conceive conscious-ness simply as a state or passive process of being aware, as little as perception in general can be conceived as a passive process of receiving stimuli (the old concept of perception as passive recep-tion of sense data). Just as perception is an act of organizing, not simply registering data, so is consciousness. Consciousness of intrapsychic processes, then, is an activity that organizes, not merely registers, intrapsychic "data." And just as primary proc-esses tend to become automatic, so secondary processes—which as they first arise recreatively repeat primary processes—tend to become automatic; their modes of operation become estab-lished patterns of organization. Their recathexis, when called into activity, is equivalent to a reproductive repetition of that established pattern, and insofar as it is no more than that, i.e., insofar as it is automatic, it is not conscious (habits, for instance).

I spoke of the appeal to the patient to understand his uncon-scious as his own, to view his dream as dreamed by him, his repetitive fate as "arranged by himself" (Freud, 1920), although unconsciously. Such appeal is contained in Freud's phrase: where id was there ego shall become. It is a moral appeal. Freud shrank from making this explicit, averse as he was to the idea of impos-ing moral standards on the patient—nor can or should they be imposed. But there can be no question that he lived by this stand-ard (as a patient of mine once put it in a different context: to practice what you do not preach) and the success of psychoana-lytic treatment depends on the patient's aroused propensity to heed this appeal. This is implicit in the therapeutic or working alliance. To acknowledge, recognize, understand one's uncon-scious as one's own means to move from a position of passivity in relation to it to a position where active care of it becomes pos-sible, where it becomes a task worthy of pursuit to make one's business and concern those needs and wishes, fantasies, conflicts and traumatic events and defenses that have been passively experienced and reproduced. This change from passivity to activity is the analogue in the psychic field to the one Freud described in the play of his little grandson who "at the outset . . . was in a passive situation—he was overpowered by the experience [of his mother's departures]; but, by repeating it, unpleasurable as it was, as a game, he took on an active part" (1920, ch. II).

Such appeal, to begin with, comes from the outside and becomes internalized as an aspect of the superego.[2] Psychoanalysis as a method of treatment, it seems to me, has this tension toward assuming responsibility for oneself, that is to learn by being instructed in self-knowledge, in repeating oneself knowingly, to take over this function of active repetition: to become a self. I know that with such remarks I am treading on dangerous ground as far as analysts are concerned. Everything seems safe as long as we talk about the psychological roots of morality, but is to acknowledge and understand the moral roots of our psychology still science? I believe it is not unscientific to know ourselves also in the sense of exploring the moral implications of our therapeutic goals and of our scientific passions. Is it truly scientific to limit our field of vision in such a way as to neglect the fact that consciousness and conscience are closely related, not only linguistically, that the so-called observing ego and the superego are closely related, and that to know oneself makes it impossible to remain the same, even if only anxiety or guilt or shame is aroused? We cannot deny that we value, as analysts, the aim of psychosexual maturity, of achieving non-incestuous object relations as a re-creative repetition of the oedipal relationships, that we aim at this achievement for our patients because we believe it to be *their* aim, inherent in the evolutionary tension of their unfolding as human beings. And I think it is an unwarranted limitation, at this stage of our science, to maintain that self-knowledge, making the unconscious conscious, transforming id into ego, is a purely "objective" matter of self-observation and self-understanding, and not a moral phenomenon and activity in

2. When I say "appeal" I imply, of course, that there is something to be appealed to, as in the baby who "has it in him" to learn to walk and to talk.

and of itself. In this respect our theory is far behind the best in our practice and technique.

Kierkegaard, in his essay on "Repetition," dealt with repetition from this vantage point. As to recollection and repetition, he writes: "When the Greeks said that all knowledge is recollection they affirmed that all that is has been; when one says that life is a repetition one affirms that existence which has been now becomes." And further: "Recollection is the pagan life view, repetition is the modern life view." That human life is a sequence of repetitions of some crucial prototypical events is a notion that appears to have been held since ancient times in many different societies and civilizations, manifesting itself in a great variety of cultural institutions, ceremonies, and rituals, as well as in religious and philosophical views. As I have tried to point out, this notion is no stranger to psychoanalysis, although "neurotic" repetitions have been stressed more in psychoanalytic writings than repetition as a "normal" phenomenon. Nevertheless, the whole conception of psychosexual development, of the stages of libidinal development, and of the crucial importance of early libido stages and early object relations, of typical "traumatic" experiences beginning with the birth trauma, of prototypical complexes and conflicts and imaginés, in determining the life course of the individual, undoubtedly contains the general notion of repetition, in one form or another, of prototypical events and complexes which took place and shape in the early days of the individual. Of equal importance in psychoanalytic thinking, as I mentioned earlier, is the concept of repetition as contained in the theory of identification and internalization.

Psychoanalytic understanding of human life implies the conception of it as repetition, and it contains elements of interpreting repetition in the sense in which Kierkegaard speaks of it: the possibility of repetition as a directed, self-realizing (although not necessarily conscious) activity of the person, repeating his past, as exemplified by certain prototypical crucial experiences and early levels of organization of experience, creatively in the present. The stance of psychoanalysis as a therapeutic procedure implies this possibility, and a clinical psychoanalysis to the extent to which it lives up to its potentialities, is such a creative repetition. When Kierkegaard says that repetition (in the sense of active repetition) is the modern life view, he means that in the course of the historical development of the race the emphasis has shifted: it is no longer the prototypical past that confers weight and dignity on the present, where the present is seen as a shadowy reproduction of some archetypes of enduring potency, where what happens now is only, in essence, a pale recollection. This would be the pagan view, and we will see how this understanding of the pagan view may be onesided and distorted. The modern life view, he maintains, puts the emphasis on the present whose weight, dignity and potency reside in repeating the past in novel transformations. This view affirms the prototypical importance of the past, but here a prototype exists to be creatively transformed in the act of repetition, not to be imitated or reproduced as best one can, nor to be eliminated. The formation of the superego as a new psychic structure arising out of the internalization of oedipal events and imaginés might be an example of such transformative repetition in the history of the human race.

In the pagan view, what is real in reality is that which is immutably there, forever, and human life has reality insofar as it can be shown to participate in and perpetuate the durable prototypes by imitation and reproduction—it is an essentially static view. Eliade points out that for what he calls pre-modern, archaic, or traditional societies the present gains its dignity from the past. To be more precise, what has weight in the life of societies and men is that which is forever and has been forever. Present vicissitudes and actions in human life count only insofar as they can be understood as being repetitions of what was before. They are replicas of archetypal events, and real insofar as they are such replicas. The important thing is that these archetypal events always take place, then and now; the replicas are not pale images of them (this seems to be a later interpretation) but are evidence of their continuous presence now. In this fashion present events and actions share in what is essential, real, forever; all else is worthless and unreal, although it occurs. It is remarkable how similar this is to certain observations and insights we have of the behavior of children (and incidentally also to an early psychoanalytic emphasis on the unconscious as the true psychic reality). To a child—and this is more so the younger the child—the important thing may not be that he is doing something now that he saw done by his parent, that he is repeating it himself. Frequently it is most important to him that what he is doing is the same as what his parent does or did, participating in this fashion in power and permanence, and more: in this way only has he any identity, any weight. At a later stage this may be attenuated to the importance of being watched by the parent while performing some action. I do not in any way wish to minimize the element of pride and satisfaction in his achievement as his own; but seeing only the latter and neglecting the former element is a good example of the particular bias of the modern life view, which fails to do full justice to a life view inherent in earlier stages of development.

In the view of repetition as described by Eliade for premodern societies, repetitions are neither recollections, indices of (unconscious or conscious) memories, nor repetitions in Kierkegaard's sense of becoming now, of active re-creation where the emphasis is on the present creator. They are, instead, re-issues or continuations of archetypal events. There is no emphasis on individuality, nor on process with a direction either into the past (recollection) or into the future (becoming), and no emphasis on actively establishing a relationship of sameness or similarity between past and present and future, which *activity* would give dignity to the present.

Such a life view gives us moderns the impression that it ignores duality and the flow of time, it dwells this side of time and duality, it clings to oneness. It is static, whereas the modern view is dynamic. We moderns affirm, even thrive on duality, conflict, individuality, process in time; we affirm the direction of time as going into the future. For us the past is important insofar as it foreshadows present and future; it is the present that counts, as activity leading into the future, in contrast to the pre-modern present, which is meaningless unless it proves that what is now has been and has not perished. The import of repetition in the modern life view lies in its aspect as active re-creation (Kierkegaard's "existence which has been now becomes"). It is repetition with its face towards the future while aware of the past (might this be a hidden meaning of the analytic arrangement whereby the patient faces away from the analyst with whom he relives and works out his past and who is behind him?). And the aspect of repetition that is stressed is the individual act of repeating in the present. "The dialectic of repetition," Kierkegaard says, "is easy; for what is repeated has been, otherwise it could not be repeated, but precisely the fact that it has been gives to *repetition* the character of novelty." Diametrically opposed to this is the concept of repetition inherent in the life view of traditional, archaic societies as explained by Eliade (p. 86):

Basically . . . the life of archaic man (a life reduced to the repetition of archetypical acts . . .), although it takes place in time, does not bear the burden of time, does not record time's irreversibility; in other words completely ignores what is especially characteristic and decisive in a consciousness of time.

Do we not recognize here the timelessness and the repetitions of the id? Eliade points out that the mystic, and the religious man in general, in this sense is similar to the primitive; "he repeats the gestures of another and, through this repetition, lives always in an atemporal present," not unlike the child I spoke of before. This is not the last word on "religious man" and his way of repeating, and Eliade is well aware of it. But it perhaps points to a deep reason for Freud's bias against religion. Kierkegaard, a most religious man although no mystic in the usual sense, saw repetition very differently from primitive man.

I have considered the concept and phenomenon of repetition from a number of different angles and viewpoints. In so doing I hope I have been able to shed some light on the problem, on how psychoanalysis views repetition and how as a treatment process it *is* repetition.

REFERENCES

Bibring, E. (1943): The conception of the repetition compulsion. *Psychoanal. Quart.* 12: 486–519.

Eliade, M. (1949): *Cosmos and History: The Myth of the Eternal Return.* New York: Harper, 1959.

Freud, S. (1914): Remembering, repeating, and working-through. S.E. 12.

––––––. (1919): The uncanny. S.E. 17.

––––––. (1920): Beyond the pleasure principle. S.E. 18.

––––––. (1925): Some additional notes on dream interpretation as a whole. (B) Moral responsibility for the content of dreams. S.E. 19.

_____. (1926): Inhibitions, symptoms, and anxiety. S.E. 20.

Kierkegaard, S. (1843): *Repetition: An Essay in Experimental Psychology*. Princeton: Princeton University Press, 1946.

Rapaport, D. (1953): Some metapsychological considerations concerning activity and passivity. *Collected Papers*. New York: Basic Books, 1967.

8

ON MOTIVATION AND INSTINCT THEORY

Psychoanalysis is interpretation. Freud called his basic work *The Interpretation of Dreams*. The essential activity of the psychoanalyst is to interpret. The psychic life of the individual is interpreted in new ways whereby it assumes meanings and an inner coherence which heretofore were not apparent. Consequently, the meaning of what we call psychical or mental has changed. Man has gained a new power of understanding, and of thereby influencing, human life by the observation and discovery of phenomena and events hitherto unknown or unheeded, by interpreting them in a manner that so far had not been applied to psychic life, and by bringing known psychological observations and activities within the context of that new interpretation, i.e., by understanding them differently.

Interpretation: we have no other way of applying our mind, whether in observation and understanding or in action. It is only in a context of meanings, when interpretations have become commonplace, that we speak of the material in question as "facts." Then we tend to deal with the material in the manner of our dealings with chairs and tables, forgetting or disregarding the mental activity of interpretation that is embodied in it but is now hidden. Even chairs and tables are such only within the context of our understanding use of them and are oddly shaped and assembled pieces of stuff outside this context.

Psychoanalysis is, however, a special case. Its essence is

I gratefully acknowledge the help for this work provided by a grant from the Robert P. Knight Fund.

In this paper I have condensed the first three chapters of a projected book that is concerned with aspects of psychoanalytic theory. While my views should ultimately be judged within that wider context, I offer them at this stage of work in progress as a contribution to the ongoing discussion of the psychoanalytic concept of instinct [1971].

interpretation. The psychoanalyst interprets dreams, slips of the tongue, symptoms, fantasies, thoughts, behavior, moods, emotions, memories, plans, actions, decisions, choices made or contemplated, physical illness, life circumstance—in principle anything and everything the patient lets be known or that can be deduced from what he reveals. The psychoanalyst's interpretations are based on and make use of a fundamental assumption: whatever transpires is personally motivated. This assumption is the all-embracing interpretation that constitutes the foundation for all individual interpretations.

This founding interpretation has components that are condensed in the expression "personally motivated": (1) What the patient reveals is motivated within and not simply chance occurrence or merely determined by forces external to him. (2) The fact of his revealing it to the analyst and the time at which he does so are personally motivated; personal motivation is involved in the past and current events he reveals, as well as in his present activity of revealing them. (3) We must also hear something else that is evoked in the expression "personally motivated," namely that motivations, while residing in the person motivated, have something to do with relations with other persons who themselves are centers of motivation. These others involved in the motivational network are the important persons in the patient's past and current life, pre-eminently including his psychoanalyst.

Such an interpretative assumption or set of assumptions as a new organizing principle has a power, a tendency, a tension of its own. This tension can be yielded to and made his own, step by step, by the "object" under consideration, i.e., by the person being analyzed, since he has organizing power of the same order as that of the analyst. This is what happens in the course of a successful analysis (as, on a much different level, in the successful upbringing of a child). The fact that the patient can make this interpretation his own is unique for psychoanalysis as a scientific endeavor; there is no other field of scientific activity where the order of organizing potential is the same in the "object" and the "investigator." In nonpsychoanalytic psychology the object of psychological investigation is never the individual in his full range of potentialities. This is also the reason that psychoanalysis is more than a science in the classical sense, calling forth as it does the investigator in the one investigated. But it also makes for one of the intrinsic problems of psychoanalysis: the "object" of investigation can never truly be made to stand still and be an object. Thus it seems that psychoanalysis also cannot help being less than a science in the classical sense.

I have implied that the object of psychoanalysis is the individual human person. Only in this entity do we encounter what psychoanalysis calls psychic life and psychic reality. It is the unit with which we deal. This, of course, does not mean that no general statements and propositions can be made about this reality. But it does mean that psychoanalytic statements and propositions are valid specifically in respect to this entity as conceived in the basic interpretative assumption mentioned and as apprehended in the psychoanalytic method which is determined by this assumption. Psychoanalytic statements are not necessarily valid in respect to other units, such as for instance family or society, even though these are composed of individuals; nor are they necessarily valid or pertinent for psychological phenomena taken out of the context of the unit constituted by the individual, as is the case in experimental or general psychology.

That the individual's life is, in principle, personally motivated is an interpretation that flows from a particular understanding of man implied in monotheism—the belief in a personal God as exemplified in Western Judaeo-Christian religion and civilization; but this self-understanding has been radicalized and modified by the decline of that belief. Psychoanalysis is an exponent and promoter of this decline. Freud's uncompromising strong stand against Judaeo-Christian religion is certainly not incidental to his lifework, but I shall not go into these matters here.

That the life of the human individual is personally motivated does, of course, not mean that it is initiated, brought into existence by the individual. It does mean that it has the *potential* of being conducted by the person himself, that the course and conduct of one's life, within certain limits, can be, or can be helped to be, in one's own hands.

The interpretation, fundamental to all specific psychoanalytic interpretations, that anything occurring in one's life is personally motivated, has a momentum that tends to transform what is being interpreted. This is, in a sense, true for any interpretation: it has the tendency to transform, to restructure that which is subject to the interpretation. The theories of modern physics and their results and consequences show this clearly. A statement of fact restates something in known and accepted terms; an interpretation changes the terms, declares that which is being interpreted to be differently structured, to have a different meaning, and to be in a different context.

The momentum, the dynamic power of an interpretation, in psychoanalysis manifests itself as personal influence.[1] The interpretation of personal motivation is a statement about potentiality rather than actuality insofar as unconscious motivation is concerned; thereby it tends to render actual what has been potential. We make a woman, plagued by the compulsion to murder her child, understand that she harbors feelings of hate against the child that are related, for example, to a disturbed relationship with her husband, which in turn is connected with certain feelings toward her father. While in the actuality of this woman's psychic life such motivational concatenations have previously not been apparent, they now are discovered because of a certain kind of psychic work she performs in conjunction with the analyst. What was an impersonal, unrelated compelling force becomes inserted in a linkage of personal motivation; it becomes open to the dynamics of personal motivation.

The psychic work performed by the patient has one of its sources of motivation in the psychic work of the analyst, in his work of understanding and interpretation, which is a motivating force when it is directed toward the patient as another center of motivational activity. It is a kind of facilitation within a constellation or field of motivational activity composed of two centers of such activity. The interpretation, then, through its own motivational momentum and the expression this takes in content and manner of interpretation, assists the patient in making a motivational concatenation actual, while previously it existed only "in the Unconscious."

The concept "unconscious," as a negative term, refers to potentiality: something is not what it might (or might not) be or become. This something is considered from the standpoint of what it might be but is not. The interpretation of personal motivation, by making statements about unconscious motiva-

1. Interpretation in psychoanalysis must be seen in the context of the personal relationship that the psychoanalytic situation represents.

tion, tends to raise the level and complexity of psychic organization, by "speaking to the Unconscious," as we say, from the standpoint of a higher organizational level, from the standpoint of what it might become. As analysts we speak, in interpretations of unconscious motivation, from the level of consciousness to the unconscious.

The term "id," as a positive term, denotes what is signified by it directly, not from the viewpoint of consciousness. Apart from other reasons for its choice, the term makes it more feasible to visualize the coexistence of mental processes of different organizational levels, without the implication, suggested by the negative term "unconscious," of mutual exclusion or of the active removal of consciousness (repression). On the other hand, the term unconscious is indispensable since it points to consciousness and indicates potential mutual transformation from one into the other.

What was (pre)conscious can become unconscious—the phenomenon of repression. Repression itself is a term that speaks from the level of (pre)conscious mental organization and, as initially conceived, of an activity performed on that level. By initially equating the unconscious and the repressed, and by tending to equate repression and (pre)conscious mental activity, great difficulties were created. The concept of repression, which had its origin and justification in a circumscribed area of observation, became overextended (as did the concept of defense) and was given more duties than it could perform. The unconscious, on the other hand, was forced into a bed of Procrustes where only what was repressed was allowed to be part of it. Furthermore, it became apparent that the repressive motivational forces themselves could be unconscious (not merely preconscious), and this could not be accounted for by the equation of the unconscious and the repressed. Nor could it be understood how "unconscious mental contents" could become conscious (as in psychosis), i.e., return from repression, without losing those characteristics that were supposed to be theirs by virtue of their being repressed. Freud's shift to the subdivision id–ego–superego undoubtedly made things easier. But when we are concerned with the mutual relations between these substructures and with the mental processes involved in these relations and in the substructures themselves, much remains to be understood and conceptualized differently.

I have mentioned these issues here in a preliminary way because repression and defense, and the conceptualization of, and the very term, the Unconscious, are crucially, although not exclusively, determined by the basic psychoanalytic interpretation of personal motivation. Freud originally (i.e., before he distinguished between preconscious and conscious) saw repression and defense as conscious motivations in the sense of conscious acts of will. For example, in "The Neuro-Psychoses of Defence" (Freud, 1894) he wrote:

. . . *the splitting of the contents of consciousness* [in one form of conversion hysteria] *is the result of an act of will on the part of the patient*; that is to say, it is initiated by an effort of will whose motive can be specified [p. 46]. [Or:] the most unambiguous statements by the patients [suffering from obsessions and phobias] give proof of the effort of will, the attempt at defense, upon which the theory lays emphasis [p. 52].

This clearly was Freud's starting point, and he contrasted this (as far as hysteria is concerned) with the etiological notions of "an innate weakness of the capacity for psychical synthesis" (Janet) and of a hypnoid state (Breuer) (1894, p. 46), in other words with etiological factors conceived as nonmotivational in nature. Freud also was at that time still inclined to doubt whether unconscious processes should be called psychic processes at all.[2] This means, in the present context, that personal motivation was still to be understood as conscious motivation insofar as psychical processes and consciousness were still considered to be coterminous. On the other hand it also means

2. "The separation of the sexual idea from its affect and the attachment of the latter to another, suitable but not incompatible idea [the 'false connection' operative in obsessions]—these are processes which occur without consciousness. Their existence can only be presumed, but cannot be proved by any clinico-psychological analysis. Perhaps it would be more correct to say that these processes are not of a psychical nature at all, that they are physical processes whose psychical consequences present themselves as if what is expressed by the terms 'separation of the idea from its affect' and 'false connection' of the latter had really taken place" (p. 53). It should be noted that Freud in these sentences by implication speaks of interpretation (the existence of these processes can only be "presumed") and of potentiality ("as if" they "had really taken place").

that unconscious processes, if they were to be interpreted in psychological terms, to be inserted in a psychological nexus, should—to the extent to which this is possible—be interpreted in terms of personal motivation.

Not enough attention has been paid to the intriguing fact that in psychoanalysis unconscious processes and phenomena are interpreted in terms of personal motivation, while conscious processes and especially volitional acts—whether of thought or deed—tend to be viewed as less personally motivated than superficially appears to be the case but as determined by instinctual-unconscious forces. It is as though what counts in mental life takes place on a kind of middle ground between two poles, and the two poles are being interpreted in terms of each other. Interpretation of unconscious mental life in terms of personal motivation has, under favorable circumstances, a power to move organization of mental processes in the direction of consciousness. Interpretation of conscious-volitional mental life in terms of unconscious-instinctual motivation has a power to move organization of mental processes in the opposite direction, the direction of unconscious-instinctual life. In clinical psychoanalysis this is clearly visible and made use of by the analyst. The analyst oscillates between "id interpretations" and "ego interpretations," between interpretations downward and interpretations upward (to use and extend a term employed by Bornstein [1949] and Loewenstein [1951]). The overall direction of a psychoanalytic investigation seems to be not so much toward consciousness per se, but toward an optimal communication, an interpenetration and balance of the two forms of mental processes and of the psychic structures their activities bring about.

But we now must attempt to clarify what is meant by personal motivation and how it operates. Freud's model for personal motivation, at least as far as repression and defense are concerned, was, as we have seen, conscious will. In contrast to "wish," it is a concept that he rarely considered or used subsequently.[3] Later a distinction was made between repression, an unconscious "mech-

3. The concept of will, however, is implied whenever Freud speaks of choices the patient is able to make once the unconscious sources of his behavior are understood by him, i.e., have become conscious, so that gratification of a wish may be sought or renounced by the ego.

anism," and suppression connoting conscious intent. But of course it is instinct that moved into the center of the psychoanalytic consideration of motivation, instincts as unconsciously motivating forces.[4] Instincts, the Unconscious, the id—these words evoke the impersonal, the depth hidden beneath the surface, concealed by the surface mask of the person as an organized, conscious human being (the Latin *persona* = mask of an actor). They also suggest involuntary action, innate impulse, elementary and untamed forces, compelling, irrational, unreasoning. The id is called daemonic. A daemon is something that possesses us, that has power in us or over us; in Greek religion it is a divine power, not definitely personified, a power of lesser stature than a personal god, yet more personal than the forces of nature.

Once repression and other "mechanisms" of defense were no longer acts of will, once their unconscious nature was acknowledged, they too moved into the area of the impersonal or less-than-personal and became manifestations of the ego instincts.[5] Later the distinction between ego instincts and sexual instincts (libido) was given up in favor of a classification which used different criteria, whereby a share of ego instincts and sexual instincts joined forces in the concept of narcissism (ego libido or narcissistic libido versus object libido) to become a much widened libido; while another share of what formerly had been subsumed under ego instincts and libido (in the forms of self-preservative instincts, repression, and sadism) became the aggressive instinct; and various kinds of fusion and defusion of sexual and aggressive instincts accounted for a variety of instinctual manifestations.

---

4. As in the *Standard Edition,* the German *Trieb* is here translated as "instinct" and not as "instinctual drive" or "drive." The arguments advanced by Strachey (1966) in his "Notes on Some Technical Terms Whose Translation Calls for Comment" in favor of "instinct" have persuaded me to adopt that translation. Besides, the fact that the English standard text of Freud's writings now uses the term, for better or worse, weighs heavily in favor of it.

5. Strachey (Editor's Note to "Instincts and Their Vicissitudes," Freud, 1915a, p. 115) states that "Freud introduced the term 'ego instincts' and identified these on the one hand with the self-preservative instincts and on the other with the repressive function." He refers to Freud's introduction of the term in "The Psycho-Analytic View of Psychogenic Disturbance of Vision" (1910), where Freud clearly speaks of repression as a function of the ego instincts that oppose the sexual instincts (p. 213).

Nevertheless, motivation had become instinctual, as had repression and defense, in contrast to the early notion of personal will. Psychic life is motivated by sometimes conflicting, sometimes confluent, sometimes fused, sometimes defused, instinctual forces. There seems to be no room for *personal* motivation. Yet I have claimed that personal motivation is the fundamental assumption of psychoanalysis. We now seem to see that, on the contrary, psychoanalytic psychology postulates instinctual, unconscious, impersonal forces as the motives of our psychic life. Where is the person? Where is the ego or self that would be the source and mainstay of personal motivation?

The problem is not resolved by hypotheses about a primary autonomy of the ego, primary ego apparatuses, and the like (Hartmann, 1939). They make the psychoanalytic ego into a biological entity with a psychological superstructure and make use of an energy concept which is biological or physical. The energy postulated in such hypotheses, while called psychic energy, is nonpsychic, i.e., nonmotivational, and instinctual motivation becomes secondary where it counts most: in the understanding of the structuring of the personality by the organization and transformation of instincts. Inborn apparatuses are nothing but a euphemism for neurophysiological and neuroanatomical substrates, they have no psychological status. Instinct (*Trieb*) does have psychological meaning and the term has its legitimate use in psychoanalysis only as a psychological concept, and not as a biological or ethological one. Nobody of course denies neurophysiological processes and neurological structures, or the maturation of such structures. But to speak of inborn ego apparatuses is speaking of a Hamlet who is not the Prince of Denmark. In psychoanalytic psychology the ego is a psychic structure that cannot be found anywhere in biology or neurology, just as an organism cannot be found anywhere in physics, or a superego in sociology. It makes sense to speak of the development of the id and the ego out of an undifferentiated phase, in which there is as yet no differentiation of id, ego, and environment, as long as the concept of the undifferentiated phase is not biologized and it is recognized that as psychoanalysts we cannot go back beyond that limit.

Ego and id are psychoanalytic constructs that do not make use of the distinction conscious or unconscious, although they must, of course, be considered in juxtaposition to that distinction. But they do make use of the concept of instinctual energy (as the first or most primitive form of psychic energy in general) by postulating free or mobile and bound energies as well as gradations in the degree and complexity of mobility and binding. They also make use of the conception of the equivalence of energy and structure (structure is bound energy and energy is unbound or potential structure), a conception that has been used in physics and has revolutionized it. Psychology has been no less revolutionized by the use of that conception in psychoanalysis, which is not to say that Freud was clearly aware of using it. It is an idea that was "in the air" and was made use of in various contexts, among them physics and psychoanalysis. In itself it is an idea that does not derive from physics as an established body of knowledge and observations but which, when applied in its investigations, restructures the whole field (compare Freud's introductory paragraph to "Instincts and Their Vicissitudes," which, with good reason, is praised as a lucid statement about such matters). That the same conception has been used in psychoanalysis does not mean that psychoanalysis has taken it over from physics or that it is physical in nature and thus not really applicable in psychological discourse. Neither do the concepts of energy and structure have of necessity physical connotations. They became conventional scientific concepts with specific physical connotations through their use in physics, but they are not by nature physical concepts or entities. Even less so is instinct by nature a biological concept or entity. On the other hand, something like myelinization or neutron or superego are terms invented within contexts of specific sciences, and they cannot be used elsewhere except by metaphor.[6]

Ego and id, conceived as psychic structures, come into being within the psychic unit the neonate is about to become by intricate interaction processes between conflicting, converging, and merging psychic energy currents surrounding and within the emerging psychic system; such interactions result in the organization of psychic structure. It cannot be stressed enough that such organization is most vitally codetermined by the fact

6. See Schur's (1966, p. 42f.) brief discussion of the concept of psychic energy and his references.

of the far higher complexity and organization of psychic energy obtaining in the (for the observer) surrounding or environmental psychic systems. It is by the interaction with them that motivational forces of various orders of complexity and integration, and stable motivational structures of any kind, come into being within the newly emerging psychic unit, the child. On that basis, but never without maintaining further interaction with psychic forces of the environment, interactional processes within the new psychic system can be built into various forms of structured organization, whereby higher levels of motivation come about. Structures are understood as more or less systematic and stable organizations of psychic energy; they bring their higher potential to bear on mobile instinctual energy, thus transforming its currents into higher orders of motivational energy. Freud's use of the concept of hypercathexis in "The Unconscious" is in keeping with such a formulation. To my understanding he described such a course of events, with a view on memory and perception and within the topographic framework, when he writes: "The system *Ucs.* contains the thing-cathexes of the objects, the first and true object-cathexes ['first and true' because instinctual]; the system *Pcs.* comes about by this thing-presentation being hypercathected through being linked with the word-presentations corresponding to it [words as symbols, as higher-order 'presentations' originally provided by the environment]. It is these hypercathexes, we may suppose, that bring about a higher psychical organization and make it possible for the primary process to be succeeded by the secondary process which is dominant in the *Pcs.*" (1915*b*, p. 201). Freud clearly speaks here of both higher-order structures (systems) and higher-order processes.

We are now prepared to give a preliminary answer to the question about personal motivation. Motivation, in the course of psychic organization, becomes increasingly personalized. The higher forms into which instinctual motivations become transformed, and the more highly organized instinctual energy conformations which we call higher psychic structures, assume dominance to a greater or less degree within the developing individual. But instincts as the original motive forces never become extinct, nor do the structures corresponding more closely to these primitive forces. Thus the id is never superseded by the ego's increasing dominance, whereas the ego may "regress," decrease in organization to a state closer to that level of psychic energy organization that we call id. It may be noted that the concepts of sublimation and instinctualization and of controlled regression conform to this picture of things.

The interpretation of personal motivation restructures what is less organized, or kept out of the overall organizational context of the person (repression), into a higher, more individually centered order of motivational energy and structuralization of such energy. This can occur only to the extent to which the organizational process of psychic development can be laid bare and revived, for no reorganization takes place by mere superimposition. The latter, on the contrary, should be taken as a method of defense against reorganization (for instance, in many obsessional and "normal" characters). In the context of the just-quoted passage from "The Unconscious" Freud (1915*b*) writes: "Now, too, we are in a position to state precisely what it is that repression denies to the rejected presentation in the transference neuroses: what it denies to the presentation is translation into words *which shall remain attached to the object*" (p. 202; my italics). Superimposition is this lack of "attachment" of words to objects, lack of the link between the unconscious and the preconscious presentation in Freud's language, a form of insulation where hypercathexis has not taken place. What Freud describes here as attachment or link is the same phenomenon, although viewed in a different context, which he calls transference in chapter 7 of *The Interpretation of Dreams*: "an unconscious idea is as such quite incapable of entering the preconscious and . . . it can only exercise any effect there by establishing a connection with an idea which already belongs to the preconscious, by transferring its intensity on to it and by getting itself 'covered' by it. Here we have the fact of 'transference', which provides an explanation of so many striking phenomena in the mental life of neurotics" (1900, p. 562).

To lay bare the organizational process of psychic development means to enter into the organizational process as a new factor, to become a new factor in the process. The disorganizational and reorganizational movements taking place in the analytic process are codetermined by a new motivational factor, the analyst; and his activity is governed by his interpretation and integration of himself as personally motivated.

The interpretation of personal motivation, basic to the whole conception of psychoanalysis, is founded on a specific, though most comprehensive, self-interpretation of man. It has motivational impact on oneself and others. It tends to restructure lower-order motivational forces (such as instincts), by making possible the transformation of a share of them into forces of greater complexity, which can then be redeployed within the nexus of higher levels of motivational organization. But only by the constant or repeated "transference" (of the intensity, as Freud puts it) from lower to higher levels can the viability and vitality of higher structures and higher motivational forces themselves be guaranteed and maintained.

It would seem that the redeployment I spoke of makes it understandable that unconscious motivating forces and "contents," i.e., their manner of representation, are by no means absent from the ego (which thus is not equivalent to the *Pcs.*) but are there rearranged in a different nexus. In the course of ontogenetic development, then, instincts, while also remaining active as such, become transmuted into higher forms of that psychic excitation which we describe as motivation, such as will.[7] And further, all motivational forces, including unmodified, unreconstructed instincts, enter into new, higher-level organizational formations which are conceptualized as psychic substructures.

II

In the preceding section I started with personal motivation, worked my way toward instinctual motivation, and back again to the personal—all this to introduce these matters; they have

7. In "The Neuro-Psychoses of Defence" (1894) Freud says that it is "a peculiarity of all states resembling sleep that they suspend the distribution of excitation on which the 'will' of the conscious personality is based" (p. 50). What we call will is, according to this terminology, a particular distribution or form of psychic excitation, and instinct is a less developed form or distribution of such excitation in the hierarchy of psychic organization. The term "excitation" (like the terms "energy" and "instinct"), although used here by Freud in analogy to physiological processes, can and must be divested of its physiologic-biological connotations, which it did not have from the start but which it acquired by being used in specific sciences. "Excitation" has a perfectly legitimate general meaning that becomes specified in and for a specific science. "To be excited" in ordinary language is used for a state of mind or mood or feeling tone. The word was not taken from physiology but given to it, or appropriated by it.

not yet been thoroughly discussed. Let me now start at the other end, instincts, and enter into things more fully and in detail. Two issues are of particular interest: (1) What is the status of the instincts in relation to the total organization we call the psyche? (2) What is the relation of instincts to objects?

The consideration of both questions involves fundamental aspects of psychoanalytic theory. In the course of the discussion I shall refer to specific theoretical formulations and examine their explicit content and their implications as I understand them, without losing sight of the fact that terms and concepts frequently have much richer meanings and connotations than is readily apparent when they are used in highly theoretical formulations—formulations that are much determined by certain theoretical-scientific preconceptions and "conventions," as Freud calls them (1915a, p. 117), and that in any event, as definitions and elaborations of definitions, cannot avoid a certain rigidity. But such formulations are precisely the ones that become enshrined in the body of psychoanalytic knowledge and theory, with a resulting shrinkage and impoverishment of its compass and depth.

What is the status of instincts in relation to the total psychic organization? Are instincts to be understood as elemental component forces of the psyche, or are they forces impinging on the psyche and thus, by definition, themselves nonmental? The problem, I believe, is analogous to the question whether the unconscious is to be understood as psychical, part of mental life, or not. Freud, after initial doubts (see footnote 2), became unalterably committed to viewing unconscious processes as mental processes—which was a decision to establish psychoanalysis as a psychological science—regardless of the nature of their correlation to physical processes, a correlation which is to be presumed as well in regard to conscious processes in any event. But he appears to have wavered in this respect when it comes to instincts. I have already stated that I consider instinct a psychoanalytic psychological concept, which should be kept free of biological and ethological connotations (although the relations between the psychoanalytic concept and nonanalytic instinct concepts may, of course, be profitably discussed). It has to be borne in mind that in such matters a decision is involved to assign the status of phenomena, processes, and events having a grammar and logic of their own—in short, the status of an autonomous field of science—to sequences and relations previously unknown or not systematically investigated; these were previously considered only in respect to their being concomitant with other sequences and relations of a different order.[8] Perhaps we will be able to gain some understanding of the reasons for Freud's indecision in regard to instincts in the course of the ensuing discussion.

In "Instincts and Their Vicissitudes" (1915a, p. 118) an instinct is said to be "a stimulus applied to the mind." The concept "stimulus" is taken from physiology in this context. Instinct is a stimulus which "does not arise from the external world but from within the organism itself." Freud says an instinctual stimulus might better be called a need. "What does away with a need is 'satisfaction'." Instinct here is seen as a factor that operates upon the mind, from within the organism, to be sure; it is called internal here in contrast to the external world of the organism's environment, but is operating from outside of that mind. Freud finds it important to call attention to the fact that "postulates" concerning the properties of the system that is being stimulated are implied in his discussion of instincts as organic stimuli (for instance, in the sentence: "What does away with a need is 'satisfaction'"). The most important postulate "runs as follows: the nervous system is an apparatus which has the function of getting rid of the stimuli that reach it, or of reducing them to the lowest possible level; or which, if it were feasible, would maintain itself in an altogether unstimulated condition" (the constancy principle). And he appears to describe something like the evolution from such a physiological system to a "psychic apparatus" when he says that instinctual stimuli "oblige the nervous system to renounce its ideal intention of keeping off stimuli" and to "cause it to undertake involved and interconnected activities by which the external world is so changed as to afford satisfaction to the internal source of stimulation."

But we obtain a somewhat different picture of "instinct" if we consider mental life from what Freud here calls a biological point of view. "If now we apply ourselves to considering mental life

8. For some of the epistemological-philosophical issues pertinent here compare Michael Polanyi's book *Personal Knowledge* (1958).

from a *biological* point of view, an 'instinct' appears to us as a concept on the frontier between the mental and the somatic, as the psychical representative of the stimuli originating from within the organism and reaching the mind, as a measure of the demand made upon the mind for work in consequence of its connection with the body" (p. 121). Instinct now is not a physiological stimulus but is the "psychical representative" of the latter. The meaning of the term "representative" is left open, and the nature of the connection of the mind with the body is left undetermined. Instinct, understood as a psychical representative (*Repräsentant*), is not a stimulus impinging on the psychic apparatus but is a force within or of the psychic apparatus; a force which represents stimuli originating in the body in a different (psychical) form. While organismic stimuli "reach the mind," in this version instincts are not these stimuli themselves, but they represent such stimuli. If we wish to call instincts stimuli, they would be mental stimuli, stimuli which form part, are elements, of the mind. They act as dynamic forces *of* the mind and not *upon* it from the outside.

The concepts "representative" and "representation" will have to concern us at considerable length on a later occasion, but two points should be mentioned here: (1) We must distinguish between psychic representative (*Repräsentant* and *Repräsentanz*) and representation in the sense of idea (*Vorstellung*). The meaning of representation, as used in the word representative, is wider than that of representation as idea. Psychical representation in the wider sense includes, for instance, such nonideational phenomena as affects and, of course, as we have seen, instincts. (2) Mental or psychical representatives are hierarchically structured in such a way that representatives of a lower order can be re-represented—not *necessarily* in the form of ideas—on higher mental levels. This is implied when we speak of primary and secondary process and when Freud speaks of thing presentations and word presentations and of the hypercathexis of the former by the latter (1915*b*, p. 201).[9]

Instincts then, considered from a so-called biological point of

9. Compare Strachey's discussion on the "ambiguity in Freud's use of the term '*Trieb*' (instinct) and '*Triebrepräsentanz*' (instinctual representative)" (1915*a*, p. 111). In "The Unconscious" (Freud, 1915*b*), *Vorstellung* is translated as "idea" or "presentation."

view, are mental stimuli. The system in which physiological stimuli are represented as instincts is capable of representing. What may be said to be stimulated by physiological, organic stimuli (and, we may assume, by other kinds of physical stimuli as well) is this faculty of representing, an activity that is then seen as inherent in the mind and not brought to it from the organismic needs. The organismic needs may stimulate this activity, they do not introduce it into the mind. The property of the system that is being stimulated, according to our discussion, is no longer the one Freud postulated when he considered instinct from a physiological point of view (the function of getting rid of organic stimuli), but is the property or function of representing (in the wide sense of representation). Whether or how in the course of evolution mental activity has developed out of physiological activity, is another matter.

A crude analogy may help to clarify the state of affairs: the fact that a transformer is capable of transforming electric currents of a certain frequency into currents of another frequency is not explained by the frequency or the force of the incoming current. That mental, "representing" activity is in some way correlated with (or powered by) neurophysiological activity also is not denied. A radio, in order to perform its function, has to have a power supply which is precisely independent of the stimuli that reach it and that stimulate the radio to perform its work. The neurophysiological activity in the nervous system that we assume to underlie or power mental activity is something quite different from the somatic needs Freud calls instincts in his first ("physiological") formulation and are said to be represented by instincts in his second ("biological") formulation. In terms of Freud's model, the organismic needs or stimuli reach the mind and demand work from it. The mind's work consists in "representing" (in the wide sense of representation), in generating mental representatives, and not in "getting rid," of the stimuli that reach it; and this work, the functioning of the mind, may be said to be powered by neurophysiological activity. The mind's "connection with the body" (1915a, p. 122) is therefore twofold: (1) the mind's work is *powered* by neurophysiological activity; and (2) this work is *stimulated* by the organismic needs. The work itself, on this level, consists in instinctual activity, which is defined as representing organismic needs.

Let me emphasize once more: the basic postulate concerning the general function of the psychic apparatus is no longer that of getting rid of the (organismic) stimuli that reach it, but that of generating mental representatives of these stimuli, i.e., generating instinctual activity. And my accent is not on the fact that instincts are mental representatives of organismic stimuli, but on the fact that they are mental representatives. Freud perhaps gave a hint of his being uneasy about the idea that the mental apparatus has the function of getting rid of stimulation when he redefined, in that same passage, its task more broadly as that of stimulus-mastery [*Reizbewältigung*], an expression that is less prejudicial as to the manner of dealing with stimuli (1915a, p. 120).

We come to the conclusion that instinct in psychoanalysis, following Freud's definition of it as a mental representative of organismic stimuli, is a mental force or stimulus and may be described as the most primitive element or unit of motivation. It is a motivational stimulus, constituent of the stream of mental life, and not a biological stimulus operating upon that stream.[10] But it must be admitted that Freud was not consistent in using instinct as a strictly psychological concept, in part because of the equivocal meaning of the term representation throughout psychoanalytic theory.

Let us now briefly consider a particular, but central aspect of the apparatus model. An instrument or apparatus, like a microscope, telescope, or camera is a tool or a machine made use of by some other agency or agencies for certain purposes, which are defined by that other agency. The apparatus itself is at rest unless used by another agency. The mind, in this respect to be compared to an organism, is itself a center of activity, has purposes of its own, as it were.[11] An organism is embedded in its environment in such a way that it is in living contact and interchange with it; it modulates and influences the environment by its own activity, and its activity is modulated and influenced

10. For a discussion of the definition of instinct (instinctual drive) as a psychic representative versus the definition as somatic stimulus, and of the conception of instinct as motivational force in a hierarchy of motivational forces, see Schur (1966, especially pp. 29–46).

11. In reference to this question, as well as to the whole problem of motivation and of instincts as motives, see Rapaport (1960).

by the environment. Although misleading in some crucial respects, to compare the mind with an organism is much more
appropriate than to compare it with a tool or machine (or, for
that matter, than to use the reflex arc model); not only because an
organism is a center of activity in its own right, differentiated
from but in continuous active interchange with its environment,
but also because its activity is of the same or a similar order as
that of the living environment. I shall have occasion to refer to
the organism analogy at various times, but it must be kept in
mind that it is an analogy from another field which, while closer
to our field than physiology, physics, mechanics, and optics, has
a different conceptual framework, is structured by different
founding postulates, and deals with a different order of "data."
The degree of objectivation possible in biology—since we apply
our mind to something that by definition of the field has no mind,
is not mental—is far greater than that possible in psychoanalysis
as a psychological science.

I believe that the structural model, in contrast to the topographic one, is a model built in analogy to an organism; this is
one of the reasons why it is, in many respects, more usable in
psychoanalysis.[12] The structural model does not conceive of
instincts as organic stimuli which are extraneous to the mind
and impinge on it, and it does not conceive of the mind as an
instrument—however complex—that processes incoming stimuli
to discharge them again in some modified form and whose
operations are simply set in motion and determined by another
agency.

To avoid misunderstanding I wish to state that such schematic descriptions, machine model and organism model, apply
to the conceptual models used and not to the flesh and blood of
Freud's discoveries and formulations, which much of the time
far transcend the models used or even disregard them. In introducing the topographic model and the simile of a microscope or
camera in *The Interpretation of Dreams,* Freud (1900, p. 536)
writes:

I see no necessity to apologize for the imperfections of this or of any

12. For detailed discussions of the two models or "theories" see Merton Gill (1963)
and Arlow and Brenner (1964). See also my review of the latter work (Loewald, 1966;
reprinted in this volume).

similar imagery. Analogies of this kind are only intended to assist us in our attempt to make the complications of mental functioning intelligible by dissecting the function and assigning its different constituents to different component parts of the apparatus. . . . We are justified, in my view, in giving free reign to our speculations so long as we retain the coolness of our judgement and do not mistake the scaffolding for the building.

Freud's reminder is important for any such undertaking and applies to his later metapsychological writings and to the structural model as well. But it must also be said that the general nature of the scaffolding used indicates something about the plan and standpoint adopted for erecting the building and delimits its extension and scope of function. In other words, the theory or model does not always do justice to the discoveries and insights of psychoanalysis, and theory may have to be brought to conform to them more closely and to understand them differently, by something more than mere additions and refinements. Freud's new conception of the structural theory is one example; another example is provided by his continued attempts to revise and change his instinct theory.

With the formulation of the structural theory the conceptualization of instincts and of the mind changed. This change did not come about suddenly, and it was not consistently adhered to after its culmination in *The Ego and the Id.* In some respects the change may even have been more apparent than real. If one tries to look at Freud's work as an organic whole, similar perhaps to the organization of the psyche itself, comparisons come to mind with the interplay and conflict of active forces and between various organizational layers, with progressive and regressive directions and movements and influences, as they occur during the lifetime of an individual. Nevertheless, in an overall way one can say that in the structural theory the psyche is conceptualized as consisting in and constituted by an interplay of psychic forces and structural layers in a manner that could not be achieved by the apparatus model. The view of the relations between the inside and the outside of the psyche, of the relations between the inner forces and the forces external to the psyche, changed quite radically and had much to do with the emergence of the structural theory, as will become clearer in section IV.

The conceptualization of instincts changed in a number of ways. Since the psyche was now being conceived more like an organism (this is exemplified in Freud's comparisons of it with an amoeba and its pseudopodia, and in his description of the ego as an outer layer of the id, which has been modified by the external medium on which it borders), instincts tended to become forces within this organism. But there was no longer any particular emphasis on an instinct's being a psychical representative. In fact, in "The Unconscious" (1915h), especially in the discussion of unconscious emotions, it becomes doubtful whether Freud continued to adhere to this view. In Beyond the Pleasure Principle (1920) instinct became a more global concept for "an urge inherent in organic life to restore an earlier state of things" (1920, p. 36). This harks back to the constancy principle. In the "physiological" view of instincts in "Instincts and Their Vicissitudes," the psychic apparatus dealt with instincts, understood as organic stimuli, in accordance with this principle; the psychic apparatus had the function to restore that earlier state of things, namely, the state of rest, nonexcitation. Now, however, instincts themselves have become expressions of this principle; they are no longer forces that interfere with it or call it into operation. This means that they are forces, urges of an organism, whether biological or psychical, manifesting the constancy principle, not stirring it into action. The gain, from the present point of view, was that instincts and the psyche were no longer at loggerheads with each other, as they had been when instincts were seen as disturbing an apparatus that wanted to be unstimulated and was intrinsically inactive and opposed to activity; instincts now were active forces constituting the dynamic elements of the psyche. But the emphasis on their being psychical representatives was lost.

Since 1920, instincts are conceived as broad polar forces of living matter, the life or love instinct, Eros, and the death instinct, Thanatos. They lose their distinction as psychic forces, although they also manifest themselves in psychic form. This conforms to a tendency, always present in Freud, to view and implement psychoanalysis as a biological science. But it is one thing to consider the correlations and illuminating analogies between psychoanalysis and biology, or to put psychoanalytic findings within an overall framework of biological or even cosmic evolution. It is quite another thing to reduce psychoanalytic data and concepts to biological ones, as though a psychology were possible without postulating psychic life and psychic reality, without being committed to the mind's existence (whatever form or meaning of existence may be involved from a philosophical point of view). Freud, like many before and after him, did not always avoid the fallacy of thinking that the switch from psychological to biological or physical concept formation could make psychology more objective. But such a switch only dissolves psychology. As long as the human individual is apprehended by himself and by other individuals as a center of activity distinct from other centers of different kinds of activity — be they stars or nebulas, atoms, plants, or animals — psychology as an understanding of the mind as mind will then have to be recreated. To the extent to which Freud, in *Beyond the Pleasure Principle,* places psychoanalysis in a continuum whose referent is not mind but living matter, he loses the subject of psychoanalysis.

It is now possible to answer the first question I raised at the beginning of this section: what is the status of instincts in relation to the total psychic organization? Instincts, whether defined as psychic representatives of organismic stimuli or needs, or, much more broadly, as urges inherent in organic life (including psychic life as a special case), are forces within the psychic organization and not stimuli which operate on that system from without. The system itself is conceived as something akin to or analogous to an organism, and not as an apparatus made use of by an organism. A duality of instincts in their interplay, confluence and conflict, constitutes the activity of this organization. It is assumed that the system is a center of endogenous activity (whatever the ultimate reason for that activity may be) that consists, in its primitive form, in what we call instinctual activity. True, there is, according to Freud, the death instinct, the tendency to die, to return to a state of rest. But the opposing tendency to live, the life instinct, also is an intrinsic motive force; it is not imposed upon the system by forces outside of it.

From this point of view, insofar as the death instinct can be

equated with the constancy–inertia–unpleasure principle,[13] the
death instinct is nothing startlingly new in Freud's theory. The
constancy or unpleasure principle always regulated the psychic
apparatus and in that sense was intrinsic to it, in contrast to the
instincts conceived as stimuli extrinsic to it. But in an apparatus
such a principle could not be conceptualized as an instinct. When
the psyche was conceived of as an organic entity, as a living
structure, the abstract principle became an instinct. What *is* new
in Freud's new instinct theory and in the structural theory is the
life instinct as an intrinsic motive force of the psyche paired with
the death instinct.[14]

III

Before going on to a discussion of the second question, the
relations of instincts to objects, some more general remarks
about instincts and an "instinct psychology" (*Trieb-Psychologie*)
are in order. They will also serve as a corrective to the preceding
discussion in respect to instincts as biological forces. One concern of Freud's, especially in the beginning, was to free psychology of its intellectualistic orientation, of its bias in favor of
consciousness, and, from the point of view of then-current
morality, of its preoccupation with the "higher," rational, and
morally acceptable reaches of the mind. He was not alone in his
interest in and emphasis on the irrational in life and human
nature, the importance of primordial, archaic, infantile, and
primitive forces in human life and the life of the mind, including
those existing "in consequence of its connection with the body."
But he was the one to bring these matters most forcefully within
the compass of psychiatry and psychology, and to penetrate and
articulate them with the methods of scientific investigation and
conceptualization.

13. This equation, in my opinion, is valid only up to a point. Freud's conception of the
death instinct also contains other elements which are not under discussion here (see
footnote 14).

14. For brief discussions of the connections between the constancy–unpleasure principle and the death instinct, and between a separate pleasure principle and the life
instinct, see Freud (1924, p. 159), and Schur (1966, especially pp. 146–52). For comments
on the regulatory principles and the death instinct, see also my discussion of Schur's
paper on "The Regulatory Principles of Mental Functioning," reprinted in this volume
(chapter 5).

Triebe were, however, for Freud not just abstract constructs or concepts in a theory of motivation or personality, to be sorted out from other forces of motivation, to be classified and distinguished from affects, perceptual and cognitive processes, and somatic needs. Triebe, instincts, were—much more than scientists, doctors, ministers, judges ("the educated circles") wanted to admit or know—what made the human world go around, what drove people to act and think and feel the way they do, in excess as well as in self-constriction, inhibition, and fear, in their daily lives in the family and with others, and in their civilized and professional occupations and preoccupations as well. They dominated their love life and influenced their behavior with children and authorities. They made people sick and made them mad. They drove people to perversion and crimes, made them into hypocrites and liars as well as into fanatics for truth and other virtues, or into prissy, bigoted, prejudiced, or anxious creatures. And their sexual needs, preoccupations, and inhibitions turned out to be at the root of much of all this. Rational, civilized, measured, "good" behavior, the noble and kind deeds and thoughts and feelings so highly valued were much of the time postures and gestures, self-denials, rationalizations, distortions, and hideouts—a thin surface mask covering and embellishing the true life and the real power of the instincts.

The life of the body, of bodily needs and habits and functions, kisses and excrements and intercourse, tastes and smells and sights, body noises and sensations, caresses and punishments, tics and gait and movements, facial expression, the penis and the vagina and the tongue and arms and hands and feet and legs and hair, pain and pleasure, physical excitement and lassitude, violence and bliss—all this is the body in the context of human life. The body is not primarily the organism with its organs and physiological functions, anatomical structures, nerve pathways, and chemical processes.

If Freud had not had all this in view, and the vagaries and foibles of people, his own and those of his patients, he would never have been able to write his case histories and to create a scientific psychoanalysis as distinct from both neurology and academic psychiatry and psychology. He would not have been able to understand dreams and jokes and neurosis and the psychopathology of everyday life. He created, partly in spite of his inclinations and not without grave misgivings, an entirely new method and standard of scientific investigation which went counter to scientific principles and methods derived from or devised for a different realm of reality—principles and methods that stultified an appropriate approach to and grasp of psychic life. He could do this because he was unwilling to accept the narrow limitations imposed on science by the science of his day, whose child he remained nevertheless. He broke out of those limits and widened the field of scientific action, while loath to accept the consequences of such a venture in all its implications. But had he not in such a way brought science and life as it is lived together again, psychoanalysis would never have had the impact on modern life and scientific thought that we see today.

Instincts and the life of the body, seen in the perspective sketched above, are one and the same. They become separate only when we begin to distinguish between soma and psyche. But once this is done—and without this distinction there is neither physiology–anatomy nor psychology—instinct in psychoanalysis must be understood as a psychological concept. I believe it means reintroducing the psyche into biology and physics if one speaks of Eros and Thanatos as universal cosmic tendencies. Whether this is legitimate or not remains, in my opinion, an open question; this psyche, however, would in any event not be psyche or mind in terms of human psychology. Within the framework of psychoanalysis as a science of the human mind we must, if we accept the Eros–Thanatos conception (or its less "metaphysical" form, the duality of libido and aggression), speak of instincts as psychic representatives, and of life and death instincts as such representatives.

IV

I turn now to the second question raised about instincts: *What is the relation of instincts to objects?* This is possibly the most complex and most important problem for psychoanalytic theory today, and perhaps one of the most controversial issues as well. In this paper I shall approach the problem only from a few selected angles. In its wider implications it is the problem of object relations and of what has been termed object–relations theory (for a recent extensive discussion see Modell, 1968). My limited treatment of this broad issue here is intended as a first approach toward it.

The status of objects in psychoanalytic theory has undergone a gradual and profound change in the course of time. In broad outline, one may say that objects were first conceptualized predominantly as means for providing satisfaction of instinctual needs, i.e., as possible sources of "pleasure" and, by the same token, possible sources of unpleasure and frustration of such needs. Satisfaction, be it noted again, was understood as that process which, in conformity with the pleasure-unpleasure principle, leads to the elimination or reduction of excitation (stimulation), or is the result of such a process. Objects were taken as givens and no psychoanalytic questions were raised about them and their status in psychoanalytic theory. Such a psychoanalytically naive conception of objects, despite subsequent changes, still pervades much of psychoanalytic theory.

But gradually it became apparent that, at least in regard to early psychic stages—and these are of specific importance for instinct theory—objects are not givens. On the contrary, a highly complex course of psychic development is required for environmental and body-surface stimuli to become organized and experienced as external, in contrast to internal, and for such sources of stimulation, gratification, and frustration eventually to become objects, in any acceptable sense of that word, for a subject or self. Hand in hand with this came a growing recognition of the fact that, what from an external (i.e., nonpsychoanalytic) observer's point of view are called objects, are indispensable and crucial factors in the organization of psychic functioning and psychic structure. In other words, what is naively called objects plays an essential part in the constitution of the subject, including the organization of instincts as psychic phenomena and of the subject's developing "object relations"; and what is naively called subject plays an essential part in the organization of objects (not merely of object representations). A detailed reconsideration of the concepts of object and object representation in psychoanalysis must be reserved for a later occasion. At that time the relation of instincts to objects will have to be re-examined.

In order to provide a focus of orientation the following thesis is proposed: *instincts, understood as psychic, motivational, forces, become organized as such through interactions within a psychic field consisting originally of the mother–child (psychic) unit.* (This formulation implies that neither objects nor instincts are any longer taken as givens or as concepts simply appropriated from other sciences.)

When Freud (1915a) undertook "to discuss certain terms which are used in reference to the concept of an instinct," he significantly included, together with "pressure," "aim," and "source" of an instinct, the term "object." While he thus acknowledged that the object of an instinct is something intrinsic to instinct, he immediately gave the object a special status by saying that it "is not originally connected with" the instinct, "but becomes assigned [zugeordnet] to it only in consequence of being peculiarly fitted to make satisfaction possible." And by defining object as "the thing in regard to which or through which the instinct is able to achieve its aim," by saying that "the aim of an instinct is in every instance satisfaction," by specifying that satisfaction "can only be obtained by removing the state of stimulation at the source of the instinct"—the source being "the somatic process which occurs in an organ or part of the body" (p. 122)—he remains with or reverts to a somatic instinct concept, remains within the purview of the constancy principle (satisfaction or pleasure equals reduction or abolition of stimulation), and narrows down the object to a means of satisfying somatic needs which primarily have nothing to do with the environment. It must be left to biologists to decide whether the closed system model is really serviceable in their field; it certainly is not in psychology.

With the introduction of the concepts of narcissism, narcissistic identification, and "introjection" (in the sense in which Freud [1915a, p. 136] uses the term), the problem of the development and organization of intrapsychic processes and structures was definitely raised and approached, mainly in terms of ego and superego development. But the instinct concept, and id theory by and large, were left out of consideration in this new approach. I do not mean to say, of course, that Freud did not consider the relations of narcissism to the instinct problem. The concept of narcissism was in fact introduced mainly to gain an understanding of the instinctual processes subsumed under the term narcissistic libido (in contradistinction to object libido). But this did not lead Freud to a reconsideration of the instinct *concept* in terms of the relationship between instinct and environment ("object"). By and large, he continued to operate—despite his definition of instinct as psychic representative—with a somatic and "innate" instinct concept, and he discussed instincts psychoanalytically only when he took up what he called their vicissitudes.[15] If instincts are resolutely conceptualized as psychic forces, these vicissitudes are not something that happens to instincts (once they are there, as it were) but are the processes by which they become organized as instincts, by which, we might say, somatic processes become transformed into psychic processes, into psychic representatives.

This transformation, the organization of instincts *qua* psychic forces, comes to pass, I maintain, through interactions within the mother–child psychic field. If one views the problem from the vantage point of the organization of psychic reality, the question whether objects are or are not "originally connected" with instincts is nonsensical. Phenomena such as instincts and objects gradually become constituted, by differentiation and integration, in those interaction processes. Neither instinct nor object, to begin with, is there to become or not to become connected with the other. Once each can be differentiated from the other as an internal or external phenomenon because of the interactions by which they come into being, each "contains" elements of the other. Saying that an object is primarily, psychoanalytically understood, a libidinal object, implies this situation.

If we use the language of the fully developed adult objective

---

15. As late as 1938 he wrote: "The forces which we assume to exist behind the [need-] tensions of the id are called *instincts*. They represent the somatic demands upon the mind" (1940, p. 148). (I have slightly modified Strachey's translation in the interest of precision; Freud does not speak of "tensions caused by the needs of the id," as Strachey translates, but of need-tensions [*Bedürfnisspannungen*]. No cause-effect relationship is implied between the needs of the id and the tensions; needs of the id *are* tensions for Freud, they do not *cause* tensions.) It is true that the word "represent" is used ("they represent the somatic demands upon the mind"), but the whole passage makes it clear that instinct itself is conceived as somatic force *behind* the need-tensions of the id. Since the id is a province of the mind (not a biological-somatic entity or concept), forces behind the id act *upon* the mind, not *within* it as mental processes, so that Freud reverts here to his "physiological" approach to instincts (see section II).

reality to which we are accustomed in ordinary scientific terminology,[16] we would have to say that the object does not become
"assigned" to the instinct (understood as psychic force) but
contributes crucially to the organization of instincts *qua* instincts, just as instinctual forces crucially contribute to the
organization of objects *qua* objects. In this sense the object is no
less an original element of the instinct than its pressure, aim, or
source.

Speaking in terms of the ontogenesis of psychic reality, I
would say that the neonate's incoherent urges, thrashings, and
reflex activities become coordinated and organized into instincts
and assume aims and direction by activities and responses
coming from the environment. And here we should include in
our consideration the meaning of "satisfaction." The responsive,
attuned activity of the primary caring person does not simply
provide satisfaction in the sense of being a means for abolishing
excitation. The experience of satisfaction, I believe, is a "creative"
process in which appropriate environmental activity does not
necessarily or only reduce or abolish excitation but also *engenders* and *organizes* excitation processes. So-called "mnemic
images" are thus created, which are not additions to but constituents of instincts. Mnemic image must be understood here in the
sense in which Freud speaks of motor or kinesthetic images
(*Bewegungsbild*) in his discussion of satisfaction in the "Project"
(1895, p. 318).[17] In the "Project" Freud barely mentions instincts,
but his discussion of the "Experience of Satisfaction" (p. 317),
with its emphasis on the "specific action" brought about by the

16. I regret that a very much needed clarification of the meanings and ramifications of
the term "objective" would lead us too far afield in the present context. In any psychoanalytic investigation the subject–object antithesis creates great methodological and
terminological difficulties. It should be noted that Freud mentions this problem (1915a,
p. 134): "The antithesis ego–non-ego (external), i.e. subject–object, is ... thrust upon the
individual organism at an early stage.... This antithesis remains, above all, sovereign in
our intellectual activity and creates for research the basic situation which no efforts can
alter." I do not believe, however, that this latter dictum can be taken as the last word on
the matter.

17. Mnemic "images" of this kind are neither visual images nor ideas, but action
patterns comparable to those in hysterical "reminiscences" (Breuer and Freud, 1893–95,
p. 7). "Acting out" is a higher form of this type of mnemic process-structure. These
mnemic activities are of utmost importance for the psychoanalytic theory of memory and
especially of unconscious memory and so-called "memory traces." In another connection
they are the prototypes of identification processes.

"extraneous help" on the part of an "experienced person," adumbrates this understanding of the psychological genesis of instincts as psychic representatives.

The fact that such mnemic action patterns become established as constituents of instincts does not mean, however, that at this stage a differentiation of internal (intrapsychic) and external has already occurred. In the mnemic action pattern, urge and response, environmental engenderment, and the subject's excitation are not differentiated from one another, so that a repetition of such action patterns remains at first a re-enactment of a global event. Only repeated occurrences of such re-enactments, due to the combined effects of recurring need-tensions, environmental responsive actions, and satisfaction events (in the sense outlined above), in alternation with delays and temporary absences of the experience of satisfaction by virtue of differentials between— objectively speaking—subject and environment, lead eventually to a subjective differentiation of mnemic "image" and "actual satisfaction." In such a way, that is, differentiations between something like an internal action pattern (a "memory") and an external factor operating in the effective reinforcement, perpetuation, and revival of that action pattern come about.[18]

In the process of a mother's caring activities, which consist of spontaneous stimulations as well as responses, instincts come into being in the child. The pressure [*Drang*] of the uncoordinated urges that become instincts results from separation events, particularly and most prominently from the event of birth, of physical separation from the mother organism. Rapaport, I believe, has ideas similar to mine when he writes that "*Motives* are characterized by appetitiveness implying a coordination of the instinctual drive discharge [what I would call uncoordinated urges biologically determined] with a definite (even if broad) range of objects," while "*Causes* [nonmotivational] have only a direction which does not change, that is, causes do not 'home' appetitively on the object by changing the direction and path as the place or conditions of the object change." He also emphasizes that "the role of the object in instinctual drive discharge also

---

18. An original nondifferentiation of cognitive-memorial and instinctual processes is implied here, as is the view that cognitive-memorial processes are instinctually based. For a discussion of memory and memory traces, see chapter 10.

involves the 'summation' of the excitation provided by the object
as a stimulus and the excitation provided by instinctual drive
energy. When the accumulation of instinctual drive energy has
not yet reached threshold intensity, this 'summation' may raise it
to that intensity and thus bring about discharge" (1960, p. 878). I
differ with him inasmuch as I hold that the "summation" of these
two sources of excitation creates the instinct (qua psychic,
motivational force), and is generated or mediated by the stimu-
lating-responsive activity of the "object" that gathers, sums up,
something for the infant. While Rapaport speaks of instinctual
drive discharge, I stress, in keeping with my view of the psychological organization of instincts, not the conditions for discharge
of instinctual drive energy but the conditions for the formation
of instincts as psychic phenomena.[19]

In my view, then, based on the definition of instinct as a
psychic representative, the neonate's incoherent urges and thrashings, of which I spoke, are not instinctual. They, like bowel
movements or breathing or the crying of the neonate, are not
psychic representatives; they are as yet no more than somatic
manifestations of stimulation and organic need. In this connection it may be questioned whether the stimulation that becomes
psychically represented as instinct can be confined to "inner,"
organismic stimulation, if "external" stimulation by the mother
enters into the formation of instinct. Inasmuch as the entire
psychic life of the baby is in the early stages apt to be characterized as instinctual [triebhaft], in response to organic as well as
"external" stimulations, what we call instinctual in psychoanalysis seems at that stage to have more to do with the primitive
character of motivation, of psychic organization, than with
"organic" versus "environmental." Everything is still close to the
body and its "language" and expression, not just organic needs.
This would be in contradiction to Freud's distinction between instinctual and "physiological" stimuli (1915a, p. 118). This problem as well as Freud's emphasis on the difference between the
constant force of an instinctual stimulus and the momentary
impact of an external stimulus cannot be discussed in this paper.

19. In his paper "On the Psychoanalytic Theory of Motivation," from which the
quotations in the text are taken, Rapaport discusses many problems of the instinct concept, which are of great importance but must be left out of consideration here. The term
"synergic action" perhaps would be preferable to "summation."

A few words need to be said about the concept of primary narcissism in relation to the concept of instinct advanced here. In "Instincts and Their Vicissitudes" Freud writes:

Originally, at the very beginning of mental life, the ego is cathected with instincts and is to some extent capable of satisfying them on itself. We call this condition "narcissism" and this way of obtaining satisfaction "auto-erotic." At this time the external world is not cathected with interest . . . and is indifferent for purposes of satisfaction. During this period, therefore, the ego-subject coincides with what is pleasurable and the external world with what is indifferent (or possibly unpleasurable, as being a source of stimulation). [Thus, there is an original situation] in which the ego loves itself only and is indifferent to the external world [p. 134]. [On the basis of this view of primary narcissism the distinction is made between a "purely narcissistic stage" and an "object-stage" (p. 137). The latter is an advance that is said to come about in the following way:] Those sexual instincts, which from the outset require an object [i.e., are not capable of autoerotic satisfaction], and the needs of the ego-instincts, which are never capable of auto-erotic satisfaction, naturally disturb this state and so pave the way for an advance from it [p. 134n].

Our present conception of the original situation of mental life called primary narcissism is different. We no longer understand it as a stage where "the external world is not cathected with interest" and is indifferent or hostile (unpleasurable), but as a stage which Freud in *Civilization and Its Discontents* (1930) described as follows:

An infant at the breast does not as yet distinguish his ego from the external world as the source of the sensations flowing in upon him. . . . He must be very strongly impressed by the fact that some sources of excitation, *which he will later recognize as his own bodily organs,* can provide him with sensations at any moment, whereas other sources evade him from time to time—among them what he desires most of all, his mother's breast—and only reappear as a result of his screaming for help. *In this way there is for the first time set over against the ego an "object," in the form of something which exists "outside."* . . . In this way, then, the ego detaches itself from the external world. Or, to put it more correctly, originally the ego includes everything, later it separates off an external world from itself. Our present ego-feeling is, therefore, only a shrunken residue of a much more inclusive—indeed, an all-

embracing—feeling which corresponded to a more intimate bond between the ego and the world about it. [pp. 66–68; my italics].

In the "primal psychical situation" [*psychische Ursituation*]
(Freud, 1915a, p. 134) of primary narcissism, understood in this
new light, ego and external world, ego and "object" are still one
undifferentiated psychic field. And it would not be correct to describe this primal situation as though the external world were
not cathected with interest and were indifferent (or unpleasurable) while the ego–subject would coincide with what is
pleasurable. Pleasure and unpleasure, at this stage at any rate,
are not distributed between inside and outside, or pleasure
attributed to what is internal and unpleasure to what is external.
Pleasure and unpleasure, at this stage, are global states of being.
And an adequately empathic mother is, as a matter of fact, a
participant in this state of being, no less or hardly less than the
infant.[20]

What are the implications of the revised conception of primary
narcissism for the instinct concept? What indeed is the ego of
which we speak at such a stage? It clearly is not the structure we
have in mind when we think of the mental structures id, ego, and
superego. In the passage I quoted from "Instincts and Their
Vicissitudes" the word ego is used in the sense of "the whole
subject"; at one point Freud uses the term "ego-subject" to make
this clear.[21] The word ego is used in the same sense in chapter I of

20. Any sufficiently empathic observer of the mother–infant relationship and interaction can see (and can learn from perceptive mothers) that this is the case; that there is a
mutual correspondence and responsiveness, a reciprocal heightening and decrease of
states of pleasure and unpleasure, including physical pleasurable and unpleasurable
sensations in the mother. In somewhat later stages we tend to describe such phenomena
as emotional contagion or identification, as for instance in the nonverbal transmission of
anxiety from mother to child or vice versa. Any competent psychotherapist is aware of
similar events in the treatment of sensitive or "regressed" patients. It therefore remains
an important question to what extent an investigation and understanding of early
psychic stages is at all possible if the focus of observation does not encompass the
mother together with the infant. If this is done, we are, I believe, much less at the mercy of
reconstructive *speculations* in regard to early stages than is often assumed. Compare
Winnicott's paper on "Primary Maternal Preoccupation" (1956).

21. I advisedly avoid using the term "self" in this connection and at this psychic stage.
Self denotes a "Person's or thing's own individuality or essence, person or thing as object
of introspection or reflexive action" (*The Concise Oxford Dictionary*, 1938); see also
Webster's *International Dictionary* (1958) under: self, n., especially 3. In psychoanalytic
literature the term is used far too loosely and equivocally. Accordingly, I cannot agree
with a definition, as proposed by Hartmann (1950), of narcissism as cathexis of the self in
contradistinction to cathexis of the ego.

Civilization and Its Discontents from which I quoted. A reading of the whole first chapter of that book makes it clear that Freud is not dealing with the ego as a mental substructure. To put it another way, the meaning of ego as a mental substructure dissolves when we concern ourselves with early "ego states" and with their later equivalents. When, in "Instincts and Their Vicissitudes" Freud writes that "at the very beginning of mental life the ego is cathected with instincts [*triebbesetzt*]," or when he speaks of a body ego or pleasure ego, a distinction between what he later would call id and ego clearly could not be intended, given the stage of mental development to which he refers. The ego–subject (to use Freud's specifying term) at this stage *is* an instinctual one.[22]

Due to "various promptings" (Freud, 1930, p. 67), by gradual development (see above) there is an "object" being set over against the ego or—and this is saying the same thing—an instinctual ego over against the "object." That Freud describes the ego's primal state as narcissism is in itself a fact which makes it clear that instinctual life is the referent here. (The introduction of the concept of primary narcissism is an "extension of the libido theory" [Freud, 1914, p. 75].) We cannot have one theory in regard to the constitution or organization of the ego, and another one in regard to the organization of instincts. The early development of the ego, as adumbrated by Freud in *Civilization and Its Discontents,* is the organization and development of instincts understood as psychic representatives. Freud did not make this explicit and did not revise his instinct concept in accordance with the new insights into early mental development. Among the reasons for his not doing so are his theoretical bias in favor of a biological instinct concept, and his reluctance, amounting to an aversion, to involve himself deeply in the investigation of mental stages and states where the subject–object polarity does not hold.[23]

In this context Freud's concepts of the original reality ego and

22. Winnicott (1956, p. 305) writes: "In reconstructing the early development of an infant there is no point at all in talking of instincts, except on a basis of ego development. There is a watershed: Ego maturity—instinctual experiences strengthen ego. Ego immaturity—instinctual experiences disrupt ego. Ego here implies a summation of experience."

23. See Freud's comments on the oceanic feeling (1930, pp. 64, 72). Compare also his letter to Hollos (written in 1928), which clearly shows such an aversion, and Schur's discussion (1966, pp. 21–23). Cf. my paper "Ego and Reality" (this volume, pp. 9–10), which deals with this problem from another angle.

the purified pleasure ego (1915a) should be reconsidered; here I can state only that in the light of the revised conception of primary narcissism neither concept can be retained in its original form.

As a preliminary conclusion, the following may be said about the relation of instincts to objects: objects are "originally connected" with instincts in such a way that the problem is not how they become connected in the course of time and development, or why they become connected. Rather, seen from the standpoint of instinctual life, the problem is: how what later is distinguished as object from subject, becomes differentiated, in the course of mental development, from instincts. Only if instincts are conceptualized as organismic, biological stimuli impinging on a pre-ordained "psychic apparatus" which is not itself instinctual but stimulated by such instincts, and if instincts are conceived merely as biological urges pressing for discharge—only then can the idea arise that the "object" is not an original element of "instinct." At the same time, I have suggested that, in order to speak of the relation of instinct to object in a truly psychoanalytic discourse, the object concept itself must be freed of its naive connotations rooted in nonanalytic epistemological preconceptions.

REFERENCES

Arlow, J. A., and Brenner, C. (1964): *Psychoanalytic Concepts and the Structural Theory.* New York: International Universities Press.

Bornstein, B. (1949): The analysis of a phobic child: Some problems of theory and technique in child analysis. *The Psychoanalytic Study of the Child* 3/4: 181–226.

Breuer, J., and Freud, S. (1893–95): Studies on hysteria. S.E. 2.

Freud, S. (1894): The neuro-psychoses of defence. S.E. 3: 43–68.

———. (1895): Project for a scientific psychology. S.E. 1: 281–397.

———. (1900): *The Interpretation of Dreams.* S.E. 4/5.

———. (1910): The psycho-analytic view of psychogenic disturbance of vision. S.E. 11: 209–18.

———. (1914): On narcissism: An introduction. S.E. 14: 69–102.

———. (1915a): Instincts and their vicissitudes. S.E. 14: 109–40.

_____. (1915*b*): The unconscious. S.E. 14:159–215.

_____. (1920): Beyond the pleasure principle. S.E. 18:3–64.

_____. (1923): The ego and the id. S.E. 19:3–66.

_____. (1924): The economic problem of masochism. S.E. 19: 157–70.

_____. (1930): Civilization and its discontents. S.E. 21:59–145.

_____. (1940 [1938]): An outline of psycho-analysis. S.E. 23: 141–207.

Gill, M. M. (1963): *Topography and Systems in Psychoanalytic Theory* [*Psychological Issues*, Monograph 10]. New York: International Universities Press.

Hartmann, H. (1939): *Ego Psychology and the Problem of Adaptation.* New York: International Universities Press, 1958.

_____. (1950): Comments on the psychoanalytic theory of the ego. *The Psychoanalytic Study of the Child* 5:74–96.

Loewald, H. W. (1951): Ego and reality. *Int. J. Psycho-Anal.* 32: 10–18.

_____. (1966): Review of: *Psychoanalytic Concepts and the Structural Theory*, by J. A. Arlow and C. Brenner. *Psychoanal. Quart.* 35:430–36 (reprinted in this volume).

_____. (1971): Discussion of *The Id and the Regulatory Principles of Mental Functioning*, by M. Schur. In: *The Unconscious Today: Essays in Honor of Max Schur*, ed. M. Kanzer. New York: International Universities Press, 1971 (reprinted in this volume).

Loewenstein, R. M. (1951): The problem of interpretation. *Psychoanal. Quart.* 20:1–14.

Modell, A. H. (1968): *Object Love and Reality.* New York: International Universities Press.

Polanyi, M. (1958): *Personal Knowledge: Towards a Post-Critical Philosophy.* London: Oxford University Press.

Rapaport, D. (1960): On the psychoanalytic theory of motivation. In: *The Collected Papers of David Rapaport*, ed. M. M. Gill. New York: Basic Books, 1967, pp. 853–915.

Schur, M. (1966): *The Id and the Regulatory Principles of Mental Functioning.* New York: International Universities Press.

Strachey, J. (1966): Notes on some technical terms whose translation calls for comment. S.E. 1:xxiii–xxvi.

Winnicott, D. W. (1956): Primary maternal preoccupation. *Collected Papers.* New York: Basic Books, 1958, pp. 300–05.

9

THE EXPERIENCE OF TIME

I

Time and the experience of time are of central importance in mental life. Yet psychoanalytic contributions dealing with the subject in more than a tangential fashion are sparse, although there has been some increase in recent years. Despite our vast experience with time, despite our dealing with time in one way or another every day, and despite our common-sense knowledge of it, the phenomenon of time and what is meant by the concept have through the ages remained most elusive and may well be incomprehensible to the human mind. "It is impossible," Whitehead (1920, p. 73) said, "to meditate on time and the mystery of the creative passage of nature without overwhelming emotion at the limitations of human intelligence." Freud (1933, p. 74) has expressed similar feelings of frustration in regard to the problem of time. Nevertheless, the experience of time, temporal phenomena, and the concept of time play an essential role in psychoanalysis, both as a method of treatment and research and as a body of theory.

Here are some of the temporal phenomena and concepts that most obviously are of importance in psychoanalysis: memory, forgetting, regression, repetition, anticipation, presentation, and representation; the influence of the past on the present in thought, feeling, and behavior; delay of gratification and action; sleep–wakefulness and other rhythmicities in mental life; variations and abnormalities in the subjective sense of elapsed time; the so-called timelessness of the id; the role of imagination and fantasy in structuring the future; values, standards, ideals as future-

This paper consists of the Chairman's introductory contribution to the Panel on "The Experience of Time," held at the Fall Meeting of the American Psychoanalytic Association, New York, on December 18, 1971.

oriented categories; concepts such as object constancy and self identity; not to mention the important factor of time in the psychoanalytic situation itself, in technical aspects, appointments, length of hour, etc.

More generally, psychoanalysis as a scientific discipline is unthinkable without the theory of evolution and of ontogenesis of mental development. In this regard psychoanalysis is in the mainstream of modern science and its "Discovery of Time" (see the book of that title by Toulmin and Goodfield, 1965): time, the historical dimension, having gained equal importance in the natural sciences and in the social sciences.[1] In psychoanalysis, more than in any other form of psychological research and treatment, man is taken as a historical being, a being that as a race and as an individual has a history, has run and continues to run through a course of development from something simple and primitive to something complex and "civilized." We are aware of the parallels, in certain respects, between archaeology and psychoanalysis. This time dimension, and the fact that human beings become, to a greater or less degree, aware of their history and their historicity, determine mental life. Furthermore, fixations, delays, detours, arrests, and developmental spurts are considered to be prime factors in shaping the course of mental life and its disturbances, all of them factors crucially involving the dimension of time. We hold that emotional-intellectual understanding and reworking of such developmental factors of the past in the present—in the psychoanalytic situation—may lead to a more harmonious, less disturbed integration of the personality. That man can own up to his past and thus gain some measure of mastery of his present life and the shape of his future, is part of his experience of time and implicit in the whole undertaking of psychoanalysis.

The "experience of time" may be understood as referring to the question: how is time, objectively measured by clocks as duration, subjectively experienced; what distortions of objective world time can we observe and how can we understand and explain such distortions? Further, phenomena such as *déjà vu* and

1. For those who have more than a passing interest in the problems of time, I mention the book *The Voices of Time*, edited by J. T. Fraser (1966), being, in the words of the subtitle, "A cooperative survey of man's views of time as expressed by the sciences and the humanities." See also the review of this book by Blank (1967).

other paramnesias, screen memories, amnesias, contraction of time in dreams and fantasy, fall under the rubric of time experience and its variations. We ask how time is experienced by children and in the various stages of life including old age; there is the problem of life cycles, the relationships between aging and its physical changes and time experience. What symbolic meanings of time play a role in mental life (Father Time, death, etc.)? There is the question how the sense and the concept of time as duration and succession of events in physical time-space develop; what determines the rise of this time concept in secondary process ideation?

In an earlier contribution (1962) I have attempted to outline a conception of time which is not based on the time concept of physical science and present-day common-sense experience, but which considers time in terms of the reciprocal relations between past, present, and future as active modes of psychic life. In this sense the experience of time, as a psychoanalytic topic, refers to the interactions and interrelations between these three temporal modes of psychic activity, as we discern them in our psychoanalytic work, for instance, in the play of transference, in the impact of unconscious and conscious remembering and anticipating on the present, in the interplay between primitive (stemming from the past) and higher-order ("present") motivations. In this conception time is understood neither as a dimension of objective external reality, nor merely as a form of our cognition or apprehension of this reality (Kant).

There is another aspect of the experience of time which deserves mention here. Is the course of our lives seen as propelled by forces of the past, by a *vis a tergo* (absolute determinism), or is it seen as pulled by the attraction or prospect of future possibilities or purposes (conscious or unconscious)? In the early stages of psychoanalysis, with its emphasis on id psychology, there was a decided tendency to understand psychic life as wholly determined by our unconscious past: unconscious forces from the past explained the development and vicissitudes of life; and future was nothing but a time when a past state would be attained again. With the ascendancy of the structural theory and ego psychology, with the growing importance of object relations in psychoanalytic theory, this time perspective shifted. The shift is perhaps most clearly exemplified by Freud's stipulation of a life or love instinct, which works in opposition to as well as in cooperation with a death instinct. The idea of a life instinct bespeaks an orientation toward a view in which life is not altogether motivated by forces of the past but is partially motivated by an attraction coming from something ahead of us. Our experience, I believe, tends to oscillate between these two time perspectives. It is the latter which makes it difficult to eliminate teleological considerations from biology and psychoanalysis.

Having taken this cursory glance at temporal phenomena and concepts relevant to the psychoanalyst, I now turn to the specific subject of my communication.

II

There are two experiences, at the opposite poles of time, which may throw some light on the problem of time. Both are exceptional in the sense that they rarely, for many people never, come to full awareness. In our present civilization they are apt to be seen as pathological, because they constitute extreme limits beyond which our accustomed, normal organization of the world no longer obtains.

At one extreme is the experience of eternity where the flux of time is stayed or suspended. Eternity is to be distinguished from sempiternity or everlasting time. Scholastic philosophers speak of the nunc stans, the abiding instant, where there is no division of past, present, and future, no remembering, no wish, no anticipation, merely the complete absorption in being, or in that which is. Insofar as that which seems to last forever, even in change such as the revolutions of the sun and stars, appears not to partake of a past and future different from the present, what lasts forever is confused with the eternity of the abiding instant. But the experience of eternity does not include everlastingness. Time as something that, in its modes of past, present, and future, articulates experience and conveys such concepts as succession, simultaneity, and duration is suspended in such a state. Inasmuch as this experience, however, can be remembered, it tends to be described retrospectively in temporal terms which seem to approximate or be similar to such a state.

States of this kind have been described by mystics and are in some respects akin to ecstatic states occurring under the influence of certain drugs or during emotional states of exceptional intensity. In conditions of extreme joy or sadness, sometimes during sexual intercourse and related orgastic experiences, at the height of manic and the depth of depressive conditions, in the depth of bliss or despair, the temporal attributes of experience fall away and only the now, as something outside of time, remains. In his discussion of the origins of religious feelings, Freud (1930, p. 72) briefly considers the "oceanic" feeling and its relation to the concept of eternity, connects such "ego feelings" with the primal ego feeling of the infant, prior to the differentiation between subject and object, and alludes to relations between these issues and the "wisdom of mysticism" and "a number of obscure modifications of mental life, such as trances and ecstasies."

At the other pole of time is the experience of fragmentation, where one's world is in bits and pieces none of which have any meaning. The time continuum by which we hold our world together, the interrelatedness and the connections between a past, present, and future disintegrate, are broken in the most elementary sense, so that each instant loses its relation to any other instant and stands by itself, not embraced in a time continuum. While in the experience of eternity—which objectively may last only for a small fraction of time—temporal relations have vanished into a unity which abolishes time, in the experience of fragmentation time has been abolished in the annihilation of connectedness. To express this in a different way: in the experience of eternity, all meaning is condensed in the undifferentiated, global unity of the abiding instant, the *nunc stans*, and may flow out from there again to replenish the world of time with meaning; while in the experience of fragmentation, meaning, i.e., connectedness, has disappeared, each instant is only its empty self, a nothing. There are probably, here too, genetic affinities with early stages of psychic functioning in which the connectedness of experience—which is temporal—as yet is not, or not firmly, established. Experiences of estrangement, depersonalization, derealization may approximate such fragmentation.[2] The fact that experiences of eternity and fragmentation are often best under-

2. There are relations between the experience of fragmentation and Pious's (1961) concept of nadir.

stood as defenses against anxiety, as escapes from the world of temporal reality, does not invalidate their status as genuine representatives of transtemporal states.

I mentioned that the experience of eternity may itself last only for a fraction of time, and the same is true for fragmentation. When we say this, we speak of time as observed duration, of so-called objective time, which can be clocked and measured. In that sense such experiences are of course not outside of time; in that sense they are moments or episodes in time, have a beginning and end and duration, may be located in the past and remembered, or feared or wished for in an anticipated future. By this standard of objective time we view such experiences as representatives of so-called subjective time. Subjective time here means a sense of time that conforms or does not conform to, or is a distortion of, observed time as duration which can be measured objectively.

I submit that this concept of time, as adequate as it may have been or still may be in the physical sciences, and as useful as it is for our orientation in what we have come to perceive as objective reality, is inadequate for a psychoanalytic investigation of time. If this is true, it follows that we have to abandon the concept of subjective time, insofar as the viewpoint from which we define subjective time is that of objective time as duration, as clock time. Even if one takes into account recent findings regarding biological time, internal clocks, circadian rhythms, etc., findings that raise fascinating questions about the relations between subjective and objective time and about a possible "objective" validity of "subjective" time—even then the time concept involved in such investigations remains essentially unchanged.

When we consider time as psychoanalysts, the concept of time as duration, objectively observed or subjectively experienced, loses much of its relevance. We encounter time in psychic life primarily as a linking activity in which what we call past, present, and future are woven into a nexus. The terms themselves, past, present, and future, gain meaning only within the context of such a nexus. The nexus itself is not so much one of succession but of interaction. Past, present, and future present themselves in psychic life not primarily as one preceding or following the other, but as modes of time which determine and shape each other, which differentiate out of and articulate a pure now. There is no irreversibility on a linear continuum, as in the common concept of time as succession, but a reciprocal relationship whereby one time mode cannot be experienced or thought without the other and whereby they continually modify each other. As terms they are correlative, like the terms father and son; as experiential phenomena they interpenetrate.

The phenomenology of transference may serve as example: not only is the present relationship to the analyst partially determined by the patient's past (which is, as we say, still active in the present) and by a wished-for or feared future (itself codetermined by the past). It is also true that the present relationship, and the expectations it engenders, activate the past and influence how it is now experienced and remembered. This reintegration of the past, in its turn, modifies the present relationship with the analyst (and of course with other people as well) and has a bearing on the envisaged future. The modification of the past by the present does not change "what objectively happened in the past," but it changes that past which the patient carries within him as his living history.

Similar reciprocal relations between past, present, and future can be ascertained in the connections between day residue and infantile, unconscious wish in the construction of dreams (and I would add: in the construction of reality). Freud (1900) speaks of the need for attachment between one and the other. Without such mutual attachment, between the contemporary day residue and the past infantile wish, neither gains ascendancy in psychic life. The important and still poorly understood complex of problems subsumed under such titles as self or identity and object constancy (the latter being correlative to "ego identity") is directly related to the interactions between past, present, and future.

Such time phenomena, where the three temporal modes appear as active agents in mental life, are those which in my view are of primary concern to the psychoanalyst; the time concept of classical physical science and of everyday clock time is of little value or relevance here.

In the experience of fragmentation the reciprocal relationship between past, present, and future, taken as active agents, is broken, and the three words no longer carry meaning. What is experienced is a meaningless *now*, not a present as element in a temporal context. In the experience of eternity that context is not broken up but ceases to exist as a nexus by virtue of a fusion of its elements into a unitary *now*. This *now* does not lose but overflows its meaning, goes beyond meaning in the accepted sense in which meaning comes into being by connections, linkings between elements. We are familiar with momentary and isolated fragmentation, as when we focus on a word, perhaps by repeating it several times, and the very focusing may make the word into a meaningless sound; the same kind of thing may happen with visual objects if stared at long enough. There are hypnagogic and hypnopompic phenomena, especially regarding one's own mental processes, which are of a similar order. The connections between elements are broken or, to put it more correctly, are not re-created.

This leads to another aspect of time as active agent in psychic life. It concerns what I may call the microdynamics of memory. The examples just cited are not instances of all-including fragmentation of self and object world, but of minute fragmentations in the texture of mental processes, perceptions, etc. It is the memorial activity of the mind by which a before, now, and after in their meaningful connections, as well as the simultaneity of occurrences, are created. This memorial activity links what otherwise would be disparate bits into a nexus which has meaning and gives meaning to each element by virtue of the reciprocal relationship created between them. That this linking activity is automatic and unconscious in most of our daily life obscures the fact that it *is* an activity; in fragmentation this activity is interrupted. Related to such interruption of memorial processes is the compartmentalization engaged in by obsessive-compulsive characters. On the other hand, fragmentation in certain instances may be the starting point for novel linking processes which create new meanings.

When we consider time in mental life, time and memory are inseparable—memory here understood as mental activity (the words, mind and memory, are etymologically related), and not as a *fait accompli* that we find as one of the functions of the mental apparatus, perhaps ultimately based on so-called memory traces imprinted on a waxtablet brain. Memory, memorial activity, is understood here as a linking activity in which either a global event becomes articulated, a unity becoming a textured manifold ("analysis" in the literal sense of the word), which is held together by inner connections, or in which bits of events get linked together ("synthesis").

The microdynamics of memory is the microcosmic side of historicity, i.e., of the fact that the individual not only *has* a history that an observer may unravel and describe, but that he *is* history and makes his history by virtue of his memorial activity in which past–present–future are created as mutually interacting modes of time. Psychoanalysis is a method in which this memorial activity, shared by patient and analyst and more or less strongly defended against by the patient, is exercised, reactivated, and promoted. The personal myth, with the pathological aspects of which Ernst Kris (1956) has dealt, but in the creation of which every individual is unconsciously and sometimes consciously engaged, is a precipitate of this history-making or time-weaving memorial activity. A patient, after considerable analytic work had been done on his relationship to his father, once put it this way: you have to create your own history. Myth here is used not in the sense of a lie, or of an *ad hoc* invented fable, although reconstructions in analysis, for example, may sometimes come dangerously close to the latter. Myth, in other words, is not meant here as the opposite or as a distortion of historical truth, of "how things actually were." Its use here emphasizes that any historical truth—whatever Freud might have thought of the status of objective reality and of the truth of objectivity—is a reconstruction or construction which restructures in novel ways what already at the time when it actually happened had been a mental construction, a memorial structure unconsciously built by the time agents of the mind.[3]

---

3. For an original and pertinent philosophical discussion of time see St. Augustine, *Confessions*, book XI.

REFERENCES

Blank, H. R. (1967): Review of J. T. Fraser: *The Voices of Time.* *Psychoanal. Quart.* 36:297–300.
Fraser, J. T., ed. (1966): *The Voices of Time.* New York: George Braziller.
Freud, S. (1900): *The Interpretation of Dreams.* S.E. 4/5: 564.
———. (1930): Civilization and its discontents. S.E. 21:59–145.

_____. (1933): New introductory lectures on psycho-analysis. S.E. 22:3–182.

Kris, E. (1956): The personal myth: A problem in psychoanalytic technique. *J. Amer. Psychoanal. Assn.* 5:653–81.

Loewald, H. W. (1962): Superego and time. *Int. J. Psycho-Anal.* 43:264–68 (reprinted in this volume).

Pious, W. L. (1961): A hypothesis about the nature of schizophrenic behavior. In: *Psychotherapy and the Psychoses,* ed. A. Burton. New York: Basic Books, pp. 43–68.

Toulmin, S., and Goodfield, J. (1965): *The Discovery of Time.* New York: Harper & Row, 1966.

Whitehead, A. N. (1920): *Concept of Nature.* Cambridge: Cambridge University Press.

10

PERSPECTIVES ON MEMORY

I

Memory, for the psychoanalyst, is not just a faculty or function of the intellect by virtue of which the mind registers, retains, and may remember experiences, events, and objects. For him, memory also has something to do with separation, loss, mourning, and restitution, and often carries with it a sense of nostalgia, especially as we get older. The words commemoration and memorial remind us of such connotations.

The past would be irretrievably lost without memory; in fact there would not be any past, just as there would not be any present that has meaning or any future to envisage. The fact that memory lets us have a past means that we experience loss and the irretrievability of the past and yet can recover the past in another form.

Memory, however, does not simply enable us to hang on to

This paper was presented as the Brill Memorial Lecture to the New York Psychoanalytic Society on November 14, 1972.

When Merton Gill and Philip Holzman, as editors, asked me to contribute to a volume of essays in memory of George Klein, I offered them this paper, having in mind Klein's interest in problems of memory, as documented in his paper "The Several Grades of Memory" (1966). They accepted my article and the volume was later published under the title: *Psychology Versus Metapsychology: Psychoanalytic Essays in Memory of George S. Klein* (1976). My intention in contributing the paper was to honor George Klein with whom I had had, over some years, a number of cordial, spirited, and fruitful exchanges of views. It was not my intention to participate in a controversy over whether or not metapsychology has a place in or is relevant to psychoanalysis.

The text will show that I use metapsychological concepts, reformulating or reinterpreting some of them, and attempting to integrate them within a broader framework than that in which they were originally stated. In view of the fact that the paper first appeared together with several contributions that consider metapsychology as nonpsychoanalytic or nonpsychological, I wish to make it clear that I do not share that position. At the same time I do think that what goes under the name of metapsychology both needs and deserves renewed thought, elaboration, and reinterpretations.

the past in some way; it gives meaning to the present and helps to shape a future. Memory is connected with our whole experience of time. It is not merely a faculty of reviving or reproducing the past, nor is it simply the faculty of recording and retaining present but fleeting perceptions so that they may last in some other form. By virtue of memory, our experiences become connectible, are woven into a context, and extend into a past and a future. In an important sense, memorial activity is linking activity. A before, now, and after are created in this linking and become mutually influential; continuity of our life as individuals comes into being. By these memorial processes, what would otherwise be at best bits of impressions, only to perish immediately, are made to remain as inner state, image, or idea to be linked with fresh impressions and experiences. To move from one eventful moment to the next without having lost the first one —so as to be able to link and match one with the other—requires memorial activity. Without the mind's activity of holding and rebuilding its impressions and its own acts, affects, perceptions, ideas, images, and fantasies, an activity in which present reality is organized by matching and comparing with what has been and what, in anticipation, might be—without all this there would be for us neither past nor present nor future. These are the modes of time, the mutually dependent articulations of experience that arise through memorial activity. Without such inner reproductive holding, in which consists the linking together of before, now, and after, we would experience neither duration nor change. Memory, in this broadest sense, is the activity by which, above all, some sort of order and organization and some sense of permanence, as well as of movement and change, come into our world.

Such a broad conception of memory, in which the word refers to that central, all-pervasive activity of the mind by which our world and our life gain breadth and depth and continuity in flux, and change in continuity, by which, in other words, our life and world acquire dimension and meaning, makes memory virtually synonymous with mind itself. This broad definition, however, is not so much an arbitrary overextension of the accepted sense of the word, but rather a return to an ancient close relation, if not identity, of the two words mind and memory, a relation documented by their common root and still visible in such English words as mindful and remind, or in the German *Gedächtnis* (from *denken,* to think). To stay with language for another moment, memory and mourning are also closely related etymologically. And the other German word for memory, *Erinnerung,* derives from German *inner,* internal, the same "inner" that appears in *Verinnerlichung* (internalization) which, considering its motivational aspects, brings us back to loss, mourning, and restitution.

In many ways, the following discussions owe much to the work and thought of others. Apart from Piaget and Freud himself, I mention only a few: Bartlett, Kris, Mahler, Spitz, Winnicott, Rapaport, George Klein, I. H. Paul, and Heinz Werner. It would be most useful and would contribute greatly to the clarification of my own formulations if my considerations could be correlated with their research, but the limitations of time and mental energy make this impossible here.

The genetic-motivational aspects of memorial processes (I use the plural to stress their variety, and in order to avoid the notion of a monolithic "memory function")—including their instinctual-affective roots and genetic derivations—are of particular relevance to a psychoanalytic study. It is important to emphasize again that memorial processes are activities, despite the fact that they may, on the one hand, become automatic (operating then without needing added cathexes) and, on the other hand, evolve into enduring process patterns that we tend to call structures.

By thinking of memory as active process—and not only in regard to unconscious or conscious and intentional remembering, but specifically also in regard to the more deep-seated memorial processes we call registration and retention—we will avoid the temptation to visualize the latter two aspects, and especially registration, as some sort of record that lasts by virtue of the inertia of matter, like indentations on a phonograph disk or on the wax slab of Freud's (1925) famous mystic writing pad. It is necessary, if these processes deserve the name of memory at all, also to conceive of registration–retention as activities, as patterned forms of low-key cathectic processes, which will resonate to corresponding new cathectic processes (as in recall) and may be amplified or modified and restructured by them. Something can be revived only if it is still living or if, as with the phonograph disk, activity can be simulated by setting the system in motion by artificial means. The principle of the insusceptibility to excitation of uncathected systems (Freud, 1917) applies here. Freud, of course, always assumed the activity of "the unconscious," including unconscious "memory traces." It is precisely the fact that the wax slab of the mystic writing pad cannot reproduce the writing from within that makes the analogy with memory break down. If the wax slab could make writing on the celluloid visible from within, it would, as Freud said, be a mystic pad indeed (1925, p. 230). The recall of a childhood memory, for example, is to be understood as a reinforcement or restructuring, by virtue of new cathectic processes based on new experiences, of the reproductive activity constituting the unconscious registration–retention of that infantile experience; and that unconscious reproductive activity itself, like the unconscious wish in dreams, continues to determine the character of the present experience, in fact helps it to be significant and not meaningless. This applies, I believe, not only to those intermediary memorial process–structures called unconscious ideas or fantasies, but also to the underlying so-called mnemic images or memory traces that in psychoanalytic theory have tended to be taken as ultimate givens or mechanical replicas of sensory data.

In passing, I should like to mention a difficulty regarding the conventional distinction between registration and retention. Freud was repeatedly preoccupied with the question whether anything ever registered by the mind could be truly destroyed. If we are inclined, as Freud was, to assume that such destruction does not occur, then the distinction between registration and retention is difficult to maintain. The reasons not to assume such destruction have to do with the very notion of unconscious memory and its continuing effect on subsequent mental life, and with the coexistence of early and later stages of mental development in the structure and dynamics of the mind. If nothing recorded in the mind is ever truly destroyed—extinguished rather than merely altered—and if through the alterations the psychoanalyst can still perceive or guess the original text that continues to be active and have its own impact, then registration amounts to retention. One meaning of the timelessness of the unconscious depends on

this consideration. The term retention, then, would be reserved
for those subsequent memorial processes that elaborate and
alter original registrations.

I have so far not specifically mentioned that aspect of memory
which is called remembering. Remembering, for psychoanalysts,
is an equivocal term, insofar as Freud has distinguished, notably
in his paper "Remembering, Repeating and Working-Through"
(1914b), between remembering and repeating, while pointing
out at the same time that repeating, as in acting out, is the
patient's way of remembering. He subsumes both under reproducing and speaks of reproduction in action (repeating) versus
reproduction in the psychical field (remembering in the narrower
sense). But there can be no question that both acting out (or
hysterical reminiscences and transference manifestations in the
analytic situation) and remembering "in the old manner" (Freud,
1914b) are memorial processes. Their differences and their relations to each other will have to occupy us later on. A character
common to both, and to other memorial processes, is that they
are reproducing something.

Let me now return to the motivational aspects of memorial
processes and specifically to what I have called their instinctual-
affective roots and genetic origins. My exposition and discussion
in what follows will of necessity be condensed and schematic
and will leave many misgivings, doubts, and questions, which
either cannot be resolved or answered within the present context, or which are complex theoretical issues beyond my capacity
for further organization and penetration at the present time.

When I speak of instinctual forces and of instincts or instinctual drives, I define them as motivational, i.e., both motivated
and motivating, and as being the most primitive psychic forces
in the motivational, hierarchically organized network of psychic
forces. As intrapsychic motivations, they arise within and develop from a psychic matrix or field constituted essentially by
the mother–child unit. Instincts are here defined as what Freud
has called psychic representatives, not as biological forces, and
as forces that ab initio manifest themselves within and between
what gradually differentiates into individual and environment
(or ego and objects, or self and object world—allowing these
terms for the moment to be equivalent). Instincts remain relational phenomena, rather than being considered energies within

a closed system, to be "discharged" somewhere (see Loewald, 1971). The differentiation, within the original matrix, of individual and environment involves the differentiation of narcissistic and object cathexis. Here, narcissistic cathexis means instinctual currents between elements within the emerging individual (or ego system); object cathexis means instinctual currents between individual and environment (or objects). Narcissistic and object cathexes, once portions of instinctual cathexis have thus been differentiated (other portions remain undifferentiated), interact with and influence each other; they do not simply each go their own way. It is the instinctual interactions within the ego system that deserve par excellence to be termed narcissistic, although the state prior to the differentiation of object cathexis and narcissistic cathexis is referred to as primary narcissism, a designation that is justified insofar as we consider that prior state in regard to the prospect of intrapsychic development. It is true that, once an ego system or internal world has developed, it may itself be cathected as a totality, and we speak of this process, too, as narcissistic. For our present purposes, let it be clear only that one has to distinguish, on the one hand, between cathectic processes *within* the system that give it its character as an organization, and, on the other, cathectic processes that are deployed *upon* the system by itself.

A few terminological comments are unavoidable. I use the word ego here in the sense in which Freud has used it, for example in the paper "On Narcissism" (1914a) and again in *Civilization and Its Discontents* (1930) (*after* the formulation of the structural theory), i.e., in the general sense of the totality of the psyche as an organization, and not in the sense specified when we speak of id, ego, and superego as substructures of the total psyche. Despite that ambiguity, I prefer ego in the present context, because the term self, which Hartmann has used in the definition of narcissism, in my opinion is equally if not more ambiguous and is in need of much further clarification as an analytic concept. I wish to stress again that I have in mind primarily the cathectic interactions *within* the ego (or self) system. To me, it seems preferable to reserve the term self for a stage in the individual's development when the structuralization into id, ego, and superego is rather definitively established. To my mind, the word object is the most problematic term but so ingrained in psychoanalytic language that it is difficult to circumvent it. If the ego is a unity that has to develop and not something "there" from the beginning of psychic development, this is also true for the object. It is misleading to speak of objects when referring to stages in development where the differentiation of inside and outside, or ego and object, is at best *in statu nascendi,* where, in other words, there is as yet no subject as a psychic unity that may cathect or interact with something that is differentiated as an external unity.

I believe that Freud did not come to distinguish clearly between narcissistic cathexes in interaction with the ego system as a whole and narcissistic cathexes that constitute and organize that unity, i.e., which are employed in the ego's internal organization. It is the latter, I suggest, that are involved in the genesis of memory. But I believe this thesis to be in accord with Freud's own ideas regarding the role of introjection–identification in ego and superego formation, although he does not explicitly speak of memory in this connection. It should be clearer now why I have gone into some detail about the differentiation of narcissistic and object cathexis. This differentiation runs parallel to that of memory and perception in early psychic life. Possibly it is the selfsame differentiation as considered from the instinct side. It seems to me that there have been two parallel theories in psychoanalysis, one in terms of perception and memory (the "topographic" model), with a tendency to equate perception with consciousness and memory with the unconscious, and the other in terms of instincts and motivation and libidinal development. I believe that the concept of narcissistic libido (and its aggression complement, masochism) provided a bridge between the two theories and led to an attempt at unification in the structural theory.

Considering memory with regard to the distinction between it and perception, we may ask what it is that is registered and how it is registered. In reply to the first question, one might be inclined to say: perceptions are registered. It is now generally agreed that perception is not a passive process, not something that happens to a "perceptual apparatus," but a process that involves activity on the part of the perceiver. The act of perception is an interaction, and what is registered would be that interaction. The mental activity involved in perceiving, its modification in the interaction with the perceptual stimulus, is reproduced, or rather one should say, is continued, in the registering act. This is an act that, seen from the standpoint of an outside observer, reproduces or continues internally a process that has occurred between the subject and an object or stimulating agent. Perceiving, in the beginning of mental life, is an instinctual activity, and the stimulus perceived is by that very fact an instinctual stimulus. The internal reproduction of that instinctual interaction is equally an instinctual activity. Indeed, from the standpoint of that bundle of instincts which is the primitive infantile psyche, interaction with something outside and internal interaction are indistinguishable; nor does the infantile psyche differentiate a perceptual act (having occurred) from a memorial act (occurring now). Memory, as registration or recording, and perception are identical for the infant.

Let us consider the primitive experience of satisfaction, an instinctual-perceptual experience in which cognition and conation have not yet fallen asunder. This experience is reproduced, we assume, in the process of hallucinatory wish fulfillment, a first sign—again viewed only from the observer's point of view—of memory. For the infant, there is no difference between the actual event of satisfaction and its reproduction. But the exigencies of life are such that the hallucinatory experience does not remain satisfying, i.e., the instinctual urge eventually has to be satisfied again by the repetition of the perceptual experience. Its internal reproduction does not last for long or remain strong enough without further external reinforcement. This latter fact remains true, to a much attenuated degree, for the rest of one's life, but it is the more obvious the farther back we go into the origins of mental life. This consideration may throw some new light on the problem of the destructibility of memory that I mentioned earlier: Is the indestructibility of the unconscious contingent on a minimum degree of nourishment from object-libidinal interactions?

As mentioned before, the internal interaction called registration (to be understood in the same active sense as perception) is best viewed, it seems, as a continuation of the perceptual experience, a reproduction in the sense in which a reverberating echo is a reproduction, and not as the resumption of a process that had come to an end. Memory would basically be an instinctual, narcissistic activity modulated and patterned by interactions with environment, which gradually gains a high degree of autonomy, but which, in order to become preconscious or conscious, requires periodic reinforcement through perceptions (object-cathecting activity) that "revive memories."

The experience of satisfaction, brought about by a mutually responsive interaction with environment, would be continued, at least for a while, as a "registration." The hypothetical hallucinatory wish fulfillment, as an inner revival of the experience of satisfaction, is based on such registration and is conceivable only inasmuch as a renewed wish may now be temporarily satisfied through the internal interaction called registration, which is a continuation of the experience of satisfaction. If registration is the continuation, internally or mentally, of a satisfying interaction with environment, it is at the same time a continuation of the system's intrinsic instinctual activity *as modified by the satisfying response*. The perceptual experience tends to pattern internal excitation in the experiencing system in novel ways, so that internal processes gain in complexity and richness.

Our preoccupation with the fact that renewed "specific action" on the part of environment eventually becomes necessary has perhaps led us to neglect a consideration of the psychic activity that takes place during the period between the satisfying experience with environment and the renewed necessity for it. The general quiescence of the baby in a state of satisfaction does not mean that psychic activity has ceased. Instead of assuming that during such periods the psyche has returned to a state of rest (as postulated by the constancy or inertia principle), it is, in my opinion, far more reasonable to assume that the interactions with the world continue to reverberate, are reproduced, and thus lay the foundations for the development of an internal world, in the form of memorial processes. Instead of thinking of static memory traces or mnemic images as the model for registration—traces that supposedly are utilized by a function called memory—registration and its elaborations in retention are seen here as an active (although "silent") process of continued reproduction of interactional activities that is in itself a linking. It is in the process of internal reproduction that the identity, and later the similarity, with the initial stimulating experiences comes about. The similarity does not reside in static traces which then may be used by memory. The terms memory trace or mnemic image already *contain* the problem of memory; they do not explain or elucidate it.

The controversy over schema versus trace in memory theory may perhaps be clarified, if not resolved, in the following way: schema refers to the intrinsic instinctual activity of the system, whereas trace refers to the modifying or patterning influence brought to bear on that activity by the responsive environmental activity. The proponents of schema insist on the observation that perceptual material is in some way organized by memory and not just passively received. On the other hand—and this refers to trace—the perceptual material undoubtedly modulates and organizes the intrinsic activity into certain process configurations. What is registered (reproduced) is just that mutual organization. This reproduction—and here we go a step further in our discussion of perception and memory, and object cathexis and narcissistic cathexis—this memorial product, while being itself further organized by new perceptions, in its turn further organizes perceptual material. That perception and memory have a reciprocal influence on each other is a clear implication of my reminder that perception is an active process and not a purely passive reception. The mental "schemata," themselves increasingly articulated by perceptual material, increasingly participate in the organization of perceptions, so that percepts more and more acquire structure. Perception, rather than being the forever fresh and pure receptivity that Freud often claimed it to be, is shot through with memory. Because this memorial element in perceptions is for the most part unconscious and automatic, we take the so-structured material as what we call objective external reality. That mode of schematizing which is objectivation of reality appears to us to be encountered in external reality, as though it were contained already in the material itself and not the product of the meeting between mind and world. That this meeting may produce other ways of experiencing reality is well known to us from our observation of children, from primitive mentality, and from creative moments in ourselves and in others —creative in the sense that mental schemata are not rigid and lose their automatic character. But the largely automatic objectivation of experience makes us view that particular schematization as the unquestioned standard of truth.

In a similar way, when thinking of memory traces, we have

already built into their countenance that objectifying schematization, which our mental, memorial processes only gradually
develop. We tend to visualize the original primitive "memory
traces" as more or less faithful tracings of what we, dominated
as we are by secondary-process mentation (a highly complex
form of schematization), have come to see as objective data given
us by nature. These traces, however, in which experiences are
reproduced, cannot be reproductions or continuations of anything other than quite primitively organized interactions between
a primitively organized mind, dominated by primary process,
and a therefore primitively organized or schematized environment—where, in addition, a distinction between individual and
environment, between memory and what is memorized, is barely
in the making, and where sense impressions are likely to be
global, all-engulfing, and engulfed coenesthetic receptions. (I am
referring here to Spitz's [1965] distinction between coenesthetic
and diacritic perception.) We must assume that at early developmental levels registrations, being continuations, reproductions,
reverberations of interactions between mind and world, are subject to the laws of primary process no less than these interactions
themselves.

The development of diacritic perception is related to the distinct sensory modalities that arise out of a welter of undifferentiated global sensory experiences; and any registering-retaining
activities would have the same global character at such stages.
We have reason to assume that in early psychic stages (as well as
in certain exceptional or abnormal "ego states" that hark back to
them) the child does not distinguish between his mouth and the
mother's breast, or between the activity of sucking and mouth
and breast. Also, one moment is not distinguished from the next,
or memory from the remembered event, nor, even at a somewhat
later time when we can begin to speak of emotions, is the
mother's smile or assuring appearance distinguished from the
baby's own delight.

In sum, what is perceived and can be registered in reproductive activity is determined on the one hand by material, insofar
as it is available and needed, and on the other by how and to
what degree this material is differentiated and integrated. The
kind of mind, so to speak, that organizes the material, the fashion
and degree of schematization—including even that degree of

minimal schematization where neither is the perceiver distinguished from the perceived nor the moment of initial interaction ("perception") from the moment of reproduction ("memory")— these are the conditions to be considered, together with the properties of the material for memorial processes, i.e., the kind of environmental responsive stimulation. In primitive hallucinatory wish fulfillment, i.e., in the recathexis of the registration of an experience of satisfaction, there would be no distinction between the past or present state of being or between external and internal reality.

I will mention only in passing that Freud's (1895) early concept of motor or kinesthetic image (*Bewegungsbild*) and Rapaport's (1942) distinction between drive organization and conceptual organization of memories are related to these considerations. But two points have to be emphasized and integrated here, although I am unable to do more than mention them in this presentation: (1) the development from a minimal degree of schematization in "coenesthetic reception" to the various differentiations implied in "diacritic perceptions" is itself codetermined by the higher schematizations provided by the environment, schematizations that are embedded in the manner in which the environment encounters and interacts with the developing individual. (2) Insofar as schemata are considered as constituents of memory, that is, of the mind that organizes and reproduces material at the same time it is being organized by it, memorial processes, as mentioned before, enter into the very fabric of perception. If memory is that aspect of our activity as humans that links events and phenomena together so that they are more than unrelated bits and pieces, namely, by holding an experience in reproductive continuation while the next one occurs, then perceptions as organizations of stimulation events cannot exist without memory.

I have said that we cannot assume a cessation of psychic activity during the period of general quiescence that occurs when a baby is in a state of satisfaction. During such periods, it seems plausible to assume, the foundations for the development of an internal world are built in the form of unconscious memorial processes by which the satisfying interaction with environment is continued, without any need for further external interaction. Maternal "cathexes" leading to satisfaction, by being continued or reproduced after they have ceased externally, pattern or structure hitherto undifferentiated instinctual activity in such a way that the maternal stimulating responses become part of the internal repertoire. Not only does the baby have instinctual needs, but the mother also stimulates the baby in many ways and thus increases and enriches his instinctual-perceptual capacities and activities. These, in turn, if appropriately responded to, further contribute to internal, memorial activity. The quiescent periods during which memorial processes continue—which in fact are needed to provide a chance for memorial activity to evolve an internal world without interference by unceasing or overstimulating external interactions—might be compared to the latency period of childhood, when the consolidation and elaboration of the internal world in the wake of the oedipal period takes place.

If nothing else would, the resolution of the Oedipus complex, with its relinquishments and the internalization–repression of oedipal object relations, reminds us that we have so far left out a most important aspect of the problem of memory. Memory seems to be inextricably interwoven with experiences of separation, loss, object withdrawal, or cessation of satisfying external interactions. Loss or separation from a love object appears to be a most powerful stimulus for the activation of memorial processes. I mentioned in the beginning that the words memory and mourning are closely related etymologically. Memory and "object loss" are so intimately connected and yet so much in an oppositional relation to each other that it often looks as though they are the two sides of the same coin. Although memorial processes often appear to be motivated by object loss, there would be no loss but only emptiness if the object were not already remembered in some form. And yet, one must also say that, in a deeper sense, only by virtue of the differentiation of subject from object— which is the primordial separation—does memory arise.

It would seem that those memorial processes that are set in motion by loss, whether they are conscious recollections or unconscious remembering as in the identifications of the mourner, are revivals of deeper memories. On the basis of retention, that is, of the internal, continuous, though unconscious, reproduction of interactional experiences, what otherwise would be inner emptiness or rage due to disruption, may become a longing that produces the experience of missing or realizing the absence of something, under the impact of renewed instinctual pressures. This something has continued in inner reproduction and therefore may be longed for and missed and sought again on the outside or revived inside. For the very young infant, the absence of the needed mother is not so much an experience of separation or loss as one of total helplessness and emptiness, insofar as memorial processes are only fleeting and seem to cease or fall below a threshold of effectiveness without reinforcement by interaction with the mother. It is for this reason that I began the discussion of memory development with the satisfying experiences of infancy. At a later level, only sufficiently gratifying oedipal experiences lead to further psychosexual development through the resolution (internalization) of oedipal relationships. There can nevertheless be no question that external deprivation and consequent inner conflict and pain are powerful determinants in promoting, although probably not founding, memory development, that is, the elaboration of an internal world. Memory is the child of both satisfaction and frustration.

I have said there would be no (experienced) loss if the object were not remembered in some form. The object, or rather the infant–mother interaction, is "narcissistically" continued into what we call memorial reproduction. Would this not occur if external interaction were to continue? Such a hypothetical case plays havoc with what we know about the periodicity of biological and psychic processes. The infant at some point, which ideally coincides with the mother's withdrawal of the breast, is satisfied and goes to sleep. Instinctual activity, however, no less than vital biological processes, continues within the infant. It does not cease, but is transposed to a different arena, as it were. Biological processes, digestion, assimilation, etc., continue within the infantile organism to maintain and develop the internal processes and structures that constitute biological growth. From the point of view of the infant's growth, the aim and purpose of the biological interactions between infant and mother are his maintenance and development, and it is these internal biological processes and their results that count; from this viewpoint, the mother–infant interactions are means to an end. Similarly, those reproductive memorial processes that take over and continue internally what was external interaction are, from the viewpoint of individual mental growth, the end to which early "object ties" are the means. The infant becomes satisfied and—speaking from an outside observer's standpoint—withdraws from the external world as much as the mother "withdraws" from the infant. The infant no longer avails himself of the mother, except as a continued "internal" presence; in his sleep he digests and reproduces internally what had transpired in the actual feeding event.

Here we have to remind ourselves of the fact that such reproduction is more than a continuation: it is a continuation in which something changes. It increasingly involves a metamorphosis analogous to biological metabolism. Retention involves more or less profound changes, restructuralizations, elaborations, and integrations with other interactional processes. The initial registrations become integrated into the total context and dominated by it. This perpetual reorganization materially influences how we perceive and how we interact with the world, even as new external interactions influence internal reorganizational processes by continuing to alter memorial processes.

The relation between initial registrations and their retention may be compared to a musical theme and its variations; the latter may become so complex and elaborate that the theme is hardly recognizable in them, yet it remains the basic structure. At times the theme is repeated at the end in all its simplicity, highlighting the complexity and richness of the whole composition and making more explicit the transformational relations between the theme and the variations as well as amongst variations themselves. At the same time, the theme repeated at the end seems to say: this—despite all the artistry and grandeur in between—is what it all comes down to in the end.

Memorial activity appears to be, if not initiated, at any rate promoted or activated by experiences of deprivation as well as by experiences of satisfaction. The same problem comes up in regard to identification and its motivation. For instance, many identifications leading to superego formation are thought of as the result of renunciations forced upon the child by external prohibitions and frustrations; and this is true as well in the work of mourning. But we know also that early identifications with the parents occur under circumstances that have nothing to do with deprivation or loss, but with a closeness amounting to lack of separateness, as though what is perceived or felt in this intimacy, by that very lack of distance, becomes an element in the child or helps to form his character—as though the parent's trait is continued into the child, without his having to give up anything. Insofar as this state of affairs, this felt identity cannot permanently be maintained because of unavoidable "untimely" separations and disruptions of intimacy, what we call the internal world or character of the child—although for him it is neither inner nor outer but still undifferentiated—becomes strengthened if the conditions are not too disruptive. That is, the memorial processes that were promoted by the intimacy (which was "satisfying") gain prominence, begin to predominate *due to the disruption,* and increasingly acquire the status of inner versus outer. The satisfying original identity is renounced to a degree, or the importance of sensory contact as a condition for identity recedes. It looks as though the experience of satisfaction leads to or permits the giving up of intimacy or identity with environment if it alternates with experiences of deprivation or loss. Most likely, the alternations and combinations of experiences of satisfaction and deprivation that occur in life under ordinary circumstances make it possible that either and both may have the same result: experiences of satisfaction may lead to renunciation and internalization under the impact of experiences of deprivation which alert to that danger, while experiences of deprivation may lead there too, under the sway of experiences of satisfaction, which permit the former not to become truly traumatic and alert the psyche to the possibility of satisfaction by internalization. Neither one nor the other experience alone would eventuate in psychic development.

What I have said implies something I have so far not specifically mentioned: experiences of deprivation themselves are continued in memorial reproduction once the foundations for memory have been laid by sufficient satisfying intimacy. Let me also mention again a factor one tends to lose sight of: the infant's inherent tendency toward withdrawal from sensory contact as a result of satisfaction, which under optimal conditions is reciprocated by the environment and which is a component element in the alternations I have spoken of.

I have so far mainly discussed aspects of memory that have to do with its genesis and have maintained that memorial processes deserve to be called narcissistic, in contrast to object-cathecting processes. I have tried to describe briefly the differentiation of narcissistic and object libido out of the undifferentiated matrix of an instinctual force field constituted by the mother–child psychic unit. And I have suggested that the differentiation of memory and perception in early development runs parallel to that of narcissistic and object cathexis; perhaps at bottom is the same differentiation process viewed from the cognitive side. This would imply an original unity of instinctual and cognitive mental processes and would accord with the conception of an undifferentiated phase out of which id and ego develop, with one—to my mind ineluctable—amendment: at the level of that phase there also is no differentiation of subject and object or inside and outside or of temporal modes. Only when there is developed in mental life something like an experience of internality and externality and of temporal modes, only then can we distinguish between memory and perception and between narcissistic and object cathexis.

II

When something is reproduced that in some form has become part of the inner life, either in action or affect or in imagination and ideation, we speak of remembering. Since recording and retaining themselves reproduce experience and are reproductions in the sense delineated earlier, remembering is a way of reproducing reproductions, a potentiated form of memory.

I have already mentioned Freud's (1914b) distinction between reproduction in action and reproduction in the psychical field as two forms of remembering. I propose to go beyond Freud's formulation, which was geared to considerations of psychoanalytic technique, and to speak of enactive and representational remembering. The first includes not only acting out and transference repetitions, but also identificatory reproductions, as in the following example. In contrast to offering recollections of his father's overbearing behavior toward him, a patient may at times behave in just that overbearing fashion toward his son, or he may show such behavior toward the analyst in the analytic hour. He may even first *describe* his father's behavior toward him in more or less objective terms and then subtly shift to *enacting* the father's behavior in what I have just called identificatory reproduction.

Such shifts from representational to identificatory reproduction are not uncommon during analysis, although we are perhaps more familiar with shifts from enactive to representational reproduction, the latter being the analyst's aim when he interprets the patient's behavior as an identification with his father. Perhaps it would be more correct to say that the analyst's aim is to establish links between the two forms of memorial reproduction, to allow one to be illuminated by the other in a mutual recognition that leads to higher psychic organization (cf. hypercathexis).

Characteristic for the enactive form of remembering is that, as remembering, it is unconscious, i.e., the individual is not aware that he is reproducing something from the past. But this is only a superficial way of looking at it: the remembering is unconscious in a much deeper, dynamic sense, inasmuch as it shares the timelessness and lack of differentiation of the unconscious and of the primary process. In my example of the patient's identification with his father, the patient re-enacts what we assume to be his earlier identification, his earlier dedifferentiation from object relation, involving secondary process, in the direction of primary-process mentation; and in this re-enactment there is no past as distinguished from present. From the point of view of representational memory, which is our ordinary yardstick, we would say that the patient, instead of *having* a past, *is* his past; he does not distinguish himself as rememberer from the content of his memory. In representational remembering, the mind presents something to itself as its own past experience, distinguishing past from present and himself as the experiencer from what he experienced.

It is to be noted that any significant degree of affect present in representational remembering brings it closer to re-enactment: the patient may, as we say, be overcome by his memory so that the index of pastness and the distinction between himself as the agent of reproduction and the remembered content are diminished. The inner distance required for representational remembering appears to decrease in proportion to an increase in affect. I will not be able to enlarge here on the important relations between affect and memory, but can only stress that affective states and moods may often be understood as forms of nonrepresentational remembering (cf. anniversary reactions).

We have encountered characteristics of the nonrepresentational, enactive forms of memory before: we discussed original registrations as reproductive continuations of interactional experiences and said that in its primitive beginnings there is no differentiation of an internal process ("memory") from an interplay of primitive psyche and environment ("perception"), and no distinction between present (the moment of reproducing) and past (the time when what is reproduced occurred). This, of course, also means that there is as yet no difference between the agent and the product of his activity, between registering and its content.

Let me now attempt to fit these various considerations into a larger metapsychological framework. In doing so, I am fully aware of the unsolved theoretical difficulties that remain and of the fact that the following condensed conceptualizations are not always in keeping with accepted psychoanalytic theory, and may raise new problems. But I believe that progress in our field, and especially advances in psychoanalytic theory, will depend on formulating new propositions and on reorganizing available psychoanalytic knowledge and observation.

The distinction between enactive and representational memory resolves itself into that between unconscious and preconscious memory. Unconscious memory follows the laws of primary process, whereas preconscious memory is determined by secondary process. There is thus a primary memorial system, which consists in the aggregate of identifications and internalizations that enter into the organization of the psychic substructures id, ego, and superego. From this point of view, the latter are memorial structures on different levels of organization. Representational or, more generally speaking, preconscious memory constitutes a secondary memorial system, which arises and branches off from the primary system on the basis of the organization of the ego and as a result of that organization. I distinguish between the ego's structure as a self-organizing system of narcissistic interactions, and the ego's functions in relation to the world and to itself, which its structure makes possible. Similarly, a biological structure like the lung comes about by various intrauterine developmental processes which enable it to function as a respiratory organ after birth. The developmental processes leading to the organization of the ego as a psychological structure, however, begin at birth and come to their relative completion only during and through the oedipal period. The secondary, pre-conscious memorial system is a function of the ego insofar as secondary-process mentation characterizes the ego's functioning in relation to the outer and inner worlds.

Leaving out of consideration the id (the structure resulting from the organization—to an extent separate and autonomous—of instinctual life), both ego and superego are creatures of the internalization processes described by Freud (1923) although not so termed by him. In that respect they are memorial structures. Without going into any detail here about internalization, I should say that I conceive of it, broadly speaking, as the process by which interactions within the original mother–child psychic matrix, and later between the growing individual and his environment, become transmuted into internal interactions constituting the individual psyche and creating, maintaining, and developing an internal world. This internal world has to be distinguished from the representational world (Sandler and Rosenblatt, 1962) or inner world or "map" (Rapaport, 1957, pp. 696–697) constituted by mental representations of objects and their relations to each other. The latter is the secondary or representational memory system; it arises on the basis of the development of the ego and as a function of it. Internalization in the sense intended here is not a process involving the representation of objects and object relations, but it involves, to speak in Freud's language, their dissolution or destruction. In the identifications that may lead to internalization, it is precisely the object character of a person that is either not yet established (as in those early identifications preceding object cathexis), or is suspended or annihilated by a process of dedifferentiation of subject and object. The object is not represented by the ego to itself, but it becomes deobjectified and depersonified, and the former object relation becomes a dynamic element of the reorganized ego.

I have said that unconscious memory follows the laws of primary process while preconscious memory is determined by secondary process. A clarification of the terms primary and secondary is in order. I suggest that a deeper meaning may be discovered in these terms, deeper than merely indicating that the former is more primitive and comes first and the latter develops out of it and comes second. Mental and memorial processes are primary if and insofar as they are *unitary*, single-minded, as it were, undifferentiated and nondifferentiating, unhampered, as Freud (1933) has described it, by laws of contradiction, causality, and by the differentiation of past, present, and future and of subject and object, i.e., by the differentiation of temporal and spatial relations. Condensation and displacement, considered as indications of the influence of primary on secondary process, are regressive influences in the direction of an original density where all our distinctions and dichotomies do not hold sway. Mental processes are primary to the extent to which they are nonsplitting, to the extent to which they do not manifest or establish duality or multiplicity, no this and/or that, no before and after, no action as distinguished from its agent or its goal or its object. It is clear that into this category fall what we call magical thinking, omnipotence of thought and movements and gestures, as well as identification, coenesthetic reception, and many other phenomena of so-called primitive mentality such as the "oceanic feeling" and ecstatic experiences.

The secondary process is secondary insofar as in it *duality* becomes established, insofar as it differentiates; among these differentiations is the distinction between the perceiver and the perceived. The ego as agency of the secondary process presents something to itself, whether this is material from the outer or the inner world. Mental processes, in the development from primary to secondary process, undergo a splitting of themselves by which an inner encounter arises, which leads to all the distinctions and dichotomies characteristic for secondary process. This dichotomous reflexion—I am not speaking here of conscious reflection—is set in motion or made possible by the fact that the parents actively reflect the child to the child by their responsive encounters with him, encounters that become elements in the child's eventual inner reflexiveness. It is this mirroring of the child on the part of the parents, a mirroring that inevitably, because of the parents' higher mental development, reflects "more" than the child presents, which leads to the development of secondary process. Words provided by the environment are one prominent example of this mirroring "hypercathexis," which, according to Freud, makes it possible for the primary process to be succeeded by the secondary process. The interpretations given to the patient in analysis, especially, in our context, when enactive remembering is interpreted in terms of representational memory, are highly developed forms of such hypercathecting reflection, which the patient may then make his own.

I believe that these considerations, sketchy and incomplete as they are, are in accord with Freud's (1933, for example) ideas about the intimate relations between the ego and the preconscious system and "external reality." The unconscious and preconscious, considered from the viewpoint of memory, are primary and secondary memorial systems. (This, incidentally, is consistent with Freud's diagram of the psychic apparatus in chapter VII of *The Interpretation of Dreams* [1900].) The term preconscious indicates something about the character of secondary process. The essential characteristic of preconscious mental processes is not that they lack conscious awareness, but that they involve that internal splitting by which what I would call an inner *conscire* arises in mental life. We are most familiar with this *conscire*, with this splitting into different psychic elements which thereby may encounter and know each other, from consciousness. But it is not conscious awareness of such things that establishes that knowing. In consciousness, we only become aware, in a reflective movement of a higher order, of representational or, as I will call it, *conscient* mentation. The latter is recathected in conscious recall.

In primary memorial activity, such inner splitting and *conscire* is lacking. If memory is linking production and reproduction of experience, in primary memory activity the links are links of action, or, from another viewpoint, links of the continuity and urge of instinctual process. Through "hypercathexis," of which Freud's "word presentations" joining with "thing presentations" (1915) are an example, and which originates in the mother's mirroring interpretation and organization of the child's urges, feelings, and actions — through such processes the links of action and feeling become links of meaning. The various elements of action and feeling begin to encounter and "know" each other; they become a context of meaning, which is one way of describing the organizing function of the ego. Freud increasingly insisted on the ego's character as a coherent organization. In his later writings, he more and more tended to the view that the main characteristic of the repressed is that it is excluded from the coherent ego, i.e., excluded from an overall context of meaning, thereby regressing toward primary process, toward a nondiacritic, nonrepresentational form of mentation. As such, the repressed is a reservoir of primary memorial processes, which through interpretation (meaning-giving on the part of the analyst) may combine with or again become part of a context of meaning.

With all this, the status of unconscious fantasies and unconscious ideas remains problematic. Similar to the latent dream thoughts, they appear to be combinations of elements from the two realms, the primary and secondary memorial systems, or the unconscious and the preconscious. Perhaps the most we can say is that a so-called unconscious idea, like a latent dream thought, is a construction or reconstruction of something dynamically unconscious in terms of, or in the language of, preconscious thought processes. An unconscious idea would not be something that as such has an existence in the primary memorial system. The unitary, enactive memorial process–structure, for an empathic observer, corresponds to a dual, secondary memorial structure that is isolated from the former and readily available only to the analyst as agent of secondary-process mentation. The unconscious structure, in and through the act of interpretation as a hypercathectic act, again becomes, in the case of derepression, an "idea," i.e., a secondary-process structure.

Becoming an idea means that the unconscious structure loses its unitary, instinctual, "single-minded" character and becomes reinserted into a context of meaning, i.e., into a context of mutually reflecting and related mental elements. The linking is no longer merely one of reproductive action; it is one of representational connection. The loss involved in the transformation of the unitary, single-minded character of primary memorial activity is, I believe, the cause for what Freud has called the resistance of the id. This loss is fended off by the "compulsion to repeat," which forever remains an active source of conflict between id and ego.

We are led back to the intricate relations between memory and mourning. In some sense, the sadness and grief of mourning perhaps also concerns that loss, that giving up of the unitary single-mindedness of instinctual life that tends to preserve in some way the primary narcissistic oneness from which we have to take leave in the development of conscient life and secondary-process mentation. That development involves being split from the embeddedness in an embracing totality, as well as that internal split in which we come to reflect and confront ourselves. The development of conscient, representational memory is a departure from that inner unity and replaces the original unity prior to individuation.[1] Individuation is our human way of memorializing and thus re-creating those origins.

The ego is, as Freud thought—and I believe this is his deepest insight into its psychology—the precipitate, the internalization of what goes on between the primitive psyche and its environment; it is an organization of reproductive action, but action on a new stage, the stage of internality. This interplay on the internal stage of action constitutes the process–structure of the ego. The ego, in its further elaboration and articulation of this reproductive action, which takes place in continuous interaction with the world, then develops toward that more remote, divided, and abstract form of mentation we call the secondary process or representational memory. This mentation is at the same time more distant and self-divided, and more lucid and free—shall we say sadder and wiser? By virtue of the secondary process, the ego exercises its functions, including that function by which the individual becomes an object of contemplation and care and love to itself and can encounter others as objects in the same spirit.

Before closing, I wish to say a few words about a prime function in human life—and in psychoanalysis as an exquisitely human undertaking—of fully matured memorial activity. Through psychoanalysis man may become a truly historical being. In contrast to the ahistorical life of primitive societies and primitive man, including the primitive man in ourselves, the higher forms of memorial activity make us create a history of ourselves as a race and as individuals, as well as a history of the world in which we live. Rudiments of this history-creating activity are present even in primitive mentality, but it comes into its own in the individual in those higher forms of reflective memory wherein we encounter ourselves in all our dimensions. This is the thrust of psychoanalysis, of the endeavor to transform unconscious or

---

1. Cf. Freud (1914a, p. 100): "The development of the ego consists in a departure (*Entfernung*) from primary narcissism and gives rise to a vigorous attempt to recover that state."

automatic repetitions—memorial processes in which we do not encounter ourselves and others—into aware and re-creative action in which we know who we and others are, understand how we got to be that way, and envisage what we might do with ourselves as we are. In such memorial activity, which weaves past, present, and future into a context of heightened meaning, each of us is on the path to becoming a self. For most of us, such self-aware organization and conduct of life with others and ourselves remains a potential rather than an actuality, except for brief moments or periods. Understanding this potentiality, however, can help us to strive toward a more human life.

REFERENCES

Bartlett, F. C. (1932): *Remembering: A Study in Experimental and Social Psychology.* Cambridge: Cambridge University Press, 1967.

Freud, S. (1895): Project for a scientific psychology. S.E. 1: 283–387.

_____. (1900): *The Interpretation of Dreams.* S.E. 4/5.

_____. (1914a): On narcissism. S.E. 14:67–102.

_____. (1914b): Remembering, repeating and working-through. S.E. 12:145–56.

_____. (1915): The unconscious. S.E. 14:159–215.

_____. (1917): A metapsychological supplement to the theory of dreams. S.E. 14:217–36.

_____. (1923): The ego and the id. S.E. 19:3–66.

_____. (1925): A note upon the "mystic writing-pad." S.E. 19:227–32.

_____. (1930): Civilization and its discontents. S.E. 21:59–145.

_____. (1933): New introductory lectures on psycho-analysis. S.E. 22:3–182.

Klein, G. (1966): The several grades of memory. In: *Psychoanalysis—A General Psychology: Essays in Honor of Heinz Hartmann,* ed. R. M. Loewenstein, L. M. Newman, M. Schur, and A. J. Solnit. New York: International Universities Press, pp. 177–389. Reprinted in: George S. Klein, *Perception, Motives, and Personality.* New York: Alfred A. Knopf, 1970.

Loewald, H. (1971): On motivation and instinct theory. *The Psychoanalytic Study of the Child* 26:91–128 (reprinted in this volume).

Mahler, M. (1968): *On Human Symbiosis and the Vicissitudes of Individuation.* New York: International Universities Press.

Paul, I. H. (1967): The concept of schema in memory theory. In: Motives and Thought: Psychoanalytic Essays in Honor of David Rapaport, ed. R. R. Holt. *Psychol. Issues* Monograph No. 18/19:218–58. New York: International Universities Press.

Rapaport, D. (1942): *Emotion and Memory,* rev. ed. New York: International Universities Press, 1950.

———, ed. (1951): *Organization and Pathology of Thought: Selected Sources.* New York: Columbia University Press.

———. (1957): A theoretical analysis of the superego concept. In: *The Collected Papers of David Rapaport,* ed. M. M. Gill. New York: Basic Books, 1967, pp. 685–709.

Sandler, J., and Rosenblatt, B. (1962): The concept of the representational world. *The Psychoanalytic Study of the Child* 17: 128–45.

Spitz, R. A. (1965): *The First Year of Life.* New York: International Universities Press.

Werner, H., and Kaplan, B. (1963): *Symbol Formation.* New York: Wiley.

Winnicott, D. W. (1958): *Collected Papers.* New York: Basic Books.

11

EGO-ORGANIZATION AND DEFENSE

My remarks will focus on certain developments regarding the understanding of ego and defense that have taken place since Anna Freud's book was published, many of them being fore-shadowed or promoted by her approach. There have been advances or shifts in emphasis concerning the understanding of the ego and changes or refinements in the theory of defense, and the two are intimately related to each other.

The distinction became clarified between ego as one of the three substructures of the personality, and ego as the term for the totality of the mind or personality, sometimes called the *Gesamt-Ich* by Freud. Hartmann introduced the term self for this *Gesamt-Ich*. The clear distinction between these two uses of the term ego was not merely an advance in conceptual precision. It led to greater appreciation of the fact that the *Gesamt-Ich* or self is at first undifferentiated and that its organization is brought about by two interrelated processes: identificatory and boundary-setting interactions with environment by which self and object world increasingly become differentiated from each other and by which each undergoes processes of integration and differentiation of its own. In this way the self becomes a coherent and articulated unity (of which id, ego, and superego might be conceived as substructures), and "objects" become distinct and constant unities. These evolving object-units are increasingly experienced by the developing self as related to each other and related to the self, rather than as merged. We might speak of the

This paper, not previously published, was written as a contribution to a panel on "The Ego and the Mechanisms of Defense: A Review," held at the Twentieth Annual Freud Memorial Lecture Program, sponsored by the Philadelphia Association for Psychoanalysis, on April 28, 1973 in Philadelphia. Anna Freud had inaugurated this Program in 1954 and was an active participant in the various panels presented at the 1973 meetings. She gave the 20th Annual Freud Memorial Lecture on this occasion. It was to pay tribute to her 1936 book that this particular panel was organized.

primitive stage of self–object relatedness, prior to the differentiation of identification and object-relation, or of narcissistic and
object cathexis, as object-tie (*Objekt-Bindung*) in contradistinction to object-relation (*Objekt-Beziehung*).

In regard to ego in the narrower sense (as one of the three
agencies of the mind), emphasis shifted from ego as the agency of
defense to ego as an organization. It is an organization not only in
the sense that it is the more highly organized province of the
mind, but most importantly also in the sense of being an organizing agency, organizing both the environment (external reality)
and the psyche itself (inner or psychic reality). This does not
mean that the defense functions of the ego were lost sight of, but
that the latter now were understood in the context and from the
viewpoint of psychic organization, rather than psychic organization being viewed from the standpoint of defense. I shall briefly
return to this issue later on. Growing emphasis on adaptation
expresses this shift.

We are now paying more attention to the formation and to the
development of the psychic substructures, especially of ego and
superego, than was formerly the case. This change in emphasis
occurred in good part under the impact of increased psychoanalytic experience with character disorders, borderline conditions,
and psychoses, as well as of child analysis, analysis of adolescents and of analytically informed child observation and research. It became more apparent that the classical defense
mechanisms, observed in the psychoneuroses, are comparatively
late psychic operations that come into being only on the basis of
a relatively well-established articulation of id and ego in conjunction with the differentiation of self and object. It would
appear that the ego's defense mechanisms make use, by regression, of primitive psychic processes, which in their original stage
may better be viewed as subserving psychic organization and
boundary setting, instead of being seen as defense mechanisms
in the usual clinical sense of that term. So-called primal repression, projection, introjection–identification, the instincts' turning
around upon the self, isolation, and intellectualization are examples. Anna Freud's discussions, in "The Ego and the Mechanisms of Defense," of the genesis and complexity of identification with the aggressor, of projection, and of intellectualization
in adolescence point to such a view. Perhaps the clearest example

is introjection or identification, a psychic activity that contributes to the formation and consolidation of ego and superego,
before and besides being used by the ego for purposes of defense.

This leads to the growing discrimination between defense,
warding off of inner or outer demands or influences on the ego,
and assimilation or inclusion of these influences within the ego
organization, which may be described as internalization. Defense would be the ego's protection of its own status quo, whereas
internalization would involve expansion, further and richer
organization of the ego. The difference between repression of the
Oedipus complex and what Freud has called its destruction, may
serve as a prototype of this distinction (cf. my paper "On Internalization," reprinted in this volume).

The appreciation of the intricate vicissitudes of ego and
superego formation, expansion and consolidation, has given us a
broader perspective on a number of pathological phenomena
that earlier were seen predominantly, often exclusively, in terms
of ego defenses. In this light signs or symptoms of ego defects
came into view that should not simply be understood as caused
by the ego's defense mechanisms—the latter presuppose an
already developed, reasonably intact ego—but as relating to
early, pre-oedipal, pathogenic problems of the very organization
of the ego, connected with those primitive internalizing interactions with the parental environment that lead to that organization. Such structural deficiencies have an often decisive impact
on defense mechanisms, making them so brittle as to interfere
with their functioning even under stresses of normal proportions
and reducing them easily to their primitive prototypes. An example are projective mechanisms in narcissistic personality disorders: what appears as an ego defense against unacceptable
instinctual impulses may need to be understood and interpreted
on the deeper level of primitive blurring of boundaries between
self and object before it can be dealt with in terms of the regressive use of the latter as a defense.

My final comments have to do with the concept of defense. I
had mentioned that, instead of viewing psychic organization as
being in the service of defense, we may view defense as being in
the service of psychic organization. The first alternative implies
a defense concept which is deeply rooted in general psychoanalytic theory, that is, in the assumption of the constancy principle

as regulating psychic events. If one postulates the rule of the constancy principle, the psychological version of which is the unpleasure principle, then the whole development of the psychic apparatus with its psychic processes and structures is interpreted as a defense against unpleasure. A state of stimulation or excitation of the psychic apparatus is understood, according to the constancy or inertia principle, as unpleasure, and pleasure consists in an at least approximate return to a state of rest or non-stimulation. The equations: state of excitation = unpleasure, state of rest = pleasure, have dominated general psychoanalytic theory from the beginning. Accordingly, warding off stimulation, or its reduction and, if possible, its annulment, were seen as the function and purpose of the psychic apparatus. Excitation as such spells conflict; the state of satisfaction is nothing more than the state in which excitation is abolished. Under this perspective, defense becomes the dominant issue of psychic life, and psychic organization is ultimately a defense process. If the evolution of psychic life is not seen as a complex detour on the road to a state of rest, then psychic organization is not in the service of defense. And the ego's defense mechanisms, discovered through psychoanalytic clinical observation, rather than being confused with ultimate postulates about the evolution of organic and psychic life, can be seen in their proper proportions as protective devices against disruption and disorganization, protections that often overshoot their mark or continue to function when no longer necessary and thus become pathological, interfering with the further organization of the self and the world of objects.

12

PRIMARY PROCESS, SECONDARY PROCESS, AND LANGUAGE

The following contribution to the theory of primary and secondary process and their relations to language is limited to only a few aspects of this vast subject. Primary process and secondary process are generally considered as fundamental, perhaps the most fundamental, concepts in psychoanalytic theory. Having a high degree of abstraction and generality they subsume, in various ways, most if not all psychoanalytic findings and concepts. Primary process is directly correlated with the concepts Unconscious and Id, secondary process with Preconscious and Ego, themselves basic conceptualizations in psychoanalytic theory. With language I shall concern myself from a very narrow point of view. Conspicuous by its absence will be, for example, any reference to the important fields of linguistics and psycholinguistics, any consideration of the structure of language. Little will be said about interpretation and the symbolic function. I have set myself merely the task of attempting to throw some additional light on the two forms of mental processes that Freud distinguishes, and on the function he attributes to language in the "progression," in mental development, from primary to secondary process mentation.

Primary and secondary process are ideal constructs. Or they may be described as poles between which human mentation moves. I mean this not only in the longitudinal sense of progres-

This paper was written for vol. 3 of *Psychiatry and the Humanities,* a collection of invited articles under the title "Psychoanalysis and Language," edited by Joseph H. Smith (New Haven and London: Yale University Press, 1978). The series is published under the auspices of the Forum on Psychiatry and the Humanities of the Washington School of Psychiatry. A shorter version was presented as the 11th Freud Anniversary Lecture of the Psychoanalytic Association of New York in 1976.

sion from primitive and infantile to civilized and adult mental life and regressions in the opposite direction. Mental activity appears to be characterized by a to and fro between, an interweaving of, these modes of mental processes, granted that often one or the other is dominant and more manifestly guiding mentation and that the secondary process assumes an increasingly important role on more advanced levels of mentation. Language itself, considered in terms of these categories, partakes of those two sides of the coin of mentation. The primary process quality or suggestiveness of language is apparent in certain kinds of schizophrenic speech as well as in poetry, especially modern poetry, and in modern prose by writers such as Joyce or Faulkner. We see here that what we call dynamically unconscious processes can be compatible with conscious awareness and verbalization, as though there were a direct leap from primary process to conscious awareness, omitting preconscious, secondary process mediation, despite the fact of expression in words.

In the verbal interventions and interpretations of the analyst in psychoanalysis the secondary process aspect of language ordinarily predominates. However, when we encourage the patient to free-associate, we try to move him in the direction of primary process, or in a direction where the influence of primary process mentation on his verbal productions increases. To the extent to which the patient allows himself free association, his feelings and trains of thought are more influenced by, more embedded in his global emotional situation of the moment, including the impact the analyst's presence has on it. The injunction to express himself in words rather than to act or move about, induces the patient to funnel, as it were, his mental activity into the narrow channel of language. Speech thereby tends to gain greater intensity and to resonate more with the total emotional situation. This condition is greatly enhanced by the fact that the analyst is invisible and that the latter's communications are funneled through auditory channels. Thus language, both spoken and heard by the patient, tends to assume that greater intensity and experiential resonance.

I emphasized the embeddedness of verbalized thought and feeling in the global emotional situation, i.e., in the psychoanalytic situation with its transference significance, because of the bearing this has on the primary-process aspect of language. In the clarifying, reflective, and interpretative interventions of the analyst, on the other hand, secondary-process aspects of language are by and large dominant, insofar as these interventions question, define, highlight, and articulate the hidden connections of what the patient said. To the extent to which this happens, we may be allowed to speak of a transformation of primary-process aspects of language into secondary-process organization.

The preceding remarks on language in the psychoanalytic situation are merely meant to sketch in vague outline the problem area with which we are dealing.

Two further observations should be mentioned in these introductory comments. One is that language is typically first conveyed to the child by the parental voice and in an all-pervasive way by the mother in the feeding situation and in all her other ministrations to the infant. In these situations her speech and voice are part and parcel of the global mother–child interaction. Secondly, parental voice and speech take on a special significance for the child insofar as they come to convey the parents' closeness at a distance, their presence in absence. When the child is alone, cannot see or touch and smell the parents, hearing their voice tends to render them present in a somewhat remote and less global fashion. The parental voice, responding to the child's crying or other vocal utterance, for example in the dark, gives him a sense of their presence. Thus the child's utterances may conjure up parental presence, even if the parent does not visibly or tangibly appear.

While I have studied only a very small fraction of the vast literature relevant to my subject matter, I am indebted to many authors in the fields of psychoanalysis and developmental psychology who have stimulated and influenced my thinking. I am grateful to the participants—psychoanalytic candidates and graduate analysts—in a seminar on this topic conducted by me under the auspices of the Western New England Institute for Psychoanalysis, for many fruitful discussions. The strongest and most congenial source of stimulation and influence, outside of psychoanalysis itself, has been Werner and Kaplan's book, *Symbol Formation. An Organismic-Developmental Approach to Language and the Expression of Thought* (1963).

I

I shall begin with a reconsideration of a crucial passage from Freud's paper "The Unconscious" (1915*b*, pp. 201–02):

The system Ucs. contains the thing-cathexes of the objects, the first and true object-cathexes; the system Pcs. comes about by this thing-presentation being hypercathected through being linked with the word-presentations corresponding to it. It is these hypercathexes, we may suppose, that bring about a higher psychical organization and make possible for the primary process to be succeeded by the secondary process which is dominant in the Pcs.

In these sentences Freud sets forth essential relations between the dynamic unconscious, thing-cathexes, thing-presentation, and primary process on the one hand, and the preconscious, word-presentation, and secondary process on the other.[1] Word-presentations are said to play a crucial role in the organization of the preconscious, which is "a higher psychical organization" than the dynamic unconscious. A thing-presentation, according to this account, becomes hypercathected by being linked with the corresponding word-presentations. The nature of that cor-respondence—which seems to be the basis for the linking—remains unspecified. In any case, it is the linking of thing-presenta-tion with word-presentations by which preconscious or second-ary process mentation becomes established. We note that Freud here equates thing-cathexis (*Sachbesetzung*) with thing-presen-tation (*Sachvorstellung*). A little further on, at the end of the paragraph from which I quoted, the thing-presentation is called a psychical *act*. In as much as cathexes and presentations are psychical acts—no matter how enduring, unchanging, struc-tured, they appear to be—word-presentations also are psychical acts, although Freud does not specify this. Nor does he explicitly state that word-presentations as psychical acts are themselves cathexes.

Both, thing-presentations and word-presentations, ultimately derive from sense perceptions, via "memory traces" of the latter.

---

1. Freud's postulation of the *systems* Ucs. and Pcs. will not be discussed in this paper; it is not directly pertinent to the problems considered here.

Thing-presentations derive from global, complex perceptions, while word-presentations derive from primarily auditory perceptions (proprioceptive components in the respective memory traces would play a role in the utterance of words).

It has to be stressed that word-presentations do not constitute a higher organizational state than thing-presentations: it is the linking of the two by which higher organization comes about. This linking is a hypercathecting act, an act that intensifies and in some way modifies the already existing cathexis of the thing-presentation. But if linking of thing-presentation with corresponding word-presentations establishes hypercathexis[2] in a presentation, then word-presentations no less than thing-presentations would be hypercathected in such linking. It would be more accurate to formulate the state of affairs in the following way: the hypercathecting act, the linking of thing-presentations and word-presentations, brings about a presentation that differs from either in being a novel, more complexly organized psychical act.

At an earlier point (pp. 175–76) in "The Unconscious" Freud explains that having heard something and having experienced it are, as to their psychological nature, entirely different psychic acts. If the analyst informs the patient in words of the existence of an unconscious presentation (a thing-presentation) in the patient's mind, the patient now will "have" the word-presentations corresponding to the thing-presentation. But the patient will not be able to make adequate use of the information unless the two become linked in his mind or by his mind, through a hypercathecting act that creates a new form of mental presentation. In less abstract language we would say that in the joining of words and corresponding experience the psychic life of the patient is intensified or deepened, has gained a new dimension (as in the so-called aha-Erlebnis). No longer do unconscious presentation and presentation of the corresponding words exist side by side. There is now a novel present experience or psychical act that as such henceforth can become part of the patient's memorial repertoire. This novel mental act, I suggest, is of the nature of a per-

---

2. The term hypercathexis, like presentation, cathexis, and perception, denotes both the act of hypercathecting and the "result" of that act, i.e., the organized action pattern that act brings into being.

ception. Hypercathexis in the sense used here, then, would be something like an actual perceptual act—if we may define a perceptual act as a psychical act in which the continuum of memorial, reproductive activity interacts with novelty in such a way that "a new experience" arises, which in turn gives rise to refreshed, modified memorial activity. The two presentations are, in their interaction, lifted out of their status as separate reproductive acts and become united in one perceptual act, with the freshness and poignancy characteristic of the latter. (The perceptual act here referred to is, of course, not the patient's perception of the words spoken by the analyst, but an intrapsychic perception, although triggered or induced by the analyst's words.) Such an intrapsychic perceptual act, while often experienced in conscious awareness, in all likelihood may occur outside of awareness.

I have indicated that Freud, when speaking of the linking of thing-presentation with word-presentations corresponding to it, says nothing more about this correspondence. But it is clear that he assumes a correspondence between them that somehow pre-exists the linking and should determine what becomes linked to what in the hypercathecting act.[3] I have also maintained that in such linking not only the thing-presentation but also the word-presentations would be hypercathected, one by the other. If there is a pre-existing correspondence, the linking would re-establish some old bond that had been severed. And indeed, such severance occurs by repression. If presentations are not repressed, presentation of the thing and presentation of the word remain together. They belong together. As Freud puts it, words are the translation of the object and shall remain linked (*verknüpft*) with it. The analyst's interpretation, which translates the patient's unconscious (thing-) presentation into words originally belonging to it, helps to re-establish—once resistances are overcome—a piece of secondary process mentation, and therefore helps to re-establish the old bond between thing and word.

This clarifies things insofar as the dynamic unconscious and primary process are understood as being due to repression. If

3. The mechanism of "false (wrong) connection" or link (*falsche Verknüpfung*), adduced by Freud, especially in his earlier writings, in a variety of contexts (transference, compulsion neurosis, obsessions and phobias, screen memories), is related to the issues of linking and correspondence. See Loewald (1960, section 4, p. 248).

secondary-process, preconscious-conscious mentation is our starting point and standard, taking for granted the existence of developed language, then the phenomena of psychic conflict and defense account for the appearance of primary-process mentation and of its indications, such as condensation and displacement, in dreams, neurosis, etc. Merton Gill, in his paper on "The Primary Process" (1967), has emphasized a basic ambiguity in that concept: the primary process, on the one hand, is "motivated" (Gill's term) by defense, is due to the impact of repression on standard rational, secondary-process thinking. On the other hand, primary process is assumed to be the original form or mode of mentation according to the pleasure principle, which secondarily becomes changed by the exigencies of life, by "reality," resulting in secondary-process mentation guided by the reality principle. In a manner the ambiguity is resolved by introducing the concept of regression: defense brings about regression from preconscious to unconscious mentation. The primary process is "primary" because it is the first and more primitive. Defense, repression, leads to a regression to this old mode of mental functioning; it does not *create* primary process.

But what about language? What about the old bond between thing-presentation and word-presentations? We have said that the hypercathecting link between them re-establishes preconscious organization in as much as the old tie between thing and corresponding words is rewoven. However, in the passage quoted at the beginning Freud speaks not just of the reconstitution of preconscious presentations, of the re-establishment of higher psychical organization by the removal of repression in analysis through appropriate interpretations. He wishes to explain the origin, the emergence of the preconscious in the course of mental development, by the linking of thing-presentation and word-presentations that correspond to it.[4] The correspondence between thing and word, then, must be older than the preconscious. Where do word-presentations come from? If the unconscious is older than the preconscious, if it is true that the unconscious "thing-cathexes of the objects" are "the first and true object-

4. "... the system Pcs. *comes about* by this thing-presentation being hypercathected ..." ("... *das System Vbw entsteht* ..."). "... these hypercathexes ... *bring about* a higher psychical organization and *make possible* for the primary process to be succeeded by the secondary process ..." (1915b, p. 202; my italics).

cathexes," then thing-presentations would be older than word-presentations. Yet, a correspondence between them is assumed that precedes the emergence of preconscious mentation; that correspondence must be more ancient than the preconscious.

It is evident that during the first few months of life, when primary process mentation is unquestionably dominant, the infant does not have language at his disposal. He cannot speak; but he is spoken to. He is provided with words, as it were, but he cannot use them. Does he perhaps have word-presentations, but no words to utter them? Or, if not word-presentations, then memory traces of words he perceived, from which word-presentations eventually derive? Would he then have memory traces of things and memory traces of words, contiguous to each other? Would this contiguity constitute the ancient correspondence? We would be thrown back from a correspondence between thing-presentation and word-presentations to an underlying contiguity of the respective memory traces. This contiguity, in turn, would have come about by "thing" and "words" having been perceived simultaneously or one right after the other.

I believe that such a reconstruction is untenable. It takes for granted the separateness of thing and word and the separate perception of thing and word by the infant. According to modern developmental theory sensory perception in its initial stages is a global affair; there is no such thing as perception according to distinct sensory modalities in the beginnings of mental life. A thing, event, act, or experience given a word or words by the mother is one buzzing blooming confusion (William James) for the infant, and "the word" is part of that confusion. It must be added that during early stages the mother, unless she is out of phase with the infant's developmental stage, does not *name* things for the infant. She speaks with or to the infant, not with the expectation that he will grasp the words, but as if speaking to herself with the infant included. The words of which her speaking is composed form undifferentiated ingredients of the total situation or event experienced by the infant. He does not apprehend separate words—words separate one from the other and separate from the total experience—but he is immersed, embedded in a flow of speech that is part and parcel of a global experience within the mother–child field.

If this is correct, are we entitled to say that the infant's perception of what "in fact" happens represents a condensation of the separate elements and components of a total process? I think not. We can properly speak of condensation, a condensing, only if what is now condensed was at some prior stage separate or differentiated. This fits regression from secondary process to primary process in repression. Speaking of condensation always implies the secondary process vantage point. In primary process mentation a primordial density is given, not a condensation achieved.[5]

Our scientific conceptual language—a function of a specially developed, highly differentiated form of secondary process mentation—appears to be particularly inadequate for statements about early mental functioning and about primary-process phenomena in general. For this reason correctives and qualifications have to be applied almost constantly, in order to make even approximately adequate statements when we wish to describe or formulate in conceptual language primary-process phenomena and processes. The much maligned "anthropomorphisms" and "metaphors," not infrequently used in theoretical psychoanalytic writings, in many instances serve this corrective function. They often are closer to the phenomena in question by having an evocative quality. Just because such language is more influenced by the primary process aspects of words, by the evocative-magical qualities of language, it often constitutes a more adequate formulation of primary-process phenomena.

Words and things (or objects) in traditional psychoanalytic theory are treated as separate percepts given to a perceptual system (Pcpt./Cs.). There, sensory data or stimuli are said to be passively received and then relayed to and further processed in "memory systems" (Freud begins to take a more sophisticated view of perception in the 1925 papers on the "Mystic Writing Pad" and on "Negation"). In primary-process mentation, however, words and things are not perceptually differentiated entities, the percepts of which would then be laid down in different but contiguous memory traces.[6]

5. This statement obviously has implications for the theory of dreams and the dream work, problems that cannot be pursued here.

6. For a discussion on memory and perception see my paper "Perspectives on Memory" (1976; reprinted in this volume).

It is to be noted that "thing" (*Sache*), in "thing-presentation" (*Sachvorstellung*), is not so much or not merely a thing in the sense of material object or substance, but includes the wider sense of that word: state of affairs, event, circumscribed action, etc. The emphasis is on the distinction between words as auditory percepts and their correspondence and reference to other perceptual phenomena or experiences, not just to material objects. Thing, in this wide sense, and words, in early stages of mentation, in primary process—insofar as words come into play—are not separate. Words here are, on the contrary, indistinguishable ingredients of global states of affairs. The mother's flow of words does not convey meaning to or symbolize "things" for the infant—"meaning" as something differentiated from "fact"—but the sounds, tone of voice, and rhythm of speech are fused within the apprehended global event. One might say that, while the mother utters words, the infant does not perceive words but is bathed in sound, rhythm, etc., as accentuating ingredients of a uniform experience. The distinction between sounds as ingredients of a total occurrence, and what the heard sounds refer to or signify—this is a slowly developing achievement to which we apply the term secondary process. This is true also for sounds, "words" uttered by the growing child himself.

The linking of thing-presentation and word-presentations is a process that is secondary to an original unity where "word" is embedded in "thing." It is this original unity that constitutes the matrix for a "correspondence" between thing-presentation and word-presentations as they become differentiated from one another. Freud later acknowledged that more than language (word-presentations) is involved in secondary process formation, although language has a special status in the development of what we now may term the symbolic function. Hypercathexis comes about not only in links with word-presentations, but with various other presentations as they differentiate out of global experience.

In sum: the linking between thing-presentation and word-presentations is based on or concomitant with a differentiation of elements out of an original oneness. This differentiation is an unfolding or separating of what now are apprehended as different components or aspects of a global experience. In as much as the differentiated elements betray their common origin and respond to each other, a correspondence between them remains as the heir, the reflection, the articulate memory of the primordial oneness. The linking between thing-presentation and word-presentations in secondary process is a rejoining on a different level, by way of a creative repetition, of elements that had been at one; it is a reconciliation. The differentiating process implied in the differentiation of separate sensory modalities out of "coenesthetic reception" (Spitz, 1965) may be seen as a precursor of secondary process.

Repression, seen from this angle, amounts to a severing or loosening of the connections between thing-presentation and word-presentations. Word-presentations may remain conscious but are no longer or only loosely linked with corresponding thing-presentations. As I had stated earlier, the hypercathecting link between them constitutes a psychical act of the nature of an internal perception. This internal perception (a "preconscious" mental act), or rather its memorial presentation, in repression becomes disrupted. Thus, repression as an intrapsychic action can be understood as an unlinking. The unconscious thing-presentation as a result of repression, however, is not simply a presentation of the "thing" minus the corresponding words. Rather, the words have been reabsorbed into that old memorial formation where thing and words are not yet distinguished as different but corresponding and thus linkable elements of experience. Therefore an interpretation of unconscious presentations, communicated in words by the analyst, is capable of reestablishing differentiation of the thing-presentation in such a way that renewed linking can be achieved. It is as if the analyst's words summon the thing-presentation via the words contained in it, lifting them from the unitary thing as differentiated elements that now can be linked with other thing-elements. The analyst's interpreting words thus redifferentiate the unitary thing-presentation.

I said that word-presentations, unlinked or insufficiently linked with thing-presentations in repression, may remain conscious as such. But they are now void of or deficient in experiential meaning. They have deteriorated to more or less hollow echoes of secondary process presentations. In everyday mental functioning repression is always more or less at work; there is a relative isolation of word-presentations. Indirect (through "derivatives") or weak links usually remain, sustaining an average[7] level of mental functioning that represents a viable compromise between too intimate and intense closeness to the unconscious, with its threatening creative-destructive potentialities, and deadening insulation from the unconscious where human life and language are no longer vibrant and warmed by its fire. This relative deficiency or weakness of links between verbal thought and its primordial referents makes it feasible for language to function as vehicle for everyday rational thought and action, comparatively unaffected by or sheltered from the powers of the unconscious that tend to consume rationality.

Related, by contrast, to the issue of average mental functioning are the problems of abstract and of schizophrenic thinking and language. At the end of "The Unconscious" (1915b, p. 204) Freud expresses views on them that call for critical comment.

When we think in abstractions there is a danger that we may neglect the relations of words to unconscious thing-presentations, and it must be confessed that the expression and content of our philosophizing then begins to acquire an unwelcome resemblance to the mode of operation of schizophrenics. We may, on the other hand, attempt a characterization of the schizophrenic's mode of thought by saying that he treats concrete things as though they were abstract.

Earlier in that paper (p. 199) he writes:

In schizophrenia *words* [Freud's italics] are subjected to the same process as that which makes the dream-images out of latent dream-thoughts—to what we have called the primary psychical process.

---

7. The etymology of the word *average* throws an unexpected light on the use of it in the above context of compromise. A marginal note of this kind may not be amiss in a paper concerned with words. According to Webster (1958) the word derives from the Arabic *'awār*, loss or damage in articles of merchandise; Italian *avaria*, French *avarie*, damage to ship or cargo, port dues. It is used in Marine Law. One of Webster's entries runs as follows: "A loss less than total to cargo or ship, or a charge arising from damage done by sea perils; also, the equitable and proportionate distribution of such loss or expense among all chargeable with it." A so-called general average (in Marine Insurance) "arises from an intentional sacrifice or expense made for the safety of all the interests involved in the same adventure under pressure of a common risk." From there derives the meaning of average as "mean value" and eventually as "the usual, typical, or most frequently encountered thing, happening or person of a considerable number," "common run." Thus, the ideas of loss or damage (deficiency) and proportionate expenses "made for the safety of all the interests involved," are hidden in the word average.

They undergo condensation, and by means of displacement transfer their cathexes to one another in their entirety.

He makes a similar observation in "A Metapsychological Supplement to the Theory of Dreams" (1916, p. 229). But if this is so, abstract thought does not tend to resemble the mode of operation of schizophrenics, and the schizophrenic does not treat "concrete things as though they were abstract." Rather, the schizophrenic treats words as concrete things or actions, instead of treating words as being linked with them. This phenomenon is similar to, if not identical with, Freud's observation in "Totem and Taboo" (1913, p. 56) that "savages regard a name as an essential part of a man's personality and as an important possession; they treat words in every sense as things."

It is true that the danger in abstract thinking is to neglect the relations of words to unconscious thing-presentations. But words, in abstract thinking, do not undergo condensation and displacement in the sense in which Freud states it to be the case in schizophrenia. Rather, words tend to acquire a peculiar degree of autonomy. In the neglect of the relations of words to unconscious thing-presentations their links are weakened. Meaning and the links between thing-presentations and word-presentations are thinned out to more or less tenuous threads. In excessive abstraction verbal thought processes give the impression of acquiring a mechanical or automatic activity of their own, like puppets manipulated by invisible hands that are connected with them only by thin threads attached at certain joints. Verbal thought then may have a lifeless nimbleness all its own—very much in contrast to the concretization of verbal thought in schizophrenia. In the latter case there is no link between word and thing, not because the link is cut or too tenuous, but because the distance between thing-presentation and word-presentations vanishes; they are no longer or insufficiently differentiated. Word stands for thing, not as its symbol or representative but as being re-merged with it, or as magically summoning it into presence. The task of the therapist here is to differentiate or re-differentiate thing-presentation from word-presentations. If that succeeds (unless secondary obsessional defenses come into play) their correspondence, emerging out of identity, is not in question, and the secondary-process linking is no problem; the problem for the patient is to hold on to the differentiation. In neurotic repression, on the other hand, the therapeutic task is to reconstitute weakened or severed links, to narrow the distance between thing-presentation and word-presentation.

More than differentiation between thing-presentation and word-presentations is absent or underdeveloped in the kind of schizophrenic mentation under consideration. The same is true for the differentiation between thing and thing-presentation, and between word and word-presentation. In schematic outline, we can distinguish four types of differentiation that take place in unison in higher mental development: (1) between thing and word, (2) between thing and thing-presentation, (3) between word and word-presentation, and (4) between thing-presentation and word-presentation. It seems that no one of these four differentiations (or the lack of one of them) takes place without the others being involved as well. The differentiation between thing and thing-presentation and between word and word-presentation, of course, involves subject–object differentiation. Language, considered from the standpoint of secondary-process mentation, develops within the growing differentiation between self and object–world. The concretization of language, as in schizophrenia, whereby the distinction between word and thing collapses, is at the same time concretization in another sense: distinctions between word and word-presentation and between thing and thing-presentation collapse as well. What we call *meaning* comprises both the differentiating–linking of word and thing (their mutual reference) and that of presentation (memorial act) and percept.

I break off at this point in order to consider some of the metapsychological concepts used so far.

II

I shall begin with a digression that is related to language in a broader sense. While keenly aware of the recent debates in the psychoanalytic literature about some metapsychological concepts, pointing out their deficiencies, questioning even the relevance or validity of metapsychology itself, I shall proceed here without taking these objections into account in my discussion. But I wish to state my conviction that many of the objections raised are based on anxious clinging to unimaginative comprehension and to rigid and unduly restrictive definitions of certain Freudian concepts and theoretical formulations. If viewed within the overall context of Freud's and his followers' work, many of them allow for much freer elaboration and development of their content and meaning than has been accorded them by the majority of theoreticians. True, some scientific concepts are so narrowly conceived at the outset, or conversely so vague and ill-defined, that they have to be dropped along the way. But many Freudian concepts and terms are overdetermined and full of connotations and implications that have not been spelled out by him or that he neglected. Others he may have defined more narrowly than need be, because of special theoretical considerations of the moment.

Concepts share the potential of language and words for unfolding new meanings, for changes of meaning, return to earlier meanings, etc. There are, of course, limits to this and there is always the risk of overstepping them. Equally, however, there is the risk of being too timid or too rigid about such limits, of not utilizing, exploring, and testing the hidden potentialities of concepts. Freud's own aversion to technical terms and precise definitions of concepts undoubtedly has contributed to confusion in psychoanalytic theory and terminology. But he clearly wanted to keep his theories and concepts open to the winds of change, while not condoning changes indiscriminately. Speaking of basic scientific concepts he warns against prematurely confining them in definitions. In a well-known passage in his introductory remarks to "Instincts and Their Vicissitudes" (1915a, p. 117)[8] he writes about this issue as follows:

The true beginning of scientific activity consists . . . in describing phenomena and then in proceeding to group, classify, and correlate them. Even at the stage of description it is not possible to avoid applying certain abstract ideas to the material in hand, ideas derived from somewhere or other but certainly not from the new observations alone. Such

8. I quote this passage not only because of its immediate manifest content, but also for its relevance to the broader problem of the interrelations between language and mental activity and the "thing" intended by it. I remark in passing that for Freud the thing tends to have the implicit meaning of "objective fact" (although he recognizes in principle the unknowableness of Kant's "thing in itself"), whereas in the view presented here the thing varies with the level or degree of differentiation of the mental activity that enters into an experience.

ideas—which will later become the basic concepts of the science—are still more indispensable as the material is further worked over. They must at first necessarily possess some degree of indefiniteness. . . . So long as they remain in this condition, we come to an understanding about their meaning (*Bedeutung*) by making repeated references to the material of observation from which they appear to have been derived, but upon which, in fact, they have been imposed.[9]

. . . everything depends on their not being arbitrarily chosen but determined by their having significant relations to the empirical material, relations that we seem to sense before we can clearly recognize and demonstrate them. It is only after more thorough investigation of the field of observation that we are able to formulate its basic scientific concepts with increased precision, and progressively so to modify them that they become serviceable and consistent over a wide area. Then, indeed, the time may have come to confine them in definitions. The advance of knowledge, however, does not tolerate any rigidity even in definitions. Physics furnishes an excellent illustration of the way in which even "basic concepts" that have been established in the form of definitions are constantly being altered in their content.

What psychoanalysis needs might not be a "new language" but a less inhibited, less pedantic and narrow understanding and interpretation of its current language, leading to elaborations and transformations of the meanings of concepts, theoretical formulations, or definitions that may or may not have been envisaged by Freud. Words, including concepts used in science, are living and enlivening entities in their authentic function. In their interactions with "things" to which they refer, they are informed with increased or transformed meaning as these things become better known, even as words and concepts inform things with increased and transformed meaning. This must be heard in the term hypercathexis, although Freud appeared to speak merely of some form of intensification or heightening of cathexis in terms

---

9. The German text of the last sentence reads: "*Solange sie sich in diesem Zustande befinden, verständigt man sich über ihre Bedeutung durch den wiederholten Hinweis auf das Erfahrungsmaterial, dem sie entnommen scheinen, das aber in Wirklichkeit ihnen unterworfen wird.*" A more precise translation would be: "So long as they remain in this condition, we arrive at an agreement about their meaning by repeated references to the material of observation from which they appear to have been derived, but which actually has been subjected to them." *Sich verständigen* means to come to an agreement, a *mutual* understanding about something.

of a quantitative energy influx. Words have a potential for development and change of meaning while remaining the same words, just as things have that potential while remaining "the same." Their potentials are realized to the extent to which they engage in live interplay with each other. Concepts tend to become dead issues by narrow-minded exegesis.

What I have said also applies to the definition of metapsychology itself, although I dislike the term and am looking for a better one. In other words, I do not wish to imply that there is no room for new concepts and terms and no point in eliminating inadequate ones. Nor do I imply that definitions and precise formulations of concepts are useless.[10]

I shall briefly attempt to reformulate the meaning of the terms cathexis and primary and secondary process, and in this connection I'll reconsider the concepts preconscious and conscious (see also my paper "Perspectives on Memory," 1976). I begin with *cathexis,* especially in regard to object-cathexis and narcissistic cathexis. The notion of cathexis, as Freud used the terms *Besetzung* and *besetzen* in his theoretical writings, implies preexistent entities—whether objects or intrapsychic presentations (or memory traces)—that are infused or invested with instinctual energy. It assumes a ready-made external reality (objects) and a ready-made psychic apparatus, to which some instinctual charge is supplied. The entities so cathected would remain what they were before but would now be equipped with some charge or supercharge (hypercathexis). In my explication of hypercathexis I already tacitly changed this conception. In his later writings Freud arrived at a different understanding of the relations between ego (subject) and external reality, according to which they differentiate from and organize each other instead of being seen as accomplished facts *ab initio.* This is explicitly stated in the first chapter of *Civilization and Its Discontents* (1930). The understanding of perception as an interactive, not purely passive, process goes in the same direction. The implications for the concept of cathexis, however, were not spelled out.

10. Discussions of psychoanalytic concepts and terms, outstanding for their thoroughness and sophisticated, flexible approach, are presented in "The Language of Psychoanalysis" by Laplanche and Pontalis (1967).

In the light of such considerations, and others that would lead us too far afield here, I propose to interpret cathexis as a concept for organizing activity (in contrast to what might somewhat facetiously be described as a fuel-injection notion). Applied to object-cathexis and narcissistic cathexis this means: object-cathexis is not the investment of an object with some energy charge, but an organizing mental act (instinctual in origin) that structures available material as an object, i.e., as an entity differentiated and relatively distant from the organizing agent. Such a cathexis creates—and in subsequent, secondary cathecting activities re-creates and reorganizes—the object *qua* object. It is *objectifying* cathexis. Once objects are organized as objects in an initial cathecting act, they are then maintained or restructured in different ways by further objectifying cathexes. Narcissistic cathexis (in its metapsychological sense) is not investment of a pre-existing ego or self with some energy charge, but a mental act (instinctual in origin) in which "available material" is not differentiated from the cathecting agent, not distanced in the cathecting act; the cathexis is *identificatory*, not objectifying. Narcissistic cathexis, then, contributes to the organization and reorganization of an ego or self, as object-cathexis contributes to the organization and reorganization of an object–world. The object character of an object may be dissolved, as it were, through narcissistic, identificatory, cathecting activity if an identification "with the object" takes place.

There are all kinds of gradations, intermediate states, and interminglings of these two cathexes. Winnicott's transitional objects (or "possessions") and Kohut's self–object would be examples of such. Insofar as primary process implies lack of differentiation, narcissistic cathexis would be closely related to primary process, while object-cathexis, i.e., objectifying cathexis, would be related to secondary process. These last statements are tentative. I am on uncertain ground here; significant modifications and qualifications are likely to be required.

According to this interpretation of cathexis, there is not a given structure—object or object-representation—that is invested with a charge of psychic energy. Instead, these very structures come into being, are maintained and restructured by virtue of objectifying cathexis. Similarly, such "psychic structures" as ego or superego come into being, are maintained and modified by virtue of narcissistic cathexis.[11] Winnicott (1967, p. 371) and Kohut (1971, pp. 26, 39n.1), I believe, think about cathexis along similar lines.

The primary process has been called primary because it is developmentally the first, the earliest form of mentation, and because it is seen as more primitive than secondary process. But the process is *primary* in a deeper sense insofar as it is unitary, non-differentiating, non-discriminating between various elements or components of a global event or experience. Thinking in terms of elements or components of an experience or act already bespeaks secondary process thinking. In primary process mentation *oneness,* as against duality or multiplicity, is dominant. In secondary-process mentation *duality* and multiplicity are dominant, i.e., differentiation, division, a splitting of what was unitary, global, unstructured oneness. Earlier I spoke of the original uniform density conveyed in primary process, a density that may become reconstituted from secondary process differentiation by regressive condensation, as it occurs in repression. I also explained that the secondary process consists not simply in splitting, dividing, discriminating—the word *diacritic* in Spitz's "diacritic perception" refers to the same phenomenon—but that in this same act the original wholeness is kept alive by an articulating integration that makes a textured totality out of a global one. What was homogeneous becomes a manifold whose elements are linked together. A weakening of these links, of this connectedness, can occur that may culminate in a virtual rupture, a fragmentation of experience and thought.

Developed language is a preeminent vehicle for articulating complex experiences or thought processes, for making explicit their elements and the mutual connections between these elements, for "scanning" experience and thought point by point, thus rendering present their immanent textured structure. Without language or some other sensory-motor means or vehicle for articulating mentation, conditions are ripe for primary process. But language itself arises out of the homogeneous "thing-presen-

11. This view of narcissistic cathexis is in disagreement with Hartmann's definition of narcissism as cathexis of the self (a definition adopted by Kohut) for the reasons stated above. See Loewald (1973) for a brief discussion.

tation" or primary-process experience. Therefore words and sentences, while bringing to the fore the textured linkedness in experience and thought, themselves become linked to concrete experience in as much as secondary-process mentation differentiates vocables out of homogeneous experience as elements linked to it. I described how the mother's talking with the baby gives vocal accentuation to his experience that gradually becomes a separate but linked aspect of that experience.[12] Although in a derivative form, based on far more articulate modes of mentation to begin with, something similar takes place every time we first learn a word for a thing. In such learning, much of the time, the word is not simply added to the thing, but the thing itself becomes first defined or delimited as an alive circumscribed entity (hypercathexis). The emotional relationship to the person from whom the word is learned plays a significant, in fact crucial, part in how alive the link between thing and word turns out to be. Language, and any other mode of symbolization (visual representation, music, dance), in the course of its development may take on a life of its own, evolving its own laws in accordance with its particular sensory-motor possibilities and the limits set by them. But this "life of its own" nevertheless remains imperceptibly tied to and fed by the global experiences from which it has segregated, while at the same time giving them newly disclosed meaning.[13]

The primary form of mental acts is called unconscious, the secondary form preconscious. I shall attempt to clarify the meaning of the word *conscious,* contained in these two basic terms of psychoanalytic theory, by going beyond the ordinary understanding of consciousness as conscious awareness. Although Freud briefly mentioned the possibility of unconscious percep-

12. In language as it is used in religious service, there seems to be a tension toward such an early form of experiencing by virtue of its sing-song quality and the fact that frequently words of an ancient language are used, ununderstandable or indistinct in their specific meanings to the congregation. The ununderstood words, for the trusting, child-like congregation merge into the global religious experience.

13. For a detailed and most perceptive and illuminating study of language from a developmental point of view, I wish to call attention again to Werner and Kaplan's book on *Symbol Formation* (1963). In one sense it can be described as a treatise on the relationship between "things" and "words" or their "presentations." A lengthy quotation (with discussion) from Hellen Keller's autobiography beautifully illustrates and elaborates on the above remarks on the learning of words (pp. 110–12).

tion,[14] he generally adhered to the notion that consciousness and perception are inextricably tied together. In his dominant thought, perception is a conscious, purely passive-receptive phenomenon (occurring in the system Pcpt./Cs.). Secondly, he understands consciousness itself as a perceptual phenomenon in the just mentioned sense of perception (although he considers the possibility that consciousness involves further hypercathexis). Thirdly, he thinks of consciousness as conscious awareness.

I proposed earlier to think of the perceptual act as a psychical act "in which the continuum of memorial, reproductive activity interacts with novelty" (see p. 183). Novelty need not be material encountered in external sense-perception. In so-called inner perception the material would be internal. Nor does novelty, in the sense intended here, imply that what is encountered is brand-new and has never been met before, but only that the interaction itself, the encounter, is new, takes place now ("new" and "now" are etymologically related). We should therefore correct our definition by saying: the perceptual act is an act in which a novel, present interaction takes place between the continuum of memorial activity and material, differentiated from that activity (thus defined, we could not see identification as involving [diacritic] perception). Furthermore, I do not assume that a perceptual act is necessarily characterized by conscious awareness, nor that the word conscious *a priori* or only means conscious awareness.

The word conscious derives from the Latin *conscius, conscire,* to know together. In secondary-process mentation the differentiation of uniform experience involves a knowing-together (as belonging together) of the now differentiating elements of that experience. The hypercathecting linking of the elements, in our case of thing-presentation and corresponding word-presentations, is a perceptual act, an act of *con-scire.* The linking is a knowing-together, but a *con-scire* that is not necessarily itself known in and by the linking activity, it may happen unbeknownst to the ego or self that is engaged in this *con-scire.* Freud has called that kind of linking mentation *pre-conscious.* Traditionally, what has been emphasized about preconscious menta-

14. "It is a very remarkable thing that the Ucs. of one human being can react upon that of another, without passing through the Cs. This deserves closer investigation, especially with a view to finding out whether preconscious activity can be excluded as playing a part in it; but descriptively speaking, the fact is incontestable" (1915b, p. 194).

tion—and the prefix *pre-* suggests it—is its being a stage preliminary and close to conscious awareness, but that the attribute of awareness is lacking. If the word conscious is taken in the sense explained above, the positive characteristic of "preconscious" mentation comes into relief, namely, that in contrast to dynamically unconscious mental processes, it is a differentiating-linking, a *con-scire.* Conscious awareness[15] and verbal expression of dynamically unconscious, primary process mentation is possible, as we know from psychotic and certain other forms of verbal productions. Unconscious mental processes may be known to the ego, although the inner, preconscious *con-scire* is absent. Conscious awareness of psychic reality is not contingent on a preliminary stage of preconscious elaboration of unconscious material. In order to stress the secondary-process *con-scire* in "preconscious" mentation and to distinguish this radical meaning of conscious from the common sense meaning of self-awareness, I propose to call secondary-process mentation *con-scient* and to speak of conscient instead of preconscious mental processes. Dynamically unconscious mental processes (primary process) are non-conscient, but they may under certain circumstances be known to the subject and verbalized in that non-conscient mode of mentation.

It is to be noted that the distinction between identification and object-choice (libidinal object-cathexis) runs parallel to that between unconscious and conscient mentation. These two distinctions refer to the same mental development, the former seen from the instinctual-affective, the latter from the cognitive side. The dichotomy of instinctual-affective and cognitive mental life, of course, is itself a distinction arising in secondary-process mentation.

III

In the concluding part of this study I shall very briefly consider that aspect of language which I will call here its magical-

---

15. Freud thought that conscious awareness involves the institution of a second "censorship between the Pcs. and the Cs.," "that becoming conscious is no mere act of perception [perception understood here as purely passive-receptive], but is probably also a *hypercathexis*, a further advance in the psychical organization" (1915b, p. 194; Freud's italics).

evocative function or quality. This aspect brings us close again to primary process. It lets us see most clearly that there is no simple, one-to-one relationship between, on the one hand, primary process and thing-presentation, and, on the other, between secondary process and word-presentations. Freud and other analysts, notably Ferenczi, have been well aware of this aspect of language. But psychoanalytic theory, to the limited extent to which it has dealt with language, has concerned itself mainly with its specific function in the development of discursive, conceptual, rational thought, consonant with Freud's valuation of scientific-rational thought as the highest form of human mentation. Partly because of this circumstance, and because of his having to embark on a fight against the prevailing equation of mind and consciousness, a distorting polarization of primary and secondary process was created. Freud recognized and combatted the cognitive-intellectualistic bias of psychology and of the dominant trends in philosophy of his formative years. But he was and remained firmly committed to a rationalistic-scientific *Weltanschauung*. One only has to read the last of his *New Introductory Lectures on Psychoanalysis* (1933).

When we think of the magical-evocational aspects of language we are concerned with the *power* of words. We are dealing then with words, not insofar as they refer to or are linked with things, but as embodying and summoning things and experiences, as bringing them to life. The relation of reference or signification, from this perspective, is merely a pale reflection, a faint echo, a highly derivative form of that original power of words to conjure up things. This power of words is intimately related to their being physical, sensory-motor events or acts. Poets and those concerned with words as the medium of poetry are keenly aware of this essential condition of words. The poet Mallarmé said: "Approaching the organism that is the repository of life, the word with its vowels and diphthongs represents a kind of flesh" (as quoted by Raymond). Raymond, in his book on modern French poetry (1947), speaks of the poetic word as "an instrument of power. Its aim is to move, in the most emphatic sense of the word, to shake the soul to its ultimate depths, to promote the birth and metamorphosis of 'open' reveries, capable of operating freely and indefinitely" (pp. 25–26). He quotes

Mallarmé as saying that "between the old methods of magic and the sorcery which poetry will remain, there exists a secret parity" (p. 26). The French poet and writer Paul Valéry, in his Oxford lecture on "Poetry and Abstract Thought" (1939, p. 75), referring to a poetic line of Baudelaire, speaks of "the inestimable value of a spell." He continues:

the momentary being who made that line could not have done so had he been in a state where the form and the content occurred separately to his mind. On the contrary, he was in a special phase in the domain of his psychic existence, a phase in which the sound and the meaning of the word, acquire or keep an equal importance—which is excluded from the habits of practical language, as from the needs of abstract language. The state in which the inseparability of sound and sense, in which the desire, the expectation, the possibility of their intimate and indissoluble fusion are required and sought or given, and sometimes anxiously awaited, is a comparatively rare state. It is rare, firstly because all the exigencies of life are against it; secondly because it is opposed to the crude simplifying and specializing of verbal notations.

At another point (p. 74) he speaks

of the miracles and prodigies of ancient magic. It must not be forgotten that for centuries poetry was used for purposes of enchantment. Those who took part in these strange operations had to believe in the power of the word, and far more in the efficacy of its sound than in its significance.

Ferenczi, in his paper "On Obscene Words" (1911, p. 137) writes: "An obscene word has a peculiar power of compelling the hearer to imagine the object it denotes, the sexual organ or function, *in substantial actuality*" (*in dinglicher Wirklichkeit*; Ferenczi's italics). He goes on to say that "obscene words have attributes which all words must have possessed in some early stage of psychical development" (p. 138). He describes how "abstract thought, thinking in words" develops out of such "imagining in substantial actuality," as memory images (*Erinnerungsbilder*) get to "being represented merely by certain qualitative remains of these images, the speech-signs." He adds (p. 139):

. . . it seems that speech-signs replacing images, i.e., words, retain for a considerable time a certain tendency to regression, which we can picture to ourselves in a gradually diminishing degree, until the capacity is attained for "abstract" imagination and thought that is almost completely free from hallucinatory perceptual elements.[16]

The magical, compelling power of words is not confined to forcing the listener to imagine the object "in substantial actuality." Language in its primordial form has the power or the significance of *action* for the *speaker*. Ferenczi, following Freud, speaks of the "original source of all speech in omitted action," adding that "on uttering an obscene joke we still have the definite feeling of initiating an act" (1911, p. 141). In other words, the power of obscene and other primordial words may be such that in the experience of the utterer the act is not omitted but committed. Frequently the listener, too, experiences obscene jokes as sexual aggression. I mentioned earlier Freud's remark that primitive man treats "words in every sense as things" (1913, p. 56), and he points out that for primitive man and for our own children, as well as for certain neurotics and to an extent for ourselves, names are important parts or possessions of the person. The same is true for words that name things. The word as a name evokes or summons the thing or person, renders them present "in substantial actuality." And the word, as an action, as naming, affects the "thing" it is addressed to because the word carries the "substantial actuality" (*dingliche Wirklichkeit*) of action.[17]

All of this is related to what I earlier pointed out about the

16. Ernest Jones, Ferenczi's translator, alternates in his translation of the German verb *vorstellen* and the nouns *Vorstellen* and *Vorstellung*. At one point he translates *Vorstellen* as "act of mental representation," at another point as "imagination." *Vorstellung* is translated as "image" in the passage quoted above; but "image" also functions as a translation for *Bild*. In the Standard Edition of Freud's works *Vorstellung* is usually rendered as "presentation" or "idea." The verb *vorstellen* is rendered by Jones as "imagine," whereas it usually is translated as "present" or "represent." The basic reason for this seeming confusion is that *Vorstellung* and *vorstellen* (literally: that which is set before oneself, and: to set before oneself) are used in the more concrete sense of inner visual or auditory image (*Bild*), as well as in the more abstract sense rendered by "presentation," "representation," or "idea." Ferenczi describes the latter as "*abstraktes Vorstellen und Denken*" which "is almost completely free from hallucinatory perceptual elements." Depending then on the degree of abstraction involved in *Vorstellung*, the sense of the word varies (in German, *Vorstellung* is also used in the sense of a stage performance as an action set before an audience).

17. *Ding* (in *dingliche Wirklichkeit*) must be understood in the same broad sense in which Freud uses *Sache* in *Sachvorstellung*. The German *Wirklichkeit* (actuality, reality) through its root word *wirken* connotes concrete action or efficacy; it is related to the English "work."

original unity of thing and vocables when the mother's flow of talking with the infant and the growing child's own utterances are still undifferentiated or poorly differentiated ingredients of global experience. Words in their original or recovered power do not function then as signs or symbols for (as referring to) something other than themselves, but as being of the same substance, the same actual efficacy as that which they name; they embody it in a specific sensory-motor medium. The sensory-motor elements of speech remain bodily ingredients of language, lending to words and sentences the aspect of concrete acts and entities that Ferenczi mentions. This aspect continues to dwell in language, although unattended to, even in its most abstract use, and in written and read language and "inner speech" as well.

I shall not discuss here the distinction between sign and symbol, despite its great importance for the understanding of language, nor the theory of symbolism.[18] Suffice it to say that the traditional, unduly narrow use of the symbol concept in psychoanalysis has more recently been criticized by analysts themselves, especially by those influenced by Melanie Klein. But already Fenichel pointed out the difference between "archaic symbolism as a part of prelogical thinking" and the traditional psychoanalytic notion of symbolism as a "distortion by means of representing a repressed idea through a conscious symbol" (1945, p. 48). This distinction clearly relates to the "ambiguity" in the concept of primary process discussed by Gill (1967).

In the course of the development of civilization, of the variegated ways in which language becomes both reduced and elevated to a vehicle for civilized human communication and expression of thoughts and feelings and for abstract thought, the primordial power and concrete impact of language become attenuated and relatively neutralized, as the density of the primary process gives way to the discursiveness and articulation of secondary process. In the most creative forms of language, such as in its authentic religious use, in oratory, poetry, and dramatic

---

18. For an illuminating discussion of this distinction and its relevance to language as magic see Werner and Kaplan (1963), pp. 35 ff., pp. 110 ff.). Regarding primitive mental life in general see Heinz Werner's *Comparative Psychology of Mental Development* (1948). For discussions by psychoanalysts on symbolism, apart from Jones's well-known paper (1916), see Milner (1952), Rodrigué (1956), and Rycroft (1956), among others.

art, the primordial power of language comes again to the fore. In great poetry and creative prose—quite consciously in much of modern literature—there is an interweaving of primary and secondary process by virtue of which language functions as a transitional mode encompassing both. We may say that language, being a vehicle for secondary process or conscient mentation, being a medium of hypercathexis that creates higher organization, in its most genuine and autonomous function is a binding power. It ties together human beings and self and object world, and it binds abstract thought with the bodily concreteness and power of life. In the word primary and secondary process are reconciled.

Let me conclude with Paul Valéry. "Poetry is an attempt to represent or to restore, by articulate language, those things or that thing, which tears, cries, caresses, kisses, sighs, etc., try obscurely to express" (as quoted by Raymond, 1947, p. 156). Of the word in its essential function he says: "It enjoins upon us to come into being much more than it stimulates us to understand" (p. 26).

Dare I say that at propitious moments this may happen in a psychoanalytic hour?

REFERENCES

Fenichel, O. (1945): *The Psychoanalytic Theory of Neurosis*. New York: W. W. Norton.
Ferenczi, S. (1911): On obscene words. In: *Sex in Psychoanalysis. Contributions to Psychoanalysis*. Trans. E. Jones. New York: Robert Brunner, 1950, pp. 132–53.
Freud, S. (1913): Totem and taboo. S.E. 13:1–161.
_____. (1915a): Instincts and their vicissitudes. S.E. 14: 109–40.
_____. (1915b): The unconscious. S.E. 14:159–215.
_____. (1917): A metapsychological supplement to the theory of dreams. S.E. 14:217–35.
_____. (1923): The ego and the id. S.E. 19:1–66.
_____. (1925a): A note on the "mystic writing pad." S.E. 19: 225–32.
_____. (1925b): Negation. S.E. 19:233–39.
_____. (1930): Civilization and its discontents. S.E. 21:57–145.

_____. (1933): New introductory lectures on psychoanalysis. S.E. 22:5–182.

Gill, M. (1967): The primary process. In: *Psychological Issues* 5, No. 2/3. Monograph 18/19. New York: International Universities Press, pp. 260–98.

Jones, E. (1916): The theory of symbolism. In: *Papers on Psychoanalysis.* 5th ed. Baltimore: The Williams & Wilkins Co., 1948.

Keller, H. (1903): *The Story of My Life.* New York: Doubleday, Page.

Kohut, H. (1971): *The Analysis of the Self.* New York: International Universities Press.

Laplanche, J., and J.-B. Pontalis (1967): *The Language of Psychoanalysis.* Trans. from the French by D. Nicholson-Smith. New York: W. W. Norton, 1973.

Loewald, H. W. (1960): On the therapeutic action of psychoanalysis. *Int. J. Psychoanal.* 41:16–33 (reprinted in this volume).

_____. (1973): Book review: The analysis of the self, by H. Kohut. *Psychoanal. Quart.* 42:441–51 (reprinted in this volume).

_____. (1976): Perspectives on memory. *Psychological Issues* 9, no. 4. Monograph 36. New York: International Universities Press, pp. 298–325 (reprinted in this volume).

Milner, M. (1952): Aspects of symbolism in comprehension of the not-self. *Int. J. Psychoanal.* 33:181–95.

Raymond, M. (1947): *From Baudelaire to Surrealism.* Trans. from the French. New York: Wittenborn, Schultz, Inc., 1950.

Rodrigué, E. (1956): Notes on symbolism. *Int. J. Psychoanal.* 37: 147–58.

Rycroft, C. (1956): Symbolism and its relationship to the primary and secondary process. *Int. J. Psychoanal.* 37:137–46.

Spitz, R. (1965): *The First Year of Life.* New York: International Universities Press.

Valéry, P. (1939): Poetry and abstract thought. In: *The Art of Poetry.* Trans. from the French by Denise Folliot. New York: Vintage Books, 1961 (Collected Works of Paul Valéry, vol. 7, Bollingen Foundation).

Webster's International Dictionary (1958): 2d ed.

Werner, H. (1948): *Comparative Psychology of Mental Development.* New York: Science Editions, Inc., 1961.

Werner, H., and B. Kaplan (1963): *Symbol Formation. An Organismic-Developmental Approach to Language and the Expression of Thought.* New York: John Wiley & Sons.

Winnicott, D. W. (1967): The location of cultural experience. *Int. J. Psychoanal.* 48:368–72.

13

INSTINCT THEORY, OBJECT RELATIONS, AND PSYCHIC STRUCTURE FORMATION

I can best pay tribute to Margaret Mahler's outstanding contributions to psychoanalysis in honor of her 80th birthday, by presenting some facets of my own work in psychoanalytic theory and its conceptualization. I trust that in the course of my presentation, necessarily quite brief and condensed, it will become apparent how much I owe to her observations and concepts, although my conceptual language in a number of ways differs from hers. I know how much I have learned from her ways of perceiving psychological material with the eyes, ears, and other perceptual organs of a psychoanalyst, while I often organize such data in a somewhat different, but I believe congenial, manner. In part this is the case because my psychoanalytic experience is based exclusively on therapeutic work with adults, however regressed or infantile they may have been in aspects of their personalities. In part the differences, not in approach but in conceptualization, derive from my abiding special preoccupation with certain issues of psychoanalytic theory and concept formation, issues that have not been in the forefront of her work.

I shall define, provisionally, individuation as that group of psychic processes or activities by which the separateness of subject and object as distinct psychic organizations becomes increasingly established. Since the formulation of the structural theory, the organization of the mind or personality has progressively been conceived of as a more or less orderly sequence, and

Paper presented at the Margaret Mahler Symposium on "Symbiosis and Separation—Individuation Theory and Instinct Theory," Philadelphia, Pa., May 21, 1977. The Symposium was organized by the Department of Psychiatry, Section of Child Psychiatry, Medical College of Pennsylvania, and The Children's Unit, Eastern Pennsylvania Psychiatric Institute, and co-sponsored by the Philadelphia Psychoanalytic Institute and the Philadelphia Psychoanalytic Society.

synthesis, of differentiating-integrative processes by which id, ego, and superego become constituted as the three substructures of the individual psyche.

These processes begin with the differentiating activities taking place within the "dual unity" of the infant–mother psychic matrix, equivalent to Mahler's early symbiotic phase. In terms of the structural theory, individuation can be described as the total of the activities culminating in psychic-structure formation. Individuation or intrapsychic-structure formation is brought about, not by unilateral activities on the part of the infant organism, but by interactions taking place at first within the infant–mother unitary field, and progressively between elements that become more autonomous as differentiating activities within that field progress. The mother's various ministrations to the infant, although prompted by biological necessities and interactions of infant and mother, are organized on a far more advanced level of mentation than that of the infant's incipient mentation. They begin to organize his vital processes in such a way that one can more and more speak of the infant's *instinctual* life in contrast to a purely biological life with its physiological prerequisites. Following a formulation of Freud's—to which he himself and other analytic theorists have not consistently adhered—I define instinct (or instinctual drive) here as a *psychic representative* of biological stimuli or processes, and not as these biological stimuli themselves. In contradistinction to Freud's thought in "Instincts and Their Vicissitudes" (1915, pp. 121–22), however, I do not speak of biological stimuli impinging on a ready-made "psychic apparatus" in which their psychic representatives are thus created, but of interactional biological processes that find higher organization on levels which we have come to call psychic life. Understood as psychic phenomena or representatives, instincts come into being in the early organizing mother–infant interactions. They form the most primitive level of human mentation and motivation. In their totality, and as mental life progresses toward more complex organization of different levels of mentation and interplay between them, instincts constitute the id as distinguishable from ego and superego. Thus I conceive instincts (considered in the framework of psychoanalytic psychology), and the id as a psychic structure, as originating in interactions of the infantile organism and its human environment (mother), that is, in what Mahler calls the dual unity of the infant–mother symbiosis.

As for ego as a psychic substructure, and superego, they too, although on already more complexly organized levels of inter-action, come into being as resultants of interactions of the indi-viduating child and its human environment. Internalization of such interactions leads to their formation. Perhaps this was more readily acknowledged in respect to the superego, because Freud began his investigations into the process we now call internalization by studying the phenomena of identification as they came to light in the area of ideal formation and superego development. But it is equally true of the ego as a coherent or-ganization that it is formed in those primary identifications taking place during pre-oedipal stages.

Several implications of this view of things should be briefly indicated. If individuation is defined as that group of processes by which increasing separateness of subject and object comes about, it means that, in and by these processes, both subject and object (in early stages, mother as object) become organized in the child's mental experience as more or less distinct entities. As I have expressed it elsewhere (Loewald, 1962, pp. 492-93), in regard to early differentiating activities internalization and ex-ternalization are processes by which internality and externality first become constituted. I shall return to this point.

I do not agree with the view that memory, perception, reality testing, etc., are ego functions pure and simple that do not have their origin and their equivalents in instinctual life. In this sense I do not see that there are ego apparatuses with primary auton-omy. Perception and memory in their primitive conformations, which remain basic ingredients of their later transformations, are unconscious instinctual activities, aspects of libidinal proc-esses that only later gain a comparatively autonomous status. Expressed differently: in assuming an undifferentiated phase, instinctual in nature, from which id and ego differentiate, we assume undifferentiated libidinal-aggressive processes that bi-furcate into what we can eventually distinguish as instinctual-affective life and cognitive functions. In such bifurcation the original global functioning, although dominated and overshad-owed by specialized modes of functioning, remains preserved: libidinal-aggressive elements remain ingredients of perception and memory, considered as ego functions, and constitute the unconscious motivational aspect of the latter. On the other hand, cognitive aspects remain implicit in affective life, being from the beginning undifferentiated aspects of instinctual processes.

I think that the now commonly accepted definition of psychic structures as simply different groups of mental functions is not tenable. Take the ego as example: the ego is not defined as a structure by having functions such as memory, perception, reality testing, etc., but by its being a coherent organization on a certain level of mental functioning. It is its *mode of functioning*, which is due to its particular differentiation and integration of mental activities and "percepts," that makes us speak of it as a psychic structure distinct from the other structures. In general, the character of being a structure is not determined by the fact that certain components are simply grouped together, whether these components are functions or material parts, but by the interrelations of the components as dominated by the organization of the whole, by the particular principles of arrangement and mutual relatedness of its component elements. We approach a psychoanalytic understanding of the structuredness or organization of a structure such as the ego or superego by understanding how it has come about, i.e., in terms of its genesis—granted that later factors may, and normally do, greatly modify and make more complex its organization and functioning. This is surely one of the reasons why we concern ourselves so much with early development. It is not only in order to understand children, but adults as well. I am not speaking in favor of reductionism. There is a vast difference between, on the one hand, deriving something from its origins and antecedents, thus reconstructing its structure and functioning, and, on the other hand, reducing some now extant structure to its original rudiments, as though no development had taken place. Without focusing on such reconstruction, we will never understand the unconscious organization and aspects of the human mind, or how where id was, ego may come into being.

It is quite likely that the notion of psychic structures being defined by their functions is due, at least in part, to confusion between the concepts of functioning, function, and process. We speak of a psychic structure as a functioning unit that can be said to be extant only inasmuch as it functions, unlike a material structure such as a building, which, if abandoned, has no function while remaining that material structure. It is one thing to say that psychic structures can be perceived or conceived as structures only insofar as they function, that they each are differently organized modalities of psychic activity or functioning. It is quite another thing to maintain that they each are clusters of specified mental functions.

Regarding process, it is true that we recognize immediately, in contrast to material structures, the process nature of psychic structures. Their structuredness consists in particularly organized activity patterns, and not in arrangements of component elements that would have the nature of material particles of some kind. Apparently the definition of psychic structures as groups of *functions* has to do with our direct awareness of the process character of psychic structures. However, while functions spell activity and process, function and process are concepts with different meanings. That functions manifest themselves in activities, have process character, and that psychic structures are process-structures par excellence, does not mean that psychic structures are groups of mental functions. Different psychic structures are characterized by different ways of *functioning*; they perform mental functions in differently organized process-patterns and configurations, rather than performing different mental functions. Sphincter morality (Ferenczi), for example, shows how what we tend to single out as superego function operates (functions) on a primitive level of mentation, that is, on a level of mentation earlier than and different from superego organization and its particular mental process-structure.

If id, ego, and superego have their origins in interactions with environment that are internalized, interactions transposed to a new arena, thus becoming intrapsychic interactions, then psychic-structure formation and individuation are dependent on *object relations*. The separateness of subject and object—I am not speaking of the objective separateness of two biological organisms—becomes established by way of internalization and externalization processes in which both infant and mother participate, and, later, the child and its broadening human environment. Disturbances of internalizing and externalizing processes, caused by deficiencies—for whatever reasons—in the

vicissitudes of attunement between child and human environment, spell disturbance of individuation, of psychic-structure
formation. Mahler's clinical research work furnishes many examples of such disturbances due to disharmonies between child
and mother both in the early symbiotic phase and in the separation–individuation subphases of differentiation, practicing, rapprochement, etc.

Individuation, the organization of instincts, of id, ego, and
superego, I have said, is dependent on object relations. The term
object relations is by tradition used in a loose and rather impre-
cise way in psychoanalysis. It comprises the relations between
child and adult—and the human environment, regardless of the
level of psychic development on which these relations occur.
Psychoanalytic theory makes the important distinctions between
object choice and identification and between object cathexis and
narcissistic cathexis. If we keep these distinctions in mind, and
if we consider more closely the concepts ego (self, subject) and
object, it becomes apparent that not all relations between child
or adult and human environment are relations between a subject
and an object. We have learned from psychoanalytic child observation and from the so-called narcissistic personality disorders
that what for an observer is an object related to a subject, may
be, for the infant or narcissistic patient, an aspect or part of himself or unspecified as to inside or outside, subject or object.

Let me give a brief clinical illustration. Some years ago I had a
patient in his middle twenties in analysis who suffered from a
narcissistic character disorder with depressive and hysterical
features. We had established a fragile rapport consisting mainly
in a volatile, easily disrupted empathic bond, with subtle indications of a powerfully demanding attitude on the patient's part,
reminiscent of the nonverbal demanding quality of a small child's
ties to his mother. Some of the patient's precarious object relations in current life had begun to come under our scrutiny. Over
one weekend I had a slight accident which made it necessary to
wear my left arm in a sling, but which did not interfere, as far as I
was aware, with attending to my work and my patients; I was
not in pain. On the following Monday I saw all my patients. With
the patient under discussion there immediately occurred a palpable disruption of our rapport. I briefly explained to him the
reason for the sling. He was able to tell me, in vague language,

that he experienced me as not being there and that he himself felt lifeless, without feelings or thoughts. Then he lapsed into silence. After some reflection I told the patient that I thought what he experienced must be like the experience of a small boy when his mother, of whom he is in need, is sick and appears unavailable; for him she then no longer exists, and together with this the boy then no longer feels alive, or dissolves. This interpretation led to gradual re-establishment of contact and of his functioning.

In her book *On Human Symbiosis and the Vicissitudes of Individuation* Mahler writes (1968, p. 220): "The danger situation in the symbiotic phase is loss of the symbiotic object, which amounts, at that stage, to loss of an integral part of the ego itself, and thus constitutes a threat of self-annihilation." Assuming the essential correctness of my interpretation, one may formulate the state of affairs, using Mahler's terms, as follows: the therapist, in this context a symbiotic object for the patient, is suddenly lost, having become a strange, unattached figure; and this coincides with, or is the same as, loss of self or annihilation. With the loss of the symbiotic object "an integral part of the ego itself" is lost. To put it in somewhat different terms, ego and object are not sufficiently differentiated, on the then dominant level of the patient's mentation, for him to experience a difference between ego and object. The patient seemed not to be bereft or anxious, but deadened. I should prefer to conceptualize this, not as a loss of symbiotic object and integral ego-part, but as a disintegration of nondifferentiated ego/object. As nondifferentiated, ego or self (I use these terms here interchangeably) and object are, so to speak, consubstantial. Disintegration of the meaningful organization of the object *is* disintegration of the ego and vice versa, insofar as they are identical in experience. This unitary organization or structure (the so-called self–object, Kohut 1971), in the developmental phase Mahler calls the symbiotic phase, is brought about and maintained by the conjoint organizing activities of mother and infant. The more this conjoint activity is dependent on the mother's contribution, that is, the more the infant is still at the mercy of his mother's organizing psychic activity for his own to be viable, the less is there differentiation of ego from object as different structures. If for some reason, as in the case of my patient, the object falls apart as a meaning-giving and meaning-ful agent, then the patient's ego disintegrates because the symbiotic object and the ego are not experienced as separate or separable. My interpretation, my organizing meaning-giving activity, presumably reactivated the patient's organizing potential so that we could reconstitute the self–object as a live psychic structure. Such an organization, undifferentiated as to id–ego and ego–object, could not be called an intrapsychic structure; internality and externality are disestablished as distinguishable worlds. On the higher level of superego formation we observe similar unitary structures where internal and external authority and constraints are not yet or no longer differentiated sufficiently to speak of superego as an internal structure. Such intermediate constraints, as we can see in children as well as in many adults, are not truly intrapsychic, but are experienced by the persons involved as taking shape and having force *between* them. They are neither internal nor external; and this is so despite the fact that an internal world, an intrapsychic id and ego of significant consolidation are established.

In psychoanalytic research on early child development and during therapeutic analysis, especially with patients suffering from narcissistic disorders, we are able to observe the organization and dedifferentiation of psychic structure and object relations as ongoing processes. We can see that object relations and intrapsychic structure formation and their maintenance are intimately interrelated. And further, that there are psychic process-structures that are not intrapsychic but in an intermediate region as it were, analogous to Winnicott's transitional phenomena.

As mentioned before, in using the terms object relations, ego, object, as applied to interactional processes within the infant–mother matrix and to identificatory interactions at later stages, we speak from a standpoint that is incongruous with the level of mental organization we wish to understand and describe. The word object categorizes the human environment in terms of the adult's advanced and dominant "objective" level of mentation, a level different from that form of mentation we attempt to comprehend in psychoanalysis when we investigate archaic mental processes. It may be permissible to speak of object relations in reference to preobjective and identificatory interactions if we keep this incongruity in mind, if we remember that we deal here with phases of mental development in which subject and object are not, or not sufficiently, differentiated. Thus we are dealing with something other than two different organizations that could be said to be in a relationship to each other. Relationship, in contrast to sameness, identity, or "symbiotic fusion," implies difference, presupposes differentiation.

I provisionally defined individuation as that group of processes by which the separateness of subject and object becomes established. Obviously, this does not mean that prior to these processes ego and object were not separate but together like two entities in one container or two ideas in the same mind; or that they were so close together that we were not aware of their separateness. It means, instead, that in beginning stages there was, as far as the mentation of the infant is concerned—and it is that mentation we want to understand—only one global structure, one fleeting and very perishable mental entity that was neither ego nor object, neither a self nor another. My patient, at the time of the episode I described, because of the intensity of the transference, at least momentarily functioned on a comparable level of mentation. For the archaic layers of the mind there is no separation experience leading to differentiation, separateness, or "separation anxiety"; but, as Mahler expresses it, there is danger of annihilation, of disruption of functioning, when there is disruption of the symbiotic unity. On the other hand, during periods of physical separation of infant and mother if they are not unduly prolonged (if the infant is in a state of satisfaction), the global organization, which is neither ego nor object, is preserved. I venture to suggest that the "good enough" mother, during certain periods or moments in early motherhood, functions on a similar level of mentation. I believe that Winnicott's understanding of early development, in which he includes the mother's archaic experience level—activated by pregnancy and early motherhood—as an integral component, is in essential agreement with such a view. We also begin to realize that the therapist, in order to work analytically with patients with narcissistic disorders, must rely on his ability to reactivate such archaic levels of mental functioning within himself, at given moments during treatment. In other words, he needs the flexibility or mental agility to suspend, when required, his ego boundaries for a long enough period, if he is to understand the patient's experience and then interpret it to him. His interpretation, if adequately attuned, raises the experience to a higher level of mental organization, a level where we can more properly speak of object relations.

If we use the term object relations for any and all psychic interactions of objectively distinguishable human beings, regardless of whether or not instincts and ego are differentiated from object, then the primary datum for a genetic, psychoanalytic psychology would be object relations. This relatedness is the psychic matrix out of which intrapsychic instincts and ego, and extrapsychic object, differentiate.

I shall conclude my remarks with some comments on the "widening scope of psychoanalysis." The scope of psychoanalytic investigation and treatment was, during the earlier phase of their development, determined by those aspects of the mental life of patients that could in essence be derived from the oedipal stage at which ego and (libidinal) object are sufficiently differentiated. Already with the tracing of libido development in terms of oral, anal, phallic, and genital stages the picture began to change. But it was the investigation of psychosis, of the archaic mentality of young children, of "savages," and of group psychology (where individuation regresses) that initiated an understanding of instinctual-cognitive processes on different levels of mentation. The comprehensive title for such investigations became: analysis of the ego, i.e., of the graded levels of more or less coherent organization. Ego, at that point, was the title for the totality of these levels *considered as a comprehensive organization.* Freud at times spoke, in reference to this ego, as the *Gesamt-Ich,* "the ego as a whole" (1921, p. 130), when he wanted to distinguish it from the ego considered as counterpart to id and superego. Organization here means organizing activity as much as the totality resulting from such activity.

Analysis of the ego in this sense means: to investigate how such an encompassing and increasingly coherent organization comes into being; what are its antecedents and ingredients? What are the processes that bring about and determine this organization? It became apparent (1) that a coherent organization of some solidity was already present by the time the object relations forming the Oedipus complex and, with that, the starting point for neurotic conflict could be discerned. (2) What became known as ego defects or deficiencies and may lead to borderline and psychotic phenomena could not be understood *on* the basis of the oedipal conflict. They antedate and are apt to distort the very development of the oedipal stage and its object relations. The organizing activities leading up to the oedipal stage, themselves, and their disturbances, became the subject of analytic investigation and, if feasible, of therapeutic repetition and reconstruction in the transference.

One can speak, following Kohut (1971), of narcissistic trans-ference—or self-object transference (Kohut, 1977)—insofar as there is a relatedness, a rapport between patient and analyst, which is mainly based on an archaic form of relatedness, close to or reproducing "symbiosis," and which is repeated in or trans-ferred to the analytic situation. There is transfer of the archaic relatedness, with its blurring or lack of ego boundaries, from the pre-oedipal prototypes to given current figures and specifically to the analyst. By virtue of the undifferentiated nature of this transference such patients have difficulty not only in distin-guishing between themselves and the analyst but also between infantile and current figures, between infantile or archaic and current, more advanced levels of relatedness: not only the dif-ferentiation of internal and external, but also that of past and present is deficient. For patients with predominantly oedipal unresolved conflicts, ego and object, as well as temporal modes, are sufficiently distinguishable.

I fail to see that the attempts at therapeutic reconstruction and interpretation of these far more archaic phases and levels of mental life, when working with more deeply disturbed patients, is any less psychoanalytic than work with the classical neuroses. It only seems that way because levels of relatedness, involving both patient and analyst, come into play that are far less familiar to most of us than oedipal and postoedipal levels. And further-more, verbal interpretation itself, the mainstay of psychoana-lytic intervention, takes on connotations and aspects of meaning-fulness—of which analysts need to be aware—that derive from or hark back more directly to that "magical" power and signifi-cance of words which plays a predominant role in the preverbal and early verbal period of life and the resonance and responses of the young child to parental verbal material.[1]

1. Some of the preceding formulations grew out of recent personal communications with Calvin Settlage.

No one who has tried such work can doubt that a great deal about early and archaic mentation can be learned from it. Only further work with patients can help us answer the question of its therapeutic value in terms of lasting change. Temporary changes undoubtedly occur with adult patients of the type under discussion. But it is not clear to me whether, given the early onset of the disturbances, and in view of the primitive nature of their object relations, sufficient true internal structure formation is likely, or whether such patients periodically will require equivalents of that "refueling" Mahler et al. (1975), following Furer, describe in the practicing subphase of individuation.

REFERENCES

Freud, S. (1915): Instincts and their vicissitudes. S.E. 14:117–40.
_____. (1921): Group psychology and the analysis of the ego. S.E. 18:69–143.
Kohut, H. (1971): *The Analysis of the Self.* New York: International Universities Press.
_____. (1977): *The Restoration of the Self.* New York: International Universities Press.
Loewald, H. W. (1962): Internalization, separation, mourning, and the superego. *Psychoanal. Quart.* 31:483–504 (reprinted in this volume).
Mahler, M., and Furer, M. (1968): *On Human Symbiosis and the Vicissitudes of Individuation.* New York: International Universities Press.
_____, Pine, F., and Bergman, A. (1975): *The Psychological Birth of the Human Infant.* New York: Basic Books.

PART II.

THE PSYCHOANALYTIC PROCESS

14

ON THE THERAPEUTIC ACTION OF PSYCHOANALYSIS

Advances in our understanding of the therapeutic action of psychoanalysis should be based on deeper insight into the psychoanalytic process. By psychoanalytic process I mean the significant interactions between patient and analyst that ultimately lead to structural changes in the patient's personality. Today, after more than fifty years of psychoanalytic investigation and practice, we are in a position to appreciate, if not to understand better, the role that interaction with environment plays in the formation, development, and continued integrity of the psychic apparatus. Psychoanalytic ego psychology, based on a variety of investigations concerned with ego development, has given us some tools to deal with the central problem of the relationship between the development of psychic structures and interaction with other psychic structures, and of the connection between ego formation and object relations.

If "structural changes in the patient's personality" means anything, it must mean that we assume that ego development is resumed in the therapeutic process in psychoanalysis. And this resumption of ego development is contingent on the relationship with a new object, the analyst. The nature and the effects of this new relationship are under discussion. It should be fruitful to attempt to correlate our understanding of the significance of object relations for the formation and development of the psychic apparatus with the dynamics of the therapeutic process. A first approach to this task is made here.

Problems, however, of more or less established psychoana-

Paper presented in two parts at meetings of the Western New England Psychoanalytic Society in 1956 and 1957. Sections I and III were read at the Annual Meeting of the American Psychoanalytic Association, Chicago, 1957. Section IV was read at the 20th Congress of the International Psychoanalytical Association, Paris, 1957.

lytic theory and tradition concerning object relations, the phenomenon of transference, the relations between instinctual drives
and ego, as well as concerning the function of the analyst in the
analytic situation, have to be dealt with. I, at any rate, found it
unavoidable, for clarification of my own thinking, to diverge repeatedly from the central theme so as to deal with such problems.

The paper, therefore, is anything but a systematic presentation of the subject matter. The four parts of the paper intend to
light up the scenery from different angles, in the hope that the
central characters will be recognizable although they may scarcely
speak themselves. A more systematic approach to the subject
would also have to deal extensively with the pertinent literature,
a task which I have found impossible to assume at this time.

Before I proceed, I wish to make it clear that this is *not* a
paper on psychoanalytic technique. It does not attempt to suggest modifications or variations in technique. Psychoanalytic
technique has changed since the beginning of psychoanalysis
and is going to continue to change. A better understanding of the
therapeutic action of psychoanalysis may lead to changes in
technique, but anything such clarification may entail as far as
technique is concerned will have to be worked out carefully and
is not the topic of this paper.

I

While the fact of an object relationship between patient and
analyst is taken for granted, classical formulations concerning
therapeutic action and concerning the role of the analyst in the
analytic relationship do not reflect our present understanding of
the dynamic organization of the psychic apparatus. I speak here
of psychic apparatus and not merely of ego. I believe that modern
psychoanalytic ego psychology represents far more than an
addition to the psychoanalytic theory of instinctual drives. In
my opinion, it is the elaboration of a more comprehensive theory
of the dynamic organization of the psychic apparatus, and psychoanalysis is in the process of integrating our knowledge of
instinctual drives, gained during earlier stages of its history, into
such a psychological theory. The impact psychoanalytic ego
psychology has on the development of psychoanalysis indicates
that ego psychology is not concerned with just another part of
the psychic apparatus, but is giving a new dimension to the con-

ception of the psychic apparatus as a whole. I shall come back to this point later on.

In an analysis, I believe, we have opportunities to observe and investigate primitive as well as more advanced interaction processes, that is, interactions between patient and analyst which lead to or form steps in ego integration and disintegration. Such interactions, which I shall call integrative (and disintegrative) experiences, occur many times but do not often as such become the focus of our attention and observation, and go unnoticed. Apart from the difficulty for the analyst of self-observation while in interaction with his patient, there seems to be a specific reason, stemming from theoretical bias, why such interactions not only go unnoticed but frequently are denied. The theoretical bias is the view of the psychic apparatus as a closed system. Thus the analyst is seen, not as a co-actor on the analytic stage on which the childhood development, culminating in the infantile neurosis, is restaged and reactivated in the development, crystallization and resolution of the transference neurosis, but as a reflecting mirror, albeit of the unconscious, and characterized by scrupulous neutrality.

This neutrality of the analyst appears to be required (i) in the interest of scientific objectivity, in order to keep the field of observation from being contaminated by the analyst's own emotional intrusions; and (ii) to guarantee a *tabula rasa* for the patient's transferences. While the latter reason is closely related to the general demand for scientific objectivity and avoidance of the interference of the personal equation, it has its specific relevance for the analytic procedure as such insofar as the analyst is supposed to function not only as an observer of certain processes, but as a mirror that actively reflects back to the patient the latter's conscious and particularly his unconscious processes through verbal communication. A specific aspect of this neutrality is that the analyst must avoid falling into the role of the environmental figure (or of his opposite) the relationship to whom the patient is transferring to the analyst. Instead of falling into the assigned role, he must be objective and neutral enough to reflect back to the patient what roles the latter has assigned to the analyst and to himself in the transference situation. But such objectivity and neutrality now need to be understood more clearly as to their meaning in a therapeutic setting.

Let us take a fresh look at the analytic situation. Ego development is a process of increasingly higher integration and differentiation of the psychic apparatus and does not stop at any given point except in neurosis and psychosis; even though it is true that there is normally a marked consolidation of ego organization around the period of the Oedipus complex. Another consolidation normally takes place toward the end of adolescence, and further, often less marked and less visible, consolidations occur at various other life stages. These later consolidations—and this is important—follow periods of relative ego disorganization and reorganization, characterized by ego regression. Erikson has described certain types of such periods of ego regression with subsequent new consolidations as identity crises. An analysis can be characterized, from this standpoint, as a period or periods of induced ego disorganization and reorganization. The promotion of the transference neurosis is the induction of such ego disorganization and reorganization. Analysis is thus understood as an intervention designed to set ego development in motion, be it from a point of relative arrest, or to promote what we conceive of as a healthier direction and/or comprehensiveness of such development. This is achieved by the promotion and utilization of (controlled) regression. This regression is one important aspect under which the transference neurosis can be understood. The transference neurosis, in the sense of reactivation of the childhood neurosis, is set in motion not simply by the technical skill of the analyst, but by the fact that the analyst makes himself available for the development of a new "object-relationship" between the patient and the analyst. The patient tends to make this potentially new object-relationship into an old one. On the other hand, to the extent to which the patient develops a "positive transference" (not in the sense of transference as resistance, but in the sense in which "transference" carries the whole process of an analysis) he keeps this potentiality of a new object-relationship alive through all the various stages of resistance. The patient can dare to take the plunge into the regressive crisis of the transference neurosis which brings him face to face again with his childhood anxieties and conflicts, *if* he can hold on to the potentiality of a new object-relationship, represented by the analyst.

We know from analytic as well as from life experience that new spurts of self-development may be intimately connected with such "regressive" rediscoveries of oneself as may occur through the establishment of new object-relationships, and this means: new discovery of "objects." I say new discovery of objects, and not discovery of new objects, because the essence of such new object-relationships is the opportunity they offer for rediscovery of the early paths of the development of object-relations, leading to a new way of relating to objects as well as of being and relating to oneself. This new discovery of oneself and of objects, this reorganization of ego and objects, is made possible by the encounter with a "new object" that has to possess certain qualifications in order to promote the process. Such a new object-relationship for which the analyst holds himself available to the patient and to which the patient has to hold on throughout the analysis is one meaning of the term *positive transference*.

What is the neutrality of the analyst? I spoke of the encounter with a potentially new object, the analyst, which new object has to possess certain qualifications to be able to promote the process of ego reorganization implicit in the transference neurosis. One of these qualifications is objectivity. This objectivity cannot mean the avoidance of being available to the patient as an object. The objectivity of the analyst has reference to the patient's transference distortions. Increasingly, through the objective analysis of them, the analyst becomes not only potentially but actually available as a new object, by eliminating step by step impediments, represented by these transferences, to a new object-relationship. There is a tendency to consider the analyst's availability as an object merely as a device on his part to attract transferences onto himself. His availability is seen in terms of his being a screen or mirror onto which the patient projects his transferences, and which reflects them back to him in the form of interpretations. In this view, at the ideal termination point of the analysis no further transference occurs, no projections are thrown on the mirror; the mirror, having nothing now to reflect, can be discarded.

This is only a half-truth. The analyst in actuality does not only reflect the transference distortions. In his interpretations he implies aspects of undistorted reality which the patient begins to grasp step by step as transferences are interpreted. This undistorted reality is mediated to the patient by the analyst, mostly by the process of chiselling away the transference distortions, or, as Freud has beautifully put it, using an expression of Leonardo da

Vinci, per via di levare as in sculpturing, not per via di porre as in painting. In sculpturing, the figure to be created comes into being by taking away from the material; in painting, by adding something to the canvas. In analysis, we bring out the true form by taking away the neurotic distortions. However, as in sculpture, we must have, if only in rudiments, an image of that which needs to be brought into its own. The patient, by revealing himself to the analyst, provides rudiments of such an image through all the distortions—an image that the analyst has to focus in his mind, thus holding it in safe keeping for the patient to whom it is mainly lost. It is this tenuous reciprocal tie which represents the germ of a new object-relationship.

The objectivity of the analyst in regard to the patient's transference distortions, his neutrality in this sense, should not be confused with the "neutral" attitude of the pure scientist towards his subject of study. Nevertheless, the relationship between a scientific observer and his subject of study has been taken as the model for the analytic relationship, with the following deviations: the subject, under the specific conditions of the analytic experiment, directs his activities towards the observer, and the observer communicates his findings directly to the subject with the goal of modifying the findings. These deviations from the model, however, change the whole structure of the relationship to the extent that the model is not representative and useful but, indeed, misleading. As the subject directs his activities towards the analyst, the latter is not integrated by the subject as an observer; as the observer communicates his findings to the patient, the latter is no longer integrated by the "observer" as a subject of study.

While the relationship between analyst and patient does not possess the structure, scientist–scientific subject, and is not characterized by neutrality in that sense on the part of the analyst, the analyst may become a scientific observer to the extent to which he is able to observe objectively the patient and himself in interaction. The interaction itself, however, cannot be adequately represented by the model of scientific neutrality. It is unscientific, based on faulty observation, to use this model. The confusion about the issue of countertransference has to do with this. It hardly needs to be pointed out that such a view in no way denies or minimizes the role scientific knowledge, understanding, and methodology play in the analytic process; nor does it have anything to do with advocating an emotionally charged attitude toward the patient or "role taking." What I am attempting to do is to disentangle the justified and necessary requirement of objectivity and neutrality from a model of neutrality which has its origin in propositions which I believe to be untenable.

One of these is that therapeutic analysis is an objective scientific research method, of a special nature to be sure, but falling within the general category of science as an objective, detached study of natural phenomena, their genesis and interrelations. The ideal image of the analyst is that of a detached scientist. The research method and the investigative procedure *in themselves,* carried out by this scientist, are said to be therapeutic. It is not self-explanatory why a research project should have a therapeutic effect on the subject of study. The therapeutic effect appears to have something to do with the requirement, in analysis, that the subject, the patient himself, gradually become an associate, as it were, in the research work, that he himself become increasingly engaged in the "scientific project," which is, of course, directed at himself. We speak of the patient's observing ego on which we need to be able to rely to a certain extent, which we attempt to strengthen and with which we ally ourselves. We encounter and make use of, in other words, what is known under the general title: identification. The patient and the analyst identify to an increasing degree, if the analysis proceeds, in their ego activity of scientifically guided self-scrutiny.

If the possibility and gradual development of such identification is, as is always claimed, a necessary requirement for a successful analysis, this introduces then and there a factor which has nothing to do with scientific detachment and the neutrality of a mirror.[1] This identification does have to do with the development of a new object-relationship of which I spoke earlier. In fact, it is the foundation for it.

The transference neurosis takes place in the influential presence of the analyst and, as the analysis progresses, more and more "in the presence" and under the eyes of the patient's observ-

---

1. I am speaking here of "mirror" in the naive sense in which it has mostly been used to denote the "properties" of the analyst as a "scientific instrument." A psychodynamic understanding of the mirror as it functions in human life may well reestablish it as an appropriate description of at least certain aspects of the analyst's function.

ing ego. The scrutiny, carried out by the analyst and by the patient, is an organizing, "synthetic" ego activity. The development of an ego function is dependent on interaction. Neither the self-scrutiny, nor the freer, healthier development of the psychic apparatus whose resumption is contingent upon such scrutiny, take place in the vacuum of scientific laboratory conditions. They take place in the presence of a favorable environment, by interaction with it. One could say that in the analytic process this environmontal clcmcnt, as happens in the original development, becomes increasingly internalized as what we call the observing ego of the patient.

There is another aspect to this issue. Involved in the insistence that the analytic activity is a strictly scientific one (not merely using scientific knowledge and methods) is the notion of the dignity of science. Scientific man is considered by Freud as the most advanced form of human development. The scientific stage of the development of man's conception of the universe has its counterpart in the individual's state of maturity, according to Totem and Taboo. Scientific self-understanding, to which the patient is helped, is in and by itself therapeutic, following this view, since it implies the movement towards a stage of human evolution not previously reached. The patient is led towards the maturity of scientific man who understands himself and external reality not in animistic or religious terms but in terms of objective science. There is little doubt that what we call the scientific exploration of the universe, including the self, may lead to greater mastery over it (within certain limits of which we are becoming painfully aware). The activity of mastering it, however, is not itself a scientific activity. If scientific objectivity is assumed to be the most mature stage of man's understanding of the universe, indicating the highest degree of the individual's state of maturity, we may have a vested interest in viewing psychoanalytic therapy as a purely scientific activity and its effects as due to such scientific objectivity. Beyond the issue of a vested interest, I believe it to be necessary and timely to question the assumption, handed to us from the nineteenth century, that the scientific approach to the world and the self represents a higher and more mature evolutionary stage of man than the religious way of life. But I cannot pursue this question here.

I have said that the analyst, through the objective interpretation of transference distortions, increasingly becomes available to the patient as a new object. And this not primarily in the sense of an object not previously met, but the newness consists in the patient's rediscovery of the early paths of the development of object-relations leading to a new way of relating to objects and of being oneself. Through all the transference distortions the patient reveals rudiments at least of the core of himself and "objects" that has been distorted. It is this core, rudimentary and vague as it may be, to which the analyst has reference when he interprets transferences and defenses, and not some abstract concept of reality or normality, if he is to reach the patient. If the analyst keeps his central focus on this emerging core he avoids moulding the patient in the analyst's own image or imposing on the patient his own concept of what the patient should become. It requires an objectivity and neutrality the essence of which is love and respect for the individual and for individual development. This love and respect represent that counterpart in "reality," in interaction with which the organization and reorganization of ego and psychic apparatus take place.

The parent–child relationship can serve as a model here. The parent ideally is in an empathic relationship of understanding the child's particular stage in development, yet ahead in his vision of the child's future and mediating this vision to the child in his dealing with him. This vision, informed by the parent's own experience and knowledge of growth and future, is, ideally, a more articulate and more integrated version of the core of being that the child presents to the parent. This "more" that the parent sees and knows, he mediates to the child so that the child in identification with it can grow. The child, by internalizing aspects of the parent, also internalizes the parent's image of the child—an image that is mediated to the child in the thousand different ways of being handled, bodily and emotionally. Early identification as part of ego development, built up through introjection of maternal aspects, includes introjection of the mother's image of the child. Part of what is introjected is the image of the child as seen, felt, smelled, heard, touched by the mother. It would perhaps be more correct to add that what happens is not wholly a process of introjection, if introjection is used as a term for an intrapsychic activity. The bodily handling of and concern with the child, the manner in which the child is fed, touched, cleaned, the way it is looked at, talked to, called by name, recognized and re-recognized—all these and many other ways of communicating with the child, and communicating to him his identity, sameness, unity, and individuality, shape and mould him so that he can begin to identify himself, to feel and recognize himself as one and as separate from others yet with others. The child begins to experience himself as a centered unit by being centered upon.

In analysis, if it is to be a process leading to structural changes, interactions of a comparable nature have to take place. At this point I only want to indicate, by sketching these interactions during early development, the positive nature of the neutrality required, which includes the capacity for mature object-relations as manifested in the parent by his or her ability to follow and at the same time be ahead of the child's development.

Mature object-relations are not characterized by a sameness of relatedness but by an optimal range of relatedness and by the ability to relate to different objects according to their particular levels of maturity. In analysis, a mature object-relationship is maintained with a given patient if the analyst relates to the patient in tune with the shifting levels of development manifested by the patient at different times, but always from the viewpoint of potential growth, that is, from the viewpoint of the future. It seems to be the fear of moulding the patient in one's own image that has prevented analysts from coming to grips with the dimension of the future in analytic theory and practice, a strange omission considering the fact that growth and development are at the center of all psychoanalytic concern. A fresh and deeper approach to the superego problem cannot be taken without facing this issue.

The patient, in order to attain structural changes in his ego organization, needs the relatedness with a consistently mature object. This, of course, does not mean that during the course of the analysis the analyst is *experienced* by the patient always or most of the time as a mature object. In the analyst it requires the establishment and exercise of special skills during the analytic hour, similar in structure to other professional skills (including the fact that as a skill it is practiced only during the professional work period) and related to the special, but not professionally articulated and concentrated attitudes of parents when dealing with their children.

I am trying to indicate that the activity of the analyst, and specifically his interpretations as well as the ways in which they are integrated by the patient, need to be considered and understood in terms of the psychodynamics of the ego. Such psychodynamics cannot be worked out without proper attention to the functionings of integrative processes in the ego-reality field, beginning with such processes as introjection, identification, projection (of which we know something), and progressing to their genetic derivatives, modifications, and transformations in later life stages (of which we understand very little, except insofar as they are used for defensive purposes). The more intact the ego of the patient, the more of this integration taking place in the analytic process occurs without being noticed or at least without being considered and conceptualized as an essential element in the analytic process. "Classical" analysis with "classical" cases easily leaves unrecognized essential elements of the analytic process, not because they are not present but because they are as difficult to see in such cases as it was difficult to discover "classical" psychodynamics in normal people. Cases with obvious ego defects magnify what also occurs in the typical analysis of the neuroses, just as in neurotics we see magnified the psychodynamics of human beings in general. This is not to say that there is no difference between the analysis of the classical psychoneuroses and of cases with obvious ego defects. In the latter, especially in borderline cases and psychoses, processes such as I tried to sketch in the child-parent relationship take place in the therapeutic situation on levels relatively close and similar to those of the early child-parent relationship. The further we move away from gross ego defect cases, the more do these integrative processes take place on higher levels of sublimation and by modes of communication which show much more complex stages of organization.

II

The elaboration of the structural point of view in psychoanalytic theory has brought about the danger of isolating the different structures of the psychic apparatus from one another. It may look nowadays as though the ego is a creature of and functioning in conjunction with external reality, whereas the area of the instinctual drives, of the id, is as such unrelated to the external world. To use Freud's archeological simile, it is as though the functional relationship between the deeper strata of an excavation and *their* external environment were denied because these deeper strata are not in a functional relationship with the present-day environment; as though it were maintained that the architectural structures of deeper, earlier strata are due to purely "internal" processes, in contrast to the functional interrelatedness between present architectural structures (higher, later strata) and the external environment that we see and live in. The id—in the archeological analogy being comparable to a deeper, earlier stratum—integrates with its correlative "early" external environment as much as the ego integrates with the ego's more "recent" external reality. The id deals with and is a creature of "adaptation" just as much as the ego—but on a very different level of organization.

Earlier I referred to the conception of the psychic apparatus as a closed system and said that this view has a bearing on the traditional notion of the analyst's neutrality and of his function as a mirror. It is in this context that I now enter into a discussion of the concept of instinctual drives, particularly as regards their relation to objects, as formulated in psychoanalytic theory. I shall preface this discussion with a quotation from Freud which is taken from the introduction to his discussion of instincts in his paper "Instincts and Their Vicissitudes" (pp. 117–18). He says:

The true beginning of scientific activity consists . . . in describing phenomena and then in proceeding to group, classify and correlate them. *Even at the stage of description it is not possible to avoid applying certain abstract ideas to the material in hand, ideas derived from somewhere or other but certainly not from the new observations alone.* Such ideas—which will later become the basic concepts of the science—are still more indispensable as the material is further worked over. They must at first necessarily possess some degree of indefiniteness; there can be no question of any clear delimitation of their content. So long as they remain in this condition, we come to an understanding about their meaning by making repeated references to the material of observation *from which they appear to have been derived, but upon which, in fact, they have been imposed.* Thus, strictly speaking, they are in the nature of conventions—although everything depends on their not being arbitrarily chosen but determined by their having significant relations to the empirical material, relations that we seem to sense before we can clearly recognize and demonstrate them. It is only after more thorough investigation of the field of observation that we are able to formulate its basic scientific concepts with increased precision, and progressively so to modify them that they become serviceable and consistent over a wide area. Then, indeed, the time may have come to confine them in definitions. The advance of knowledge, however, does not tolerate any rigidity even in definitions. Physics furnishes an excellent illustration of the way in which even "basic concepts" that have been established in the form of definitions are constantly being altered in their content.

The concept of instinct (*Trieb*), Freud goes on to say, is such a basic concept, "conventional but still somewhat obscure," and thus open to alterations in its content (my italics).

In this same paper, Freud defines instinct as a stimulus; a stimulus not arising in the outer world but "from within the organism." He adds that "a better term for an instinctual stimulus is a 'need,'" and says that such "stimuli are the signs of an internal world." Freud lays explicit stress on one fundamental implication of his whole consideration of instincts here, namely that it implies the concept of purpose in the form of what he calls a biological postulate. This postulate "runs as follows: the nervous system is an apparatus which has the function of getting rid of the stimuli that reach it, or of reducing them to the lowest possible level." An instinct is a stimulus from within reaching the nervous system. Since an instinct is a stimulus arising within the organism and acting "always as a constant force," it obliges "the nervous system to renounce its ideal intention of keeping off stimuli" and compels it "to undertake involved and interconnected activities by which the external world is so changed as to afford satisfaction to the internal source of stimulation" (pp. 118–20).

Instinct being an inner stimulus reaching the nervous apparatus, the object of an instinct is "the thing in regard to which or through which the instinct is able to achieve its aim," this aim being satisfaction. The object of an instinct is further described as "what is most variable about an instinct," "not originally connected with it," and as becoming "assigned to it only in conse-

quence of being peculiarly fitted to make satisfaction possible"
(p. 122). It is here that we see instinctual drives being conceived
of as "intrapsychic," or originally not related to objects.

In his later writings Freud gradually moves away from this
position. Instincts are no longer defined as (inner) stimuli with
which the nervous apparatus deals in accordance with the
scheme of the reflex arc, but instinct, in *Beyond the Pleasure
Principle* (p. 36), is seen as "an urge inherent in organic life to
restore an earlier state of things which the living entity has been
obliged to abandon under the pressure of external disturbing
forces." Here he defines instinct in terms equivalent to the terms
he used earlier in describing the function of the nervous apparatus itself, the nervous apparatus, the "living entity," in its
interchange with "external disturbing forces." Instinct is no
longer an intrapsychic stimulus, but an expression of the function, the "urge" of the nervous apparatus to deal with environment. The intimate and fundamental relationship of instincts,
especially insofar as libido (sexual instincts, Eros) is concerned,
with objects, is more clearly brought out in "Inhibitions, Symptoms and Anxiety," until finally, in *An Outline of Psychoanalysis,*
"the aim of the first of these basic instincts [Eros] is to establish
ever greater unities and to preserve them thus—in short, to bind
together." It is noteworthy that here not only the relatedness to
objects is implicit; the aim of the instinct Eros is no longer formulated in terms of a contentless satisfaction, or satisfaction in the
sense of abolishing stimuli, but the aim is clearly seen in terms of
integration. It is: "to bind together." And while Freud feels that it
is possible to apply his earlier formula, "to the effect that instincts
tend towards a return to an earlier [inanimate] state," to the
destructive or death instinct, "we cannot apply this formula" to
Eros (the love instinct) (pp. 148–49).

The basic concept Instinct has thus indeed changed its content since Freud wrote "Instincts and Their Vicissitudes." In his
later writings he does not take as his starting point and model
the reflex arc scheme of a self-contained, closed system, but
bases his considerations on a much broader, more modern biological framework. And it should be clear from the last quotation
that it is by no means the ego alone to which he assigns the function of synthesis, of binding together. Eros, one of the two basic

instincts, is itself an integrating force. This is in accordance with his concept of primary narcissism as first formulated in "On Narcissism, an Introduction," and further elaborated in his later writings, notably in "Civilization and Its Discontents," where objects, reality, far from being originally not connected with libido, are seen as becoming gradually differentiated from a primary narcissistic identity of inner and outer world (see my paper on "Ego and Reality," 1951).

In his conception of Eros, Freud moves away from an opposition between instinctual drives and ego, and toward a view according to which instinctual drives become moulded, channelled, focused, tamed, transformed, and sublimated in and by the ego organization, an organization which is more complex and at the same time more sharply elaborated and articulated than the drive organization that we call the id. But the ego is an organization that continues, much more than it is in opposition to, the inherent tendencies of the drive organization. The concept Eros encompasses in one term one of the two basic tendencies or "purposes" of the psychic apparatus as manifested on both levels of organization.

In such a perspective, instinctual drives are as primarily related to "objects," to the external world as the ego is. The organization of this outer world, of these objects, corresponds to the level of drive organization rather than of ego organization. In other words, instinctual drives organize environment and are organized by it no less than is true for the ego and its reality. It is the mutuality of organization, in the sense of organizing each other, which constitutes the inextricable interrelatedness of "inner and outer world." It would be justified to speak of primary and secondary processes not only in reference to the psychic apparatus but also in reference to the outer world insofar as its psychological structure is concerned. The qualitative difference between the two levels of organization might terminologically be indicated by speaking of environment as correlative to drives, and of reality as correlative to ego. Instinctual drives can be seen as originally not connected with objects only in the sense that originally the world is not organized by the primitive psychic apparatus in such a way that objects are differentiated. Out of an "undifferentiated stage" emerge what have been termed part-

objects or object-nuclei. A more appropriate term for such pre-
stages of an object-world might be the noun "shapes"; in the
sense of configurations of an indeterminate degree and a fluidity
of organization, and without the connotation of object-fragments.

The preceding excursion into some problems of instinct
theory is intended to show that the issue of object-relations in
psychoanalytic theory has suffered from a formulation of the
instinct concept according to which instincts, as inner stimuli,
are contrasted with outer stimuli, both, although in different
ways, affecting the psychic apparatus. Inner and outer stimuli,
terms for inner and outer world on a certain level of abstraction,
are thus conceived as originally unrelated or even opposed to
each other but running parallel, as it were, in their relation to the
nervous apparatus. And while, as we have seen, Freud in his
general trend of thought and in many formulations moved away
from this framework, psychoanalytic theory has remained under
its sway except in the realm of ego psychology. It is unfortunate
that the development of ego psychology had to take place in relative isolation from instinct theory. It is true that our understanding of instinctual drives has also progressed. But the extremely
fruitful concept of organization (the two aspects of which are
integration and differentiation) has been insufficiently, if at all,
applied to the understanding of instinctual drives, and instinct
theory has remained under the aegis of the antiquated stimulus–
reflex arc conceptual model—a mechanistic frame of reference
far removed from modern psychological as well as biological
thought. The scheme of the reflex arc, as Freud says in "Instincts
and Their Vicissitudes" (p. 118), has been given to us by physiology. But this was the mechanistic physiology of the nineteenth
century. Ego psychology began its development in a quite different climate already, as is clear from Freud's biological reflections in *Beyond the Pleasure Principle*. Thus it has come about
that the ego is seen as an organ of adaptation to and integration
and differentiation with and of the outer world, whereas instinctual drives were left behind in the realm of stimulus–reflex
physiology. This, and specifically the conception of instinct as
an inner stimulus impinging on the nervous apparatus, has
affected the formulations concerning the role of objects in libidinal development and, by extension, has vitiated the understand-

ing of the object-relationship between patient and analyst in psychoanalytic treatment.[2]

III

Returning to the discussion of the analytic situation and the therapeutic process in analysis, it will be useful to dwell further on the dynamics of interaction in early stages of development.

The mother recognizes and fulfils the need of the infant. Both recognition and fulfilment of a need are at first beyond the ability of the infant, not merely the fulfilment. The understanding recognition of the infant's need on the part of the mother represents a gathering together of as yet undifferentiated urges of the infant, urges that in the acts of recognition and fulfilment by the mother undergo a first organization into some directed drive. In a remarkable passage in the "Project for a Scientific Psychology," in a chapter which has been called "The Experience of Satisfaction," Freud discusses this constellation in its consequences for the further organization of the psychic apparatus and in its significance as the origin of communication. Gradually, both recognition and satisfaction of the need come within the grasp of the growing infant itself. The processes by which this occurs are generally subsumed under the headings identification and introjection. Access to them has to be made available by the environment, here the mother, who performs this function in the acts of recognition and fulfilment of the need. These acts are not merely necessary for the physical survival of the infant but necessary at the same time for its psychological development insofar as they organize, in successive steps, the infant's relatively uncoordinated urges. The whole complex dynamic constellation is one of mutual responsiveness where nothing is introjected by the infant that is not brought to it by the mother, although brought by her often unconsciously. And a prerequisite for introjection and

2. It is obvious that the conception of instinct as an internal stimulus is connected with Freud's discovery of infantile sexuality as stimulating sexual fantasies, which earlier he attributed purely to environmental seductive traumatization. It should be clear, however, that the formulation of that problem in such alternatives as "internal" fantasies versus "environmental" seduction is itself open to the same questions and reconsiderations that we are discussing throughout this paper.

identification is the gathering mediation of structure and direction by the mother in her caring activities. As the mediating environment conveys structure and direction to the unfolding psychophysical entity, the environment begins to gain structure and direction in the experience of that entity; the environment begins to take shape in the experience of the infant. It is now that identification and introjection as well as projection emerge as more defined processes of organization of the psychic apparatus and of environment.

We arrive at the following formulation: the organization of the psychic apparatus, on the basis of given neuroanatomical structures and neurophysiological potentiality-patterns, proceeds by way of mediation of higher organization on the part of the environment to the infantile organism. In one and the same act—I am tempted to say, in the same breath and the same sucking of milk—drive direction and organization of environment into shapes or configurations begin, and they are continued into ego organization and object organization, by methods such as identification, introjection, projection. The higher organizational stage of the environment is indispensable for the development of the psychic apparatus and, in early stages, has to be brought to it actively. Without such a differential between organism and environment no development takes place.

The patient, who comes to the analyst for help through increased self-understanding, is led to this self-understanding by the understanding he finds in the analyst. The analyst operates on various levels of understanding. Whether he verbalizes his understanding to the patient on the level of clarifications of conscious material, whether he indicates or reiterates his intent of understanding, restates the procedure to be followed, or whether he interprets unconscious, verbal or other, material, and especially if he interprets transference and resistance—the analyst structures and articulates, or works towards structuring and articulating, the material and the productions offered by the patient. If an interpretation of unconscious meaning is timely, the words by which this meaning is expressed are recognizable to the patient as expressions of what he experiences. They organize for him what was previously less organized and thus give him the distance from himself that enables him to understand, to see, to put into words and to "handle" what was previously not visible, understandable, speakable, tangible. A higher stage of organization, of both himself and his environment, is thus reached, by way of the organizing understanding which the analyst provides. The analyst functions as a representative of a higher stage of organization and mediates this to the patient, insofar as the analyst's understanding is attuned to what is, and the way in which it is, in need of organization.

I am speaking of what I have earlier called integrative experiences in analysis. These are experiences of interaction, comparable in their structure and significance to the early understanding between mother and child. The latter is a model, and as such always of limited value, but a model whose usefulness has recently been stressed by a number of analysts (see for instance René Spitz, 1956) and which in its full implications and in its perspective is a radical departure from the classical "mirror model."

Interactions in analysis take place on much higher levels of organization. Communication is carried on predominantly by way of language, an instrument of and for secondary processes. The satisfaction involved in the analytic interaction is a sublimated one, in increasing degree as the analysis progresses. Satisfaction now has to be understood, not in terms of abolition or reduction of stimulation leading back to a previous state of equilibrium, but in terms of absorbing and integrating stimuli, leading to higher levels of equilibrium. This, it is true, is often achieved by temporary regression to an earlier level, but this regression is "in the service of the ego," that is, in the service of higher organization. Satisfaction, in this context, is a unifying experience because of the creation of an identity of experience in two systems, two psychic apparatuses of different levels of organization, thus containing the potential of growth. This identity is achieved by overcoming a differential. Properly speaking, there is no experience of satisfaction and no integrative experience where there is no differential to be overcome, where identity is simply given, that is existing rather than to be created by interaction. An approximate model of such existing identity is perhaps provided in the intra-uterine situation, and decreasingly in the early months of life in the symbiotic relationship of mother and infant.

Analytic interpretations represent, on higher levels of interaction, the mutual recognition involved in the creation of identity of experience in two individuals of different levels of ego organization. Insight gained in such interaction is an integrative experience. The interpretation represents the recognition and understanding that makes available to the patient previously unconscious material. "Making it available to the patient" means lifting it to the level of the preconscious system, of secondary processes, by the operation of certain types of secondary processes on the part of the analyst. Material, organized on or close to the level of drive organization, of the primary process, and isolated from the preconscious system, is made available for organization on the level of the preconscious system by the analyst's interpretation, a secondary process operation that mediates to the patient secondary process organization. Whether this mediation is successful or not depends, among other things, on the organizing strength of the patient's ego attained through earlier steps in ego integration, in previous phases of the analysis, and ultimately in his earlier life. To the extent to which such strength is lacking, analysis—organizing interaction by way of language communication—becomes less feasible.

An interpretation can be said to comprise two elements, inseparable from each other. The interpretation takes with the patient the step towards true regression, as against the neurotic compromise formation, thus clarifying for the patient his true regression level, which has been covered and made unrecognizable by defensive operations and structures. Secondly, by this very step it mediates to the patient the higher integrative level to be reached. The interpretation thus creates the possibility for freer interplay between the unconscious and preconscious systems, whereby the preconscious regains its originality and intensity, lost to the unconscious in the repression, and the unconscious regains access to and capacity for progression in the direction of higher organization. Put in terms of Freud's metapsychological language, the barrier between Ucs and Pcs, consisting of the archaic cathexis (repetition compulsion) of the unconscious and the warding-off anticathexis of the preconscious, is temporarily overcome. This process may be seen as the internalized version of the overcoming of a differential in the *interaction process* described above as integrative experience. Internalization itself is dependent on interaction and is made possible again in the analytic process. The analytic process then consists in certain integrative experiences between patient and analyst as the foundation for the internalized version of such experiences: reorganization of ego, "structural change."

The analyst in his interpretations reorganizes, reintegrates unconscious material for himself as well as for the patient, since he has to be attuned to the patient's unconscious, using, as we say, his own unconscious as a tool, in order to arrive at the organizing interpretation. The analyst has to move freely between the unconscious and the organization of it in thought and language, for and with the patient. If this is not so—a good example is most instances of the use of technical language—language is used as a defense against leading the unconscious material into ego organization, and ego activity is used as a defense against integration. It is the weakness of the "strong" ego—strong in its defenses—that it guides the psychic apparatus into excluding the unconscious (for instance by repression or isolation) rather than into lifting the unconscious to higher organization and, at the same time, holding it available for replenishing regression to it.

Language, when not defensively used, is employed by the patient for communication which attempts to reach the analyst on his presumed or actual level of maturity in order to achieve the integrative experience longed for. The analytic patient, while striving for improvement in terms of inner reorganization, is constantly tempted to seek improvement in terms of unsublimated satisfaction through interaction with the analyst on levels closer to the primary process, rather than in terms of internalization of integrative experience as it is achieved in the process which Freud has described as: where there was id there shall be ego. The analyst, in his communication through language, mediates higher organization of material hitherto less highly organized, to the patient. This can occur only if two conditions are fulfilled: (i) the patient, through a sufficiently strong "positive transference" to the analyst, becomes again available for integrative work with himself and his world, as against defensive warding-off of psychic and external reality manifested in the analytic situation in resistance. (ii) The analyst must be in tune with the patient's productions, that is, he must be able to regress within himself to the level of organization on which the patient is stuck, and to help the patient, by the analysis of defense and resistance, to realize this regression. This realization is prevented by the compromise formations of the neurosis and is made possible by dissolving them into the components of a subjugated unconscious and a superimposed preconscious. By an interpretation, both the unconscious experience and a higher organizational level of that experience are made available to the patient: unconscious and preconscious are joined together in the act of interpretation. In a well-going analysis the patient increasingly becomes enabled to perform this joining himself.

Language, in its most specific function in analysis, as interpretation, is thus a creative act similar to that in poetry, where language is found for phenomena, contexts, connections, experiences not previously known and speakable. New phenomena and new experience are made available as a result of reorganization of material according to hitherto unknown principles, contexts, and connections.

Ordinarily we operate with material organized on high levels of sublimation as "given reality." In an analysis the analyst has to retrace the organizational steps that have led to such a reality level, so that the organizing process becomes available to the patient. This is regression in the service of the ego, in the service of reorganization—a regression against which there is resistance in the analyst as well as in the patient. As an often necessary defense against the relatively unorganized power of the unconscious, we tend to automatize higher organizational levels and resist regression out of fear lest we may not find the way back to higher organization. The fear of reliving the past is fear of toppling off a plateau we have reached, and fear of that more chaotic past itself, not only in the sense of past content but more essentially of past, less stable stages of organization of experience, whose genuine reintegration requires psychic "work." Related to it is the fear of the future, pregnant with new integrative tasks and the risk of losing what had been secured. In analysis such fear of the future may be manifested in the patient's defensive clinging to regressed, but seemingly safe levels.

Once the patient is able to speak, nondefensively, from the true level of regression which he has been helped to reach by analysis of defenses, he himself, by putting his experience into words, begins to use language creatively, that is, begins to create insight. The patient, by speaking to the analyst, attempts to reach the analyst as a representative of higher stages of ego reality organization, and thus may be said to create insight for himself in the process of language-communication with the analyst as such a representative. Such communication on the part of the patient is possible if the analyst, by way of *his* communications, is revealing himself to the patient as a more mature person, as a person who can feel with the patient what the patient experiences and how he experiences it, and who understands it as something more than it has been for the patient. It is this something more, not necessarily more in content but more in organization and significance, that external reality, here represented and mediated by the analyst, has to offer to the individual and for which the individual is striving. The analyst, in doing his part of the work, experiences the cathartic effect of "regression in the service of the ego" and performs a piece of self-analysis or reanalysis (cf. Lucia Tower, 1956). Freud has remarked that his own self-analysis proceeded by way of analyzing patients, and that this was necessary in order to gain the psychic distance required for any such work (Freud, 1954, p. 234).

The patient, being recognized by the analyst as something more than he is at present, can attempt to reach this something more by his communications to the analyst, which may establish a new identity with reality. To varying degrees patients are striving for this integrative experience, through and despite their resistances. To varying degrees patients have given up this striving above the level of omnipotent, magical identification, and to that extent are less available for the analytic process. The therapist, depending on the mobility and potential strength of integrative mechanisms in the patient, has to be more or less explicit and "primitive" in his ways of communicating to the patient his availability as a mature object and his own integrative processes. We call analysis that kind of organizing, restructuring interaction between patient and therapist which is predominantly performed on the level of language communication. It is likely that the development of language, as a means of meaningful and coherent communicating with "objects," is related to the child's reaching, at least in a first approximation, the oedipal stage of psychosexual development. The inner connections between the development of language, the formation of ego

and of objects, and the oedipal phase of psychosexual development, are still to be explored. If such connections exist, as I
believe they do, then it is not mere arbitrariness to distinguish
analysis proper from more primitive means of integrative interaction. To set up rigid boundary lines, however, is to ignore or
deny the complexities of the development and of the dynamics of
the psychic apparatus.

IV

In the concluding part of this paper I hope to shed further
light on the theory of the therapeutic action of psychoanalysis by
re-examining certain aspects of the concept and the phenomenon
of transference. In contrast to trends in modern psychoanalytic
thought to narrow the term transference down to a very specific
limited meaning, an attempt will be made here to regain the
original richness of interrelated phenomena and mental mechanisms which the concept encompasses, and to contribute to the
clarification of such interrelations.

When Freud speaks of transference neuroses in contradistinction to narcissistic neuroses, two meanings of the term transference are involved: (i) the transfer of libido, contained in the
ego, to objects, in the transference neuroses, while in the narcissistic neuroses the libido remains in or is taken back into the ego,
not transferred to objects. Transference in this sense is virtually
synonymous with object-cathexis. To quote from an important
early paper on transference (Ferenczi, 1909): "The first loving
and hating is a transference of autoerotic pleasant and unpleas-
ant feelings on to the objects that evoke these feelings. The first
'object-love' and the first 'object-hate' are, so to speak, the primordial transferences." (ii) The second meaning of transference,
when distinguishing transference neuroses from narcissistic
neuroses, is that of transfer of relations with infantile objects on
to later objects, and especially to the analyst in the analytic
situation.

This second meaning of the term is today the one most frequently referred to, to the exclusion of other meanings. I quote
from two recent representative papers on the subject of transference. Waelder, in his Geneva Congress paper, "Introduction to
the Discussion on Problems of Transference" (1956) says: "Trans-

ference may be said to be an attempt of the patient to revive and re-enact, in the analytic situation and in relation to the analyst, situations and phantasies of his childhood." Hoffer, in his paper, presented at the same Congress, on "Transference and Transference Neurosis" (1956) states:

The term "transference" refers to the generally agreed fact that people when entering into any form of object-relationship . . . *transfer* upon their objects those images which they encountered in the course of previous *infantile* experiences. . . . The term "transference," stressing an aspect of the influence our childhood has on our life as a whole, thus refers to those observations in which people in their contacts with objects, which may be real or imaginary, positive, negative, or ambivalent, "transfer" their *memories* of significant previous experiences and thus "*change the reality*" of their objects, invest them with qualities from the past.

The transference neuroses, thus, are characterized by the transfer of libido to external objects as against the attachment of the libido to the "ego" in the narcissistic affections; and, secondly, by the transfer of libidinal cathexes (and defenses against them), originally related to infantile objects, on to contemporary objects.

Transference neurosis as distinguished from narcissistic neurosis is a nosological term. At the same time, the term *transference neurosis* is used in a technical sense to designate the revival of the infantile neurosis in the analytic situation. In this sense of the term, the accent is on the second meaning of transference, since the revival of the infantile neurosis is due to the transfer of relations with infantile objects on to the contemporary object, the analyst. It is, however, only on the basis of transfer of libido to (external) objects in childhood that libidinal attachments to infantile objects can be transferred to contemporary objects. The first meaning of transference, therefore, is implicit in the technical concept of transference neurosis.

The narcissistic neuroses were thought to be inaccessible to psychoanalytic treatment because of the narcissistic libido cathexis. Psychoanalysis was considered to be feasible only where a "transference relationship" with the analyst could be established; in that group of disorders, in other words, where emotional development had taken place to the point that transfer of libido to external objects had occurred to a significant degree. If today we consider schizophrenics capable of transference, we hold (i) that they do relate in some way to "objects," i.e. to pre-stages of objects that are less "objective" than oedipal objects (narcissistic and object libido, ego and objects are not yet clearly differentiated; this implies the concept of primary narcissism in its full sense). And we hold (ii) that schizophrenics transfer this early type of relatedness onto contemporary "objects," which objects thus become less objective. If ego and objects are not clearly differentiated, if ego boundaries and object boundaries are not clearly established, the character of transference also is different, in as much as ego and objects are still largely merged; objects—"different objects"—are not yet clearly differentiated one from the other, and especially not early from contemporary ones. The transference is a much more primitive and "massive" one. Thus, in regard to child analysis, at any rate before the latency period, it has been questioned whether one can speak of transference in the sense in which adult neurotic patients manifest it. The conception of such a primitive form of transference is fundamentally different from the assumption of an unrelatedness of ego and objects as is implied in the idea of a withdrawal of libido from objects into the ego.

The modification of our view on the narcissistic affections in this respect, based on clinical experience with schizophrenics and on deepened understanding of early ego development, leads to a broadened conception of transference in the first-mentioned meaning of that term. To be more precise: transference in the sense of transfer of libido to objects is clarified genetically; it develops out of a primary lack of differentiation of ego and objects and thus may regress, as in schizophrenia, to such a pre-stage. Transference does not disappear in the narcissistic affections, by "withdrawal of libido cathexes into the ego"; it undifferentiates in a regressive direction towards its origins in the ego object identity of primary narcissism.

An apparently quite unrelated meaning of transference is found in chapter 7 of The Interpretation of Dreams, in the context of a discussion of the importance of day residues in dreams. Since I believe this last meaning of transference to be fundamental for a deeper understanding of the phenomenon of transference, I shall quote the relevant passages.

We learn from [the psychology of the neuroses] that an unconscious idea is as such quite incapable of entering the preconscious and that it can only exercise any effect there by establishing a connection with an idea which already belongs to the preconscious, by transferring its intensity on to it and by getting itself "covered" by it. Here we have the fact of "transference" which provides an explanation of so many striking phenomena in the mental life of neurotics. The preconscious idea, which thus acquires an undeserved degree of intensity, may either be left unaltered by the transference, or it may have a modification forced upon it, derived from the content of the idea which effects the transference (pp. 562–3).

And later, again referring to day residues:

the fact that recent elements occur with such regularity points to the existence of a need for transference. It will be seen, then, that the day's residues . . . not only borrow something from the Ucs. when they succeed in taking a share in the formation of the dream—namely the instinctual force which is at the disposal of the repressed wish—but that they also offer the unconscious something indispensable—namely the necessary point of attachment for a transference. If we wished to penetrate more deeply at this point into the processes of the mind, we should have to throw more light upon the interplay of excitations between the preconscious and the unconscious—a subject towards which the study of the psychoneuroses draws us, but upon which, as it happens, dreams have no help to offer (p. 564).[3]

One parallel between this meaning of transference and the one mentioned under (ii)—transfer of infantile object-cathexes to contemporary objects—emerges: the unconscious idea, transferring its intensity to a preconscious idea and getting itself "covered" by it, corresponds to the infantile object-cathexis, whereas the preconscious idea corresponds to the contemporary object-relationship to which the infantile object-cathexis is transferred.

---

3. Charles Fisher (1956) recently has drawn particular attention to this meaning of the term transference. His studies of unconscious-preconscious relationships, while specifically concerned with dream formation, imagery, and perception, have relevance to the whole problem area of the formation of object-relations and the psychological constitution of reality.

Transference is described in detail by Freud in the chapter on psychotherapy in *Studies on Hysteria*. It is seen there as due to the mechanism of "false (wrong) connection." Freud discusses this mechanism in chapter 2 of *Studies on Hysteria* where he refers to a "compulsion to associate" the unconscious complex with one that is conscious and reminds us that the mechanism of compulsive ideas in compulsion neurosis is of a similar nature (p. 69). In the paper on "The Neuro-Psychoses of Defence" the "false connection" is called upon to clarify the mechanism of obsessions and phobias. The false connection, of course, is also involved in the explanation of "Screen Memories," where it is called displacement. The German term for screen memories, *Deck-Erinnerungen,* uses the same word *decken,* to cover, which is used in the above quotation from *The Interpretation of Dreams* where the unconscious idea gets itself covered by the preconscious idea.

While these mechanisms involved in the "interplay of excitations between the preconscious and the unconscious" have reference to the psychoneuroses and the dream and were discovered and described in those contexts, they are only the more or less pathological, magnified, or distorted versions of normal mechanisms. Similarly, the transfer of libido to objects and the transfer of infantile object-relations to contemporary ones are normal processes, seen in neurosis in pathological modifications and distortions.

The compulsion to associate the unconscious complex with one that is conscious is the same phenomenon as the need for transference in the quotation from chapter 7 of *The Interpretation of Dreams*. It has to do with the indestructibility of all mental acts which are truly unconscious. This indestructibility of unconscious mental acts is compared by Freud to the ghosts in the underworld of the Odyssey—"ghosts which awoke to new life as soon as they tasted blood" (p. 553n.), the blood of conscious-preconscious life, the life of contemporary present-day objects. It is a short step from here to the view of transference as a manifestation of the repetition compulsion—a line of thought which we cannot pursue here.

The transference neurosis, in the technical sense of the establishment and resolution of it in the analytic process, is due to the blood of recognition, which the patient's unconscious is given to taste so that the old ghosts may reawaken to life. Those who know ghosts tell us that they long to be released from their ghost life and led to rest as ancestors. As ancestors they live forth in the present generation, while as ghosts they are compelled to haunt the present generation with their shadow life. Transference is pathological insofar as the unconscious is a crowd of ghosts, and this is the beginning of the transference neurosis in analysis: ghosts of the unconscious, imprisoned by defenses but haunting the patient in the dark of his defenses and symptoms, are allowed to taste blood, are let loose. In the daylight of analysis the ghosts of the unconscious are laid and led to rest as ancestors whose power is taken over and transformed into the newer intensity of present life, of the secondary process and contemporary objects.

In the development of the psychic apparatus the secondary process, preconscious organization, is the manifestation and result of interaction between a more primitively organized psychic apparatus and the secondary process activity of the environment; through such interaction the unconscious gains higher organization. Such ego development, arrested or distorted in neurosis, is resumed in analysis. The analyst helps to revive the repressed unconscious of the patient by his recognition of it; through interpretation of transference and resistance, through the recovery of memories and through reconstruction, the patient's unconscious activity is led into preconscious organization. The analyst, in the analytic situation, offers himself to the patient as a contemporary object. As such he revives the ghosts of the unconscious for the patient by fostering the transference neurosis which comes about in the same way in which the dream comes about: through the mutual attraction of unconscious and "recent," "day-residue" elements. Dream interpretation and interpretation of transference have this function in common: they both attempt to re-establish the lost connections, the buried interplay, between the unconscious and the preconscious.

Transferences studied in neurosis and analyzed in therapeutic analysis are the diseased manifestations of the life of that indestructible unconscious whose attachments to recent elements, by way of transformation of primary into secondary processes, constitute growth. There is no greater misunderstanding of the full meaning of transference than the one most clearly expressed in a formulation by Silverberg, but shared, I believe, by many analysts. Silverberg in his paper on "The Concept of Transference" (1948), writes: "The wide prevalance of the dynamism of transference among human beings is a mark of man's immaturity, and it may be expected in ages to come that, as man progressively matures . . . transference will gradually vanish from his psychic repertory." But far from being, as Silverberg puts it, "the enduring monument of man's profound rebellion against reality and his stubborn persistence in the ways of immaturity," transference is the "dynamism" by which the instinctual life of man, the id, becomes ego and by which reality becomes integrated and maturity is achieved. Without such transference—of the intensity of the unconscious, of the infantile ways of experiencing life that have no language and little organization, but the indestructibility and power of the origins of life—to the preconscious and to present-day life and contemporary objects—without such transference, or to the extent to which such transference miscarries, human life becomes sterile and an empty shell. On the other hand, the unconscious needs present-day external reality (objects) and present-day psychic reality (the preconscious) for its own continuity, lest it be condemned to live the shadow life of ghosts or to destroy life.

I have pointed out earlier that in the development of preconscious mental organization—and this is resumed in the analytic process—transformation of primary into secondary process activity is contingent upon a differential, a (libidinal) tension system between primary and secondary process organization, that is, between the infantile organism, its psychic apparatus, and the more structured environment: transference in the sense of an evolving relationship with "objects." This interaction is the basis for what I have called "integrative experience." The relationship is a mutual one—as is the interplay of excitations between unconscious and preconscious—since the environment not only has to make itself available and move in a regressive direction towards the more primitively organized psychic apparatus; the environment also needs the latter as an external representative of its own unconscious levels of organization with which communication is to be maintained. The analytic process, in the development and resolution of the transference neurosis, is a repetition—with essential modifications because taking place on another level—of such a libidinal tension system between a more primitively and a more maturely organized psychic apparatus.

This differential, implicit in the integrative experience, we meet again, internalized, in the form of the tension system constituting the interplay of excitations between the preconscious and the unconscious. We postulate thus internalization of an interaction process, not simply internalization of objects, as an essential element in ego development as well as in the resumption of it in analysis. The double aspect of transference, the fact that transference refers to the interaction between psychic apparatus and object-world as well as to the interplay between the unconscious and the preconscious within the psychic apparatus, thus becomes clarified. The opening of barriers between unconscious and preconscious, as it occurs in any creative process, is then to be understood as an internalized integrative experience— and is in fact experienced as such.

The intensity of unconscious processes and experiences is transferred to preconscious-conscious experiences. Our present, current experiences have intensity and depth to the extent to which they are in communication (interplay) with the unconscious, infantile, experiences representing the indestructible matrix of all subsequent experiences. Freud, in 1897, was well aware of this. In a letter to Fliess he writes, after recounting experiences with his younger brother and his nephew between the ages of 1 and 2 years: "My nephew and younger brother determined, not only the neurotic side of all my friendships, but also their depth" (1954, p. 219).

The unconscious suffers under repression because its need for transference is inhibited. It finds an outlet in neurotic transferences, "repetitions" that fail to achieve higher integration (wrong connections). The preconscious suffers no less from repression since it has no access to the unconscious intensities, the unconscious prototypical experiences which give current experiences their full meaning and emotional depth. In promoting the transference neurosis, we are promoting a regressive movement on the part of the preconscious (ego regression) that is designed to bring the preconscious out of its defensive isolation from the unconscious and to allow the unconscious to recathect, in interaction with the analyst, preconscious ideas and experiences in such a way that higher organization of mental life can come about. The mediator of this interplay of transference is the analyst who, as a contemporary object, offers himself to the patient's unconscious as a necessary point of attachment for a transference. As a contemporary object, the analyst represents a psychic apparatus whose secondary process organization is stable and capable of controlled regression so that he is optimally in communication with both his own and the patient's unconscious, so as to serve as a reliable mediator and partner of communication, of transference between unconscious and preconscious, and thus of higher, interpenetrating organization of both.

The integration of ego and reality consists in, and the continued integrity of ego and reality depends on, transference of unconscious processes and "contents" on to new experiences and objects of contemporary life. In pathological transferences the transformation of primary into secondary processes and the continued interplay between them has been replaced by superimpositions of secondary on primary processes, so that they exist side by side, isolated from each other. Freud has described this constellation in his paper on "The Unconscious" (pp. 175–76): "Actually there is no lifting of the repression until the conscious idea, after the resistances have been overcome, has *entered into connection* with the unconscious memory trace. It is only through the making conscious of the latter itself that success is achieved" (italics mine). In an analytic interpretation "the identity of the information given to the patient with his repressed memory is only apparent. To have heard something and to have experienced something are in their psychological nature two different things, even though the content of both is the same." And later (p. 201) in the same paper, Freud speaks of the thing-cathexes of objects in the Ucs, whereas the "conscious presentation comprises the presentation of the thing [thing cathexis] plus the presentation of the word belonging to it." And further: "The system Pcs comes about by this thing-presentation being hypercathected through being linked with the word-presentations corresponding to it. It is these hypercathexes, we may suppose, that bring about a higher psychical organization and make it possible for the primary process to be succeeded by the secondary process which is dominant in the Pcs. Now, too, we are in a position to state precisely what it is that repression denies to the rejected presentation in the transference neuroses: what it denies to the presentation is translation into words which shall remain attached to the object" (p. 202).

The correspondence of verbal ideas to concrete ideas, that is to thing-cathexes in the unconscious, is mediated to the developing infantile psychic apparatus by the adult environment. The hypercathexes that "bring about a higher psychical organization," consisting in a linking up of unconscious memory traces with verbal ideas corresponding to them, are, in early ego development, due to the organizing interaction between primary process activity of the infantile psychic apparatus and secondary process activity of the child's environment. The terms "differential" and "libidinal tension system," which I used earlier designate energy aspects of this interaction, sources of energy of such hypercathexes. Freud clearly approached the problem of interaction between psychic apparatuses of different levels of organization when he spoke of the linking up of concrete ideas in the unconscious with verbal ideas as constituting the hypercathexes that "bring about a higher psychical organization." For this "linking up" is the same phenomenon as the mediation of higher organization, of preconscious mental activity, on the part of the child's environment, to the infantile psychic apparatus (cf. Charles Rycroft, 1956). Verbal ideas are representatives of preconscious activity, representatives of special importance because of the special role language plays in the higher development of the psychic apparatus, but they are, of course, not the only ones. Such linking up occurring in the interaction process becomes increasingly internalized as the interplay and communication between unconscious and preconscious within the psychic apparatus. The need for resumption of such mediating interaction in analysis, so that new internalizations may become possible and internal interaction be reactivated, results from the pathological degree of isolation between unconscious and preconscious, or—to speak in terms of a later terminology—from the development of defense processes of such proportions that the ego, rather than maintaining or extending its organization of the realm of the id, excludes more and more from its reach.

It should be apparent that a view of transference, which stresses the need of the unconscious for transference, for a point of attachment for a transference in the preconscious, by which

primary process is transformed into secondary process—implies
the notion that psychic health has to do with an optimal, although
by no means necessarily conscious, communication between unconscious and preconscious, between the infantile, archaic stages
and structures of the psychic apparatus and its later stages and
structures of organization. And further, that the unconscious is
capable of change and, as Freud says, "accessible to the impressions of life" ("The Unconscious," p. 190) and of the preconscious.
Where repression is lifted and unconscious and preconscious are
again in communication, infantile object and contemporary object may be united into one—a truly new object as both unconscious and preconscious are changed by their mutual communication. The object that helps to bring this about in therapy, the
analyst, mediates this union—a new version of the way in which
transformation of primary into secondary processes opened up
in childhood, through mediation of higher organization by way
of early object-relations.

A few words about transference and the so-called real relationship between patient and analyst. It has been said repeatedly
that one should distinguish transference (and countertransference) between patient and analyst in the analytic situation from
the realistic relationship between the two. I fully agree. However, it is implied in such statements that the realistic relationship between patient and analyst has nothing to do with transference. I hope to have made the point in the present discussion
that there is neither such a thing as reality nor a real relationship,
without transference. Any "real relationship" involves transfer
of unconscious images to present-day objects. In fact, present-
day objects are objects, and thus real, in the full sense of the
word (which comprises the unity of unconscious memory traces
and preconscious idea) only to the extent to which this transference, in the sense of transformational interplay between
unconscious and preconscious, is realized. The resolution of the
transference at the termination of an analysis means resolution
of the transference neurosis, and thereby of the transference distortions. This includes the recognition of the limited nature of
any human relationship and of the specific limitations of the
patient–analyst relationship. But the new object-relationship
with the analyst, which is gradually being built in the course of
the analysis and constitutes the real relationship between patient
and analyst, and which serves as a focal point for the establish-

ment of healthier object-relations in the patient's "real" life, is not devoid of transference in the sense clarified in this paper. I said earlier: To the extent to which the patient develops a "positive transference" (not in the sense of transference as resistance, but in the sense of that "transference," which carries the whole process of an analysis) he keeps this potentiality of a new object-relationship alive through all the various stages of resistance. This meaning of positive transference tends to be discredited in modern analytic writing and teaching, although not in treatment itself.

Freud, like any man who does not sacrifice the complexity of life to the deceptive simplicity of rigid concepts, has said a good many contradictory things. He can be quoted in support of many different ideas. May I, at the end, quote him in support of mine?

He writes to Jung on 6 December, 1906 (Sigmund Freud—C. G. Jung *Briefwechsel,* p. 13; *The Freud/Jung Letters,* pp. 12–13):

I have kept to myself some things that might be said about the therapy's limits and mechanisms, or have presented them in a way that only the initiate recognizes. It will not have escaped *you* that our cures come about by the fixation of libido ruling in the unconscious (transference), which, to be sure, meets us more reliably in hysteria. It is this that provides the driving force [Triebkraft] for the understanding and translation of the unconscious; where this is withheld, the patient does not take the trouble or does not listen to us when we present to him the translation we have found. It is actually a cure through love. Transference then, too, provides the strongest, the one unassailable proof that neurosis is determined by man's love life [my translation from the original German text].

And he writes to Ferenczi, on 10 January, 1910 (Jones, 1953, p. 496):

I will present you with some theory that has occurred to me while reading your analysis [referring to Ferenczi's self-analysis of a dream]. It seems to me that in our influencing of the sexual impulses we cannot achieve anything other than exchanges and displacements, never renunciation, relinquishment or the resolution of a complex (Strictly secret!). When someone brings out his infantile complexes he has saved a part of them (the affect) in a current form (transference). He has shed a skin and leaves it for the analyst. God forbid that he should now be naked, without a skin!

REFERENCES

Ferenczi, S. (1909): Introjection and transference. In: *Sex in Psychoanalysis*. New York: Brunner, 1950, p. 49.

Fisher, Charles. (1956): Dreams, images, and perception. *J. Amer. Psychoanal. Assn.* vol. 4.

Freud, S. Instincts and their vicissitudes. S.E. 14.

――――. *Beyond the Pleasure Principle*. S.E. 18.

――――. *An Outline of Psycho-analysis*. S.E. 23.

――――. *The Origins of Psychoanalysis*, New York: Basic Books, 1954, p. 379f.

――――. *The Interpretation of Dreams*. S.E. 5.

――――. *Studies on Hysteria*. S.E. 2.

――――. The neuro-psychoses of defence. S.E. 3.

――――. Screen memories. S.E. 3.

――――. The unconscious. S.E. 14.

Freud, S., and C. G. Jung. *Briefwechsel*. Edited by William McGuire and Wolfgang Sauerländer. Frankfurt am Main: S. Fischer Verlag, 1974.

――――. *The Freud/Jung Letters*. Edited by William McGuire. Translated by Ralph Manheim and R. F. C. Hull. Bollingen Series 94. Princeton, N.J.: Princeton University Press, 1974.

Hoffer, W. (1956): Transference and transference neurosis. *Int. J. Psycho-Anal.* 37:377.

Jones, E. *The Life and Work of Sigmund Freud*, vol. 2. London: Hogarth, 1955.

Loewald, H. W. (1951): Ego and reality. *Int. J. Psycho-Anal.*, vol. 32.

Rycroft, C. (1956): The nature and function of the analyst's communication to the patient. *Int. J. Psycho-Anal.* 37:470.

Silverberg, W. (1948): The concept of transference. *Psychoanal. Quart.* 17:321.

Spitz, R. (1956): Countertransference. *J. Amer. Psychoanal. Assn.* vol. 4.

Tower, L. (1956): Countertransference. *J. Amer. Psychoanal. Assn.*, vol. 4.

Waelder, R. Introduction to the discussion on problems of transference. *Int. J. Psycho-Anal.* 37:367.

15

INTERNALIZATION, SEPARATION, MOURNING, AND THE SUPEREGO

In this paper I shall speak of the superego as a product of internalization, and of internalization in its relations to separation, loss, and mourning. A brief consideration of some aspects of the termination of analysis will be presented in this context. I shall describe some of the differences and similarities between ego identifications and superego identifications and shall introduce the concept of degrees of internalization, suggesting that the introjects constituting the superego are more on the periphery of the ego system but are capable of mobility within this system and may thus merge into the ego proper and lose their superego character. The proposition will be presented that the superego, an enduring structure whose elements may change, has important relations to the internal representation of the temporal mode future.

As an introduction to the subject it may be useful to recall that for Freud the superego is the heir of the Oedipus complex. Introjections and identifications preceding the oedipal phase and preparing the way for its development go into the formation of the ego proper. The origins of the superego are to be found also, according to Freud, in those early identifications, which he calls immediate and direct and which are not the outcome of relinquished object cathexes. But the identifications that constitute the superego proper are the outcome of a relinquishment of oedipal objects: they are relinquished as external objects, even as fantasy objects, and are set up in the ego, by which process they become internal objects cathected by the id—a narcissistic ca-

Versions of this paper have been presented to the Topeka Psychoanalytic Society (1959), to the Western New England Psychoanalytic Society (1960), and at the December meeting of the American Psychoanalytic Association in New York (1960). Refer to "Superego and Time" in this volume.

thexis. This is a process of desexualization in which an internal relationship is substituted for an external one.

Thus we can distinguish two types or stages of identification: those that precede, and are the basis for, object cathexes and those that are the outcome of object cathexes formed in the oedipal phase. The latter constitute the precipitate in the ego which Freud calls the superego; the former constitute the forerunners, the origins of the superego but are, considered in themselves, constituent elements of the ego proper. I think it is correct to say that the early ("ego") identifications take place during stages of development when inside and outside—ego and objects—are not clearly differentiated, which is to say that the stage where "objects" can be "cathected" is not yet reached or that a temporary regression from this stage has taken place. The later type of identifications, the superego identifications, on the other hand, are identifications with differentiated objects of libidinal and aggressive cathexis—objects that themselves cathect in such ways. The later identifications thus can be based on the relinquishment of these objects. In actuality, of course, there is a continuum of stages between these two types and much overlapping and intermingling of them.

I

The relinquishment of external objects and their internalization involves a process of separation, of loss and restitution in many ways similar to mourning. During analysis, problems of separation and mourning come to the fore in a specific way at times of interruption and most particularly in the terminal phases of treatment. In fact, the end phase of an analysis may be described as a long-drawn-out leave taking—too long, it often seems, from the point of view of ordinary life. In everyday life, many of us tend to cut short a farewell, perhaps in order to diminish the embarrassment, the ambiguity, and pain, even though we may be torn between the grief of separation and the eager anticipation of the future awaiting us. Others seem to wish to prolong the farewell; yet it is not the farewell they want to prolong but the presence of the beloved person so as to postpone the leave taking as long as possible. In both cases an attempt is made to deny loss: either we try to deny that the other person still exists or did exist, or we try to deny that we have to leave the beloved person and must venture out on our own. Either the past or the future is denied. At the death of a beloved person, either form of denial may occur internally as there is no possibility of realizing the denial by external action with the other person. In true mourning, the loss of the beloved person is perhaps temporarily denied but gradually is accepted and worked out by way of a complex inner process.

Analysis is not and should not be like ordinary life although it is a replica of it in certain essential features while it is fundamentally different in other respects. Compared with everyday life, the leave taking of the end phase of analysis is too long-drawn-out; compared with the leave taking involved in the resolution of the Oedipus complex, the terminal phase of an analysis is likely to be a considerably shortened and condensed leave taking. One of the differences between analysis and ordinary life is that experiences purposefully and often painfully made explicit in analysis usually remain implicit in ordinary life; they are lifted onto a level and quality of awareness that they do not usually possess in ordinary life. To gain such awareness, inner distance and perspective are needed, and to acquire them time is needed which is not often available or used in such ways in the urgency of immediate life experiences.

If the experience of parting, of ending the relationship with another person (here the analyst) is felt explicitly, consciously, and in the hypercathected mode that is characteristic of analysis and is promoted by the analytic interpretation, then neither the existence of the person from whom we part nor the anticipated life without him can be denied. In the explicit experience of parting, the person from whom we take leave is becoming part of the past, and at the same time we move into the future, which is to be without him. Neither past nor future are denied but are recognized and taken hold of in the present. The extended leave taking of the end phase of analysis is a replica of the process of mourning. The analyst who during the analysis has stood at times for mother, father, and other loved and hated figures of the patient's past is to be left. The internal relationships the patient had established with these loved and hated figures of the past have become partially external again during analysis. The internalizations by which the patient's character structure became established in earlier years have been partially undone in the analytic process and have been replaced by relationships with an external object—the analyst standing for various objects at different times. In other words, internalizations have been, to a degree, reversed; internal relationships constituting elements of the ego structure have been re-externalized.

Analysis, understood as the working out of the transference neurosis, changes the inner relationships which had constituted the patient's character by promoting the partial externalization of these internal relationships, thus making them available for recognition, exploration, and reintegration. By partial externalization, psychic structures in their inner organization are projected onto a plane of reality where they become three-dimensional, as it were. However, the analyst, as was the case with the original parental figures, is only a temporary external object in important respects. The relationship with the analyst, like that with parental figures in earlier ego development, has to become partially internalized—a process which to varying degrees goes on during all but the initial stages of analysis, but which is to come to its fruition and more definitive realization during the terminal phase. The pressure of the impending separation helps to accelerate this renewed internalization, although the process of internalization will continue and come to relative completion only after termination of the analysis.

The death of a love object, or the more or less permanent separation from a love object, is the occasion for mourning and for internalization. The unconscious and conscious experiences of threats to one's own existence as an individual, heightened by the increasing awareness of one's own eventual death, are, I believe, intimately connected with the phenomenon of internalization. It seems significant that with the advent of Christianity, initiating the greatest intensification of internalization in Western civilization, the death of God as incarnated in Christ moves into the center of religious experience. Christ is not only the ultimate love object, which the believer loses as an external object and regains by identification with Him as an ego ideal, He is, in His passion and sacrificial death, the exemplification of complete internalization and sublimation of all earthly relationships and needs. But to pursue these thoughts would lead us far afield into unexplored psychological country.

Loss of a love object does not necessarily lead to mourning and internalization. The object lost by separation or death may not be mourned, but either the existence or the loss of the object may be denied. Such denial is the opposite of mourning. Instead of internalizing the relationship, external substitutions may be sought. One patient, for instance, used all available figures in the environment as substitutes for the lost parents, clinging forever to relatives and friends of his parents and from his own childhood, appealing to them, often successfully, for care and love. But he was unable to establish lasting new relationships and lasting and effective sublimations; his capacity for productive work was severely limited; his superego development was rudimentary. Both the ability to form lasting new external relationships and the capacity for stable sublimations appear to be based on, among other things, firmly established internalizations.

Another patient appeared to be the victim of his father's denial of the death of the father's beloved brother. The patient became the substitute for the brother and the father now clung to him with all the force of this never-relinquished attachment. The patient had great difficulty in emancipating himself from his father because of the guilt involved in severing this tie. Of course this was only one aspect of the patient's neurotic attachment to his father. For many complex reasons, a third patient denied the existence of his sister with whom he had had an early overt sexual relationship. This sister, now married, remained strongly attached to the patient while he denied the early relationship as well as any present feeling for her by complete condemnation of her and refusing to have anything to do with her. In the analysis he kept "forgetting" her existence, as well as the significance of the childhood relationship in his current life, despite its prominent evidence. For this patient the process of mourning was something to be avoided; for instance, even a temporary separation had to be abrupt and he would not let friends or relatives accompany him to the station if he were going away on a trip. When we began to think of termination of the analysis, he had a strong impulse to terminate practically from one day to the next, and insisted that after the analysis we would never meet again.

An analysis is itself a prime example of seeking a substitute for the lost love objects, and the analyst in the transference promotes such substitution. The goal, however, is to resolve the transference neurosis, a revival of the infantile neurosis. The failure to resolve the Oedipus complex can be understood as a failure to achieve stable internalizations based on true relinquishment of the infantile incestuous object relations, leading to faulty superego formation. The resolution of the transference neurosis is thus intimately related to the achievement of true mourning by which relationships with external objects are set up in the ego system as internal relationships in a process of further ego differentiation. This is the reason why it is so important to work through the separation involved in the termination of analysis.

Ideally termination should culminate in or lead into a genuine relinquishment of the external object (the analyst) as an incestuous love object and, in the transformation of the external relationship, into an internal relationship within the ego–superego system. Such internalization does not necessarily imply that a relationship, once it becomes internal, cannot further develop as an internal relationship. To avoid misunderstanding I should like to stress again that a sharp distinction must be maintained between a relationship to fantasy objects and an internal relationship that is a constituent of ego structure.

II

It is time to consider more closely the problem of internalization and its relation to separation and mourning. I use the term "internalization" here as a general term for certain processes of transformation by which relationships and interactions between the individual psychic apparatus and its environment are changed into inner relationships and interactions within the psychic apparatus. Thus an internal world is constituted and it in turn entertains relationships and interactions with the outer world. The term "internalization" therefore covers such "mechanisms" as incorporation, introjection, and identification, or those referred to by the terms "internal object" and "internalized object," as well as such "vicissitudes of instincts" as the "turning inward" of libidinal and aggressive drives. The word "incorporation" most often seems to emphasize zonal, particularly oral, aspects of internalization processes. "Introjection" ordinarily is used for ego aspects of the same processes. "Identification" probably is the term that is most ambiguous. There are reasons to assume that internalization per se is only one element of at least certain kinds of identification and that projection plays an important part in them. The term "identification," in accordance with general psychoanalytic parlance, is used here in a somewhat loose fashion so as not to prejudge what might be implied in the concept.

The significance of separation has been of concern to psychoanalysis since its beginnings, and in many different contexts and ramifications. To name some at random: separation anxiety, castration fear, birth trauma, loss of the love object, loss of love, the implications of the oedipal situation (relinquishment of the libidinal object, incest barrier), mourning, depression, ego boundaries and early ego development (detachment from the environment), superego origins, oral aggression, frustration, and others beside. If one asks how human beings deal with the anxieties and frustrations of separation and loss, the answer may be: either by external action designed to reduce or abolish the sense of separation and loss, or by an internal process meant to achieve the same end. Yet separation may be experienced not as deprivation and loss but as liberation and a sign of mastery. Separation from a love-hate object may be brought about by oneself in an attempt to effect emancipation from such objects, or it may be facilitated by others, even the love objects themselves; if it is not facilitated, or if it is prevented by others, the lack of separation may be experienced as deprivation. However, it seems that emancipation as a process of separation from external objects— to be distinguished from rebellion, which maintains the external relationship—goes hand in hand with the work of internalization, which reduces or abolishes the sense of external deprivation and loss. Whether separation from a love object is experienced as deprivation and loss or as emancipation and mastery will depend, in part, on the achievement of the work of internalization. Speaking in terms of affect, the road leads from depression through mourning to elation.

In the event of aggression and overwhelming intrusion and invasion from the outside, the need for separation may become imperative. Such a need may be satisfied by removal of the aggressor or of oneself. On the other hand, under such circumstances the need for union may become imperative (identification with the aggressor); through such union aggression is re-moved by a different means. As we explore these various modes of separation and union, it becomes more and more apparent that the ambivalence of love–hate and of aggression–submission (sadism–masochism) enters into all of them and that neither separation nor union can ever be entirely unambivalent. The deepest root of the ambivalence that appears to pervade all rela-tionships, external as well as internal, seems to be the polarity inherent in individual existence of individuation and "primary narcissistic" union—a polarity that Freud attempted to concep-tualize by various approaches but that he recognized and insisted upon from beginning to end by his dualistic conception of in-stincts, of human nature, and of life itself.

The relinquishment of the oedipal love objects and the con-comitant identifications are generally seen as being enforced by these very objects (castration threat, threat of loss of love, incest taboo). But if this development be a necessary evil, it is the kind of evil that is turned into a virtue in the course of human evolu-tion. It is an example of the "change of function" which led Hart-mann to the concept of the secondary autonomy of the ego.[1] As pointed out before, separation from love objects, while in one sense something to be overcome and undone through internali-zation, is, insofar as it means individuation and emancipation, a positive achievement brought about by the relinquishment and internalization of the love objects. The change of function taking place here is that a means of defense against the pain and anxiety of separation and loss becomes a goal in itself.

But can we be satisfied with the description of these internali-zations as originating in defensive needs even though we grant that they are important elements in oedipal identifications? The oedipal identifications, constituting the elements of the superego, are new versions—promoted by new experiences of deprivation and loss—of identifications which precede the oedipal situation. The narcissistic cathexis, replacing object cathexis in internali-zation, is secondary and is founded on an older, "primary" nar-

---

1. Heinz Hartmann, *Ego Psychology and the Problem of Adaptation*, New York: International Universities Press, Inc., 1958, pp. 25–26. Certain aspects of internalization and of the all-important phenomenon of change of function in biology and mental life were seen clearly by Nietzsche. He used the term "internalization." Cf. his *The Genealogy of Morals* (1887), Garden City, New York: Doubleday Anchor Books, 1956.

cissism of which it is a new version. The same appears to hold true not only for the libidinal but for the aggressive aspects of oedipal identifications. If we accept Freud's views on primary aggression, behind aggression turned inward, as manifested in phenomena of guilt and masochism, lies what Freud called "primary masochism," which, in terms of the aggressive drives, corresponds to primary narcissism. Without going into further details here, the conception is that in ontogenetic development a primitive stage of primary narcissism and primary aggression (death instinct) is followed by some process of externalization. Once such externalizations have occurred, reinternalizations may take place and sexual and aggressive drives may be turned inward. Yet they are not quite the same drives as they were before externalization; they have been qualified and differentiated by externalization, that is, by having become object-cathected. (Freud wrote: "The shadow of the object fell upon the ego.") Figuratively speaking, in the process of internalization the drives take aspects of the object with them into the ego. Neither drive nor object is the same as before, and the ego itself becomes further differentiated in the process. Internalization is structure building.

But we must go one step further. It has been recognized recently that we have to understand the stage of primary narcissism and primary aggression not as a stage where libido and aggression are still cathected in a primitive ego rather than in objects, but as a stage where inside and outside, an ego and an object-world, are as yet not distinguishable one from the other. To quote from a recent summary of views on early ego development, ". . . no difference exists between the 'I' and the 'non-I' in the first weeks of life. The first traces of such distinction begin in the second month. This lack of boundaries is a prerequisite for both projection and introjection."[2] To ask whether externalization preceded internalization or vice versa becomes, in the light of this insight, meaningless. There are primary externalizations and internalizations, and there are secondary externalizations and internalizations. In secondary externalization something that was internal becomes external, and in secondary internali-

2. Panel on *Some Theoretical Aspects of Early Psychic Functioning,* reported by David L. Rubinfine. *J. Amer. Psychoanal. Assn.* 7:569.

zation something that was external becomes internal. The meaning of the terms externalization and internalization, when we speak of the primary forms, is different: primary externalization signifies that *externality is being established*; primary internalization signifies that *internality is being constituted*. On this level, then, we cannot speak of externalization (projection) and internalization as defenses (against inner conflict or external deprivation); we must speak of them as boundary-creating processes and as processes of differentiation of an undifferentiated state. It is true, nevertheless, that defenses against inner conflict and against outer deprivation promote and color such differentiation.

Hence the relinquishment and internalization of oedipal objects, while "enforced" by these objects in the oedipal situation, must at the same time be seen as a resumption on a new level of boundary-creating processes. Ego, objects, and boundaries of and between them—at first nonexistent, later still indistinct and fluid—gradually become more distinct and fixed, although by no means in an absolute or definitive fashion. Side by side with object relations, processes of identification persist and re-enter the picture in new transformations representing resumptions of boundary-setting, differentiating processes, notwithstanding their prominent aspects as defenses against loss of love objects.

Earlier I referred to the end-phase of an analysis as an extended leave taking and as a replica of the process of mourning. Mourning involves not only the gradual, piecemeal relinquishment of the lost object, but also the internalization, the appropriation of aspects of this object—or rather, of aspects of the relationship between the ego and the lost object which are "set up in the ego" and become a relationship within the ego system. This process is similar to the relinquishment of the oedipal objects that leads to the formation of the superego. A relationship with an external libidinal-aggressive object is replaced by an internal relationship. In the work of mourning (a lost relationship, lost by death or actual separation) the change from object cathexis to narcissistic cathexis is a repetition, within certain limits, of the previous experience of the relinquishment of oedipal object relations and of their being set up in the ego. There is, of course, an important difference between the resolution of the Oedipus complex and mourning in later life: in the oedipal situation the external objects not only remain present during the resolution of the conflict, but the fact that they remain present actively promotes the process of internalization. The parents remain present during this period but change their attitude; they promote a partial detachment, a decathexis of libidinal-aggressive drives from themselves as external objects so that an amount of such drive energy is freed for narcissistic recathexis. Moreover, some drive energy becomes available for eventual recathexis in nonincestuous external relationships: parents promote emancipation. Decathexis of drive energy from the incestuous object relations promotes, in varying proportions, both narcissistic recathexis (internalization) and recathexis in nonincestuous object relations. However, to the extent that incestuous object cathexis does not undergo some degree of internalization (change into narcissistic cathexis) prior to recathexis in external object relations, the new external object relations remain incestuous in character; without further differentiation of the inner world no further differentiation of the object world takes place. The latency period exemplifies, in its essentials, such a silent phase of internalization.

The promotion by the parents of partial decathexis from themselves as libidinal-aggressive objects, and of narcissistic recathexis (omitting in this context the recathexis in new object relations), is not merely in the interest of the child's development but represents a developmental change in the parents: they themselves achieve a partial decathexis of libidinal-aggressive drive energy from the child as *their* external object, leading to further internalizing processes in themselves and modifications of their own ego structures.[3] Such mutuality, to use Erikson's term, is essential for normal resolution of the Oedipus complex and development of the superego.

If the resolution of the Oedipus complex is a prototype of mourning, it is this prototype, achieved through the interaction between the objects involved in the oedipal situation, that enables the individual to mourn external objects in later life without the object's interacting help. The analytic situation re-embodies this

3. Compare Therese Benedek, *Parenthood as a Developmental Phase. J. Amer. Psychoanal. Assn.* 7:389–417, and pertinent formulations in many of Erik Erikson's writings.

interaction and the termination of analysis leads, if things go well, to a healthier resolution of the Oedipus complex than the patient had been able to achieve before, and to a more stable superego. Patients at the termination of treatment frequently express a feeling of mutual abandonment that, if analyzed, becomes the pathway to the relinquishment of the analyst as an external object and to the internalization of the relationship. This is similar to the experience of emancipation in adolescence, which repeats the oedipal struggle on a higher level.

Internal and external relationships, of course, continue to supplement and influence each other in various ways during adult life; there are more or less continuous shifts and exchanges between internal and external relationships. Freud first alluded to them in his paper, "On Narcissism."

III

"Ideal ego" and "ego ideal" were the first names Freud gave to the "differentiating grade in the ego," which he later called the superego. The ideal ego, by identification with the parental figures—perceived as omnipotent—represents, in Freud's view, a recapturing of the original, primary narcissistic, omnipotent perfection of the child himself. It represents an attempt to return to the early infantile feeling of narcissistic sufficiency, so rudely disillusioned by the inevitable frustrations and deprivations inherent in the conditions of extrauterine existence. This presumed omnipotent sufficiency appears to be maintained, for a time, by the close "symbiotic" relationship with the mother, and is gradually replaced by reliance on the seeming parental omnipotence. The ideal ego, in contrast to the child's .frequent experience of an impotent, helpless ego, is then a return, in fantasy, to the original state; it is an ego replenished, restored to the wholeness of the undifferentiated state of primary narcissistic union and identity with the environment, by identification with the all-powerful parents. The process could be described— naively yet perhaps quite aptly—as one whereby the child reaches out to take back from the environment what has been removed from him in an ever-increasing degree since his birth: identification that attempts to re-establish an original identity with the environment. This identity of the past, at first "halluci-

nated" by the child in the manner of hallucinatory wish fulfilment, gradually becomes something to be reached for, wished
for in the future. Representatives of such a future state of being
are parents, perhaps siblings, and later other "ideals."

If the ideal ego represents something like a hallucinated or
fantasied state of perfection, the term "ego ideal" indicates more
clearly that this state of narcissistic perfection is something to be
reached for. Insofar as this wholeness is the original state of the
infant in his psychic identity with the environment, and insofar
as (from the point of view of the disillusioned observer) the
parental environment is far from such a state of omnipotent
wholeness and perfection, we must describe the identifications
just mentioned as containing an element of projection. Undoubtedly such infantile projections evoke responses in the parent
which in turn help to shape the child's developing conception of
ideals, just as in general the parents' responses to his needs,
demands, and expectations contribute to the character of his
idealizations. But the child's ideals are also shaped by the
parents' own projections, by *their* idealizations of the child, and
by their demands, expectations, and needs in respect to the child.
In a sense, both the child and the parents can be said to have
fantasies—some would say illusions—about the other's state of
perfection and wholeness, or at least about the other's perfecti-
bility.

But let us not scoff at such fantasies. The demands and expectations engendered by them are essential for the development
and maintenance of a sound superego in the object of such expectations—provided that the expectations are allowed to be con-
tinuously shaped and tempered by an increasing realistic ap-
praisal of the stage of maturity and of the potentialities of the
object. The inevitable elements of disillusionment are no less
important for superego development in the one so disillusioned,
for it is such disillusionment that under reasonably favorable
circumstances (if frustration is not overwhelming) contributes
to the internalization of expectations and demands. Regarding
the child, then, parental projective fantasies of the child's narcissistic perfection and wholeness, as well as infantile projective
fantasies of the parent's omnipotent perfection, have an important bearing on the development of his superego. Such fantasies,
based on old longings in all concerned, in normal development

are gradually being cleared and modified in accordance with a more realistic comprehension of the potentialities and limitations of the object relation involved. The parents are to be the guides in this process of clearing and resolving that leads to a more rational mutual relationship externally, as well as to a reasonably balanced internal relationship within the ego–super-ego system insofar as the internalized demands lose their archaic insistence on narcissistic perfection.

The term "superego"—in accordance with Freud's view that the superego is the heir of the Oedipus complex—is used after the distinction between ego and objects, and the distinction between heterosexual and homosexual objects, is relatively firmly established, and after boundaries of and between ego and objects, and limitations of the oedipal object relations, are acknowledged. (In the particular context of this paper, I can only allude to the paramount importance of the sexual differentiation of objects and of self for the superego problem and must leave further consideration of this issue for another occasion.) It is only then that an external and an internal world can be said to exist in the experience of the child and that ideals and demands are more definitely sorted out into external and internal. There are now external and internal authorities, with their demands, their love and hate, their images of what should be, their rewards and punishments. The superego is constituted of those authorities that are clearly internal and have become a "differentiating grade in the ego," thus being clearly differentiated from external love-hate authorities and ideal images.

Demands, expectations, hopes, and ideals change in the course of development. Some are reached and fulfilled and are no longer beckonings from a future; others are not. Some are given up, others remain as ideals and demands though never reached and fulfilled. New demands and ideals arise. Some are realized for a time but then are lost or become remote again. Clinical evidence, particularly clear in some psychotic and borderline states because of the fragility and transparency of the ego structure, indicates a mobility of so-called introjected objects within the ego system, suggesting shifting degrees of internalization and externalization which bring the introjects more or less close to the ego core. If we think in such terms as "degrees of internalization," of greater or lesser "distance from an ego core," it is of great importance to keep in mind that the modification of external material for introjection, brought about by internalization, varies with the degree of internalization. A comparison with physiological assimilation is suggested whereby organic compounds are ingested and subjected to catabolic and anabolic changes in the course of assimilation into the body substance. Underlying the concept of the superego as a differentiating grade in the ego is the idea of a distance from an ego core. Unless there is a degree of tension between this ego core and the superego, they are not distinguishable.

Let me give a simple example of progressive internalization and re-externalization, taken from precursory stages of superego development. Ferenczi spoke of sphincter morality, and there can be no doubt that the expectation of sphincter control becomes increasingly internalized as an expectation. But a point is reached where such control is established and no longer an external or internal demand which may or may not be realized; it becomes an automatic control which now can be said to be a rather primitive ego function. Since maturation must have advanced to a state where such expectations become feasible, it is obvious that a correspondence between external and internalized expectation, on the one hand, and internal potentiality, on the other hand, is very important. Sphincter control, under certain conditions of stress, may be lost temporarily, at which time it regains the quality of a demand. Or it may retain this quality unconsciously from early times; for instance, if the original parental expectation of it was not in tune with the maturational stage of the child—a lack of empathic interaction that interferes with internalization.

A second example is taken from the experience of mourning. The outcome of mourning can show something like a new intake of objects into the superego structure insofar as elements of the lost object, through the mourning process, become introjected in the form of ego-ideal elements and inner demands and punishments. Such internalization of aspects of a lost love object, if observed over long periods of time (we must think in terms of years in adults) may be found to be progressive, so that eventually what was an ego-ideal or superego element becomes an element of the ego proper and is realized as an ego trait rather than an internal demand. We see this, for instance, in a son who increasingly becomes like his father after the father's death. It is as though only then can he appropriate into his ego core given elements of his father's character. It would lead too far to give clinical examples from psychotic conditions, although shifts in degrees of internalization and externalization, because of the instability of the ego structure, are often particularly impressive here.[4]

The foregoing discussion leads to a conception of the superego as a structure, and enduring as a structure whose constituent elements may change.[5] Elements of it may become elements of the ego proper and may, under conditions of ego disorganization and reorganization, return, as it were, into the superego and even be further externalized.

During analysis we can observe the projection or externalization of superego elements onto the analyst. During periods of psychic growth—in childhood as well as in adult life—the change of superego elements into ego elements is a continuing process, it seems. The superego itself, in its turn, receives new elements through interaction with the object world. The changing of superego elements into ego elements involves a further desexualization and deaggressivization; it involves a return, as in a spiral, to the type of identifications characterized as ego or primary identifications—the person thereby regaining a measure of narcissistic wholeness which inevitably, as in childhood, leads again to giving up such self-sufficiency by further involvement with others. The progressive differentiation and enrichment of the ego during life, to the extent to which it occurs, is a return in a new dimension to an identity of ego and objects, on the basis of which new reaches of the object world become accessible. The ripening of the personality in adult life, whether through analysis or other significant life experiences, is based on the widening and deepening relations that the enriched and more differentiated ego entertains with external reality, understood and penetrated in new dimensions.

4. Norman Cameron, *Introjection, Reprojection, and Hallucination in the Interaction Between Schizophrenic Patient and Therapist. Int. J. Psycho-Anal.*, vol. 42, parts 1–2, 1961.

5. See also Samuel Novey, *The Role of the Superego and Ego Ideal in Character Formation. Int. J. Psycho-Anal.*, vol. 36, 1955. He speaks of the superego as a "functional pattern of introjection rather than as a fixed institution."

Inner ideals, expectations, hopes, demands, and, equally, inner doubts, fears, guilt, despair concerning oneself—all this is reaching toward or feeling defeated by a future. The voice of conscience tells us what we should do or should have done, speaking from a future that we ask ourselves to reach or tell ourselves we are failing to reach—perhaps a future which should bring back a lost past, but certainly a future whose image in the course of development becomes imbued with all that is still alive from the hopes, expectations, demands, promises, ideals, aspirations, self-doubt, guilt, and despair of past ages, ancestors, parents, teachers, prophets, priests, gods, and heroes. Maturation and development, which are movements into a future, are promoted, defined, and channeled, or hindered and inhibited, by the hopes and expectations, fears, doubts, and demands, by the guidance and positive and negative examples given by parents and other authorities, depending on whether or not they are commensurate with the stage and speed of development and with the potentialities of the child, and depending on the superego development of the authorities themselves. Seen from the other side, parental expectations, fears, and hopes, the guidance and examples of authorities, their standards, prohibitions, and punishments for the child are promoted and channeled, or inhibited and frustrated, by the child's maturation and development, which bring some new potentialities into the parents' view and limit and exclude others. The superego, inasmuch as it is the internal representative of parental and cultural standards, expectations, fears, and hopes, is the intrapsychic representation of the future. Only insofar as we are ahead of ourselves, insofar as we recognize potentialities in ourselves, which represent *more* than we are at present and from which we look back at ourselves as we are at present, can we be said to have a conscience. The voice of conscience speaks to us as the mouthpiece of the superego, from the point of view of the inner future which we envision. One might say that in the voice of conscience the superego speaks to the ego as being capable or incapable of encompassing the superego as the inner future toward which to move.

As an aspect of the inner future of the ego becomes an inner actuality, this superego element merges into the ego as an element no longer differentiated from the ego. Guilt in respect to this element vanishes, as guilt is a form of tension between ego and superego. We have a sense of guilt concerning past or present thoughts, feelings, and deeds, but only inasmuch as they represent a nonfulfilment of the inner image of ourselves, of the internal ideal we have not reached, of the future in us that we have failed.

The greater or lesser distances from the ego core—the degrees of internalization of which I spoke—perhaps are best understood as temporal in nature, as relations between an inner present and an inner future. Such structuralization obviously is not spatial. Physical structures are in space and organized by spatial relations. It may be that we can advance our understanding of what we mean when we speak of psychic structures if we consider the possibility of their mode of organization as a temporal one, even though we do not as yet understand the nature of such organization. It might well be useful to explore further not only the superego in its relations to the temporal mode future, but also the time dimensions of id and ego and their relations to the temporal modes past and present.

SUMMARY

The formation of the superego, as the "heir of the Oedipus complex," is considered in its relation to the* phenomena of separation and mourning. Separation is described in its aspect as the occasion for processes of internalization, especially as it is related to mourning. The work of mourning is not confined to a gradual relinquishment of the lost object but also encompasses processes of internalizing elements of the relationship with the object to be relinquished. Such internalizations, insofar as they occur as part of the resolution of the Oedipus complex, lead to further differentiation of the ego of which the superego is a "differentiating grade." Some illustrations of the psychological processes involved in separation are given and there is a brief discussion of the termination of analysis from this point of view.

Separation from love objects constitutes a loss and may be experienced as deprivation. But separation, in certain crucial events in human life, also has the significance of emancipation and lack of separation may be experienced as deprivation. It is suggested that the emancipation involved in the normal resolution of the Oedipus complex, as well as in subsequent separations in which successful mourning takes place, can be understood in two ways: first, as an internal substitution for an externally severed object relationship (internal "restitution of the lost object"), and second, as a resumption of early boundary-setting processes by which a further differentiation and integration of the ego and of the object world on higher levels of development takes place. In other words, so-called superego identifications represent an undoing, so to speak, of separation insofar as object loss is concerned and they also represent the achievement of separation insofar as boundary setting and further ego and object differentiation is concerned. The differences and similarities between so-called primary and secondary identifications, as well as between primary and secondary narcissism and between primary and secondary aggression, are briefly discussed from this point of view. It is pointed out that both internality and externality, an inner world and an outer world, are constituted by the primary forms of these processes and that their secondary forms, notwithstanding their defensive aspects, continue to contribute to the further organization of an inner and an outer world.

Some concrete aspects of superego formation through the interaction between child and parents are briefly cited, and the duality or polarity of individuation and primary narcissistic identity with the environment is emphasized as a basic phenomenon of human development underlying the ambivalent significances of separation and of internalization.

The concept of degrees of internalization is advanced. This implies shifting distances of internalized "material" from the ego core and shifting distances within the ego–superego system, as well as transformations in the character of the introjects according to the respective degrees of internalization. The superego is conceived as an enduring structure pattern whose elements may change and move either in the direction of the ego core or in an outer direction toward object representation. Thus elements of the superego may lose their superego character and become ego elements, or take on the character of object representations (externalization). It is postulated that the superego has the temporal character of futurity inasmuch as the superego-ego ideal may be understood as the envisioned inner future of the ego. Conscience, as the voice of the superego, speaks to the ego from the point of view of the inner future toward which the ego reaches or which the ego has failed. It is suggested that the degrees of internalization, the distances from the ego core, are temporal in nature, representing relations between an inner present and an inner future, although we but vaguely grasp the nature of such temporal structuralization.

16

PSYCHOANALYTIC THEORY AND THE PSYCHOANALYTIC PROCESS

I

An investigation of the relationship of psychoanalytic theory to the psychoanalytic process and method is fraught with difficulties and pitfalls, as the many recent efforts to elucidate and, where necessary, to redefine and revise, theoretical concepts and formulations have demonstrated. In this attempt it is important that psychoanalytic theory (or metapsychology), though being on a high level of abstraction and generalization, keep faith with our work as analysts. This work, whether we consider it as scientific or as therapeutic or as both, has given us the insights into psychic reality, into the processes and structures of the human mind, on which the theory is founded. Yet, in the attempt to arrive at a general body of theory, following the lead and premises of other sciences, we have come to divorce, to a significant degree, theory from method and process of investigation; we have neglected the implications which the unique conditions in our field—that aspect of reality with which psychoanalysis deals—have for our method and for theory formation. To evolve theory as though our methods and processes of study were essentially the same, or could be the same, as those of other sciences, or could be disregarded when it comes to theory, implies a view of reality that is no longer tenable, least of all in that ambiguous area which we call psychic reality. Nevertheless, all of us are still more or less captives of an erroneous understanding of objectivity and objective reality, and this is one reason for the difficulties.

Based on a lecture presented at the Plenary Session of a Midwest Regional Conference arranged by the Chicago Psychoanalytic Society, Chicago, February 21–22, 1970.

I gratefully acknowledge a grant by the Robert P. Knight Fund that helped support part of the work on which this paper is based.

277

I mentioned that the unique conditions prevailing in our field of study have specific implications for its method and theory. The scientific fiction—I use that word here in its nonpejorative sense—of a field of study to which we are in the relation of extraneous observers cannot be maintained in psychoanalysis. We become part and participant of and in the field as soon as we are present in our role as analysts. The unit of a psychoanalytic investigation is the individual human mind or personality. We single it out—for reasons deeply rooted in that human mind of which we ourselves are specimens—as a subject worthy of study, as a universe in its own right. "Universe" has been defined as "any distinct field or province of thought or reality conceived as forming a closed system or self-inclusive and independent organization" (Webster). The individual's status in this regard, however, is questionable and cannot be taken for granted. If nothing else, the phenomena of transference and resistance, encountered in both analysand and analyst during the investigation of our object of study, demonstrate the precariousness of that status and show that the individual cannot be studied psychoanalytically as though he were simply a closed system investigated by another closed system. In fact, a psychoanalytic investigation must take into account and include in its investigation the phenomena of transference and resistance as essential parts of what we want to study and of our investigative method.

For the purpose of study, we have to become an integral, though in certain ways detached, part of the "field of study." The object of investigation, the analysand, as well as the investigator, the analyst, although each has a considerable degree of internal psychic organization and relative autonomy in respect to the other, can enter a psychoanalytic investigation only by virtue of their being relatively open systems, and open to each other. And each in his own ways must renounce a degree of autonomy for the sake of the investigation. Neither the object of investigation nor the investigator can be dealt with theoretically as though a simple subject–object confrontation obtained. We even have to qualify our speaking of investigator and object, insofar as the object, by the very nature of the psychoanalytic process, becomes an investigator of himself, and the investigator–analyst becomes an object of study to himself. At the same time the analysand, although not in a scientifically and professionally informed and skilled way, "studies" the analyst in the analytic process, and the analyst must hold himself open as an object of the analysand's search (by this, of course, I do not mean that he must answer questions and tell the analysand about himself). The analysand's search proceeds under the surface, often unconsciously, and the analyst is not always aware of being the object of such a search. That the analytic relationship is an asymmetrical one, and that it has to be that if analysis is to proceed, is unquestioned.

All this is confusing—our customary categories and distributions of role and our traditional views on the constellation of an investigation do not fit. Implied in the foregoing considerations, but to be made more explicit, is that the two systems, the two would-be universes, the one that is studied and the one that investigates, are the same kinds of organizations: individual psychic organizations. The mental processes and structures we study in our patients are essentially the same as our own and of the same order of reality (psychic reality), as well as of the same order as the processes and structures by means of which we study them. Our traditional standard of objectivity implies that making something an object of investigation means to subject it to procedures, ultimately mental ones, which are in principle extraneous and superordinated to the processes inherent in the object. There are differences between analysand and analyst in the degree to which their mental processes are developed and organized, and these differences make for the possibility of relative objectivity. But the differences must not be too great; if they are, the psychic processes in the object of investigation are no longer within the ken of psychoanalytic investigation. The case of the infant or of the deeply regressed psychotic (as extreme examples) introduces factors that interfere with psychoanalytic investigation, because the latter is based on the premise that analysand and analyst are both participants and that the analysand, too, is capable of a measure of objectivity toward himself as well as toward the analyst. The analysand must, at least to some extent, have developed an "observing ego" in order to get the analytic investigation off the ground.

In contrast to physics or biology, for instance, psychoanalytic knowledge and explanation depend not so much on the differences between the processes obtaining in the scientist and those obtaining in his object, but on their similarity and interrelatedness. It is a commonplace fact that introspection and empathy are essential tools of psychoanalysis, and that we can analyze others only as far as we have been analyzed ourselves and understand ourselves. To this there is the corollary: we understand ourselves psychoanalytically by seeing ourselves as others (objectivating introspection), and our self-understanding is greatly enhanced by analyzing others, as every analyst knows. This is so not only because in the external other we can often see ourselves more clearly, but also because in this concentrated and minutely scrutinized relationship, in this specially focused and heightened field of psychic forces, the analyst's intrapsychic field gains in vitality and vivid outline. The analysand in this respect can be compared to the child who—if he can allow himself that freedom—scrutinizes with his unconscious antennae the parents' motivations and moods and in this way may contribute—if the parent or analyst allows himself that freedom— to the latter's self-awareness. Internal communication, on which self-understanding is based, and communication with another organization of the same rank of reality—the psychic reality of another individual—are inextricably interwoven.

There are still other important elements inherent in the analytic process and method of psychoanalytic research and these should be encompassed in a psychoanalytic theory worthy of that name. One such fundamental characteristic of the human psyche is the capacity to change. "Where id was, there ego shall become" (Freud, 1933)[1] is not simply a statement of therapeutic goals. This dictum says that by being understood psychoanalytically and by understanding ourselves we tend to change. Our psychic organization tends to increase its range and level of functioning or, on the other hand, to become disorganized by virtue of the investigation itself. Disorganization and higher organization often go hand in hand; the balance or confluence of the two may be precarious or disrupted, but they are part of the investigative process itself. By opening up the channels of intrapsychic and interpsychic communication our psychic life is altered, even if this opening up has only increased anxiety and

1. Strachey's translation, "Where id was, there ego shall *be*" (p. 80) does not do justice to the original, "Wo Es war, soll Ich *werden*" (*Gesammelte Werke*, vol. 15, p. 86).

guilt and heightened defenses. Here we have the problem of our conventional distinction between scientific investigation and therapy, between psychoanalysis as a "research tool" and as treatment. Again, the facts of psychic life and of what the psychoanalytic study of another person involves do not fit these traditional distinctions. The dichotomy of pure and applied science may be applicable, to quite a degree at least, in other scientific disciplines; it is not applicable in ours.

Psychoanalyzing someone means to intervene in his psychic life. For this reason we enter into such an investigation only upon the request and with the active consent of the analysand (and we attempt to make sure that the consent is as informed as it can be at the outset of the venture). We must decide as best we can, beforehand or during the initial stage, whether such an intervention "makes sense" for the other person or is contraindicated because of the dangers involved in the process. If psychoanalysis is not indicated in a given case, this is not only a matter of the patient's being too vulnerable or not sufficiently able to be part of the analytic process; the investigation per se would not get very far without the patient's active participation and capacity for psychic work.

From each individual investigation, of course, we learn a great deal about human nature, about psychic reality in general. In this process we use not only the data accumulated by others and the theories that have been constructed on the basis of these data. In addition to using these as guidelines, we may also try to contribute further empirical data and to refine or revise or enlarge the theory. But in our field the theory has to encompass and organize not only what we consider the "objective data" observed or inferred by us from what the analysand presents, but more fundamentally also what we learn about the nature of psychic reality from the investigative process itself. This requirement increases in measure as the level of abstraction becomes higher.

The investigative process furnishes insights into the formation, disorganization, maintenance, enrichment, and impoverishment of psychic processes and structure, into the determinants of conflict and conflict resolution, etc.—all being of the greatest relevance precisely for psychoanalytic theory; more so, I believe, than, for instance, the sorting out, definition, and clarification of the various "functions" (from the point of view of adaptation) of the psyche and its substructures. I agree with Hartmann and Loewenstein (1962) who stress the difference between genesis and present level and range of functions of a substructure such as the superego and emphasize that these two points of view should not be confused. But it is the genesis and history of the superego that can explain the dynamic and economic processes that go into forming its functions and constitute the superego as a structure. This is not a preference of the genetic point of view over other "metapsychological points of view." When Rapaport and Gill (1959) added the genetic and adaptive points of view to the three others, they considered that these two might be on a different level of discourse. I believe this to be true, but cannot explore the question further in this context.

I only wish to emphasize here that genetic-historical understanding is of the essence of psychoanalysis as a science and as a form of treatment. From the scientific point of view, the genetic approach makes possible the mental reconstruction of psychic structures and processes and of their functions, a unique undertaking and contribution of psychoanalysis, comparable only to the reconstructive analysis of physical structure and physical processes of modern physics, in the implications both for understanding and for altering, i.e., destroying and composing or recomposing, structure. Psychoanalysis is in this sense as dangerous and as promising an undertaking as atomic physics, depending on how we use this emerging power of understanding the formation, composition, decomposition, and reorganization of the human psyche.

The psychoanalytic data we obtain from the analysand are forever "contaminated" by transference and resistance, but they can be obtained only through transference and resistance. The three structures (id, ego, superego) postulated by Freud are, from all we know, mutually interdependent. They have been formed and they are maintained and, within limits, can change by intercourse with other persons: they are not only mutually interdependent but also interdependent with the psyches of others. The genesis of the individual psyche and of its substructures is thus not merely something that happened in the past but an ongoing process, granted that it slows down after childhood and adolescence and that this genesis may and often does come to a relative standstill as times goes on. But insofar as psychic life is active and does not proceed by rote alone and automatically, the genesis of psychic structure continues, although more imperceptibly. When Freud said: where id was, there ego shall become, he had in mind this growth potential, especially in regard to the analytic process, where the genesis and the vicissitudes of the genesis of psychic organization become perceptible again in the transference illness and its resolution.

As does early psychic development, the resumption of psychic development in the concentrated form of analysis takes place within a psychic matrix: the psychoanalytic situation. Recently the similarities between that situation and the early mother–child relationship have been stressed by Stone (1961), Gitelson (1962), Greenacre (1966), me (1960), and others. As happens frequently, in emphasizing certain aspects of a problem, other aspects tend to be neglected or not sufficiently stressed to keep a balanced view. There are radical differences between the two situations which deserve careful consideration and further elucidation; moreover, the preoedipal, dyadic matrix has been stressed at the expense of the oedipal situation and its much more familiar similarities to the analytic situation as evinced in the classical transference neurosis. Changes in our perspective on psychic development, probably changes in our case material, and other factors such as increased interest in the earliest phases, have contributed to this slant, which needs correction. Nevertheless, through analytic work with so many patients who clearly show differences and deviations from the classical neuroses— even though perhaps sometimes not as many as we tend to think —we have gained deeper insight into the genesis of the psychic substructures and into the defects and deformations of ego and superego particularly.

This insight has come to us primarily, although not exclusively, from the often painful and laborious work of understanding what goes into and what interferes with the analytic process when we attempt to analyze such patients. Transference and resistance are again our guiding lights, but on deeper, more primitive levels, and therefore on levels of less differentiation, intrapsychically, i.e., between id, ego, and superego, but also interpsychically. The differentiation between patient and analyst, between object of investigation and investigator, is less, sometimes minimally, advanced, and primitive levels of psychic functioning are called into operation. It is important to realize that the analysand's operating on such levels entails the analyst's operating on such levels—if he can and will do it—although the analyst, of course, does so within the secure framework of and steered by his mature overall organization. This implies, by the nature of such psychic primitivity, a loosening or even suspension of the subject–object split. Communication with the other person than tends to approximate the kind of deep mutual empathy which we see in the mother–child relationship. By the same token, lack of communication tends to approximate an event of annihilation, insofar as the unsufficiently differentiated matrix is disrupted.

Empathy, whether in this intense form or others, involves, in contrast to sympathy, a suspension of the subject–object split. A psychic organization operating on such a level experiences lack of communication, of empathic understanding, as a disruption of organization, and not simply as being separate from another person. While the analyst is easily capable of calling forth or ascending to higher levels of psychic functioning, the patient cannot do so to the same degree. For the theoretical grasp of that aspect of analytic work which involves empathy, the notion of the loosening or suspension of the subject–object split is essential, as it is for the understanding of true identification. The subject–object split can be suspended because it did not always exist in psychic development, because psychic development takes its beginning in a psychic matrix which comprises, stated from the viewpoint of an outside observer—a nonpsychoanalytic observer—mother and infant. Stated from a reconstructive, psychoanalytic viewpoint, this matrix is a psychic field from which the infantile psyche gradually becomes differentiated as a relatively autonomous focus of psychic activity, by processes of internalization and externalization taking place within the total original field.

What we call object relations represents a highly developed form of psychic interactions in which relatively autonomous and in themselves highly organized centers of psychic activity interact with each other. But each such center originates in a primitive interactional field and depends for its further development and maintenance on remaining within the compass of increasingly wider and more complex interactional fields, even though it is now itself a comparatively autonomous, highly organized psychic field within such fields.

The psychoanalytic situation, in this regard, represents a novel interpsychic field in which more fully developed features of psychic fields, object relations, merge with or are strongly influenced by coexisting primitive features. Not that more primitive features do not form part of ordinary adult relationships; they do, as analysts well know. But the analytic method and process, by focusing on intrapsychic and interpsychic events and forces per se and on their genetic reconstruction, intervene in the very organization of the individual psyche because such special focusing and care themselves alter the field we study. As analysts we become, whether we want to or not, a weighty element and force in it. The tension, during significant periods of analysis, is in the direction of transformations from intrapsychic organization toward re-externalization of internal relationships and conflicts, and from there toward reconstitution of the psychic characteristics of the primitive matrix.

Psychoanalysis is an activity of the human mind which we as analysts exercise upon and in conjunction and cooperation with another person and his mental activity—whether we think in terms of "pure" psychoanalytic investigation or in terms of therapeutic analysis. The method we employ comprises prominently the use of verbal symbols as the means of communication, free association, free-floating attention, self-reflection and introspection, confrontation, clarification, interpretation, etc. And psychoanalysis is the body of knowledge and theory resulting from this activity and method. When I say: "the method we employ," it means not only: we as analysts, but: we, analyst and analysand. If the analytic process "takes" at all, the method becomes common good, although with significant differences between analyst and analysand. There can be no analysis as a going process in which the analysand, after a period of time which we may call the time of induction, does not engage to a varying extent in the procedures listed above. In respect to some of them, such as free-floating attention, interpretation, self-reflection, this may happen only in identifying conjunction with the analyst, whereby an interpretation, for instance, is "accepted" by the analysand. Such acceptance, if genuine, involves the free reproduction of the interpretive act on the part of the analysand. An advanced analysand may and often does perform such acts on his own. The analyst, on the other hand, does not merely engage in free-floating attention, interpretations, etc., but he uses introspection, self-reflection as well as free association (although usually not verbalized) in the service of understanding the patient.

While verbalization is the prominent means of communication (and this itself, of course, involves far more than the uttering and hearing of words and sentences), the range of communicative interaction is vast. It actually excludes only visual means, especially the visual eye-to-eye contact and grasp of facial expression, and body contact and locomotion. The psychic range may vary from the most intimate mutual understanding and empathic merging to highly abstract dialogue and argumentation. I recently had the—for me at least—unique experience of an analytic hour by telephone. The particular situation was such that I consented to the patient's request, made over the phone when he called me at the time of the beginning of his regular hour—he had to be in another city on that day, to have us proceed with his analytic hour then and there. I was struck by the fact that the funneling of communication exclusively through voice and ear seemed so extraordinary, although we are apt to think that this is what more or less happens in every analytic hour. What was lacking was personal presence, the simple being together in the same room, whether visible or not. The hour was not unproductive, but it seemed clear to me that it could be only an exception within the context of the usual analytic situation. I mention this incident because it vividly brought home to me the global nature of personal presence and the likelihood that such presence involves more than the usually listed perceptual and communicative modalities. There was—this is the best way I can describe it—a contraction of the operational psychic field that entailed a far greater effort of concentration on my part, with a deficit of free-floating attention.

II

The investigations which led to the creation of psychoanalysis were carried out as psychotherapeutic endeavors to cure emotionally disturbed patients, and psychoanalysis, once its outlines as a method *sui generis* were established, continued along this path. Transference and resistance came into view by this route. But by whatever route they might have been discovered, there can be no question that they are basic phenomena, interactional phenomena, of psychic life, and that no psychoanalytic investigation is possible without their making their appearance and being taken into account. Looked at from the viewpoint of scientific research, the object of investigation, the analysand, develops a particular kind of relationship with the analyst–investigator. This fact is part of the investigative process and of the situation in which it is carried out. In fact, a significant part of the investigation increasingly devolves on just that relationship, albeit as a vehicle for a more general understanding of the analysand's psychic processes and as a means for decontaminating, as it were, our field of vision. But it must be noted immediately that transference and resistance "contaminations" are themselves, of course, psychic phenomena and therefore part of what we want to study; that they are actually not contaminants but determinants of psychic behavior; and that such "decontamination" affects, and is intended to affect, the object no less than the investigator. The particular relationship, clinically described as transference neurosis or transference illness, develops by the nature of psychic processes, whether or not the analysand is suffering from an illness in a psychiatrically definable sense. A viable psychoanalytic process and investigation cannot develop without the development of transference. Transference and its correlate, resistance, however, not only are elements of what we intend to study, they also are "means" by which we study them ("countertransference" and "counterresistance" would be the terms applicable here, but these are open to many misunderstandings).

If transference and resistance are basic ingredients and determinants of a psychoanalytic investigation, the extent to which such an investigation is "objective" is limited by them. The investigative process itself, being carried out by the analyst who inevitably takes on all kinds of crucially important features for the analysand—and this happens not only if the latter is "sick"—continually affects the analysand's psychic processes. The analyst's interpretations, whether transference interpretations or not, are essential elements of the investigation. From the research point of view, they test and verify surmised connections and relationships between different aspects of the psychic material we perceive, and open up new avenues of approach and new psychic layers. In order to proceed with the investigative work, they have to be communicated to the analysand. If an interpretation is correct and resistance does not interfere—and this we judge from the patient's response—the communication not only verifies a connection or clarifies a piece of material for the analyst, it does the same for the analysand; better, it establishes or re-establishes connections within him, i.e., it changes something in the nexus of his psychic processes. As investigators we have, then, an object that is and must be affected by the investigative process itself if the investigation is to proceed.

Transference and resistance are basic determinants of a psychoanalytic investigation in regard to the analyst as well. Since a psychoanalytic investigation can be carried out only by a human mind, we cannot conceive of one in which the analyst's transference and resistance are not the warp and woof of his activity. Through his own analytic experience and training he has a significant measure of insight into this dynamic source of his motivations, is capable of allowing for this dynamism and of a considerable degree of self-regulation. But far from eliminating his transference and resistance, these capacities enable him to use them in the service of his work.

The phenomena of transference and resistance alone make something particularly clear in our field—though it is becoming increasingly clear in other sciences too—namely, the inextricable interrelationship between what we call subject and object. In psychoanalysis the object of study is an object in the psychoanalytic sense, another individual. In forming a theory about that object, we cannot abstract from the method we use to make it available to us, nor from what we learn from the method, more than from any other instrumentality, about the interrelationship and complementarity of subject and object. At the same time, the theory has to encompass the genesis of the subject–object split and cannot start from a basis that presupposes the latter, especially since the psychoanalytic process is based on as well as documents the merely relative existence of that split in terms of psychic reality.

Other psychoanalytic insights, gained in the pursuit of the analytic process itself and from analytically informed observation of early developmental stages and of psychotic material, point even more in the same direction. The formulation and elaboration of the concepts of narcissism, identification, introjection, and internalization represent milestones on the path toward a more adequate foundation of psychoanalytic theory. As a consequence the model of the psyche no longer is an apparatus that processes stimuli in certain ways or that, in its encounter with objects, uses them to discharge energy potentials (satisfaction = abolition of excitation in a closed system). The psyche now is conceived as an emerging organization that evolves through an active and ever more complex interchange[2] with developed organizations of the same kind, i.e., people from whom it becomes differentiated as a separate psychic entity by slow and gradual processes of individuation. Implicit and essential in this new conception are that interaction processes between what initially are focal elements in a unitary psychic field become internalized within one focal element, which by this process increasingly assumes the properties of a psychic field in its own right. This newly established intrapsychic field then entertains modified and more complex interactions with what has become external to it. The first outline of such an idea of the formation of intrapsychic structure was given by Freud (1921) in his discussions on the formation of the superego. Speaking of the ego ideal as "a differentiating grade in the ego," he writes:

The assumption of this kind of differentiating grade in the ego as a first step in an analysis of the ego must gradually establish its justification in the most various regions of psychology. In my paper on narcissism I have put together all the pathological material that could at the moment be used in support of this differentiation. But it may be expected that when we penetrate deeper into the psychology of the psychoses its significance will be discovered to be far greater. *Let us reflect that the ego now enters into the relation of an object to the ego ideal which has been developed out of it, and that all the interplay between an external object and the ego as a whole, with which our study of the neuroses has made us acquainted, may possibly be repeated upon this new scene of action within the ego* [p. 130; my italics].

2. In this conception, the processes of introjection, identification, and internalization as well as projection and externalization are prominent examples of this interchange.

The interplay between an external object and the ego as a whole is repeated upon a new, internal scene of action: this is internalization. Freud's formulation applies specifically to the superego. Only on the level of superego formation can one speak of an established ego and of external objects. But this formulation can be generalized to the effect that ego formation, too, is governed by comparable processes of internalization, with the proviso that by these primitive internalizations (and externalizations) internality and externality become constituted, whereas the more complex ones augment and enrich internality and externality.

The concept of internalization envisaged here is different from, although related to, Hartmann's (1939) and Hartmann and Loewenstein's (1962) definition of internalization. The main though not the only difference is that in their definition they include thought processes and what Rapaport (1957) has termed the internal map of external events and phenomena (representations), while I hold that thought processes and ideas are not of the same order as the processes which lead to ego and superego formation and, therefore, should not be subsumed under the same term.[3]

The concept of internalization, as the essential process in intrapsychic structure formation or, to put it differently, in individuation, presupposes neither the subject–object split nor the assumption of a separate psychic apparatus or organization, however primitive, from the beginning; it posits an original psychic field or matrix, the mother–infant unit, within which individuation processes start. If one thinks in terms of an original undifferentiated phase of psychic life, this then would refer not only to id–ego as intrapsychic potentials, but equally to the psychic undifferentiation of psyche–environment, of internal and external. Later internalizations, such as those constituting superego formation, can be conceived as taking place within a widened and far more complex psychic field, such as the oedipal situation. The latter also represents a psychic field whose focal elements, child, mother, father, are relatively autonomous psychic fields themselves, not just for a nonpsychoanalytic observer, but also for the child and from the viewpoint of the child. Inter-

3. See my paper, "On Internalization," reprinted in this volume.

actions can now be described as an interplay between external objects and an ego. In the process of superego formation the internality of the ego and the externality of objects, both previously limited, become extended and consolidated, and the superordinate psychic fields widen and gain in complexity.

The subject–object split or differentiation, having evolved in the growth process toward the oedipal situation, is suspended or superseded again in further internalizations which lead to higher orders of differentiation and interaction between subject and object. What becomes internalized—to emphasize this again— are not objects but interactions and relationships. Freud's insistence on seeing the superego not only as a representative of parental authority but also as a representative of the oedipal child's id impulses is in accord with this view. By the internalization of interactions an internal system of interactions, relationships, and connections between different elements and different genetic levels becomes established. This internalized, internally bound force field constitutes, it seems to me, what we call intrapsychic structure.

Despite the revolutionary insights implied in Freud's formulations of narcissism, identification, ego, and superego formation; despite the early recognition of the fundamental role of transference and resistance in both analysand and analyst; despite increased understanding of the analytic process and of early developmental stages—despite all these, psychoanalytic theory still clings to the model of a given psychic apparatus and starts out with the assumption of the existence of a primitive individual psyche. The fact that on the physical and biological level we observe a separate organism at birth does not imply that we also deal with a separate psychic organization, however primitive, at birth, and with immanent psychic energies and forces which, as instinctual drives, become secondarily related to objects. I suggest, in accordance with what I said earlier, that we seriously consider the proposition that instinctual drives, as psychic forces, are processes taking place within a field—the mother–infant psychic matrix; and that their character as instincts as well as the character of the emerging individual psyche are determined by the changing characteristics of that matrix-field and of its evolution into differentiated but related separate psychic fields. The psyche should neither be conceptualized as an apparatus on

which organismic and external stimuli impinge, thus compelling
it to perform work, nor should it be conceptualized as originally
being a unit of immanent instinctual forces which seek discharge
by whatever means they find (discharge by way of "autoerotic"
activities or upon or through "objects"). The discharge concept
itself is inadequate insofar as it signifies that some amount of
energy or excitation is, by whatever means available, emptied
out of a closed system.

Instinctual drives, at the stage of the mother–infant matrix,
would consist in differentiating and integrating processes within
this psychic matrix and not in unilateral processes emanating
from the infant. I am not denying the existence of biological
needs and urges in the neonate; rather, I am saying that instinctual drives as their "psychic representatives," as Freud (1915a)
called them, i.e., as motivational psychic forces, are formed by
interactions within the original psychic matrix. Instinctual
drives, in a further advanced psychic individual organization,
have been modified by narcissistic transformations, by the
changing of "object libido" into narcissistic libido (and aggression), whereby the relational character of drives becomes to a
variously limited degree internalized. This internalization leads
to a more complex organization of infantile psychic structure
and of the drives themselves. In a schematic way one might say
that now a portion of drive elements is deployed internally,
while another portion, although modified by narcissistic transformations, continues to be deployed within wider psychic fields.
At that stage instinctual drives are "internal motivational forces,"
but they never relinquish their character as relational phenomena. Their quality and intensity, their mutual balance and imbalance in regard to their fusions and defusions, remain determined by the original and subsequent "environmental contributions." That is, they are determined by the original psychic
matrix in which they arose as drives, and are variously modified
by present psychic fields of which the individual has become a
relatively autonomous constituent.

I believe that such a conception of the origin and nature of
instincts is supported by much recent work on early psychic
development, drive organization, and individuation (see Mahler,
1968; Spitz, 1965; Winnicott, 1965). Far from doing away with
intrapsychic structure and conflict (a tendency inherent, for

instance, in Sullivan's interpersonal theory), such a theoretical formulation is based on the reconstruction of the individual psyche from its component elements and takes into account the organizing currents which shape the individual psychic structure and its internal conflicts. A theory which starts out with intrapsychic immanent instinctual drives on the one hand, and external objects becoming cathected or introjected on the other hand, presupposes a dichotomy, which according to present understanding of early development does not exist *ab initio* and which in many circumstances once it does exist, is loosened or superseded. Such loosening or suspension, under certain conditions, may fall under the category of "regression in the service of the ego." What I emphasize instead is that such regression involves temporary dedifferentiation of subject–object no less than temporary dedifferentiation of intrapsychic organization, that the latter implies the former.

The psychoanalytic process is the arena *par excellence* for studying the underlying psychic activities that enter into the organization, maintenance, and growth of the individual mind. We have become increasingly aware of the fact that this process, although on quite a novel level of operation and organization, repeats and reveals essential features of the formative stages of psychic development. This understanding, implicit in the concept of the classical transference neurosis and the healthier resolution of the oedipus complex in analysis, is being supplemented and deepened by the more recent recognition of the impact of pre-oedipal disturbances on the analytic process. This has led, when called for, to certain modifications of technique, which are no less psychoanalytic because they take into account insights into and requirements of more primitive stages of development and of mental disturbance. But it is true that reorganization of psychic functioning, where early disturbances play a predominant role, is more questionable. Early, pre-oedipal, disturbances tend to interfere with the impact of psychoanalytic interventions on our accustomed verbal level of operations, because in such patients the later levels of mental development are not sufficiently stable. Moreover, the earlier a significant disturbance in mental development sets in, the more permanent seems to be its damage. In these circumstances, furthermore, far greater demands are made on the analyst's repertoire of operational psychic levels and on his agility to move back and forth between such levels, so that he finds it harder to be equal to this expanded task.

When Freud (1937) spoke of the professional hazards of analytic work, comparing them to the radiologist's exposure to dangerous X-rays, he alluded to the fact that by analyzing we become part of a psychic force field. A delicate balance has to be kept between becoming damaged by its inherent tensions and strains and resisting its power altogether. If we do the latter, we can neither pursue analytic research nor be of service to the patient, since it is by virtue of the establishment of such a new force field—the psychoanalytic situation—that the patient can resume and reorganize his mental development. The former is the case—and this, too, serves neither research nor the patient— if we overtly or covertly give in to the patient's neurotic demands and entangling propensities, instead of analyzing them. Analyzing them, as we know, means neither gratifying them, by lending ourselves as objects through which instinctual discharge is achieved, nor rejecting them, by lack of response or condemnation.

Analysis of the patient's demands and conflicts in essence involves having him put into words, whenever possible, his feelings, thoughts, fantasies, etc. Recognizing them as manifestations and derivatives of the underlying instinctual conflicts, we then interpret them by fitting them into a wider psychic context. This involves our linking them with the patient's past experience and establishing or re-establishing freer communication between different levels of integration of his past and present experiences. Such linking has been conceptualized by Freud (1915b) as hypercathexis. Hypercathexis, by virtue of the analyst's presence and pressure in that direction, is called forth in the patient as he manages to verbalize his feelings, fantasies, wishes, memories, and conflicts instead of expressing them in nonverbal actions and behavior; and hypercathexis is fostered, significantly augmented, and qualitatively changed by our interpretations if they are accepted, i.e., if the patient, by reproducing the interpretative act, makes it his own.

In his early writings Freud spoke of the patient's verbalization of his feelings in terms of abreaction in words and associative absorption. This implied the recognition that giving words to feelings is not simply a delay of gratification, or not only that, but is a kind of gratification by verbal action, by establishing communicative links between different psychic elements and levels, both within the patient himself (intrapsychic communication) and between the patient and the analyst.[4] I may use the dubious shortcut of saying that the gratification is a sublimated one— dubious because we do not yet understand much about sublimation, although its connections with identification (as a pathway, as Ernst Kris, in a personal communication, once put it) and with neutralization give us some hints.

If we urge the patient to put his feelings into words and to allow himself to associate freely, and then interpret the material to him, we respond to his longings and conflicts by calling forth his own hypercathectic resources and by providing ours for his use. His hypercathectic resources originated in the infant's and child's fields of psychic interactions with his mother, father, and others. In the psychoanalytic situation these original situations are revived and repeated on new levels and with a new person. The new level, of course, can be operative only to the extent to which it can be based upon and linked with pre-existing, though pathological or underdeveloped, intrapsychic structure and functioning. Words, language, and the linking of what Freud (1915b) called thing representations and word representations, are by no means the only media of hypercathexis, but they do have a special and prominent place in the higher organization of psychic life.

Hypercathexes, according to Freud, "bring about a higher psychical organization and make it possible for the primary process to be succeeded by the secondary process" (p. 202); the operation of hypercathexis has ceased in repression. Hypercathexis, I believe, cannot be adequately understood if we fail to take into account that it originates within a supra-individual psychic field. Expressed in traditional psychoanalytic terms, the essential factor is that cathected objects are themselves cathecting agents. The subject which cathects objects is at the same time being cathected by those objects, although on quite different and not drive-dominated levels of cathexis. The subject (the individual) is not only the subject but is at the same time the

---

4. In this respect we have to distinguish between what we have come to understand, often in a pejorative sense, as abreaction and the concept of abreaction through words as Freud used it in his early papers (see Loewald, 1955; reprinted in this volume).

object for *his* cathected objects. Object relations are relations
between mutually cathecting agents, and the cathecting of each
partner is a function of the other's cathecting. Because the individual who cathects, the subject, is an object for *his* cathected
objects, the individual can become an object to himself, can
gain distance from himself. The higher-order cathecting activity
of his libidinal objects (parents) constitutes, as it were, the first
hypercathexis. Insofar as the objects' cathecting operations are
on secondary process levels (although they are by no means
exclusively so), they have the potential of hypercathexes in
terms of the subject's psychic processes; and the internalization
of relationships makes for what I called the hypercathectic resources of the individual.

III

Psychoanalytic research, in the sense of analyzing another
person, and therapeutic analysis are inseparable. As I said
earlier, the dichotomy of pure and applied science does not hold
in our discipline. But I do not labor under the illusion that a
therapeutic analysis consists, or could consist, only of strictly
psychoanalytic procedures and interventions. This is decidedly
not the case. An actual analysis, as an undertaking extending
over a number of years, contains, apart from the attempts to
enforce the rules of the procedure, many elements, which in
themselves are not psychoanalytic, but which are intended to
underline, bring back to mind, and promote the specific task of
analysis or to prevent the patient from engaging in activities that
interfere with the analysis or from self-destructive moves in his
life. The less mature the patient is, the more are such interventions at times necessary. While ideally and ultimately such
moves on the part of the patient are to be understood as resistances and analyzed, these and other types of resistance, especially
during earlier phases of analysis, often cannot be dealt with
analytically. The foundations for the patient's analytic understanding of his behavior may not yet be firm enough. The patient
may for shorter or longer periods of time go along with the
analytic procedures not because of his grasp of their rationale
but because he wishes to please the analyst, like the child who is
afraid of the loss of love or the love object and complies with

demands for the sake of keeping the parent's attachment, which is still vital to the integrity of his own psychic organization. We would go along with this as long as it serves the analysis. We utilize this lever with the patient, not by threats, withdrawal, or punishment, but by not analyzing such "transference love" prematurely and by relying on it in our educative interventions. These often are similar to educative measures employed by affectionate and sensible parents.

If we look at the totality of an analysis as a stretch of life experience, there are striking similarities with periods of the oedipal phase or adolescence, for instance, with their ups and downs of love and hate, of dependence and rebellion, of clinging and emancipation, submission and self-assertion. Much more has gone into it, from the patient's as well as the analyst's point of view, in terms of personal investment, than strictly psychoanalytic work in the sense of detached, dispassionate research. Parenthetically, I doubt whether any scientific work proceeds in a strictly detached, dispassionate way, motivated solely by the wish to find the truth, except for those most significant moments and episodes which set for us the standard of the scientific spirit.

It also needs to be said that the love of truth is no less a passion because it desires truth rather than some less elevated end. In our field the love of truth cannot be isolated from the passion for truth to ourselves and truth in human relationships. In other fields, too, the scientist is filled with love for his object precisely in his most creative and "dispassionate" moments. Scientific detachment in its genuine form, far from excluding love, is based on it. In our work it can be truly said that in our best moments of dispassionate and objective analyzing we love our object, the patient, more than at any other time and are compassionate with his whole being.

In our field scientific spirit and care for the object certainly are not opposites; they flow from the same source. It is impossible to love the truth of psychic reality, to be moved by this love as Freud was in his lifework, and not to love and care for the object whose truth we want to discover. All great scientists, I believe, are moved by this passion. Our object, being what it is, is the other in ourselves and ourself in the other. To discover truth about the patient is always discovering it with him and for him as well as for ourselves and about ourselves. And it is discovering

truth between each other, as the truth of human beings is revealed in their interrelatedness. While this may sound unfamiliar
and perhaps too fanciful, it is only an elaboration, in nontechnical
terms, of Freud's deepest thoughts about the transference neurosis and its significance in analysis.

   In the various perspectives I have tried to sketch, a psychoanalytic investigation is, by its very nature, potentially therapeutic, granted that in order to bring it about, foster it, keep it
going, eliminate interferences, many nonpsychoanalytic measures are often called for. In this respect, too, analysis may be
compared to surgery. The work of the surgeon does not consist
exclusively in the operation itself. There are preoperative and
postoperative procedures, dressings, dietetic measures, and the
like. The same *mutatis mutandis* goes for the researcher in any
field. In our zeal to be "pure" analysts we tend to forget all this;
but we do have to be on the lookout for unnecessary or interfering
extra-analytic interventions.

                                 SUMMARY

   I have looked at psychoanalysis mainly from the point of
view of its being a scientific endeavor. It is far more than that, as
is shown in the pervasive influence that psychoanalysis has had
on many facets of modern Western civilization. And psychoanalysts should be the last to ignore or disregard this fact. Psychoanalysis, as practiced by some of its best, though often unknown
representatives, is an art even more than a science. But here I
have looked mainly at its scientific and theoretical face. I have
emphasized that as a scientific theory it cannot be content to
model itself after the traditional scientific theories constructed
by such sciences as physics, chemistry or biology. Their subject
matter, as viewed and investigated by these sciences, implies
and presupposes a subject-object dichotomy, which is, so to
speak, what puts them in business.

   Although psychoanalysis took those theories as its model, it
soon had to depart from them in essential ways, without being
able or willing to make this explicit. The phenomena of transference and resistance as inherent and necessary ingredients of a
psychoanalytic investigation do not conform to such a model.
Hence, there was a tendency to relegate them to the lower

echelon of "clinical theory" and not to admit them to the high plane of "metapsychology," even though Freud spoke of transference, for instance, in chapter VII of *The Interpretation of Dreams,* in what would now clearly be considered a metapsychological context. The new structural theory, based on the conceptions of narcissism, "primary masochism," identification, introjection, and the formation of the superego, implied and expressed a new awareness of the fundamental importance of object ties for the formation of psychic structure. Although these ideas led further away from the old model, psychoanalysis nevertheless continued to cling to its theoretical premises. In many quarters there still seems to be a tendency to put up a "no admittance" sign when metapsychological considerations point to object relations as being not merely regulative but essential constitutive factors in psychic structure formation.

I have maintained that the psychoanalytic process and deepened understanding of psychotic and early developmental processes reveal the interactional origin and nature of psychic reality, and have expressed my belief that a theory of the mind, of the psyche as it shows itself to psychoanalytic research, should start with the hypothesis of a psychic matrix within and from which individuation proceeds. In this regard I have tried to describe parallels between the psychoanalytic situation as a novel force field and earlier fields of psychic forces within which differentiated and autonomous psychic entities and structures arise and develop.

I have given a brief account of the processes of internalization and externalization which are involved in individuation and continue to be instrumentalities by which individuation in increasingly complex forms takes its course in human life. I have stressed that what is internalized are dynamic relations between psychic elements of a field of which the internalizing agent is one element. In accord with these views I reformulated the concept of instinctual drives and suggested a somewhat novel interpretation of the concept of hypercathexis.

It seems to me that most of the views I have advanced are at least implicit in Freud's work and that of many other psychoanalysts. Perhaps my contribution consists mainly in making some things explicit and drawing some unfamiliar conclusions.

REFERENCES

Freud, S. (1900): *The Interpretation of Dreams.* S.E. 4 & 5.
_____. (1914): On narcissism. S.E. 14:67–102.
_____. (1915a): Instincts and their vicissitudes. S.E. 14: 109–40.
_____. (1915b): The unconscious. S.E. 14:159–215.
_____. (1921): Group psychology and the analysis of the ego. S.E. 18:67–143.
_____. (1933): New introductory lectures on psycho-analysis. S.E. 22:3–182.
_____. (1937): Analysis terminable and interminable. S.E. 23: 209–53.
Gitelson, M. (1962): The curative factors in psycho-analysis: The first phase of psycho-analysis. *Int. J. Psychoanal.* 43: 194–205.
Greenacre, P. (1966): Problems of overidealization of the analyst and of analysis. *The Psychoanalytic Study of the Child* 21: 193–212.
Hartmann, H. (1939): *Ego Psychology and the Problem of Adaptation.* New York: International Universities Press, 1958.
Hartmann, H., and R. M. Loewenstein (1962): Notes on the superego. *The Psychoanalytic Study of the Child* 17:42–81.
Jacobson, E. (1964): *The Self and the Object World.* New York: International Universities Press.
Kris, E. (1955): Neutralization and sublimation. *The Psychoanalytic Study of the Child* 10: 30–46.
Loewald, H. W. (1955): Hypnoid state, repression, abreaction, and recollection. *J. Amer. Psychoanal. Assn.* 3: 201–10.
_____. (1960): On the therapeutic action of psycho-analysis. *Int. J. Psychoanal.* 41:16–33.
Mahler, M. S. (1968): *On Human Symbiosis and the Vicissitudes of Individuation.* New York: International Universities Press.
Rapaport, D. (1957): A theoretical analysis of the superego concept. *Collected Papers.* New York: Basic Books, 1967, pp. 685–709.
Rapaport, D., and M. M. Gill (1959): The points of view and assumptions of metapsychology. *Int. J. Psychoanal.* 40:153–62.
Sandler, J. (1960): On the concept of the superego. *The Psychoanalytic Study of the Child* 15:128–62.

Sandler, J., and B. Rosenblatt (1962):The concept of the representational world. *The Psychoanalytic Study of the Child* 17: 128–45.

Spitz, R. A. (1965): *The First Year of Life.* New York: International Universities Press.

Stone, L. (1961): *The Psychoanalytic Situation.* New York: International Universities Press.

Webster's New International Dictionary of the English Language, 2d ed. Springfield, Mass.: G. & C. Merriam, 1956.

Winnicott, D. W. (1965): *The Maturational Processes and the Facilitating Environment.* New York: International Universities Press.

17

THE TRANSFERENCE NEUROSIS: COMMENTS ON
THE CONCEPT AND THE PHENOMENON

An unusually gifted and inhibited young man of 19, an only child, ill at ease and intense, came for analysis because of grave concerns about his prolific sexual fantasies (mainly heterosexual), fears of homosexuality (no overt activity ever, as far as I know), absence of heterosexual involvement, and restriction of his social life. It soon became apparent that his relationship to me, from the very beginning, tended to be a duplicate of his relationship to his father, which seemed to be a kind of slavish adoration, imitation, and submissive love, with some evidence of rebellion against that position, deep resentment, and of attempts to extricate himself from it. The patient's love for his father seemed as excessive as his hatred and contempt for his mother, who was described as an impulse-ridden, chaotic woman with a host of fads, superstitions, and prejudices. This was in contrast to the father, who was pictured as a passionately rational, rigidly balanced, hardworking man, successful in his work, studious, and retiring. The mother appeared to be slavishly devoted to her husband, looking up to him with childlike respect and admiration, but making great demands on his composure and forbearance by her irrational, anxiety-ridden attitudes toward the family and views on life—the very opposite to his.

Here seems to be an example of a very rapidly developing transference neurosis. Although many other currents, of course, were present, the patient was in an ambivalent love relationship with his father, showing a mixture of attempted identification with an ideal and a feminine, masochistically oriented object relationship with him, which had the earmarks of an unconscious identification with his mother. This constellation was quickly

Expanded version of a contribution to the panel on "The Current Status of the Concept of Transference Neurosis," held at the Annual Meeting of The American Psychoanalytic Association, Boston, May, 1968.

transferred to me. One aspect of the prominence and compulsive nature of heterosexual fantasies was that they represented a defensive struggle against succumbing to this libidinal position, although elements of a positive oedipal position were by no means absent. I shall not go into the details of the case or describe the course of the analysis. I have greatly oversimplified things in this brief sketch and have concentrated on some salient features that made their appearance very early in the analysis, through his verbal accounts as well as in the form of verbalized and un-verbalized transference manifestations. The patient had, from the beginning, considerable awareness of his behavior and feel-ings toward me and was quickly able to grasp some of their his-torical determinants.

One might raise the question whether one should speak here of a transference *neurosis,* inasmuch as the transference was so immediate and massive. But the patient had a remarkable capac-ity for gaining or regaining perspective on himself, for self-observation and reflection. He showed what Freud and Ferenczi have called a passion for transference—then considered charac-teristic for hysteria—together with a capacity for insight. Granted that there were many pre-oedipal problems, it is fair to say that he had reached the oedipal phase, however slanted and distorted, but had not passed beyond it in many crucial aspects. In fact, no significant progress appeared to have occurred in his psycho-sexual development since the oedipal period. There was evidence of only superficial repression of his Oedipus complex during the latency period. A fairly straight line seemed to lead from the oedipal period to the time he came for treatment, without any significant modification. He still was in the oedipal period, as documented by the nature of his transference and by many de-tails of his extensive fantasy life. His intellectual development, however, had proceeded well, and this not merely in the area of his special field of interest, but in many areas, including his ability to apply his intelligence and powers of observation to his own psychic life. He had many obsessive-compulsive character traits. One is tempted to say that the development of certain ego functions had outstripped, probably since early childhood, the development of his instinctual-emotional life, in the sense in which Freud has spoken of it in "The Disposition to Obsessional Neurosis" (1913, p. 325).

The transference clearly had a primitive quality, perhaps not unlike that of children who are seen prior to the latency period. It was soon apparent that the transference, while desirable in the interest of maintaining rapport with this isolated patient who only too easily retreated from contact with people, worked as a powerful resistance, in the sense of his tending to repeat the neurotic entanglement en bloc in the analysis. Having become reasonably certain of the patient's capacity for reflection, for taking distance from himself, I began cautiously, but very early, to interpret in genetic terms certain of his transference manifestations, and, from the beginning, to engage and utilize his interest in and capacity for self-understanding. Such a course, that is, to make early transference interpretations, seemed possible also just because of the massive transference, which combined with his vivid descriptions of childhood and current events made important features of the transference situation much more transparent than they often are at such an early stage of an analysis. Furthermore, in the face of a quickly developing transference neurosis—in contrast to a slow, gradual development of it which would need to be facilitated and promoted—resistance analysis, in terms of slow, painstaking work on complex character defenses, was not called for at this time. The major resistance, in this respect not unlike many hysteria cases, was the transference itself. Thus it needed analytic work from the start. To avoid misunderstanding, I should underline that the patient talked freely about his past and current life, perhaps even somewhat compulsively, so that in terms of time spent on it my interpretative activity was minimal.

I have chosen this case to introduce the subject, not as a typical example of a transference neurosis, or to demonstrate that there is such a thing, but in order to give a clinical illustration that would point to the difficulties and complexities of the issue. These difficulties stem, at least in part, from the problems inherent in the modern concept of neurosis. What are the distinguishing features of neurosis compared with borderline cases, character disorders, and psychosis; and to what extent do we still understand neurosis as a distinct, circumscribed illness in an otherwise relatively healthy individual, or at any rate in an individual who is impaired mainly by this circumscribed illness?

An illness, furthermore, which would be comparable to an acute physical illness which has become chronic and requires an acute exacerbation in order to be treated successfully? Do character neuroses fit such a comparison, and if not, should they be classified as neuroses? There is also the fact that a neurosis with a more or less distinct symptomatology (such as conversion symptoms, phobias or obsessive-compulsive symptoms) for which the patient seeks help, usually if not always, on closer observation, shows a degree of character pathology, i.e., traits of a character neurosis.

My concern in this case was the danger of an early stalemate or disruption of the analysis because of the massive transference that would tend in the direction of a mere transference repetition. But does transference neurosis not mean repetition of the infantile neurosis, reactivation of it, with the assumption that in the course of the analysis a new and healthier outcome can be achieved? What kind of repetition? In his paper, "Remembering, Repeating and Working-Through," Freud (1914) distinguishes between reproduction by action and reproduction in the psychic field. Reproduction or, if I may be permitted this substitution, repetition in the psychic field by remembering, reflecting, and working-through is the therapeutic path of analysis. This path cannot be taken unless the infantile neurosis is reactivated in the transference, as transference neurosis. Intellectual insight is not enough; fruitful and effective self-understanding cannot be achieved unless the significant experiences and inner conflicts which led to the neurosis become alive again in the present and regain a measure of immediacy and urgency in the transference neurosis. On the other hand, reliving of the infantile neurosis, per se, is fruitless. Many patients in various disguised, or not so disguised, ways relive or continue their infantile neuroses in their everyday lives before they ever come to analysis. But they don't know it. If repression and other defenses are successful enough and not too crippling, the need for treatment does not arise, at least not on the grounds of feeling significantly handicapped or sick. This is often a problem with people who start analysis for professional reasons, such as psychoanalytic candidates, psychiatric residents, psychologists, and others. Their childhood neurosis often has—for purposes of everyday life—

been successfully repressed. Ego restrictions and unresolved conflicts become apparent and troublesome mainly in their professional work.

We are here in the area of character problems and problems of character analysis, and it is in this area, it seems to me, that the question frequently arises: where is the transference neurosis? This often is a question not only with the so-called normal patient, but with the many patients who come for analysis because of character difficulties, general feelings of inadequacy or unhappiness, slow-burning depression, marital difficulties, or work problems. In contrast to the old-fashioned symptom neurosis, one might say that their neurosis is spread over much of the whole personality. No well-defined symptomatology, no well-defined infantile neurosis, and thus no transference neurosis, in that sense, can be detected. Of course, these patients, too, show transference manifestations of various kinds and intensities, but these tend to remain diffuse, seemingly disconnected and sporadic; to arrive at the delineation of a neurosis as a more or less coherent, sequential, circumscribed development seems difficult or impossible. In fact, it sometimes seems that trying to do that forces the material into uncongenial channels.

Perhaps we need far more observation and research on the differences in the infantile antecedents which in one case make for a character neurosis and in another for what presents as a symptom neurosis. I do not, however, wish to imply that clear dividing lines can be drawn here. Our progressive understanding of neurosis has led us to recognize character problems in "symptom neurosis" which earlier were not recognized or not subjected to analytic work. In the course of character-analytic work, "new" symptoms may make their appearance; somatic ailments, as for instance, headaches, backaches, sore throats, colds, disturbances of the digestive system, may reveal themselves as equivalents of neurotic symptoms.

From clinical impressions I would venture to suggest that differences in parental attitudes and child rearing have something to do with differences in neurotic development, at least in certain cases. I am reasonably convinced that such factors, rather than, or in addition to, innate disposition, play, in a number of cases, a far greater role than was recognized in the analytic work of earlier days. In a large number of families, many problems of psychosexual development and growing up tend to be pushed under the rug, so to speak, often because of the parents' own personality restrictions and uncertainties, their tendencies to evade direct confrontations, prohibitions, and injunctions, but no less to evade the more open, unabashed expression of their own love-hate involvement with their children and of their own emotional-instinctual needs and urges. Such trends, tending to diffuse, repress, and suppress clear-cut feelings toward their children as well as in their children, may have some bearing on the diffusion and spread of neurosis over the total personality development, resulting in what we call character neurosis. Defenses would become more insidious in proportion to the insidiousness and blunting of instinctual life and affect expression. In such measure as there is less unhampered and unselfconscious communication, negative and positive, with one's children, there is perhaps less "trauma" but also less bliss and joy in childhood, and more of a climate favoring a general formation of character, which in its very structure is more defensive, cautious, and often bland and colorless. The occasions for symptom formation would be lessened.

The analytic situation, to the extent to which the analyst, owing to the requirements of noninvolvement, tends to suppress his own instinctual-affective currents instead of being cognizant of them and "sublimating" them, is apt to play into such character defenses and reinforce them. Because of the emotional tensions inherent in the analytic process in combination with the requirement for noninvolvement, the analytic situation lends itself only too easily to a perpetuation or reinforcement of this type of defensive character. It has impressed me that people with outspoken symptomatology, whether hysterical or obsessive-compulsive, often seem able to function outside the area invaded by their symptoms more fully and whole-heartedly than many of the less obviously sick character problems we see in analysis today.

There are those who tend to think that the concept of transference neurosis is no longer useful, and that searching for or trying to promote the transference neurosis leads too often only to frustration and skepticism on the part of candidates and others who attempt to find it in their patients. In addition to what I have described, many character disorders and borderline cases are genetically to be derived not so much, certainly not so exclusively, from an infantile neurosis originating in the cluster of oedipal problems, but from deficiencies and deformations of ego development antedating the oedipal period and the development of an infantile neurosis in the classical sense, based, as the latter are, on problems of relatively advanced ego development.

While this is true, perhaps our modern emphasis on ego problems and functions and on ego analysis, carries with it the danger of concentrating too heavily on autonomous ego functioning, and of losing sight of the instinctual-affective, experiential roots and determinants of ego development, thus neglecting the infantile neurosis and its object-related instinctual nature. Emphasis on the autonomy of the ego did not intend to lead to a relative neglect of the transference neurosis, but may nevertheless have done so.

As I see it, the concept of transference neurosis has not lost its value. But it is true that the picture and consequently our concept of neurosis have changed so as to include most prominently what we call character neurosis, a form of neurosis which is more formless and more hidden; and the same can be said for the transference neurosis. Furthermore, the prominence of pre-oedipal problems and of deviations and distortions of ego formation at early stages, in many patients seen nowadays, tends to obscure the clear delineation of a transference neurosis. As distinguished from the character neuroses, here the specifically neurotogenic problems of the oedipal period are intertwined with early developmental problems and colored by them. The latter, arising in a period of development prior to the relatively unblurred differentiation between self and object world, would make for complex constellations of relatedness in the analytic setting (primitive identifications, projective and introjective processes) that are different from classical transference phenomena.

Let me now come back briefly to what I consider the important and enduring aspect of the concept of transference neurosis: it defines the analytic process as an active, preconscious-conscious repetition of early pathogenic experiences and their intrapsychic pathological vicissitudes, in the interest and as a method of mastering and resolving them in new ways. Freud, again in "Remembering, Repeating and Working-Through," says that it is mainly the handling of the transference that is the means by which we can tame and master the compulsion to repeat and transform it into a motive for remembering. What has to be done is to give "all the symptoms of the illness a new transference meaning" and to replace the patient's "ordinary neurosis by a 'transference neurosis' of which he can be cured by the therapeutic work" (1914, p. 154). If we do not cling to the word "symptoms," but include the wider areas of character and of ego pathology, this still stands today as the procedure at which we aim. In this sense transference neurosis is not so much an entity to be found in the patient, but an operational concept. We may regard it as denoting the retransformation of a psychic illness which originated in pathogenic interactions with the important persons in the child's environment, into an interactional process with a new person, the analyst, in which the pathological infantile interactions and their intrapsychic consequences may become transparent and accessible to change by virtue of the analyst's objectivity and of the emergence of novel interaction possibilities. The illness, which had become an autonomous process and an automatic response regardless of environmental changes and reactions and even attracting and provoking pathogenic reactions similar to the original ones, becomes alive again and clarified as originating in pathogenic interactions with the environment. Our therapeutic work has its limitations insofar as the original illness is not a response to environmental influences, but is due to innate deficiencies; and to the extent to which the intrapsychic consequences of pathological interactions may be irreversible. The latter is more likely, the earlier the pathological interactions took place.

Understood in this light, the transference neurosis is indeed a creature of the analytic situation and not simply a repeat performance or continuation of the old illness, as seemed to be the case with the patient described in the beginning of this presentation. The patient's initial behavior was automatic, as it would be with any other person in his environment who fit certain paternal characteristics. His transference was immediate and was a resistance; his transference neurosis, which is not to be confused with resistance, was still to develop. The difference between such transference manifestations and transference neurosis or transference illness, then, would be that the former are essentially automatic responses, signs and symptoms of the old illness; whereas the transference neurosis is a creation of the analytic work done by analyst and patient, in which the old illness loses its autonomous and automatic character and becomes reactivated and comprehensible as a live responsive process and, as such, changing and changeable. New and different transference manifestations arise as signs of this new process. As promoted by the analyst, the transference neurosis is curative; as taking place in the patient, it is a healing process. What makes it into an illness different from the infantile and from the presenting one is that the forces operative in the latter are given different responses or no responses feeding the old processes. The more complex, diffuse, and hidden the old neurotic processes are, as in character neurosis, the more complex, diffuse, and hidden is the transference neurosis. The latter is not and could not be more obvious and tangible as a delimited process than the illness which brought the patient to the analyst.

"The transference," Freud continues in the same paper, "thus creates an intermediate region between illness and real life through which the transition from the one to the other is made. The new condition has taken over all the features of the illness; but it represents an artificial illness which is at every point accessible to our intervention. It is a piece of real experience, but one which has been made possible by especially favorable conditions . . ." (1914, p. 154). The intermediate region between (old) illness and real life is the transference neurosis. It is a "piece of real experience" made possible by our presence and our interventions, just as the infantile neurosis was "a piece of real experience," "made possible" by the presence and the pathogenic interventions of the original environment.

It is not Freud's opinion that this new artificial disease, the transference neurosis, is an artifact unilaterally created by the analyst. It is brought about by man's libidinal nature, by the fact that the patient will, if he is not too "narcissistic," form an attachment to the analyst, repeating the characteristics of his attachments and responses to the original love objects—as ambivalent as they are likely to have been—and by the analyst's different responses. What the analyst promotes in the handling of the transference is not so much the attachment to the analyst but the patient's awareness of his attachment (and defenses against it), of the nature of this attachment, of its historical determination;

and the analyst does this by his empathic and interpretative responses and by abstaining from repeating the pathogenic responses of the past. Giving a new meaning, a transference meaning to the illness, does not signify that a new meaning is invented, nor does it merely signify that the old meaning is newly revealed to the patient, but that a meaning is created, by the interactions between patient and analyst, which has new dynamic tensions and engenders new, healthier motivations of its own.

The transference neurosis, in this sense, is the patient's love life—the source and crux of his psychic development—as relived in relation to a potentially new love object, the analyst, who renounces libidinal–aggressive involvement for the sake of understanding and achieving higher psychic organization. From the point of view of the analyst, this means neither indifference nor absence of love–hate, but persistent renunciation of involvement, a constant activity of uninvolving which tends to impel the patient to understand himself in his involvement instead of concentrating exclusively, albeit unconsciously, on the object. The resolution of the transference neurosis consists in achieving such higher psychic organization which gradually replaces the transference illness, and by virtue of which object involvement on a more mature level becomes possible.

In many respects, similar developments, under favorable conditions, take place in the healthy transition from the oedipal phase to the latency period, and again in the transition from adolescence to adulthood. Spontaneous, "nonartificial" incestuous involvements are partially relinquished and transformed so that individuation and new involvement can proceed. This is facilitated and promoted by parental instinctual disengagement.

Looking at it from another angle, perhaps one might think of the concept, transference neurosis, as an ideal construct. The ideal construct structures, and thus always oversimplifies, a complex aggregation of events, brings some order into an at first chaotic constellation and sequence of events; it functions as an organizing principle that is gradually distilled out of the events when investigated in a certain perspective; it is neither arbitrarily imposed on them nor can it be found in them as an entity in pure culture.

On the other hand, let us also not forget the experiential meaning of such words as neurosis, illness, etc. It cannot be too

unusual for patients—I certainly remember it from the time I
was a patient on the couch—to experience, at least at times,
being in analysis as an illness, insofar as it is a regressive and
unsettling experience, not dissimilar to the passions and conflicts
stirred up anew in the state of being in love, which from the point
of view of the ordinary order and emotional tenor and discipline
of life feels like an illness, with all its deliciousness and pain.

The main enduring value of the concept of transference neurosis, then, to my mind, lies in its defining the nature, scope, and
point of impact of psychoanalysis as mental therapy. The issue
is that the patient's illness, neurosis, maladjustment, character
disorder, regarded as originating in his life experiences from
early on, is drawn into a new context, the analytic relationship
developing between patient and analyst. In this new context the
crucial pathogenic experiences, and the patient's ways of assimilating them, of defending against them, and of letting himself be
defeated by them, gain new intensity and urgency. This makes
them available for fresh psychic work. Insofar as the pathogenic
experiences and pathological ways of coping with them are still
active, in the sense in which a volcano is said to be still active,
the "passion for transference"—as in the case I described—
amounts to no more than a continuation of an acute automatic
process transported into the new setting of the analytic situation,
which then creates the potential for the development of a transference neurosis. In many other cases, processes that had become
subterranean or slowed to a standstill or frozen are apt to become
more active again in the analytic situation, and all the defensive
forces of the patient tend to be mobilized against such reactivation. Here, for long periods of time the prominent task will have
to be the analytic work on the defenses in the form of demonstrating them as resistances in the transference setting, i.e., of
giving them a transference meaning. In the first type, schematically speaking, resistance against the analytic development of a
transference neurosis consists in the direct, unmediated transferred instinctual currents (and of primitive blocks, rather than
complex defenses, against them). It is resistance against that
aspect of the analytic work that has to do with renewed psychic
organization. In the second type, resistance is directed against
the disorganization (regression if you will) that is required to
make reorganization possible.

Needless to say, almost any actual treatment situation will show both phases or aspects in different combinations, with one or the other predominating at different periods of treatment or depending on the nature of the case. Depending on how far the treatment can be truly psychoanalytic in scope, with the goal of significant psychic reorganization as distinguished from the various superficial, if often at least temporarily helpful rearrangements and readjustments, the point of impact is the transference, and the process of treatment and of change consists in a creative repetition of the disease as transference neurosis. The field of origin and initial action of pathogenic events is the field of interaction between the child and his human environment. The intrapsychic process we call illness, by entering and then being actively engaged in the new interactional context of the analytic field of forces, becomes transformed into the transference neurosis. The transference neurosis represents "an intermediate region between illness and real life" as well as a transitional stage between disease process and healing process.

Much takes place in psychoanalytic treatment that does not reach such depth or is preparatory to reaching it and has only delayed and indirect effects. A decisive engagement, such as is represented by a fully developed transference neurosis, may never or not distinctly come to pass in an analysis. Yet the repercussions of what has occurred may turn out to be deeper and more far-reaching than anticipated. A struggle may be won or lost far from the battlefield and by roundabout ways. Significant movements in the process of the transference illness or significant advances toward its resolution may go unnoticed by patient and analyst or may not be available for even disguised communication. The transference neurosis is by no means in all instances or at all times clearly visible and may even be largely a silent process without necessarily losing its impact. Some patients, throughout the analysis, maintain a distance from open emotional involvement with the analyst, and the analytic work may mostly take place at a considerable remove from the transference arena itself. This may but does not necessarily mean that these patients remain isolated from affect and that their gains in self-understanding and self-mastery and release are shallow. But it does probably indicate that such patients have to maintain a kind of narcissistic screen behind which significant inner reorganization may take place, as though the poignant interactions and strong passions of the transference neurosis have to be filtered through this protective screen in order to be bearable and useful.

REFERENCES

Freud, S. (1913): The predisposition to obsessional neurosis. S.E. 12:311–26.

——. (1914): Remembering, repeating and working through. S.E. 12:145–56.

18

FREUD'S CONCEPTION OF THE NEGATIVE THERAPEUTIC REACTION, WITH COMMENTS ON INSTINCT THEORY

It is hard to gain an unambiguous view or a consensus regarding the concept of the negative therapeutic reaction. The theoretical issues involved are as complex and difficult as is its clinical management. If one adheres more or less to what Freud appears to have meant by the term, the Pandora's box of the unconscious sense of guilt, masochism, and the death instinct soon opens. I say Pandora's box, because I believe it is not as easy as many psychoanalysts seem to think, nowadays, to dispose of Freud's ideas on the relations between the problems of guilt and masochism and the death and life instincts. Analysts by and large are comfortable with the dual instinct theory formulated in terms of sexual and aggressive drives, but most of them, including theoreticians, shy away from life and death instincts, Eros and Thanatos, and especially from the notion of inner and silent workings of the death instinct.

On the other hand, if one refuses to allow oneself to be confined by Freud's understanding of the negative therapeutic reaction as a term referring specifically to the sense of guilt, masochism, and the workings of the death instinct, then the field threatens to widen so much that almost any negative reaction to analysis and the analyst, at least any deep-seated and ingrained resistance, may fall into this category. It is, of course, quite legitimate to say that a negative therapeutic reaction in analysis may be due to motivational causes quite different from those assumed by Freud. But for purposes of this discussion I shall adhere rather closely to Freud's definition as discussed in "The

Slightly modified version of a contribution to the Panel on Negative Therapeutic Reaction, held at the Fall Meeting of The American Psychoanalytic Association in New York, December, 1969 (Chairman: Milton H. Horowitz, M.D.).

Ego and the Id" (1923) and elsewhere (1924), and particularly in "Analysis Terminable and Interminable" (1937). I have chosen to discuss the concept in the light of certain theoretical positions and assumptions that may profitably be reconsidered.

The negative therapeutic reaction, in Freud's sense, bespeaks a deep-seated unconscious resistance, which is said to come from the superego, more precisely from certain relations between ego and superego. But in relating this resistance to the death instinct, Freud goes beyond that formulation. In "Analysis Terminable and Interminable" he speaks of

a force which is defending itself by every possible means against recovery and which is absolutely resolved to hold on to illness and suffering. One portion of this force has been recognized by us, undoubtedly with justice, as the sense of guilt and need for punishment, and has been localized by us in the ego's relation to the superego. But this is only the portion of it which is, as it were, psychically bound by the superego and thus becomes recognizable; other quotas of the same force, bound or free, may be at work in other, unspecified places. If we take into consideration the total picture made up of the phenomena of masochism immanent in so many people, the negative therapeutic reaction and the sense of guilt found in so many neurotics, we shall no longer be able to adhere to the belief that mental events are exclusively governed by the desire for pleasure. These phenomena are unmistakable indications of the presence of a power in mental life which we call the instinct of aggression or of destruction according to its aims, and which we trace back to the original death instinct of living matter. It is not a question of an antithesis between an optimistic and a pessimistic theory of life. Only by the concurrent or mutually opposing action of the two primal instincts—Eros and the death instinct—never by one or the other alone, can we explain the rich multiplicity of the phenomena of life. [1937, pp. 242–243].

The negative therapeutic reaction, then, is understood by Freud as ultimately based on the prevalence of the death instinct in the economy of psychic life. The sense of guilt represents the workings of that portion of the death instinct which is "psychically bound by the superego." I believe that this should be interpreted to mean that the aggressive share of the superego—composed of the aggressive forces of the introjected oedipal imagos and the subject's aggressive impulses—constitutes a structured representative of the death instinct, while other portions of the latter may manifest themselves in ways that seem analytically inaccessible since they have not attained definitive or circumscribed psychic representation. Somatic illness and physical decline, certain phenomena of severe depressive illness, among others, would fall into this category, as well as that element in the negative therapeutic reaction that appears to be inaccessible to analytic work under the best of circumstances, where shifts from one form of suffering to another may at best be all that happens.

This leads to an aspect of the negative therapeutic reaction not frequently considered. If it bespeaks an unconscious resistance against improvement, it implies that this resistance, while turning up in the course of analysis, would manifest itself in any other form of treatment as well, as soon as signs or intimations of improvement make their appearance. If the resistance is against improvement per se, by definition the results of shock or drug treatment, or forms of psychotherapy other than psychoanalysis, would also in some unconscious way be vitiated by the patient. Thus defined, the negative therapeutic reaction is not specific for psychoanalysis. But in the course of analysis we may have a chance to gain some understanding of this general phenomenon and perhaps to effect some change in whatever the balance of motivations of such resistance may be.

If we call the negative therapeutic reaction a form of resistance, we have done more than describe a phenomenon, we have made a psychoanalytic interpretation: we have given it a psychoanalytic meaning or have assumed it to have a meaning that could be discovered only in the context of psychoanalytic psychology. By calling it a resistance, we imply that this reaction is motivated behavior. Thus, while it would be a behavioral phenomenon nonspecific for psychoanalysis (resistance against an interpretation would be specific), to call it resistance is to draw it into the circle of our psychoanalytic understanding of human beings. In this sense it becomes a specific psychoanalytic phenomenon—not because the phenomenon may be observed only during psychoanalysis but because we consider it from a psychoanalytic point of view.

I return to the death instinct. Freud's late instinct concept in the duality of Eros-Thanatos is quite different from his earlier, far more circumscribed concept. It is as though he stresses, more than before, the pitfalls of a strict or rigid division of the psyche into id, ego, and superego, and emphasizes the roles of these two instincts in the formation of these provinces of the mind and in bringing about that very division. Thus, ego and superego, no less than id and the interrelations between the three, are manifestations of the interactions of Eros and Thanatos and the two instincts are seen to express themselves even in ways that show them "at work in other, unspecified places." "The behavior of the two primal instincts, their distribution, mingling and defusion [are] things which we cannot think of as being confined to a single province of the mental apparatus, the id, the ego or the superego" (1937, p. 242).

The death or destructive instinct manifests itself in various guises in human life, certainly, according to Freud, in some superego phenomena; in the intractable unconscious sense of guilt; in the resistance against the uncovering of resistances; in the unanalyzable residue of masochism; in the need for suffering; and, last but not least, in a propensity for inner conflict. Whether or not he was influenced by Nietzsche, Freud proposes to understand inner conflict in terms of a thesis that Nietzsche, in his "Genealogy of Morals" (1887), entertained 50 years before Freud wrote "Analysis Terminable and Interminable," namely, as the result of a process of internalization or turning inward of man's aggressiveness. This would have happened "in the course of man's development from a primitive state to a civilized one. . . . If so," Freud (1937) continues, "his internal conflicts would certainly be the proper equivalent for the external struggles that have then ceased" (p. 244). While this internalization may be viewed as a defense against the dangers of external aggression, it seems appropriate here to apply Hartmann's (1939, pp. 25–26) concept of the change of function by which internalized struggle, inner conflict, becomes a hallmark, valued in itself, of human nature.

In those people for whom suffering, and especially inner suffering, has become more or less a condition of their lives, perhaps we see extremes of such internalization. They show, in distortion, something of the glory and the misery of the human condition. In view of the sexual, libidinal elements in the phenomena of masochism, including moral masochism (Freud, 1924), it seems justifiable to include here the internalization of the sexual instincts and Eros, which would help us understand the strongly narcissistic quality of such persons. The moral masochist, in pure culture, is not only torn by his inner conflicts, by his internal sado-masochistic struggle between superego and ego, he is also bound and held together by his narcissistic libido deployed in this internal relationship.

There are patients who defend against their sado-masochistic or symbiotic or homosexual needs by not giving in to improvement, by a negativistic attitude toward the analyst and his influence. But I believe that Freud, when he considered the negative therapeutic reaction in the context of his Eros–Thanatos theory, did not primarily have them in mind. The person with an intractable unconscious sense of guilt in Freud's sense resists improvement—not because he defends against his masochistic needs, but because he is so thoroughly a masochist. Improvement to him is not a sign of giving in to his masochistic or symbiotic needs; his "identity" is not so much threatened by what he considers to be yielding, for example, to the homosexual lure or to fusion with the analyst–parent–love object. Improvement to him is a sign of a lessening of that self-punishment that he requires; in the last analysis, according to Freud, improvement represents to him abandoning the life and death struggle within him in which the death instinct always has to maintain the upper hand. Often the accent seems to be on *self*-punishment, an indication of the importance of narcissistic omnipotence, including the omnipotence of bisexuality.

We should keep in mind that the unconscious sense of guilt is a psychoanalytic interpretation in terms of superego and conscience. It is an attempt on the part of the analyst to understand, and to enable the patient to understand, instinctual unconscious forces in terms of higher mental integration of motivation. The patient for whom suffering, inner conflict, sickness, misfortune in whatever form, is a necessity, does not understand when we talk to him of his sense of guilt. We may have a measure of success if we can transform the prevalence of his "unbound" death instinct into a sense of guilt, i.e., into a higher mental form, which is potentially accessible to mental therapy, to reason, which can help in a novel way to alter the balance of forces. But this possibility, in Freud's view, is severely limited by the very predominance of the death instinct in such people, an instinct working precisely against the forces of Eros that strive toward higher organization and binding together. The death instinct strives toward the lowest potential and destruction.

The negative therapeutic reaction, in this restricted sense of Freud's, is not primarily a reaction against the therapist and his efforts, however, these may be interpreted or misinterpreted by the patient. Granted that it may be a contributing factor—perhaps sometimes a disguised form of the primary resistance—the essential factor is the resistance against improvement of his, the patient's, condition. No doubt—so Freud seems to say—there are many contributing factors based on the patient's unconscious attitudes toward the analyst. All these, at least in principle, are analyzable. What is likely to be unanalyzable is that irreducible residue that remains after all such factors have been taken into account: the deleterious balance between the inner forces of Eros and Thanatos, between self-destructive and libidinal tendencies. Irrational unconscious guilt feelings and a strongly masochistic attitude toward a sadistic superego may be expressions of this slanted balance. But in severe cases such an imbalance is rooted in problems of early psychic development, in the precursors of morality, conscience, and guilt that antedate the Oedipus complex and the formation of the superego—where destructive forces got out of hand, as it were, and affected the very fiber of the person *before* they could be bound, as Freud says, by the superego and in the tension between ego and superego. Schematically speaking, such self-destructiveness can become conscious as irrational guilt only where the proportions and fusions and defusions of aggression and libido were favorable enough in early stages of psychic development for both to be bound and manifest in the ego-superego tension. There the analysis of the Oedipus complex and its resolution—the birthplace of conscience and guilt—can provide a vehicle for understanding. Otherwise the patient cannot be persuaded that he feels guilty—he feels sick. Or if he feels guilty, this is only a later, more structured expression in terms of the Oedipus complex and conscience, of a disturbance that is rooted in earlier stages of ego development. One might say in epigrammatic form the patient does not say *no* to the therapist or to any other person, but to himself.

If we think in terms of a hierarchy of motivational forces—

which structuring leads to a containment, to fusions, transformations, and a taming of instinctual forces—then we might say that
early severe disturbances in psychic development interfere with
such hierarchical structuring, and a share of the destructive
drives remains untamed, free to roam within the psychic organization and to attach itself to whatever structures lend themselves
at a given time to such contamination.

My emphasis on pre-oedipal early disturbances in the negative therapeutic reaction is in agreement with a number of
authors and with some formulations by Olinick (1964). The
close relationship to severe depression has been stressed by
many (Panel, 1970). It remains for me to try to clarify further
some of the theoretical issues involved here. Early disturbances
in psychic development are no less codetermined by interactional
processes with early environment than the oedipal problems are
by interactions on the oedipal level; if anything, more so. Early
psychic development, early ego development, according to current views, is most importantly codetermined by libidinal-
aggressive and identificatory interactions within the dyadic
mother–child field. Early "object ties," by way of primitive identifications or introjections, contribute a heavy share to the formation of the primitive, pre-oedipal ego. But I believe that we
must go further and think of instinctual drives themselves in
terms that differ with Freud's view. Instincts are, to my mind, in
the light of the work of Mahler (1968), Spitz (1965), Winnicott
(1965), and many others, no longer to be conceptualized as internal stimuli impinging on a psychic apparatus, nor yet as forces
enclosed and immanent in the primitive psyche of the newborn,
psychic forces that would first find discharge in autoerotic-
autoaggressive activities and then turn to the outside. We assume
that at such early stages, inside and outside are not differentiated,
that there is no subject–object split. Anything we can call instinctual drives, as psychic forces, arise and are being organized
first within the matrix of the mother–child unitary psychic field
from which, through manifold interactional processes within
that field, the infantile psyche gradually segregates out as a relatively more autonomous center of psychic activity. In this view
instinctual drives in their original form are not forces immanent
in an autonomous, separate primitive psyche, but are resultants
of tensions within the mother–child psychic matrix and later

between the immature infantile psyche and the mother. Instincts, in other words, are to be seen as relational phenomena from the beginning and not as autochthonous forces seeking discharge, which discharge is understood as some kind of emptying of energy potential, in a closed system or out of it. Instinctual drives, their qualities and intensities, their fusions and defusions, and their proportional strength are codetermined by the "environmental factors" that enter into their very organization as motivational forces.[1]

In this approach to the issue of instincts, life and death instincts in a psychic organization cannot be seen as independent variables, independent of the early environmental constellation. Granting the duality of life and death instincts, they are, *qua* instincts, resultants of primitive interactions and derive the forms of their "concurrent or mutually opposing action" (Freud, 1937, p. 243), their relative flexibility or inflexibility, as well as the degree of their capacity for higher transformations, from these early formative interactions. The intensity of destructive tendencies and of their narcissistic entrenchment in the negative therapeutic reaction would depend, predominantly, on early interactions that favor a distorted organization of both destructive and libidinal, destructive and creative, drives, and favor a lack of balanced coordination of them.

If we admit such a change in the instinct concept, at least some objections to the postulation of the death instinct may fall by the wayside; because the implication follows that self-destructiveness and the distortion of narcissistic libido in the service of self-aggression have something to do with environmental forces: organism and environment in their differentiation from one another and in their interactions produce the individual's death instinct and life instinct, and their origins and vicissitudes are not primarily independent of the caring persons.

But here a warning is in place. The organization of the drives is very early business in the course of psychic development, and later modifications of their distorted early organization runs into formidable difficulties. When we are actually confronted with what Freud calls the negative therapeutic reaction, the chances

---

1. For further clarification and elaboration of this conceptualization of instinctual drives, see Loewald, 1970, 1971.

of success are not great, notwithstanding the fact that environmental forces have been instrumental in its causation. It is true, I believe, that Freud underplayed, when it comes to early psychic stages, the crucial importance of the individual psychic environment. He also perhaps did not sufficiently stress the importance of often insidious and primitively structured countertransference problems for such therapeutic failures. On the other hand he had, in contrast to some passionate and self-sacrificing healers, a healthy respect for the limitations of analysis and any therapy. And we should be realistic enough to be skeptical of the chances for significantly modifying psychic conditions and constellations that stem from such serious early distortions and imbalances of the drives themselves.

As mentioned before, if negative therapeutic reactions can be traced back mainly to ego–superego tensions and guilt, the chances for analytic influence and lessening of self-defeating tendencies are better. The patient then may be open to and profit from a modification of the ego–superego relationship, and there can be little question that the implicit attitude of the analyst as a more benevolent potential superego imago is of importance here. To lend oneself in such a way to the patient's introjective capacities, as a spontaneous expression of the analyst's own healthier ego–superego tension, is quite different from attempting to play prophet or savior, against which temptation Freud rightly warns, as being against the rules of analysis. The rule's rationale is that such personally charged influence is rooted in the analyst's own unresolved unmitigated ego–superego tensions and irrational guilt, representing a negative of the patient's problems.

SUMMARY

Freud's conception of the negative therapeutic reaction, as outlined and elaborated in some of his later writings, is re-examined, especially in terms of some of its theoretical implications regarding instinct theory. A reformulation of the concept of instinctual drives is proposed. The negative therapeutic reaction is conceived by Freud as the manifestation of self-destructive tendencies, which are not primarily a by-product of reactions against the therapist and his efforts but stem from a deeply rooted intrapsychic imbalance between libidinal and aggressive drives (or of the life and death instincts). This imbalance in favor of the destructive drives may appear in the form of unconscious guilt feelings (superego versus ego) and pervasive masochistic tendencies, or in the more primitive and intractable form of unstructured ("unbound") destructive forces that have not attained sufficient psychic representation to be assignable to the superego as a mental province. In this insidious form the negative therapeutic reaction must be attributed to distorted organization of the instinctual drives themselves, prior to their structuralization in psychic subsystems. It is in this sense that Freud ultimately traces the negative therapeutic reaction back to a prevalance of the destructive drive or death instinct in the economy of mental life. The presence of an unconscious sense of guilt already presupposes the binding of such destructive forces in the subsystem superego.

In its more intractable forms the negative therapeutic reaction is rooted in pre-oedipal, primitive distortions of instinctual and ego development and is thus hardly amenable to interpretations in terms of guilt, conscience, and need for punishment.

In this connection a revision of the instinct concept itself is proposed. It is suggested that instinctual drives, understood as psychic forces, are to be conceptualized as becoming organized through interactions within the primitive mother–child unitary psychic field rather than as constitutional or innate givens. This would imply that the prevalence of self-destructive forces has something to do with particular interactions with the primitive environment; that organism and environment in their interactions and differentiation from one another produce, as it were, the individual's life and death instincts and their relative proportions; their origins and vicissitudes are not primarily independent of the caring persons. Such a view of the organization of instinctual drives would accord with the clinical impression that severe and ingrained cases of negative therapeutic reaction are rooted in extreme pre-oedipal disturbances of primitive object-ties.

REFERENCES

Freud, S. (1923): The ego and the id. S.E. 19:3–66.
————. (1924): The economic problem of masochism. S.E. 19:
    157–70.

_____. (1973): Analysis terminable and interminable. S.E. 23: 211-53.

Hartmann, H. (1939): *Ego Psychology and the Problem of Adaptation.* New York: International Universities Press, 1958.

Loewald, H. W. (1970): Psychoanalytic theory and the psychoanalytic process. In: *The Psychoanalytic Study of the Child* 25:45-68.

_____. (1971): On motivation and instinct theory. *The Psychoanalytic Study of the Child* 26:91-128.

Mahler, M. (1968): *On Human Symbiosis and the Vicissitudes of Individuation.* New York: International Universities Press.

Nietzsche, F. (1887): The genealogy of morals. In: *The Birth of Tragedy and The Genealogy of Morals.* New York: Doubleday Anchor Books, 1956.

Olinick, S. L. (1964): The negative therapeutic reaction. *Internat. J. Psycho-Anal.* 45: 540-48.

Panel Report (1970): Negative therapeutic reaction. *J. Amer. Psychoanal. Assn.* 18:655-72.

Spitz, R. (1965): *The First Year of Life.* New York: International Universities Press.

Winnicott, D. W. (1965): *The Maturational Processes and the Facilitating Environment.* New York: International Universities Press.

19

COMMENTS ON SOME INSTINCTUAL MANIFESTATIONS OF SUPEREGO FORMATION

In the following pages certain clinical observations during the termination phase of analysis are taken as the starting point for discussing some of the vicissitudes of superego formation. The termination phase, with its specific problems of separation from and relinquishment of a love object, can give insight into such vicissitudes inasmuch as the resolution of the transference neurosis and the resolution of the oedipal conflict are intimately related to each other. Broadly speaking, the paper is concerned with the relations between instinctual drives and psychic structure. In this respect I hope to make a contribution to the much needed rapprochement between what are loosely called "id analysis" and "ego analysis," or "id psychology" and "ego psychology." I explore certain instinctual manifestations, appearing in a group of patients during the termination phase of analysis, in their significance as drive representations[1] of superego formation. The emergence in male patients of passive homosexual fantasies in regard to their male analyst during the termination phase will be discussed from the point of view of the resolution of the Oedipus complex. The appearance of such fantasies can be considered as a resumption of the task of resolving the negative Oedipus component, which leads to the relinquishment and

Versions of this paper were presented in 1961 and 1962 at meetings of the Division of Psychoanalytic Education, Downstate Medical Center, State University of New York, of the Chicago and Philadelphia Psychoanalytic Societies, and of the Western New England Psychoanalytic Society. The revision for publication owes much to the discussions following these presentations. I am particularly indebted to the late Maxwell Gitelson and to Charles Kligerman and Theodore Lidz for their extensive and enlightening discussions.

1. The term "representation," is used here in its broad sense and not its narrower meaning of "idea" or "ideational representation" (the German *Vorstellung*). The noun "representation" here refers to what Freud has called a "representative" (in German *Repräsentant* or *Repräsentanz*), which is not necessarily ideational. Cf. Strachey's discussion of these terms (Freud, 1915, pp. 111–12).

internalization of this object-relationship aspect, and thus contributes to superego formation. But such passive-receptive strivings in the male will be further considered in their more fundamental significance as instinctual representations of internalization processes in general.

In the course of the terminating phase of analysis with male patients I have been impressed with the frequent appearance of direct, undisguised manifestations of such passive-homosexual strivings toward the analyst and of defensive struggles against these strivings. I have in mind wish fantasies of being the receptive partner in anal intercourse or fellatio practices with the analyst, impregnation and pregnancy fantasies, at times expressed or accompanied by somatic representations such as intestinal, stomach, or throat discomfort, bloated feeling in the abdomen, or nausea. Not infrequently such fantasies take the form of accusations against the analyst that he has aggressive designs on the patient. These may be pictured as frank sexual aggression or as a desire on the analyst's part to subject the patient to permanent submission in the form of unnecessarily prolonged treatment. Attempts to analyze the patient's expressed wish to terminate the analysis may be construed as demonstrations of the analyst's need for continued power over the patient, even in the face of the analyst's stated agreement on a termination date. It should be emphasized that the patients in question did not come to analysis because of homosexual problems or paranoid tendencies; nor has analysis in these cases revealed significant degrees of homosexual pathology (as distinguished from normal homosexual personality trends). While homosexual fantasies in the transference had appeared at times during the course of the analysis, they did not play a prominent part prior to the termination phase.

The analyst encounters a specific difficulty during the termination phase of any analysis. Both analyst and patient may become aware of signs or intimations that termination is approaching. If the matter is first brought up by the patient, the analyst will attempt to analyze what is involved in the patient's feeling or his wish to terminate. It may be nothing but a manifestation of resistance. But one may safely say that resistance of one kind or another always plays a role in the patient's urge to terminate. The uncovering of that factor, in and by itself, is not a valid argument against terminating the analysis. Our clinical judgment must be guided by an assessment of the balance of factors involved. We cannot, at this juncture of the analysis, remain completely wedded to the analytic process itself, which is by nature interminable, but must step out of it with one foot, as it were, to survey and assess also the extra-analytic reality of the patient's life. Our analytic as well as our more broadly clinical judgment must come into play. If meaningful advances have taken place in the inner reorganization of the patient's life, sooner or later his need for independence from the analyst and from analysis will assert itself, as will reactivated wishes for continued dependence; both will be present, in varying proportions. It frequently occurs that these contradictory tendencies reinforce each other. The more the patient becomes aware of his passive strivings toward the analyst, the stronger defenses against them may grow, leading to increased insistence on termination. On the other hand, a growing awareness and assertion of adult independence may throw the patient back in the direction of submissive-dependent attachment. At such a time the homosexual wish fantasies and defensive projections may come to the surface.

The question may arise whether it is the pressure of impending termination that brings about these homosexual manifestations, or whether it is the emergence of homosexual strivings in the course of the deepening analysis that pushes the patient toward termination, as a defense against them and as a resistance against their being analyzed. If such homosexual conflicts in the transference clearly appear in the context of an ongoing analysis as part of the unfolding analytic material, without apparent provocation by the reality factor of contemplated termination, it is likely that subsequent pressure from the patient for an early termination is an expression of resistance and not much more. It is likely, on the other hand, that the emergence or re-emergence of such conflicts in the context of the termination phase represents their reactivation by the impending termination. This activation then needs to be analyzed in terms of the resolution of the Oedipus complex and of the transference neurosis and should be understood as part of the process of working through this problem.

Why does the oedipal conflict become reactivated during the

termination phase, and why in this form? Termination represents separation from and loss of a love object. We call the process of coming to terms with and working through such a loss the work of mourning. Mourning, properly understood, involves more than the gradual giving up of the love object, the detachment of object cathexis. If brought to completion, the work of mourning encompasses the internalization of elements of the lost object-relationship. A partial narcissistic recathexis of the drive energies employed in the object-relationship takes place. Anna Freud some years ago re-emphasized these two phases of mourning: "The process of mourning (*Trauerarbeit*) taken in its analytic sense means to us the individual's effort to accept a fact in the external world (the loss of the cathected object) and to effect corresponding changes in the inner world (withdrawal of libido from the lost object, identification with the lost object)" (1960, p. 58).

Mourning, in these respects, has its prototype in the resolution of the Oedipus conflict. There, too, a complex process of relinquishing and identifying with love objects takes place, involving the transformation of object libido into narcissistic libido. Such identifications lead to the formation of the superego. We may say that the first mourning, properly so-called, takes place in the resolution of the Oedipus conflict. In contrast to later mourning experiences at times of permanent loss of a love object by death or definitive separation, the mourning of the resolution of the Oedipus conflict takes place in the presence and often with the help of the external objects being mourned, i.e., the parents. If this help is not forthcoming, because of inadequacies in the parents or because of the early death of a parent, the normal resolution of the Oedipus complex is interfered with and subsequent mourning experiences are likely to show pathological characteristics. Recently there has been increased interest in the vicissitudes of the Oedipus complex in the one-parent child and in children who have lost a parent during significant periods of oedipal development, including loss through death or divorce during adolescence (for a recent review of the literature, see Miller, 1971).

I have implied an answer to the question why the Oedipus conflict becomes reactivated during the termination phase of analysis. Insofar as termination means loss of or separation from a parental love object, it is not merely one of a number of mourning experiences but is, as the resolution of the transference neurosis, to be understood as a resumption or repetition of the first mourning, of the resolution and mastery of the Oedipus conflict. Not unlike the original resolution and its further elaboration during adolescence, the work of mourning during the termination phase takes place in the presence and with the help of the parental object being mourned. Frequently, the clinical picture during termination more closely resembles the adolescent than the original oedipal phase. My earlier comments on the specific difficulty for the analyst in assessing the patient's urgings and readiness for termination apply—mutatis mutandis—in many ways to the parents' difficult position in regard to the dependence–independence problems of their adolescent child. The patients' conflicts over termination, sketched above, as well as aspects of their behavior, often are a good facsimile of adolescent conflicts and behavior. A mainly clinical discussion of the problems confronting us would have much to gain from detailed consideration of and comparison with the adolescent phase. However, in my opinion, predominantly metapsychological discussion gains more by having recourse to the model situation, the original Oedipus complex—at least at this stage of our knowledge.

My second question was why the Oedipus conflict would be reactivated in the termination phase of analysis in the specific form described above. To avoid misunderstanding, I emphasize that in this paper I focus on a particular aspect of the Oedipus complex, without any implication that it is the only aspect, the only representative of the Oedipus complex appearing during termination in these patients. I do believe, however, that the aspect under consideration here has unique, although by no means exclusive, significance for problems of termination and superego development. Why do passive-homosexual strivings, in the cases mentioned, come to the fore at that time, often for the first time with such clarity and persistence? To approach this question I will take a theoretical detour. It has become customary, often to the detriment of therapy and theory, to overemphasize the distinction between ego psychology and id psychology. Problems of object loss, of introjection, identification, and mourning are discussed as ego-psychological problems. The energy involved in ego functioning and in the cohesion of ego structure itself is said to be neutralized, desexualized, and de-aggressivized energy. It is no longer psychic energy as we know it from the object cathexes of instinctual drives. But the ego pathology with which our patients confront us is a manifestation of various kinds of faulty modification or transformation of drive energy. Equally, normal ego and superego formation and functioning are manifestations of modification and transformation of drive energy, ego autonomy notwithstanding. Seen from the perspective of ego psychology, on the other hand, instinctual conflict or instinctual manifestations have to be understood as drive expressions or drive levels of ego processes. In our daily analytic work we often find that we have a choice: to deal with a given issue, a dream, a piece of behavior, a transference manifestation, either from the point of view of the id or from the point of view of the ego. Which choice we make depends not only on the content of the material but also, and often more so, on the context in which the material is brought up, and especially on our assessment of the psychic level from which the patient is speaking or which he is tending to obscure or neglect.

When we speak of neutralization and desexualization, it is important that these terms do not become mere words, devoid of live meaning. Freud speaks of desexualization very graphically: "When the ego assumes the features of the object (by identification), it forces itself, so to speak, upon the id as a love object and tries to make good the loss of that object by saying: 'look, I am so like the object, you can as well love me.'" And he continues: "The transformation of object libido into narcissistic libido which thus takes place obviously implies an abandonment of sexual aims, a process of desexualization; it is consequently a kind of sublimation" (1923, p. 30). The relinquishment of Oedipal objects and their "restitution" in the ego, as a precipitate or differentiating grade constituting the superego, is a process of desexualization of libidinal cathexis, so that object cathexis becomes transformed into neutralized, narcissistic cathexis. Prior to and during the course of achieving this relinquishment and this narcissistic transformation of object cathexis (and partly because of the impending relinquishment) the sexual-aggressive object cathexis may actually increase. This is a dynamic-economic description of the fact that the work of mourning is indeed an achievement in which rather violent and sudden cathectic shifts (often manifested in mood swings) may occur.

We may now give a partial answer to our second question. Insofar as the resolution of the Oedipus complex in the boy involves, among other factors, the relinquishment of the passively loved father and of the boy's feminine attachment to him (the negative or inverted component of the Oedipus complex; see Freud, 1923, pp. 28–34), it is easy to understand how the impending relinquishment may heighten passive-homosexual strivings. The resumption of resolving the Oedipus complex, culminating in the relinquishment of incestuous object relations and in their partial internal restitution during the termination phase (resolution of the transference neurosis), can lead to a heightening of passive-homosexual tendencies in the male patient, as a step toward relinquishing the relationship with the analyst as an incestuous love object. This increase would be part of the mourning process and of its pronounced cathectic shifts—a last stand, as it were, in the struggle to resolve the negative Oedipus component, presaging the reconstitution of aspects of this relationship in the superego.

But there is another, and more fundamental, aspect to the resurgence of the passivity conflict in men at the end of analysis.[2] It is of a more general nature than the negative Oedipus component, although perhaps related to and enhanced by it. I spoke of the passivity conflict in terms of passive-receptive, and in that sense feminine, strivings. The symptoms were fantasies or their equivalents of oral or anal intercourse and of impregnation by the analyst. These are incorporative fantasies. The introjective component of identification is a taking-in, a psychic incorporation. Incorporation, especially oral incorporation, has always been seen as the instinctual-somatic prototype of introjection; the term "introjection" is usually employed to denote the ego aspect of such processes. In the unconscious and for the unconscious, using primary-process mentation, introjection of an oedipal object relation is an incorporation. The resolution of the Oedipus conflict, insofar as it involves an introjection of the

2. Much of this discussion would be applicable to women patients as well, but the details of their psychosexuality are sufficiently different to warrant a separate consideration of their internalization processes.

relinquished object relationship, has aspects of a receptive, incorporating process. In keeping with the progressive genitalization of sexuality, the taking-in gets represented more in genital than in pregenital terms of receptivity. I mention in passing that to my mind the fantasies of oral and anal intercourse, in the group of patients under discussion here, bespeak a genitalization of orality and anality rather than a simple, direct regression to pregenital stages of libido development. That is to say, the fantasies are hysteric-obsessional in nature rather than schizoid or depressive-paranoid. Fantasies of the latter type are seen in the more severe character disorders, whereas the fantasies discussed here represent in the main regression up to but not beyond the phallic level.

The term "passive-receptive" (as the term "feminine" itself) is easily misleading. Incorporation, taking-in, is not necessarily passive if passive is thought of as the opposite of aggressive. Incorporation can be, and often is, an aggressive process; we only have to think of the devouring quality of many incorporative acts. And indeed the resurgence of what I called "passive-homosexual strivings" in these patients frequently shows, together with submissive feelings, such aggressive-devouring aspects. The term "passive," then, should be understood to mean the direction of the act, rather than to indicate necessarily the quality of gentle or abject submission to another object. Taking-in may occur in a variety of modes; the taker may incorporate the material actively, aggressively, or he may devour it destructively; he may "passively" submit or yield or surrender. The material, on the other hand, may be offered lovingly or grudgingly; it may be forced on the taker or be withheld and yielded to him only as a result of aggressive demands. These varieties of taking and giving, as we well know, determine the character of the superego to no small degree. Also, each mode of giving and of receiving exerts an influence on its counterpart. When Freud spoke of the superego as the representative of the id, he must have had in mind, too, the varieties of taking-in in introjection.

The emergence of receptive-homosexual strivings in relation to the analyst during the termination phase can be understood as an instinctual manifestation of the introjective elements of the work of mourning involved in the resolution of the transference neurosis. We are too apt to view the Oedipus conflict, and thereby the transference neurosis, in terms of instinctual and object-relation problems, without sufficient consideration of their implications for psychic structure building, that is, for superego formation. Sandler (1960) has commented on this issue in his illuminating paper on the superego. On the other hand we are apt to view psychic structure without keeping clearly in mind the instinctual-energic side of structure formation, i.e., the libido transformations and internalizations involved in psychic structure building.

Emergence of such homosexual strivings is emergence into consciousness. What remain to be brought to awareness are not the instinctual strivings themselves but their representational relationship to the ego problems with which the patient is struggling. What leads to expansion and enrichment of the ego, to the extension of the ego's reign, is not the emergence of the instinctual strivings into consciousness per se, but the understanding that the homosexual fantasies are, on one level, instinctual manifestations of internalization problems, of the work of mourning. And it is the understanding that the work of mourning and of internalization represents transformations of incorporative-receptive instinctual processes, which allows the id to play its necessary and living part in the reorganization of the superego.

Our question was why the Oedipus conflict and its resolution would be reactivated in the specific form described, during the termination phase of analysis. The question is not yet fully answered. I hope we have come to see more clearly why passive-receptive strivings, in the sense clarified above, are reactivated. But we need to comprehend more fully why they are expressed in phallic-genital terms, in terms of frank sexual fantasies and wishes rather than in the form of derivatives of higher-level representatives. The answer lies, I believe, in the retransformation of narcissistic-masochistic cathexis into object cathexis, a retransformation that is involved in the externalization of superego introjections.[3]

---

3. The terms "narcissistic," "masochistic," "libidinal," and "aggressive" must be understood here as metapsychological, not as clinical terms. Insofar as the distinction between sexual and aggressive drives is valid, masochism (as a metapsychological concept) is the counterpart to narcissism; both are here understood as internalization modes of aggressive and sexual drives respectively. See my discussion of some of these issues in a previous paper (1962, pp. 491–93, reprinted in this volume).

We know that introjected object relations which are elements of superego structure are comparatively easily reprojected into external relationships. We see this not only in paranoid conditions but to a certain degree in every analysis, when the analyst becomes an external embodiment of features of the patient's superego. Without such transference projection, subsequent modification of the now external oedipal relationship in the transference, and, finally, reinternalization of aspects of the changed relationship, no real therapeutic change takes place. Expressed in metapsychological terms: the narcissistic-masochistic, internal relationships which constitute superego structure, and whose cathectic energies consist of (relatively) desexualized, deaggressivized energy, become deneutralized, are reconverted into sexual-aggressive cathexes in the process of transference projection. To put it somewhat differently again, and less abstractly: the revival, in the transference neurosis, of the oedipal relationship with the parents, of the conflicts and libidinal-aggressive tensions inherent in them, and of the separation experiences and renunciations inherent in their resolution—this revival means repersonification, on the plane of external object relations, of what had become, to a greater or lesser degree, dynamic forces and interrelations of psychic structure during the original Oedipus resolution. If internalization of object relations or, as Freud would say, identification with the oedipal object, implies desexualization and is, according to him, "a kind of sublimation," then reexternalization in the transference means resexualization and desublimation.

The specific task in the termination phase, where the separation from the analyst is to be worked through, is the resumption of the Oedipus-conflict resolution with its renunciations and internalizations—the restoring of the superego structure that had been partially dissolved. In primary-process thinking, based on or picturing the earliest bodily processes of incorporation, and becoming imbued with the later, progressively genital editions of them, such internalization is sexual. If the analysis has been effective, primary-process representations of internalization and of the work of mourning are activated. Expressed conversely: mourning becomes regressively transformed into the components of sexual relinquishment of and by the incestuous object, and sexual incorporation of the object, in predominantly phallic-genital terms, since this is the stage reached at the height of the Oedipus conflict.

An analysis, seen in oversimplified schematic outline, consists of two constantly intermingling and overlapping phases: a phase of rolling the infantile neurosis, in the reenactment of the transference neurosis, back toward its oedipal and pre-oedipal origins; and a phase of leading forward, from this dissolution of the infantile neurosis into its elements, by reworking the conflicts, to a healthier resolution of the Oedipus complex and to healthier ego organization. Following this scheme, the superego would be the first to be subject to a gradual dissolution, from the end point of infantile psychosexual development into its oedipal-instinctual elements. At this stage, then, intrapsychic oedipal relations constituting superego structure tend to be reconverted into oedipal object relations as manifested in the positive and negative transference. In the termination phase reconstitution of the superego takes place, to the extent to which disorganization of this structure had occurred. And the task of internalization, to the degree to which repressions have been lifted in the course of the analysis, comes up in the concrete terms of id language, in terms of undisguised instinctual manifestations.

In sum: the homosexual attachment of the male patient to his analyst, while specifically expressing the negative Oedipus attachment, the "feminine" attachment of the boy to his father, is in a more general and fundamental sense an instinctual representation of his receptivity, by virtue of which he internalizes previously established object relations to become structural elements of his superego.

It is true, of course, that what we call here the boy's "feminine attitude" expresses itself also, to a greater or lesser degree, in his attachment to his mother. In fact, children of both sexes display passive-receptive ("feminine") attitudes toward their mothers as well as toward their fathers, and active-aggressive ("masculine") attitudes toward their fathers as well as toward their mothers. These are in part determined by parental attitudes and are responded to by mothers and fathers in different ways at different times. All this depends on a great variety of intrafamilial factors and on habitual attitudes of the individuals involved in such interactions. Direct identifications, i.e., identifications which belong to a genetically earlier stage than object

relations and are not transformations of the latter, further com-
plicate the picture. Freud has called attention to these intricacies
in his discussion of the superego and the Oedipus complex in
The Ego and the Id (1923, pp. 28–34).

When we speak of "bisexuality" in this connection (bisexuality of each parent as well as of the child), the term serves as a
shorthand expression to indicate the following: insofar as the
term "feminine" has come to be associated with receptivity and
the term "masculine" with activity directed outward, both sexes,
although often in significantly different proportions, show both
attitudes. In this sense parents and children are bisexual; the
question whether and to what extent such bisexuality is biologically or culturally determined is not at issue here. One might
then speak of the "masculine" counterpart or object of the boy's
"feminine" strivings, which counterpart may be, in a given case
and at a given time, the father or the mother; just as mother or
father may be the "feminine" counterpart to his masculine strivings. The same is applicable to girls and their masculine and
feminine counterparts.[4]

Viewing the resolution of the Oedipus complex as a process
of mourning, we must say that to the extent to which the
Oedipus complex is repressed the task of mourning has not been
accomplished. While in repression drive energy is withdrawn
from object relations (and in this sense the external object relationship is relinquished), it remains sexualized and is invested
in unconscious, fantasy-object relations. The transformation of
external relationships into internal, structural ones (narcissistic
transformation of drive energy) has not been achieved in repression. Instead, relegation to the id has taken place.[5] In perversion
—and the wish fantasies of the patients cited fall into this category—given components of the Oedipus complex return from or
escape repression as well as structural neutralization and become available for direct expression in external object relations.
In this light the homosexual, conscious fantasies of these patients
can be seen as way stations on the road to either true internalization or repression. They may be regarded as equivalents of the

---

4. Perhaps it needs to be emphasized that I do not intend to minimize the decisive
impact of the biological sex differences on psychological development. Nevertheless,
familial-cultural factors decisively shape and modulate these biological determinants.

5. For a more extensive discussion of this issue see Loewald (1973).

polymorphous-perverse manifestations of childhood, which are equally way stations.

Freud has spoken of the "struggle against passivity" in men and penis envy in women as the bedrock we reach when "we have penetrated through all the psychological strata"; he understands "the masculine protest" and "the wish for the penis" as expressions of "the repudiation of femininity"—"this remarkable feature in the psychical life of human beings," . . . "part of the great riddle of sex" (1937, pp. 250–253). Is not the great riddle of sexuality, of sexual differentiation, at the same time the great riddle of individuation, of becoming a separate biological and psychological entity? Freud speaks of the repudiation of femininity, the repudiation of receiving and yielding and surrender. But what about the repudiation of masculinity, the repudiation of self-assertion, of the isolation of independence, of the exposed position of separateness? Freud stressed the fear of castration and the wish for the penis—but what about the wish for surrender and for a womb? Our patients, I believe, show both. They may show us a way to understand the great riddle of sexuality and individuation in a less one-sided fashion. The development of an internal world[6] of psychic structure, an important share of which is due to internalization, might also be a sign of man's affirmative acceptance of "femininity," no matter how much he may appear to repudiate it in his struggle for mastery of the external world and against receptivity toward men. The male's fear of castration and his struggle against passivity certainly must involve a wish for them, just as the female's tenacious wish for a penis must contain the opposite—penis fear. I believe there is clinical evidence to show that side by side with penis envy, and no less primary, there is repudiation of "masculinity" in women.

ADDENDUM (1972)

In his searching discussion of this paper, when it was presented in Chicago in 1961, Maxwell Gitelson raised an important objection to my formulation in terms of re-externalization of

---

6. Cf. Rapaport's distinction between the inner and the internal world (1957, pp. 696–97).

superego elements or of retransformation of narcissistic into object cathexis, as an explanation for the appearance of the undisguised instinctual manifestations that are the starting point of my presentation. The narcissistic, internal relationships that constitute psychic structure and whose cathectic energies consist of desexualized, neutralized energy, Gitelson maintained, refer only to the ideal normal resolution of the original Oedipus complex. To the extent to which such ideal resolution has occurred, he claims, no resexualization and desublimation in the transference would occur. "We must consider," Gitelson said, "that the elements, dynamic forces, and interrelations of psychic structure in the patient have retained their original drive qualities and that re-externalization in the transference cannot mean resexualization and desublimation, but rather explicit recapitulation in the transference of the original drive qualities of the Oedipus complex, which have survived as such in the neurosis and have been more or less successfully repressed and defended against."

Gitelson rightly emphasizes the distinction between what Freud (1924) has called the "dissolution" and the "repression" of the Oedipus complex. He maintains that my clinical data should be understood in terms of derepression; accordingly, "the original drive qualities of the Oedipus complex, which have survived as such in the neurosis" under repression, through analysis would have returned from repression and appeared in consciousness. Reading the data in this way, we would not deal with a disorganization of true superego structure (if the superego—and I agree with this view—in its ideal normal form is the result not of repression but of dissolution of the Oedipus complex), but with a return from repression of component drives of the Oedipus complex which never had been adequately desexualized and neutralized. While the clinical data cited would be manifestations of drives which now, as the result of analytic work, are becoming available for narcissistic transformation and neutralization, these drives, in Gitelson's interpretation, had not been so transformed during the oedipal period, due to neurotogenic object relations impeding true psychic structure formation.

The difference in our interpretations of these instinctual manifestations, however, is more than a disagreement about the specific genetics of the situation. The difference revolves around the question: is psychic structure (in the sense in which we use this term for a structure such as the superego) irreversible? To Gitelson, if I understand him correctly, there is no return from structural neutralization; what returns, returns from repression and true structuralization in his view is irreversible. With this view I disagree, especially when applied to superego structure. To put this problem in concrete terms: is the reactivation of the oedipal struggle in adolescence, for instance, necessarily and only based on pathological solutions during the original oedipal period, and is its revival in analysis necessarily a sign of pathology? Or is even an ideal normal resolution of the Oedipus conflict, ushering in the latency period, no more than a resolution *for the time being*, so that the issues involved will return inevitably, although on a new level of organization, during puberty-adolescence, demanding fresh solutions both internally and externally, since the adolescent is confronted with new integrative tasks? Whether and to what extent he is able to confront these tasks depends in great part, to be sure, on healthy resolution during the oedipal period. But does this mean that the oedipal struggle is not unfolded again or that his superego structure does not undergo fresh phases of disorganization, involving re-externalization and deneutralization of previously narcissistically transformed drive components—unless there was a pathological outcome of the oedipal conflict, i.e., unless the complex had been merely repressed? (cf. Freud, 1924, pp. 176–77).

There are, I believe, other stages in later life, among them the analytic situation, where internalization structures, especially superego structure, may and often do undergo phases of disorganization and reorganization. These involve what I would call the return from internalization of instinctual cathexes. The reactivation of oedipal problems at such stages, to my understanding, is not necessarily and exclusively due to unresolved oedipal problems left over from the past and repressed. Such reactivation may bespeak, rather, a healthy resiliency of the ego, undoubtedly based on earlier nonrepressive structure formation, which enables the individual to engage in a disorganization in the service of the ego, i.e., to undo, to an extent, former structural resolutions and to arrive at novel resolutions, at higher levels of organization. New integrative tasks, imposed by changing life circumstances or chosen by creative individuals, tend to trigger such reactivations. The normal adolescent revival of the Oedipus complex ushers in an *advance* in development; it is not simply a resumption of the old conflict because it had been repressed. There can be no doubt, however, that both factors, de-repression and re-externalization, are most often intermingled and hard to sort out in a given case. The lines between so-called pathology and normality can never be neatly drawn, least of all in adolescence and in the psychoanalytic situation.

Gitelson's interpretation and mine therefore are not contradictory or mutually exclusive. The difference lies in our diverging views on the question of mutability or immutability of psychic structure.

REFERENCES

Freud, A. (1960): Discussion of Dr. John Bowlby's paper (Grief and mourning in infancy and early childhood). *The Psychoanalytic Study of the Child* 15:53–62.

Freud, S. (1915): Instincts and their vicissitudes. S.E. 14:111–40.

———. (1923): The ego and the id. S.E. 19:3–66.

———. (1924): The dissolution of the oedipus complex. S.E. 19: 172–79.

———. (1937): Analysis terminable and interminable. S.E. 23: 211–53.

Loewald, H. W. (1962): Internalization, separation, mourning and superego. *Psychoanal. Quart.* 31:483–504.

———. (1973): On internalization. *Internat. J. Psycho-Anal.* 54: 9–17.

Miller, J. B. M. (1971): Children's reaction to the death of a parent; A review of the psychoanalytic literature. *J. Amer. Psychoanal. Assn.* 19:697–719.

Rapaport, D. (1957): A theoretical analysis of the superego concept. In: *Collected Papers of D. R.* New York and London: Basic Books, 1967.

Sandler, J. (1960): On the concept of superego. *The Psychoanalytic Study of the Child* 15:128–62.

20

BOOK REVIEW: HEINZ KOHUT, *THE ANALYSIS OF THE SELF*

"The subject matter of this monograph is the study of certain transference and transferencelike phenomena in the psychoanalysis of narcissistic personalities, and of the analyst's reactions to them, including his countertransferences" (p. 1). This introductory sentence indicates the clinical scope and focus of Kohut's important and complex book, the fruit of many years of the psychoanalytic treatment and study of a group of patients with whom every analyst practicing today is becoming more and more familiar. The title and subtitle of the book imply the author's theoretical approach and suggest his attempt to put the treatment of such patients on a firm metapsychological basis.

The patients under consideration fall into a category halfway between Freud's transference neuroses and narcissistic neuroses (as nosological groups). While their complaints and symptomatology vary within a considerable range, they may be characterized by two outstanding features: (1) these patients appear to have what is commonly called a sufficiently intact ego, permitting them to develop a reasonably stable and close rapport with the analyst, which makes transferences possible and enables them to engage in meaningful self-observation; (2) their psychopathology centers less around conflicts over oedipal relations which would be reactivated in the transference neurosis than around more primitive, mostly pre-oedipally determined problems of self–object differentiation. These archaic problems are reactivated in the transference relationship with the analyst and give that relationship its "symbiotic" fusion quality and, at certain times, its character of cold or haughty detachment.

The Analysis of the Self. A Systematic Approach to the Psychoanalytic Treatment of Narcissistic Personality Disorders. By Heinz Kohut. The Psychoanalytic Study of the Child Monograph No. 4. New York: International Universities Press, Inc., 1971. 368 pp.

If, with Hartmann, narcissism is defined as the cathexis of the self, then the psychopathology of such patients centers around repressed or otherwise warded-off narcissistic issues[1] that have not been resolved, resulting in a deficient development of true object-cathexis (the latter being involved in oedipal relationships). As Kohut sees it, narcissistic personality disturbances are narcissistic not in the sense that the patients are not engaged with objects, but in the sense that objects are unconsciously, or in a disavowed sector of their personality, cathected with narcissistic rather than with object libido. Objects are either predominantly "used in the service of the self and of the maintenance of its instinctual investment," or they are "themselves experienced as part of the self." He refers to the latter as "self-objects" (p. xiv). It is, according to Kohut, not the "target of the instinctual investment (i.e., whether it is the subject himself or other people) but . . . the nature or quality of the instinctual charge" that determines whether cathexis is narcissistic or object cathexis (p. 26). The transference phenomena, characteristic for these patients once their archaic problems have been reactivated in the analytic situation, accordingly are called narcissistic transferences. To call them transferences, at least in a broad clinical sense, is justified by "the unquestionable fact that the image of the analyst has entered a long-term, relatively reliable relationship with the mobilized narcissistic structures, which permits the maintenance of a specific, systematic process of working through" (p. 205). Narcissistic transference is distinguished from those transferences established in the classical transference neuroses by the fact that "the phenomenon is not produced by cathecting the analyst with object libido" but by including him "in a libidinal (i.e., narcissistic) state to which [the patient] has regressed or at which he has become arrested" (Anna Freud's personal communication, p. 205 n. 1).

The stage in development preceding the differentiation of self and object, usually referred to as primary narcissism, is followed by a stage in which "the child replaces the previous perfection (a) by establishing a grandiose and exhibitionistic image of the self:

---

1. Kohut distinguishes between repression, a "horizontal split" in the personality, and a "vertical split" akin to the disavowal described by Freud as a split in the ego, as in fetishism.

the grandiose self; and (b) by giving over the previous perfection to an admired, omnipotent (transitional) self–object: the idealized parent imago" (p. 25). This twofold process—the fixation point of the narcissistic personality disturbances—leads Kohut to divide his subject matter into two main parts, the "therapeutic activation of the omnipotent object" (part I, pp. 37–101) and the "therapeutic activation of the grandiose self" (part II, pp. 105–199). In terms of the narcissistic transferences at play, the former, i.e., the patient's relationship to the analyst *qua* omnipotent object, is called the idealizing transference; the latter, i.e., the patient's relationship to the analyst as merged with or as an extension of the self, is called the mirror transference.

The idealized self–object and the grandiose self are considered as "two facets of the same developmental phase" (p. 107). The original all-embracing (primary) narcissism unfolds into these two facets: one is not more primitive than the other, although one or the other may be more prominent in the analytic relationship. The therapeutic task in either type of narcissistic transference consists in allowing the reactivation of these primitive configurations in relation to the analyst, so that the development toward true object relations (involving the emergence of more stable and more pervasive object cathexis) and toward a more realistic (i.e., limited) self may be resumed in the working through process, thus permitting the integration or reintegration of these configurations with the more mature part of the personality.

The concept of internalization, here called transmuting internalization, is crucial for Kohut's theoretical framework. He sees psychic structure formation—referring specifically to ego and superego structure—as based on the decathexis of object imagoes (p. 49), whether these be archaic self–objects, idealized objects, or the more evolved objects of the oedipal phase, and on their transmuting internalization by which the resulting "internal structure now performs the functions which the object used to perform for the child" (p. 50). The self–object in particular is seen as the precursor of psychic structure. Kohut emphasizes the crucial difference between "(1) the narcissistically experienced, archaic self–object (an object only in the sense of the observer of manifest behavior); (2) the psychological structures (. . . built up in consequence of the gradual decathexis of the narcissistically experienced archaic object) which continue to perform the drive-

regulating, integrating, and adaptive functions—previously performed by the (external) object; and (3) true objects (in the psychoanalytic sense) which are cathected with object-instinctual
investments, i.e., objects loved and hated by a psyche that has
separated itself from the archaic objects, has acquired autonomous structures, has accepted the independent motivations and
responses of others, and has grasped the notion of mutuality"
(pp. 50–51).

The idealizing transference of narcissistic personality disorders permits the resumption of that internalizing process that
leads specifically to the consolidation of the superego in its "narcissistic dimension . . . i.e., to its idealization. . . . The internalization of the object-cathected aspects of the parental imago trans-
mutes the latter into the contents and functions of the superego;
the internalization of the narcissistic aspects accounts for the
exalted position which these contents and functions have vis-à-
vis the ego" (p. 41). The author stresses this distinction, which is
related to that between superego and ego ideal.

The mirror transference constituting the activation of the
relatedness of the primitive self to itself, as it were, permits the
resumption of that process in which the grandiose self becomes
modified. In Kohut's words: "Under favorable circumstances
(appropriately selective parental response to the child's demands
for an echo to and participation in the narcissistic-exhibitionistic
manifestations of his grandiose fantasies), the child learns to
accept his realistic limitations, the grandiose fantasies and the
crude exhibitionistic demands are given up, and are *pari passu*
replaced by ego-syntonic goals and purposes, by pleasure in his
functions and activities and by realistic self-esteem" (p. 107). It
is Kohut's implication that in the mirror transference in the analytic situation the analyst is called upon to provide these favorable circumstances—not adequately provided in infancy—at
the same time as he elucidates for the patient, appealing to the
more mature sector of the patient's personality, the genetic
sources of his deficiency or lack of development in the narcissistic
realm. In his view, a "person's ultimate goals and purposes, and
his self-esteem, carry the imprint of the relevant characteristics
and attitudes of the imagoes . . . of the persons against whom the
child's grandiose self had been reflected or whom the child had
accepted as extensions of his own greatness" (pp. 107–08); but

they "also carry the earmark of the original narcissism which infuses into the central purposes of our life and into our healthy self-esteem that absoluteness of persistence and of conviction of the right to success which betrays that an unaltered piece of the old, limitless narcissism functions actively alongside the new, tamed and realistic structures" (p. 108).

The mirror transference appears in three forms, in decreasing degrees of archaism: (1) the "archaic merger through the extension of the grandiose self" (primary identity with the analyst); (2) the alter-ego or twinship transference (the analyst is experienced as like or very similar to the grandiose self); (3) the mirror transference in the narrower sense. In this last, comparatively most mature form, "the analyst is most clearly experienced as a separate person," but he is "an object which is important only insofar as it is invited to participate in the child's narcissistic pleasure and thus to confirm it" (pp. 115–16).

That the analyst provides these favorable circumstances means that his general empathic attitude and understanding of the patient's narcissistic needs, demands, and defenses prevent his interventions from interfering with their activation in the transference, for instance, by premature or ill-timed demonstrations of their unrealistic nature, by judgmental statements, or hostile withdrawal. These are pitfalls in the treatment of such disorders to which most analysts are susceptible, since we ourselves have to struggle often enough with unresolved or recurring problems of similar vintage. The opposite, an overidentification with the patient's narcissistic needs, of course is equally uncalled for. It is my impression that Kohut is not sufficiently aware of or concerned with this latter problem. Chapters ten and eleven of the book give an instructive survey of some of the analyst's reactions to the idealizing and mirror transferences.

In order to understand Kohut's conception of narcissism in a broader perspective, it is important to make clear that he postulates "two separate and largely independent developmental lines: one which leads from autoerotism via narcissism to object love; another which leads from autoerotism via narcissism to higher forms and transformations of narcissism" (p. 220). In chapter twelve he discusses these higher forms and transformations as they occur in successful analyses of narcissistic personalities. The healthy development of narcissism as the cathexis of the self, from this point of view, may be characterized as the development of a mature, rich self. Kohut stresses, and rightly so, the importance and value of narcissism in this sense, implying, as I see it, that the development from early phases in mental life need not and does not only involve development *away* from early phases but also signifies higher development *of* early stages themselves. Specifically, this appears to be so in the case of particularly empathic or of especially creative individuals and often tends toward a certain one-sided development of specific gifts, traits or interests, at the cost of other desirable character traits, frequently making for disharmony in personality development. Kohut's warning against a common bias in favor of "object love" and against "narcissism," is well taken. But I would question how independent from each other these two lines of development are, or can be, and how useful it is to see them as two separate lines of development. We must keep in mind that either of them can undergo further development and higher transformations, as distinguished from mere hypertrophy, only in conjunction with and under the influence of higher development of the other, although a given individual may have his center of gravity, in the life he lives, more in one than in the other. In chapter twelve, when speaking of the increase and expansion of object love as one of the beneficial changes occurring through analysis, Kohut takes account of these considerations to a limited extent.

Extensive clinical discussions and numerous case illustrations throughout the book make these theoretical-genetic formulations concrete and demonstrate their pertinence and usefulness. I believe every analyst will be stimulated and enabled to review and deepen his understanding of his own case material, particularly in relation to transference–countertransference problems, in the light of Kohut's illustrations. This is true whether or not one agrees with all of his theoretical formulations or with his particular inclinations in regard to therapeutic management.

What follows are some brief critical reflections. The value of the case illustrations and clinical discussions, useful and illuminating as they are, is somewhat diminished by two factors. First, Kohut's metapsychological formulations and genetic reconstructions of the patient's psychopathology frequently overshadow his descriptive material, which is understandably abbreviated and condensed. It seems to me that the author's passion and superior ability for comprehensive and precise formulations tends to interfere with his presentation of the case material and to pre-empt the reader's own judgment.

Secondly, we are too much left in the dark about the processes by which the integration of the repressed or disavowed sectors of the narcissistic personality with the more mature sectors is supposed to come about. I gained the impression that the issues of defense and resistance in the analysis of these patients are not sufficiently developed. In my experience, there is not only resistance against the reactivation of the submerged narcissistic configurations, but there is often powerful resistance against the above-mentioned integration—a resistance that is not merely due to technical errors or countertransference reactions, although the importance of the latter is beyond doubt. Are the favorable changes one hopes for in the majority of cases simply the outcome of permitting and promoting the flourishing of the hitherto warded-off narcissistic configurations? To my mind a not inconsiderable share of the analytic work consists in more or less actively and consistently confronting these freed narcissistic needs and narcissistic transferences with what Kohut calls the mature aspects of the reality ego of the patient. Granted that such confrontations too often are ill-timed or judgmentally tinged, there are also good times for them and a balanced attitude may be maintained. Although Kohut does not altogether ignore this side of the work, it would be important to devote considerably more attention to this type of resistance than he does. Integration with the more mature sectors of the personality, in my opinion, needs working through of its own. Because of the fixation on the archaic stages they become ingrained and proliferate in the course of time—factors which render them different from the early flourishing of childhood narcissism—requiring "educational" work, which consists in repeated though not nagging or premature confrontations with, and demonstrations of, the more mature personality sectors. This aspect of the work is underplayed by Kohut. Freud's observation that the analysis of patients with immature egos comprises a good deal of "after-education," is particularly pertinent in the treatment of narcissistic personality disorders.

I should like to add that a more mature integration of the personality does not merely include an acceptance of the limitations of self and others based on resigned acknowledgment of reality—although that ingredient is always present—but also and importantly it involves an affirmation of the positive and enriching aspects of limitations. This latter element in particular is involved in the expansion of object love and true object relations. Kohut's seeming neglect of analytic work with the type of resistance I emphasized above leads to the impression that a subtle kind of seduction of the patient may be at play in his work with such disorders.

Regarding other clinical problems, there is something forced about the dichotomies set up between narcissistic and object-libidinal issues and between the warded-off immature and the more mature sectors of the personality. For expository purposes these dichotomies are most valuable, but they do not do full justice to clinical realities. Object-libidinal and narcissistic issues, while distinguishable, are frequently blended or intermingled in such a way that each can be expressed in terms of the other, and it will depend on one's clinical acumen whether one or the other aspect is chosen for interpretation. Whether one interprets given material in terms of the self and its fragility, or of self-esteem, as against interpreting the same material in terms of castration fear, for example (i.e., in its object-libidinal dimension), or goes back and forth between one and the other, depends on subtle shifts signaled by the patient between more and less developed layers of the personality, but also on one's point of view regarding the interrelations and interdependence between narcissism and object-libido. Moreover, in terms of more conventional conceptualizations I would say that Kohut is biased in favor of the analysis of the archaic ego and neglects the analysis of ego defenses.

This brings me to my concluding remarks on some strictly theoretical problems. As mentioned earlier, Kohut adopts Hartmann's definition of narcissism as the cathexis of the self. If I understand Hartmann correctly, he substitutes the term "self" for Freud's "global ego," meaning the mind as a totality, irrespective of the subdivision into the mental provinces id, ego, superego (Freud sometimes speaks of ego in this sense as *Gesamt-Ich*), and in contrast to the external world or object world. The development of the self as a cohesive organization that is experienced as different from "objects," is contingent on the differentiation

between subject and object, in contrast to their nondifferentiation
in the primitive state we designate as primary narcissism. At the
stage of primary narcissism, if we follow Freud's elaboration of
this concept as given, for example, in "Civilization and Its Discontents," such distinctions as cathexis of the self versus cathexis
of objects do not exist. This is one of the reasons why the definition of narcissism as cathexis of the self, in my view, is questionable. Object love is not in opposition to or in place of
narcissism. Rather, mature narcissism, mature cathexis of the
self in Kohut's terms, and mature object love are tied together. It
is because the narcissistic personality's self in its warded-off
sectors is so immature, because the differentiation between self
and object is so deficient, that the object cathexis is deficient. For
this reason Kohut speaks of the archaic object as self–object. But
when he speaks of the self–object as transitional, he should
stress not only that the *object* is transitional and archaic, i.e., not
a true object in the psychoanalytic sense (although an object
from the point of view of an outside observer), but that the *self*,
too, is transitional, and not a true self. (It too, is a self only from
the outside observer's viewpoint.) Neither the omnipotent object
in the idealizing transference, nor the grandiose self in the mirror
transference are sufficiently differentiated *qua* object or self.
They are, as the author himself says, facets of the same early
developmental phase. In terms of the distinction between identification and object relations, closely akin to that between narcissistic and object cathexes, identification and object relations are
just beginning to differentiate out of what Freud has called
object-tie (*Objekt-Bindung*), in contradistinction to object-relation
(*Objekt-Beziehung*).

Kohut's self–object is not only the precursor of psychic structure, but equally the precursor of the object as a cohesive and
reliable (constant) organized unit. If narcissistic and object
cathexes are not determined by the target of the instinctual
investment but by the nature and quality of the cathexis, this
means that these differentiating modes of cathexis create the self
qua self and the object *qua* object. The stimulating material, the
target, becomes an element either of self or object world through
the respective cathexes.

In my opinion Kohut's attempt to arrive at conceptual clarification of such basic terms as self in its relations to id, ego, super-

ego remains unsuccessful. While self, unlike id, ego, and superego, is not a constituent or agency of the mind, it also cannot, I believe, be conceptualized as a content of the human mind or mental apparatus, much less as "half of the contents of the human mind —the other half being, of course, the objects" (pp. xiii–xv). If self is something like Freud's *Gesamt-Ich* (the total "ego" where the distinction between id, ego, and superego remains unspecified), then, far from being a content or a structure within the mind, self would be the mind as cathected in its totality. Self, mind, personality, identity are terms referring to a totality seen from different perspectives.

I also question the by now common equation of self and self-representation, or of object and object representation, due to confused thinking in regard to the term "mental representation." While mental representations of self and objects may conceivably be called "contents" of the mind, insofar as they refer to more or less specific fantasies, images, memories, or ideas of self and of objects, these entities themselves (whatever their nature may be) are not mental representations. In a certain sense they may be characterized as mental creations, but not as structures or contents within the mind.

I wish to emphasize that grandiose self, omnipotent object, mirror transference, and idealizing transference as clinical concepts are most illuminating and valuable, and that my critique of complex metapsychological issues and of certain clinical problems in no way detracts from the value of this monograph. I consider it a major achievement. The book is apt to inspire the careful reader to review his own analytic experience in depth, to revise his analytic technique with such patients, and to devote fresh thought to many theoretical and technical problems pertaining to narcissism. We do not often come across a book which gives this kind of inspiration, and which shows such a high level of integration of clinical experience and theoretical sophistication. Any reader who does not fall prey to the temptation of considering *The Analysis of the Self* as the final word on narcissistic personality disorders and their psychoanalytic treatment, will be amply rewarded by Kohut's outstanding contribution.

21

PSYCHOANALYSIS AS AN ART AND THE FANTASY CHARACTER OF THE PSYCHOANALYTIC SITUATION

What follows does not claim to measure up to the standards of scientific rigor or conceptual precision. In the fluidity and ambiguity of thought and style, this presentation is perhaps all too much affected by its subject matter.

Most of us, whether engaged solely in psychoanalytic practice or engaged also in psychoanalytic research and theory building, stress the scientific aspects and potentialities of our discipline. Freud did so, and he rejected the suggestion that there might be something nonscientific or unscientific, something resembling art, about psychoanalysis. In the recent past there has been much emphasis on psychoanalysis as a basic science or as the foundation for or as part of a general psychology. It has been claimed that this constitutes the lasting value of psychoanalysis, and doubts have been expressed, even within the ranks of psychoanalysts themselves, with regard to its viability as a form of psychotherapy. I myself have no doubt about its therapeutic value and potentialities, although I do question whether we can expect general or ready recognition of its therapeutic worth and effects—given the anti-individualistic tendencies and simplistic behavior-modification trends in our culture.

On the other hand, because of significant shifts and changes in modern understanding of what constitutes truth, in our insight into the relations between reality and fantasy or imagination and between objectivity and subjectivity, we begin to recognize that science and art are not as far apart from one another as Freud and his scientific age liked to assume. Science's dignity is not so readily offended today by the suggestion that both art and

This paper was delivered as the Rado Lecture at the Columbia University Psychoanalytic Clinic for Training and Research on May 21, 1974.

science make use of creative imagination. Neither do we take for granted that creative imagination per se is unscientific, nor do we assume that art may not and does not ever employ the stringency of scientific or scientifically informed objectivity.

Thus, in speaking today of psychoanalysis as an art, I neither speak in an antiscientific spirit, nor do I see art as being in opposition to science. Nevertheless, while I see them as closely related, we do distinguish between them. The two words refer to different facets of the human mind's activity.

I

In one sense of art, psychoanalytic *technique* may be called the art of applying psychoanalytic knowledge and the psychoanalytic method to a particular clinical case. Perhaps the latter, the method of investigation and interpretation, may more specifically be called an art (or skill), whereas the body of psychoanalytic observations and theory—the science of psychoanalysis—is made use of in this art. Insofar as investigations and interventions are intended to have a curative effect on the patient's psychic life, psychoanalysis is a therapeutic art.

Considered as a process in which patient and analyst are engaged with each other, psychoanalysis may be seen as art in another sense: the psychoanalytic situation and process involves a re-enactment, a dramatization of aspects of the patient's psychic life history, created and staged in conjunction with, and directed by, the analyst. The idea of the transference neurosis expresses this understanding of psychoanalysis as an emotionally experienced recapitulation of the patient's inner life history in crucial aspects of its unfolding. Seen in this light, psychoanalysis shares important features with dramatic art. Aristotle defined tragedy as "the imitation of action in the form of action." Francis Ferguson, in his illuminating book on dramatic art (1949), extended this definition to include drama in all its various forms. The transference neurosis is such an imitation of action in the form of action, or, more correctly, it develops from such imitation in action of an original action sequence and remains under the formative influence of that original action, although in its total development it is uniquely a creature of the psychoanalytic process.

Viewed as a dramatic play, the transference neurosis is a fantasy creation woven from memories and imaginative elaborations of present actuality, the present actuality being the psychoanalytic situation, the relationship of patient and analyst. But in contrast to a play conceived and composed by its author as a deliberate creation of his mind to be enjoyed by an audience, the transference neurosis is an unwitting fantasy creation which is considered or clearly recognized as such—at any rate in earlier stages of the analysis—only by the analyst. The patient often has inklings of it, on his own or intimated by the analyst, even in early stages; but they tend to be swept away and drowned in the poignancy of his immediate experience, to reappear and disappear again and again. But we know that analysis is not feasible without a measure of "observing ego" that can be called upon and gradually strengthened.

The fantasy character of the transference neurosis has been referred to as the make-believe aspect of the psychoanalytic situation. In the promotion and development of the transference neurosis, analyst and patient conspire in the creation of an illusion, a play. The patient takes the lead in furnishing the material and the action of this fantasy creation, while the analyst takes the lead in coalescing, articulating, and explicating the action and in revealing and highlighting it as an illusion (note that the word illusion derives from the Latin *ludere*, to play). The patient experiences and acts without knowing at first that he is creating a play. Gradually he becomes more of an author aware of being an author, by virtue of the analyst's interventions that reflect back to the patient what he does and says, and by transference interpretations that reveal the relations between the play and the original action that the play imitates.

As director of the play, the analyst must relive, re-create the action of the play. This he is able to do on the basis of his own inner life experiences and their organization, which are sufficiently similar to those of the patient. While engaging in trial identifications with the patient, i.e., with the actors and actions of the play, the analyst is the one to keep an over-all view and to direct the actors—not by telling them what to do or how to act, but by bringing out in them what they often manage to express only fleetingly, defensively, haltingly, in inhibited or distorted fashion.

Patient and analyst in a sense are co-authors of the play: the material and the action of the transference neurosis gain structure and organization by the organizing work of the analyst. The author of a dramatic play performs both functions, that is, the function of "imitating" action in the form of action, and the function of giving organization and structure to the material.

The specific impact of a play depends on its being experienced both as actuality and as a fantasy creation. This Janus-face quality is an important ingredient of the analyst's experience in the analytic situation and becomes, if things go well, an important element in the patient's experience. A spectator, if affected by the play in the way I indicated, participates in the action vicariously. But the patient is a direct participant, as well as the initially unwitting co-author. And the analyst, far from being left to his own devices as spectator by the patient, finds himself cast in the roles of various co-actors by the patient, not dissimilar to certain recent staging devices in contemporary theater. But whereas in such modern productions audience participation ordinarily consists in assuming the assigned role, the analyst, instead of assuming that role, reflects back to the patient the role the latter has assigned to him. Thus the transference neurosis again and again is revealed as an imitation of action, a dramatic play having its roots in the memories of original action and deriving its life as a present creation of fantasy from the actuality of the psychoanalytic situation and its interactions. Whenever the analyst engages in mirroring activities and interpretations, the poignant immediacy of the transference neurosis may recede at least momentarily or to some extent without being extinguished, and its character as a fantasy creation stands out in bolder relief: the patient may take some distance from the action.

Parallels between a dramatic play and the transference neurosis could be spun out further, but at this point I wish to qualify some of the things I have said. I stated that the patient tends to be caught up in the poignant immediacy of the transference and the analyst recognizes and reveals its fantasy character. This is not always the case. An obsessive-compulsive patient may have so much distance from himself, may be such a compulsive self-observer or so obsessively entangled in psychoanalytic theory, that he remains or only too promptly reverts to being a detached spectator insisting on the unreality of the transference. It is the

analyst who then must take the lead in accentuating and intensi-
fying the patient's experience of the here-and-now immediacy of
the transference.

Another qualification: even though the analyst does not assume the roles assigned to him by the patient in the transference-
play, the analyst—by telling the patient what the assigned role
is, how it relates to the original action, or by demonstrating that
the transference has its own actuality—is a participant in an
interaction nevertheless. This participation, which is to lead to
curative influences on the patient's inner life, constitutes the
basis for the transition between the actuality of the transference
neurosis as an "artificial illness" (Freud, 1914) and the actuality
of the patient's life outside the transference neurosis. The analyst's therapeutic art does not consist in mere detached specta-
torship and in reporting to the patient what the analyst perceives
and how he interprets it, but in the responsive quality of his
observations and communications, in the tact and timing of his
interventions. It consists in the analyst's capacity and skill of
conveying to the patient how he, the analyst, uses his own emotional experiences and resources for understanding the patient
and for advancing the patient's access to his, the patient's inner
resources. And there may be at times, in addition, that other
quality to the analyst's communications, difficult to describe,
which mediates another dimension to the patient's experiences,
raising them to a higher, more comprehensively human level of
integration and validity while also signaling the transitory nature of human experience. The chorus in Greek tragedy, some
soliloquies in Shakespearian plays, or, in a different way, certain
commentaries on the action of the play by Shakespearian fools,
for example, may give an idea of this function.

The transition between transference neurosis and the patient's life outside of it, or the reciprocal communication between
them, is similar to that between a dramatic play, a fantasy creation, and the life that people lead before seeing the play and after
they come home from an evening in the theater—if the play for
them is more than a pastime.

Several questions must be raised at this juncture: what is the
original action sequence that is imitated in the transference
neurosis; what is the nature of this imitation; how do we under-

stand the term transference neurosis; what of those aspects of the psychoanalytic situation and process that are not dramatic re-enactments of the past? Finally, we cannot avoid the difficult but crucial issue of the presumed antithesis of fantasy and reality.

The original action imitated by the transference neurosis would be the so-called infantile neurosis. In the traditional view, the nucleus of the infantile neurosis is the Oedipus complex and its conflicts. Some recent papers (for example, Tolpin, 1970; Blos, 1973) stress a distinction between the infantile neurosis as an actual childhood illness caused by oedipal conflicts and characterized by given symptoms, and infantile neurosis as a term for the pathogenic oedipal conflict situation itself or for its reconstruction from the transference neurosis. This distinction is of theoretical and practical importance. But relevant in our present context is the central position of the Oedipus complex in either case. While there is no doubt that the Oedipus complex occupies a central position in psychic development, there is today general agreement that pre-oedipal developmental issues are of far greater pathogenic import than the older view of neurosis assumed or allowed for. And I am thinking here not of psychotic or borderline conditions, or even of the so-called narcissistic character disorders, but of those conditions which are characterized either as symptom neuroses or as character neuroses. I would therefore include pathogenic and pathological pre-oedipal disturbances and deficiencies as relevant for infantile neurosis and transference neurosis (cf. Ritvo, 1974).

We have also come to recognize more explicitly that the transference neurosis is not simply an imitation or resumption of infantile oedipal conflicts or of their pathological resolution, but that it is strongly influenced in the majority of cases by the reworking and revisions of such problems during adolescence. I am thus taking the liberty of expanding the term transference neurosis to include also the imitation of adolescent action.

So far, I have discussed two of the questions I raised: what is the original action that is imitated in the transference neurosis, and how is the term transference neurosis to be understood here. Let me add that each later stage in development—later, that is, than the early pre-oedipal stages—may be understood as a resumption on a higher level of fundamental issues of psychic development. Psychic development takes place in interaction with environment. The transference neurosis itself also represents such a resumption.

This last consideration leads to the question: if we characterize the transference neurosis, in thinking of it as dramatization, as an imitation of action, what, then, is the nature of such imitation? No drama or play is an imitation of action in the sense of copying the original action, or even of involving only a degree of selection and highlighting of certain events in an action, as is the case in a documentary or newsreel. The imitation of action represented by a play is a re-enactment that understands and implicitly reinterprets an action from certain points of view and in certain directions that are strongly influenced by the present actuality of the author, including the *Zeitgeist* of his epoch, and, when it comes to performance of the play, by the present actuality of directors, actors, and audience. In the tragedies of *Oedipus Rex* and *Antigone,* for example, the original action itself—not unlike the original action of the transference neurosis—is shrouded in the fogs and ambiguities of history and myth. It is transmitted to Sophocles already laden with beliefs, biases, distortions, and interpretations on the part of the generations that stand between him and the original action. Whatever he conceived of as the original action he then reorganized and reinterpreted according to his lights and those of his time. Modern dramatizations of the same theme, modern imitations of the same action reorganize and reinterpret that same theme, which meanwhile has gained new layers of understanding and misunderstanding; these are apt to have become part of what is conceived of as the original action (comparison with screen memories suggests itself). Indeed, it may now be Sophocles' tragedy that is taken as the original action to be imitated.

For analysts, not long ago it was the Oedipus complex or the failures in resolving it that represented the original action imitated in the transference neurosis. When Freud called it the Oedipus complex, he gave that name to an infantile conflict situation on the basis of his own interpretation of the Oedipus story. He also determined for a generation of analysts and others what was to be conceived as the original action to be resolved and reworked in later life, and how it was to be understood. By now the Oedipus complex itself tends to be seen as a reworking,

as a re-enactment on a higher developmental level of early infantile stages of psychic development, which latter are assuming
the status of "the original action."

From the vantage point of the transference neurosis it seems
best, at least provisionally, to consider as the original action the
conglomerate of pre-oedipal, oedipal, and adolescent action sequences. These are being imitated in the transference actions.
The analyst's insights into the historical nature and layering of
the patient's symptoms, character traits, of his inner life story,
make it possible to view his various actions in the analytic situation as transference actions, as imitations of earlier actions.

At this point it seems indicated to drop the term "imitation"
(which we had adopted for purposes of exposition from Aristotle's definition of tragedy) and to substitute for it the terms re-
enactment and repetition. Repetition as a term has its own ambiguities, but it is more familiar to us in discussions on transference
and memory. When Freud distinguished between repetition and
recollection, he characterized repetition as reproduction in action, re-enactment (1914). In the course of the development of the
transference neurosis, transference actions are revealed (interpreted) as a form of memory. As they are revealed as repetitions
of earlier action, they gradually acquire the character of so-called
make-believe, or better, of fantasy play, when viewed from the
standpoint of present actuality. Present actuality and past actuality become clearly distinguishable or differentiated for the
patient—insofar as his transference actions and reactions are
concerned—only through the common analytic work, i.e., by
virtue of the interactions of patient and analyst in the analytic
situation. The patient's recognition of the fantasy aspect of the
analytic situation cannot be taken for granted in earlier stages of
the analysis. When it comes to the transference repetitions, it is
as though the differentiation of past and present—one of the
crucial advances in early psychic development—has to be undertaken all over again. We know that this differentiation tends to
recede in proportion to the increasing intensity of affect even in
recollective remembering.

I have pointed out that the "imitation of action in the form of
action," represented by a dramatic play, is not a copy of the
original action. Such imitation or, as we term it now, such repetition in the form of re-enactment, consciously and/or uncon-

sciously reorganizes and reinterprets original action from certain
points of view and in certain directions that are strongly influenced by present actuality. Applied to the transference neurosis,
this means that the patient's presenting illness or emotional disorder, his present life circumstances, expectations, and frustrations, and in particular also the various facets and rules of the
analytic situation and of the individual analyst—that all these
factors influence the re-enactment of past experience represented
by the transference neurosis. Furthermore, the re-experience by
re-enactment of the past—the unconscious organization of the
past implied in repetition—undergoes changes during the course
of treatment. In good part these changes depend on the impact of
current experiences with the analyst that do not fit the antici-
patory set the patient brings to his experiencing another, mainly
parental, person. In this manner the way of reliving the past is
apt to be influenced by novel present experience; certain past
experiences are seen in a different light and felt differently. Inasmuch as re-enactment is a form of remembering, memories may
change under the impact of present experience. Influenced by the
analyst's nonreactive response to the patient's assigning him the
role of a castrating father, for example, the patient may for the
first time re-enact more positive interactions with his father in
the transference and may bring up recollections of his father of a
positive nature. It is thus not only true that the present is influenced by the past, but also that the past—as a living force within
the patient—is influenced by the present.

Parenthetically, a word should be said here about the so-
called corrective emotional experience. The novel experiences
with the analyst in the psychoanalytic situation that I have mentioned have nothing to do with role playing on the part of the
analyst, much less with the analyst's taking a role opposite to the
one assigned to him by the patient—connotations that the expression carries with it ever since Franz Alexander used it years
ago. Without going into detail here, I wish to point out that it is
the very fact of the analyst's ability to show the patient the role
the latter has assigned to him and the genesis of this assignment
—it is this empathic objectivity of the analyst, perceived by the
patient, that carries the potentiality for change. It is neither
insight in the abstract, nor any special display of a benevolent or
warm attitude on the part of the analyst. What seems to be of

essential importance is insight or self-understanding as conveyed, as mediated by the analyst's empathic understanding,
objectively stated in articulate and open language. This activity
of the analyst has nothing whatever in common with role playing. If defenses do not interfere, it is experienced by patient and
analyst alike as authentic responsiveness. This responsiveness
is an essential element in what we call emotional insight because
it frees the patient for nondefensive responses of his own. Interpretations of this kind explicate for the patient what he then
discovers to have always known somehow, but in the absence of
its recognition and explication by the analyst such knowledge
could not be grasped and acknowledged.

The foregoing discussions underline the complexities of the
dramatic re-enactment and the changes and shifts occurring in
the course of the transference neurosis and its gradual resolution. But I have so far said little about the fantasy character of
the transference illness. This fantasy character is apparent to
the patient if and when he distinguishes between the past and
the present and between his own inner experience of the moment
and the over-all context of his life in which the analysis takes
place. These two distinctions are intimately related, but I shall
concentrate now on the latter. There are again parallels between
the analytic situation and the situation of the various participants (including the spectator) in the performance of a play. The
deeper the spectator gets absorbed in the action of the play, for
instance, the more does he lose his over-all perspective on himself
as a person who has gone to the theater for a certain purpose and
in a certain frame of mind or mood. The actors become even more
identified with the play's action and personages. So do the
author and the director during certain phases of their work.

In the course of an analysis as a truly meaningful experience
in the patient's life, the regressive pull of the analytic situation is
more or less counterbalanced or repeatedly corrected by the
patient's life outside that situation. True, his outside life is influenced and troubled by regressive tendencies which have led him
to seek treatment. But he functions there, to some extent at least,
within the context of his present life actuality. Insofar as he has
come to the analyst for help, having decided that he needs and
wants help of this sort, having inquired who might be suitable
and available, having made the various necessary arrangements

involved and more or less adhering to them throughout the analysis—doing all this, the patient manages to function within the context of present actuality in regard to the analytic situation, too. It is principally during the analytic hour itself that this other actuality, the actuality of his fantasy life, of memories of the past, is mobilized and tends to take over.

The fantasy character of the psychoanalytic situation, the transference-neurosis aspect of that situation, is apparent to the patient at those times when he is able to juxtapose it with his present actuality, and in particular with the analytic situation in the context of his present life actuality. The clearest example is the patient with a gift for histrionic dramatization who now and then, emerging from the unmitigated expressions of his infantile wishes and frustrations in the transference, regains his perspective as an adult. As that adult he knows that he has come to another adult for help, hoping or trusting that the analyst is more experienced, more knowledgeable, and more mature in regard to emotional life than he himself. As an adult the patient also knows that he is not altogether the child he makes himself out to be, or the child he lets take over in the regressive pull of the analytic situation. For other types of patients, as indicated earlier, the problem is not their easy yielding to the regressive pull, but their clinging to the rationality of present levels of ego organization. Nevertheless, if the analysis progresses, infantile fantasy levels will be significantly experienced so that the necessary juxtaposition between transference neurosis and present actuality can take place.

Fantasy here does not mean that something takes place that is not to be taken seriously or that is unreal. Patients, when they emerge from an analytic hour where their infantile life took over, often think so, as they tend to think in regard to dreams. While analysts are more sophisticated about dreams and fantasy life, they all too frequently fall into the error of regarding fantasy as being opposed to reality, as something to be eventually discarded or relegated to a psychic enclave. But fantasy is unreal only insofar as its communication with present actuality is inhibited or severed. To that extent, however, present actuality is unreal too. Perhaps a better word than "unreal" is "meaningless." In the analytic process the infantile fantasies and memories, by being linked up with the present actuality of the analytic situation and the analyst, regain meaning and may be reinserted within the stream of the total mental life. Thereby they may resume that growth process (an element of which we call sublimation) which was interrupted or interfered with at an earlier time, leading to neurosis. At the same time, as the present actuality of the analytic situation is being linked up with infantile fantasies, this present gains or regains meaning, i.e., that depth of experience which comes about by its live communication with the infantile roots of experience. The disruption of that communication is the most important aspect of the problem of defense, of repression, isolation, etc.

We know that the further back we go from adult psychic life into infantile life, the less are fantasy and reality antithetical. The two-year-old, for example, hardly distinguishes between dream and actual life occurrences. The distinction between confabulation and objective truth has little or no meaning for him. In later childhood the child appears to distinguish between his play world and other aspects of his world, or between his play activities and his other less fanciful and more sober activities. But these two different worlds and activities each have their own dignity as something real for him. The two realities coexist and communicate with and influence each other. For the adult there is far greater separation between these two worlds. If communication between them is disrupted we have each in its own corner: a conscious and/or unconscious fantasy life which proliferates on its own (a kind of malignant growth), and opposed to it what we call objective reality which tends to lose meaning as it seems to gain in objective rationality. This is a caricature of ego and id in irreconcilable opposition. In the healthier adult, communication and interplay between the world of fantasy and the world of objectivity, between imagination and rationality, remain alive. He is aware that play or drama and actual life share reality, that one gains meaning from the other, and that a great play may tap deeper sources of reality and meaning than the sober rationality of the workaday world alone can call forth.

Psychoanalysis in its scientific approach to psychological problems, i.e., in acknowledging and exploring the unconscious, and especially also as a psychotherapeutic art, has greatly contributed to revitalizing the communication and interplay between fantasy and rationality. In many of its conceptualizations psychoanalysis, nonetheless, is still affected by the disease of the age and especially of official science—the disruption between fantasy and rationality—which it is intended to cure or ameliorate. I have no question that Freud was conscious of attempting to do more than heal neuroses of individuals. In fact, this latter purpose of psychoanalysis seemed more and more to take second place in his interests. That he and his friends spoke of psychoanalysis, not only as a science and as a form of psychotherapy, but as the psychoanalytic *movement*, that they were concerned with anthropology, mythology, and civilization and its discontents—all this shows that they had larger aims and vistas, namely to influence and change the outlook and behavior of a whole era in regard to the relationship and balance between rational and instinctual life and between fantasy and objective reality.

But Freud does not appear to have recognized that the objective reality of science is itself a form of reality organized (although not created in a solipsistic sense) by the human mind and does not necessarily manifest the culmination of mental development or represent any absolute standard of truth, as he assumed. However, his assertion of the validity of psychic reality and of the existence of the unconscious was a major step in a different direction.

II

I return to the psychoanalytic situation. I spoke of the transference neurosis as a re-enactment, a repetition by action. But a clinical psychoanalysis does not consist only of re-enactments and their interpretations by the analyst. There is a considerable part of analysis which is taken up not with dramatization but with narrative, not with dramatic play but with history. Narrative, historical account, may be regarded as imitation of action too, as a reproduction of action—not in the form of action, but in the form of memory in its more familiar mode as recollection. It is repetition of action, but here action is reproduced in mental representations (*Vorstellung*) and their symbolic expression in speech, not in re-enacting the action. The action that is narrated may be a childhood experience or a current life experience (the latter, by the way, may be re-enacted in the analytic session too, instead of being recollected; as when a patient whose anger belongs to an event relating to her husband, vents this anger at the analyst, in the manner of a displacement). In recollection and its narration, the patient has a certain distance from the action, he has made the action an object of his contemplation, has objectified the action rather than being immersed in it. As I mentioned earlier, the dividing line between the two forms of remembering or repetition is not always sharply drawn: the patient who describes an experience with a great deal of affect is more identified with that experience, is less objective about it; the past invades the present. Such narration is closer to re-enactment.

The repetition of action in the form of narrative may be compared to a novel or to a historical account, the latter perhaps the more dispassionate the account is. It is often through the patient's detailed though fractionated accounts of episodes of his history, remote or recent, that we get our first knowledge of the development and character of his inner life. The unfolding of the transference neurosis as re-enactment proceeds, in a more traditional analysis, by way of the analyst's interpreting interferences with the flow of reporting and associating, and by interpreting certain directions or timings in the drift of associations in terms of transference action. The analyst gets indications of transference action from the patient's nonverbal behavior, from certain sequences, and from the timing and affective coloring of his narrative. The injunction to free-associate rather than give a coherent narrative promotes the tension toward re-enactment because everything that encourages the influence of unconscious currents, including those generated by the actual presence of the analyst, is promoting reactivation rather than mere representational recollection of past experience.

One might be tempted to say that the patient's productions oscillate between transference dramatization and narrative (leaving reflection to one side for the moment), and there is some truth to this. But we must keep in mind that language itself is an essential element in human action once the child has progressed to the verbal stage. That element of original action, too, is repeated in drama. Language—speech—because of its central role in human action, is a dominant element in drama, even though locomotion, pantomime, and dance are also important elements in any performance. Language is not merely a means of reporting action, it is itself action; narrative has a dramatic potential of its own. When not stultified by isolation from thought and fantasy, narrative tends to bring the original action to life again for the narrator and to conjure up the listener's similar or comparable memories, thoughts, fantasies. Narrative and speech then move and act upon the narrator and the listener by their function as a symbolic expression of action.

In the course of the psychoanalytic process, narrative is drawn into the context of transference dramatization, into the force field of re-enactment. Whether in the form of free association or of more consciously, logically controlled trains of thought, narrative in psychoanalysis is increasingly being revealed in its character as language action, as symbolic action, and in particular as language action within the transference force field. The emphasis, in regard to content and emotional tone of the communications through narrative, shifts more and more to their relevance as transference repetitions and transference actions in the psychoanalytic situation. One might express this by saying that we take the patient less and less as speaking merely *about* himself, about his experiences and memories, and more and more as symbolizing action in speech, as speaking from the depth of his memories, which regain life and poignancy by the impetus and urgency of reexperience in the present of the analytic situation.

All this does not ignore the fact that many of the patient's verbal communications in narrative form are important as historical data from which we can piece together his development and past experiences. They also serve as indications of what to expect about the development of the transference illness, and they give us information about the genetic and other aspects of the patient's symptoms, character traits, and specific reactions in the analytic situation. In the course of such narrative information, many new data, new memories, may come to light that modify and correct our understanding, give us important reorientations, and help us to reorganize our material.

But none of this concerns psychoanalysis as an art and the fantasy character of the analytic situation other than indirectly. The art of psychoanalysis, with regard to the analyst, consists essentially in the handling of the transference. The fantasy character of the psychoanalytic situation is its character as play, in the double sense of children's and adults' playing and of drama as a play. Play and fantasy have their roots in life experience, draw their sustenance from it, and give life its meaning. The dramatic play is a re-enactment of life in fantasy, and this fantasy life enters actual life giving it renewed and enriching meaning. The playing of the child, and of the child in the adult, also has its roots in life experience and gives meaning to life experience. The relative freedom from constraints in play and fantasy life is not only a relief from the exigencies of life, it also allows one to see beyond those exigencies and not to be overwhelmed by their constraints in actual living.

For the small child, fantasy, play, and actual life experience are still one and the same reality. It is only later that they become separated out as facets of a reality whose meaning is established in their interconnections. Thus the transference neurosis, on a regressive level of the patient's mental life, is experienced by him as though he does not distinguish between fantasy or memory and present actuality, whereas he is capable, when functioning on more advanced mental levels, of making this distinction and to profit from the revived connections between them.

The art of the psychoanalyst, then, consists in a threefold activity that is therapeutic: (1) He promotes that regression which conjoins the patient's experiential past (memories and fantasies) with his experiential present—the actuality of the analytic situation—so that they tend to become one. (2) The analyst, by appropriately timed and appropriately responsive interpretations and other interventions that speak to the reflective levels and capacities of the patient, reminds him of the difference between past and present, between memory–fantasy and actuality. (3) In doing so, the analyst helps the patient to reestablish connections, links between these different facets of reality, links that give renewed meaning to memories and fantasy life and to the patient's actual life in the present. Insofar as the patient's experiences in the analytic situation become part of his mental life, they influence his future life. All depends on the transference neurosis being recognized as the play of fantasy—a trial action in the sense in which Freud spoke of thought as trial action—which shares in organizing reality, far from being unreal and therefore to be discarded. The resolution of the transference neurosis surely does not consist of renewed repression or any

ultimate relinquishment of recovered memories and fantasies,
but of employing them, revived and made available for development and change in the transference play, in actual living.

The developmental tasks of late adolescence in many respects
are similar to those in an analysis. The so-called idealism of
youth often is supposed to be given up in favor of the so-called
realism of the adult. This realism of the disillusioned adult, in
many quarters seen as the healthy norm or at least as all that we
can aim for, is the result of the disruption, of the lack of live
communication between youthful dreams and fantasies and
what we call actual, rational life. Reality testing is far more than
an intellectual or cognitive function. It may be understood more
comprehensively as the experiential testing of fantasy—its potential and suitability for actualization—and the testing of
actuality—its potential for encompassing it in, and penetrating
it with, one's fantasy life. We deal with the task of a reciprocal
transposition.

I said that in the course of analysis narrative is drawn into
the web of transference dramatization. In the more reflective
phases, on the other hand, the patient's distance from himself
and from the analyst gains ascendancy. What was re-enactment,
by reflection changes to that more objective repetition which
Freud has called reproduction in the psychical field, as against
reproduction by action. Re-enactive memory then changes into
that form of memory in which past and present objects and past
and present self are clearly distinguished without losing each
other. There are those phases in analysis when narrative and
reflection are drawn into and yield to the force field of transference re-enactment. And there are those other phases, not infrequently in the same hour, when re-enactment is drawn into and
yields to the force field of objectifying narrative and reflection.
To hold to an optimal balance and to keep channels of communication open between these two is part of the analyst's art.

The celebrated good analytic hour—in my own experience as
an analyst, rather an exception, but all the same a standard by
which we measure our endeavors—shows something of the
analyst's art. It shows even more that a piece of good analytic
work is an artistic creation fashioned by patient and analyst in
collaboration. For the most part such an hour does not come
about by deliberate, premeditated steps or decisions on the ana-

lyst's part; it tends to proceed by virtue of the momentum of the process in which analyst and patient are engaged at a propitious time, although the soil from which such an hour grows is likely to have been prepared and cultivated by the analyst for a long time. The progression in such an hour is quite similar to the progression of a work of art, a poem, a musical composition, a painting, at a propitious moment or period during the artist's work. There, too, it is the momentum of an active imaginative process that creates the next step, propelled by the directional tension of the previous steps. This directional tension is the resultant of the artist's imagination and the inherent force of his medium. A word, a sound, a color, a shape—in the case of dramatic art an action—or a sequence of these, once determined, strongly suggests the next step to be taken. In the mutual interaction of the good analytic hour, patient and analyst—each in his own way and on his own mental level—become both artist and medium for each other. For the analyst as artist his medium is the patient in his psychic life; for the patient as artist the analyst becomes his medium. But as living human media they have their own creative capabilities, so that they are both creators themselves. In this complex interaction, patient and analyst—at least during some short but crucial periods—may together create that imaginary life which can have a lasting influence on the patient's subsequent actual life history.

In the movement toward reflection, the transference neurosis becomes apparent in its aspect as fantasy creation, which has its own validity and function in the patient's life. While intensely experienced, the transference feelings are prevented from being acted upon, from materializing in deeds, so that the transference neurosis seems to remain in the realm of trial action. But insofar as the development, flowering, and resolution of the transference neurosis requires the active presence of, and responsive thought interaction with the analyst, and is the result of the collaboration of patient and analyst, this fantasy creation is more than an intrapsychic process, it has a form of reality different from pure thought or dreaming or daydreaming or remembering. The transference neurosis is not only, as Freud called it, a transition between illness and life, it is a transitional state between mere inner fantasy and actuality. I am here in the neighborhood of Winnicott's "third area, that of play which expands into creative living and into the whole cultural life of man" (1967). Winnicott also speaks of patient and therapist playing together. As in the child's play, such fantasy action is called forth and shaped by present actuality (including the mental life of the analyst), and shapes present and future actuality. As a fantasy creation in which both patient and analyst in their different ways participate, the transference neurosis, as it is again and again contemplated and resolved in such reflection, has the potential for materially influencing the patient's conduct of his actual life.

I shall not discuss here the impact each transference neurosis, as lived through by the analyst with his patients, has on the analyst. This would require another full-length paper. I also must forego consideration of two issues that are closely related to my subject: the Aristotelian notion of catharsis or purgation through the arousal of pity and fear, and the function of the chorus in Greek tragedy, which in some respects resembles certain functions of the analyst. To the latter I have alluded earlier.

I shall close by trying to give another dimension to the dialectic of fantasy and actuality in pointing briefly to the child's and the parents' experience of the oedipal situation. The child experiences the oedipal strivings as powerful reality. In oversimplification, the little boy seriously wishes to marry his mother, the little girl her father. For the child prior to the passing of the Oedipus complex, these wishes are not just fleeting, unrealizable fantasies, but have the status of serious intentions and prospects. Understanding parents take these wishes seriously too, but for them they are serious fantasies not to be acted upon. They also may know, although often only intuitively, that these fantasy wishes are necessary ingredients of the child's psychosexual development, expressions of the child's beginning love life. In other words, the adult may understand that they are fantasies that are not in opposition to reality. While not to be realized in present actuality or with the actual parents at some future time, the oedipal strivings contribute to the formation of the full reality of life, as seen from the parental vantage point, from the viewpoint of the child's future. They are not fantasies to be given up or that, if not given up, must by necessity proliferate, unchanged, in the repressed unconscious, but fantasies that are indispensable factors in the full development of object relations and object love. The same, *mutatis mutandis,* is true for the fantasy character of the transference neurosis, as experienced by the child in the patient and as experienced by the analyst and by the patient as a reflecting adult.

REFERENCES

Blos, P. (1973): The epigenesis of the adult neurosis. *The Psychoanalytic Study of the Child* 27:106–35.

Ferguson, F. (1949): *The Idea of a Theater.* New York: Doubleday Anchor Books, 1953.

Freud, S. (1914): Remembering, repeating, and working-through. S.E. 12:145–56.

Ritvo, S. (1974): Current status of the concept of infantile neurosis. *The Psychoanalytic Study of the Child* 29:159–81.

Tolpin, M. (1970): The infantile neurosis. *The Psychoanalytic Study of the Child* 25:273–305.

Winnicott, D. W. (1967): The location of cultural experience. *Int. J. Psycho-Anal.* 48:368–72.

22
REFLECTIONS ON THE
PSYCHOANALYTIC PROCESS AND
ITS THERAPEUTIC POTENTIAL

As a special form of psychotherapy, psychoanalysis constitutes a unique mode of personal relationship. It shares certain aspects with other kinds of personal relationships, for instance with those between child and parent, patient and physician, student and teacher, between friends, and between lovers. But the relationship between analysand and analyst is quite different from all of them. There appears to be something inherently unnatural and contradictory about it. In a certain way, it is engaged in for the purpose of a deeper understanding of human relationships and of their impact on the organization of the individual's inner life in time—although this purpose often is but vaguely, if at all, grasped by the analysand when he enters treatment. While there is this engagement, there is at the same time, and from the beginning, a countermovement of disengagement. I am not speaking here of resistance, at least not in the usual sense, but of the fact that the dissolution and abnegation of whatever factual reality the relationship tends to assume is part and parcel of the analytic method from the start. The reason is that individuation and what we consider mature object relations, while originating and culminating in intimacy, involve and are dependent on separation, alienation, and renunciations along the way from infancy to adulthood. Without these there cannot be effective internalization, that is, the building of a stable self that may maintain viable object relations.

The analytic relationship, then, comes into being as a sort of self-played dramatic play in and by which the history of the

Contribution to Panel: Conceptualizing the Nature of the Therapeutic Action of Psychoanalysis, held at the Fall Meeting of the American Psychoanalytic Association, New York, December 16, 1977.

individual is re-experienced, restructured, acquires new meanings, and regains old meanings that were lost. But this relationship is never allowed to materialize as an actual relationship. It has the substantiality and the evanescence of a play, as well as that quality of a child's play: it seems to exist for its own sake and at the same time to be a rehearsal for real life.

The psychoanalytic method of treatment requires simultaneously unusual restraints and endurance of frustration together with an uncommon quality and degree of spontaneity and freedom—and all this, although in different ways, from both partners.

Except in child analysis, both participants are adults, with the age difference often insignificant or nonexistent, yet the relationship is asymmetrical, much of the time experienced by the analysand as unjustly unequal. If the analysis progresses well, this asymmetry and sense of inequality gradually recede, not unlike what happens between parents and children as the children grow into adolescence and beyond, if things go well there.

The relationship between analysand and analyst is comparable to adolescent and oedipal relationships and their derivatives, but also to the infant–mother "dual unit." Much of the analytic work centers around oedipal conflicts, but more and more, in many cases, also around developmental defects and distortions related to those early phases of the individuation process described by child analysts. In this connection, the self–object differentiation, until recently an essential condition of what we have believed to be scientific objectivity and analytic objectivity, can no longer be taken for granted as the single or basic mode of cognition and mental interactions. Is it the relevant mode and basis for all mental transactions between analysand and analyst, or is there a deep unconscious level on which this dichotomy is not valid? If so, for the sake of a more encompassing objectivity vis-à-vis the psychoanalytic process and its therapeutic potential this needs to be further elucidated. We are far from understanding much about it.

There are other problems I want to mention, some of them related to the above. What are the preconditions for analysis? Is its scope becoming too wide or is it, as traditionally understood, too narrow? Is the psychoanalytic process one of objective investigation of psychological facts, or is it interpretation of meanings? If the latter, are the meanings there, to be uncovered by us as analysts, or are we, although not arbitrarily, providing meanings? Are the patients providing the meanings, or the psychological facts, as a function of our active receptivity as analysts? Are "meanings" something that arises in the interactions between analysand and analyst?

It is questioned, in view of rapid, sometimes radical, changes in and dissolutions of cultural norms and child-rearing methods, whether we still can speak of an average expectable environment and in conjunction with it of an "average expectable physical and mental equipment" of the child (Anna Freud, 1976, p. 259).

These and many other questions, doubts, novel conceptual approaches, often are disconcerting and troublesome; they are at times formulated too naively or too stridently, or not giving due weight to important aspects and factors involved in very complex problems. But I believe that they are raised where psychoanalysis is most alive, endangered and troubled—yes, but not in danger of ossification. At the International Congress in London in 1975 much was heard of the malaise of psychoanalysts (André Green, 1975; Anna Freud, 1976), as though it were a new phenomenon. But is malaise, *Unbehagen,* discontent, not a condition of life for psychoanalysis, one of the reasons for as well as a result of the rise of psychoanalysis? Does this go for a therapeutic analysis too? If a result of psychoanalysis is malaise, suffering, is it therapeutic? Does its therapeutic potential reside, as Freud suggested, in a subtle but crucial shift in the quality of suffering? Is malaise, as Anna Freud seemed to imply in her discussion at that Congress, incompatible with excitement and satisfaction?

Many important questions are—as is true in our clinical work—not raised in order to be answered with a yes or no or a clearcut reply, but in order to address oneself to and reflect on issues that are brought to the fore by the question or arise within its context.

Let me turn briefly to some pragmatical considerations. A therapeutic analysis, as a treatment process extending over a long period of time, is a blend consisting, even in the hands of the analytical purist, of more than verbal interpretations of free associations, fantasies, dreams, and other verbal and non-verbal material, in terms of transference and resistance. Aside from their content, the timing of interpretations, the context in which they are made, the way they are phrased, the tone of voice, are important elements of therapeutic action. Clarifications and confrontations are used, historical discrepancies are pointed out, comments and interpretations are made that are not or only indirectly related to the analytic transference itself. Tact, basic rapport and its fluctuations, the analyst's breadth of life experience and imagination, the manner in which intercurrent events in the patient's life (and before, during and after the analytic hour) are handled—all these and other factors are far more than incidental ingredients of the therapeutic action. They constitute the actual medium without which the most correct interpretations are likely to remain unconvincing and ineffective. So-called educational measures, and at times encouragement and reassurance, are used. If used judiciously they often make possible and enhance the more strictly psychoanalytic interventions in all phases of an analysis. Psychoanalysis, a distinct and unique therapeutic method, in actual practice makes use, if sparingly, of therapeutic measures that are in themselves not analytic, while inspired and guided constantly by the model of the psychoanalytic method. A clinical analysis and the nature of its therapeutic action are more complex, more lifelike than any theory or model. Attempts at conceptualizing the therapeutic action always will stress certain aspects at the expense of others.

Its conceptualization at any given historical moment also is a function of particular predilections, biases, and innovations of that moment, of preoccupations with specific clinical problems, theoretical issues, and research interests. To this must be added the impact of fashions whose origins are not always apparent and which are often determined or strongly influenced by extra-analytic cultural currents. And we often encounter reactions and overreactions against preceding slants and fashions.

I return now to more strictly psychoanalytic considerations of the psychoanalytic process. The complexities and intricacies of the relationship between analysand and analyst have come under more careful scrutiny in recent years. It is no longer only a question of investigating the patient's transference and resistance, of considering the analyst's stance as objective-empathic observer and interpreter or of his possible countertransference and counterresistance as interfering factors. The origins of the psychoanalytic exploration of the nature of the patient–analyst relationship, as a relationship, can be traced back to the teens of the century when Freud, Ferenczi, Federn, Tausk, and others began to concern themselves with the problems of narcissistic identification, introjection, projection, the ego ideal, and ego boundaries. What we term object cathexis was recognized as developing out of less differentiated "emotional ties" called identifications. The differentiation of, and the establishment of boundaries between, self and objects came into focus as developmental processes. Thus, that distinction itself could no longer be taken for granted as the unquestioned single basis for psychoanalytic investigations. There are kinds of relatedness between what conventionally we call self and object, that call into question the universal validity of these very terms. We have come to see that there are levels of mental functioning and experience where these distinctions are not made, or made only fleetingly and in rudimentary form. These are deep unconscious layers showing modes of interpsychic relatedness, of emotional ties that are active under the surface in both analysand and analyst, and thus in their relatedness, forming ingredients of the therapeutic potential. The psychic reality or validity of these more deeply hidden unconscious levels is no more dubious than the psychic reality of unconscious oedipal currents and conflicts and their manifestations in the transference—that is, seen from a perspective that goes beyond conscious mentation (the original meaning of the word "metapsychological"). But their strangeness and uncanniness are more pronounced. These layers of experience, too, coexist with the more advanced levels of mental functioning and organization of mental content, and continue to exert their influence throughout life.

Schematically speaking, in the classical transference neuroses unmastered oedipal conflicts and their derivatives are revived and reworked in the psychoanalytic situation of controlled and limited regression, which enables the analyst to interpret those unconscious contents and their forms of mentation in terms of conscious content and form of organization. The analyst has to have a flexible and firm hold on his conscious, objective, frame of reference, a frame of reference the analysand tends to lose or to maintain too rigidly. The analyst, as empathizer, in order to be able to interpret has to experience with the analysand on the analysand's primitive level of functioning. Unless the analyst's own oedipal attachments and its inherent conflicts, while having been and repeatedly being "mastered" by him, remain for him alive and available, true empathy does not take place. His interpretations, although correct as to abstract content, are not likely to touch the patient so that he can make them his own. This is a side that Freud did not dwell on, although undoubtedly he was aware of it. Freud emphasized the patient's autonomous defenses against assimilating interpretations. The validity and pertinence of such autonomy, however, recedes as we penetrate to deeper unconscious levels, where there is communication and interdependence between the unconscious of the patient and that of the analyst.

What is true for the classical transference neuroses (with their main basis in the Oedipus complex) goes also for those disturbances that are included in the widening scope of analysis. Speaking again schematically, and omitting a great many complex clinical problems, these disturbances (narcissistic disorders, borderline cases, etc.) can best be understood as rooted in those deeper unconscious levels I spoke of, where the distinction between self and object is at a vanishing point, blurred, uncertain, unstable or even non-existent. As we became more aware of and better acquainted with these forms of mental functioning, we also have come to recognize that problems in the classical neuroses, which had been seen mainly in the light of psychosexual conflicts rooted in the oedipal phase, are often importantly codetermined by disruptive, distorting and inhibiting influences occurring during earlier phases. Such recognition and the ability to work with these problems analytically is dependent on the analyst's awareness and mastery of his own problems in this area. This is an extension of the principle that an analyst can understand and help his patient only as far as he understands himself and is ahead of the patient in the degree of mastery of his unconscious. Problems of self–object differentiation, with its inherent issues of the polarity between individuation and merging union, probably are not less but more universal and deep-seated than psychosexual conflicts of the oedipal nucleus of neurosis. They are what some have called the psychotic core of our mental life, an expression that should be understood in the same sense in which we speak of the Oedipus complex as the nucleus of neurosis. Such expressions refer to pathogenicity, not to pathology itself. All of us are heirs to this psychotic core. That is the important truth in Melanie Klein's work, as much as many of us disagree with her emphasis, her metapsychological elaborations and speculations and her technical procedures.

Many patients coming to analysis have, sustained by a sufficiently favorable early environment, mastered this psychotic core enough so that no or little explicit analytic work need be devoted to it. But with many patients in analysis nowadays a good deal of work has to be devoted to the analytic revival and working through of such problems. "Nowadays" means the present world in which patients and analysts alike have grown up and live. Many patients and many analysts are different from those half a century and more ago, and so is analysis. How could it be otherwise? It is not that human nature has changed since then. But shifts in inner and outer reality and their interaction have brought to the fore differently centered conflicts and disruptive influences, revealing to the psychoanalyst levels and phenomena of unconscious processes and their derivatives that earlier could hardly have come into clear focus.

In my analytic experience oedipal conflicts—to use that shorthand expression—are no less important today than they have always been. And their neglect, when it occurs, is an overreaction to exclusive preoccupation with them. But it is not surprising that the analytic situation so frequently today is compared with that developmental stage in which the phenomena and pathogenic issues of self-object differentiation, of the initial stages of individuation, of the formation of a cohesive self and of object relations, first come into view, namely the infant-mother dyad. The mental functioning and the derivatives of that developmental phase today are a focus of analytic exploration and interpretation. These archaic levels and their sublimated equivalents in the adult are revived and become available in the analytic situation—as is true of the oedipal level—through the medium or vehicle of transference and resistance, i.e., through the analysis of the patient's relatedness with the analyst. The patient-analyst relationship in its totality is highly complex, has many facets, levels, and stages. I shall come back to this briefly later on. On the archaic level now under discussion, the patient–analyst relatedness is not an object relationship in the usual sense. On that level of his mental life—and I oversimplify here for purposes of exposition—the patient is not, does not experience himself as, a self clearly distinguishable from the analyst as an object; by the same token, the analyst is not experienced as clearly distinguishable from the patient as self. Kohut speaks of narcissistic or self–object transference—transference insofar as there is not a lack of relatedness, not a "withdrawal of libido into the ego," but a lack of differentiation between two relatable entities that could be called self and object.

Unless the analyst grasps that he is, on the now pertinent level of the patient's mental functioning, drawn into this undifferentiated force field, he will not be able to interpret adequately the transference meanings of the patient's communications. To do so, he has to be in touch with that mental level in himself, a level on which for him, too, the distance and separateness between himself and the patient are reduced or suspended. Ego boundaries, the whole complex individuating organization of self–object differentiation tend to dissolve. The difference between the patient and the analyst is that the former is at the mercy of that primitive level (inundated by it or disavowing it), whereas the analyst is aware of but not given over to it. The undifferentiatedness of that level also involves a dedifferentiation of the secondary process difference between words and their referents ("things"), i.e., between words as sound entities and their "meanings" or what they symbolize. Such dedifferentiation entails special qualities of intimacy, intensity, and poignancy of communication, both verbal and nonverbal, or, in the absence of empathy, of total, though temporary, alienation (depersonalization and derealization).[1]

The analyst—as is true, though on a relatively more advanced level, in the case of the more familiar transference manifestations—for a stretch joins the patient on a potentially common level of experience. On that basis the analyst can translate that form of experience, by means of articulate and specifying lan-

1. For a discussion of primary process and secondary process mentation in their relations to language, see Loewald (1978; reprinted in this volume).

guage, on to a level that is further differentiated, which enables
the patient to join the analyst, for a stretch, on the path to higher
differentiation and articulation of experience.

Having spoken of the archaic pole of analysis, I now turn
briefly to its overall conditions and intentions, which make
feasible and justify the whole undertaking. I come back here to
the complexity and the apparent contradictions of the analytic
relationship. I wish now to stress the risks of misunderstanding
and distortion when the analytic situation is compared with the
early parent–child dyadic relationship, as illuminating as this
comparison is in many respects. When all is said and done, the
widening scope of analysis notwithstanding, the analytic situation, in contradistinction to other, often related psychotherapeutic settings, presupposes or is encompassed in an adult overall setting (at least as far as work with adults is concerned). I am
not competent to speak of the necessary modifications and qualifications in regard to child analysis.[2] The analysis of adults, no
matter how much given to regression or immature they are in
significant areas of their functioning, is a venture in which the
analysand not only is chronologically a grown-up, but that
makes sense only if his or her adult potential, as manifested in
certain significant areas of life, is in evidence. The predominantly
verbal channeling of expression and communication, the restraints on action, the high degree of tolerance for frustration,
the required capacity for reflection, as well as the unique spontaneity and freedom of responsiveness as elements of the analytic situation—even if some or all of them are available in anything
but their optimal form—, these characteristics make psychoanalysis an adult undertaking.

Thus there is a grid of rational adult mentation through
which the analytic experience, and specifically the transference
in all its primitive and more advanced variations, is sifted or
screened. Analysis as a relatively continuous process, sustained
over a protracted period of time, not constantly disrupted by
irrational *manifest* behavior, requires the patient's capacity for
this kind of rational mediation as a fairly reliable compass and

2. It is to be considered whether, in the case of child analysis, the "adult overall
setting" is provided by the understanding "cooperation" of the parents or parent. If such
cooperation is not available, child analysis apparently tends to become difficult or
impossible.

overall guide. The engagement and development of this capacity frequently needs the active or silent support of the analyst, but the analyst cannot create it. This does not mean that analytic methods, including transference interpretations, and analytic knowledge and insights cannot be used at given times in cases where analysis as a sustained clinical process is not feasible. And it is to be emphasized that analysts can and do learn a great deal about the unconscious and about transference from patients who for practical purposes are unsuitable for sustained therapeutic analysis—often learning things about unconscious processes and transference phenomena that they then can use in their strictly analytic work. This actually has been the case ever since Freud and the early pioneers began to concern themselves with problems of psychosis.

Anna Freud (1976) spoke of the difference between "understanding a mental aberration" and the "possibility to cure it," suggesting that there is no obvious reason to assume "that any mental affliction which is open to analytic understanding is open also to analytic cure" (p. 260). This issue has interested me for years. I think that any answer to the problem has to wait for further insights concerning the structure and function of psychoanalytic understanding. At present our insight is insufficient. But I suspect that there is no psychoanalytic understanding worthy of the name that leaves that which is to be understood altogether untouched and unchanged, if one is to judge from the act of understanding that takes place in a piece of analytic work during an hour. It is true that our understanding has to be communicated to the patient in an interpretation. But it seems to me that an interpretation is not so much the result of understanding as it is the means by which understanding proceeds. This has to do with the intimate interrelations between thought and language. Understanding as an act—as distinguished from a storehouse of knowledge that we make use of for understanding—is impossible unless the patient lends himself and is open to our understanding, although he may not know that and may fight against it; and it is to *his* powers of understanding that we speak when we interpret. In this sense, while understanding does not spell "cure," it is a therapeutic step. Perhaps it could simply be said that a therapeutic step occurs if and when the patient feels understood. But it is a curious fact that unless the patient feels understood we feel that we have not fully understood him. Understanding would seem to be an act that involves some sort of mutual engagement, a particular form of the meeting of minds. As applied to self-understanding, it would involve the mutual engagement of different mental levels.

Psychoanalytic interpretations are based on self-understanding, and self-understanding is reactivated in the act of interpretation to the patient. Self-understanding originates in the early interactions between child and caring parent. For the analyst, his self-understanding is resumed, vastly increased, enriched, and deepened in his own training analysis. On that basis—firmed up and articulated by the rest of his training—he is enabled to understand the patient if the latter is open to it. Interpretation is an activity in which the analyst mediates or conveys self-understanding or its possibility to the patient, something the patient then is enabled to make his own or internalize as an intrapsychic activity.

Psychoanalytic interpretations establish or make explicit bridges between two minds, and within the patient bridges between different areas and layers of the mind that lack or have lost connections with each other, that are not encompassed within an overall contextual organization of the personality. Interpretations establish or re-establish links between islands of unconscious mentation and between the unconscious and consciousness. They are translations that do not simply make the unconscious conscious or cause ego to be where id was; they link these different forms and contents of mental life, going back and forth between them. There are interpretations upward and interpretations downward. What is therapeutic, I believe, is the mutual linking itself by which each of the linked elements gains or regains meaning or becomes richer in meaning—meaning being our word for the resultant of that reciprocal activity. In the re-initiation and promotion of this process the intrepretative activity of the analyst and the specific contents of interpretations are the enabling factors; he envisages and holds for the patient that context which makes linking possible.

One last comment, having to do with pleasure. Interpretations may gratify the patient. All of us know how patients may exploit or try to exploit the giving of interpretations for the sake of direct instinctual gratification. We also know that there are interpretations that are, at least at first, anything but gratifying to the patient. But on a different level the interpretations that the patient assimilates and makes his own are and should be gratifying the patient's desire for responsive understanding and articulation of his deepest needs and highest wishes. These are gratifications that reverberate, together with the frustrations inherent in analysis, throughout the whole spectrum of mental life. On that foundation, shaky as it still is likely to be at the termination of analysis, separation from and renunciation of the analyst become possible and an inner requirement in the end.

REFERENCES

Freud, Anna (1976): Changes in psychoanalytic practice and experience. *Int. J. Psycho-Anal.* 57:257–80.
Green, André (1975): The analyst, symbolization, and absence in the analytic setting (On changes in analytic practice and analytic experience). *Int. J. Psycho-Anal.* 56:1–22.
Loewald, H. W. (1978): Primary process, secondary process, and language. In: *Psychiatry and the Humanities.* Joseph H. Smith, ed. vol. 3, New Haven and London: Yale University Press, 1978.

23

THE WANING OF THE OEDIPUS COMPLEX

Many of the views expressed in this paper have been stated previously by others in some form. To account for my omission (barring a very few exceptions) of specific references I can do no better than quote from Breuer's introduction to his theoretical chapter in the "Studies on Hysteria" (Freud, 1893–95; pp. 185–86):

When a science is making rapid advances, thoughts which were first expressed by single individuals quickly become common property. Thus no one who attempts to put forward today his views on hysteria and its psychical basis can avoid repeating a great quantity of other people's thoughts, which are in the act of passing from personal into general possession. It is scarcely possible always to be certain who first gave them utterance, and there is always a danger of regarding as a product of one's own what has already been said by someone else. I hope, therefore, that I may be excused if few quotations are found in this discussion and if no strict distinction is made between what is my own and what originates elsewhere. Originality is claimed for very little of what will be found in the following pages.

The Oedipus complex—psychic representation of a central, instinctually motivated, triangular conflictual constellation of child–parent relations—is said to be superseded or to lose manifest importance, temporarily, during latency. The disappearance or retreat of the complex was the subject of Freud's 1924 paper, "*Der Untergang des Oedipuskomplexes.*" In the *Collected Papers* the title is translated as "The Passing of the Oedipus Complex," in the Standard Edition as "The Dissolution of the Oedipus Complex." Freud, in the body of this paper and elsewhere (1923, 1925) uses even stronger, more active words: destruction (*Zerstörung*),

Address given in Plenary Session at the Annual Meeting of the American Psychoanalytic Association in Atlanta, Georgia, on May 6, 1978. The first paragraph has been added for publication of the paper.

demolition (Zertrümmerung). The German word Untergang literally means a going under or going down. It is used for the sun's
going down in the evening (Sonnenuntergang) as well as for the
"destruction" of the world (Weltuntergang) (cf. Schreber). Speng-
ler's famous book, The Decline of the West, which was published
just a few years earlier (1922), bears the German title Der Untergang des Abendlandes, Abendland being the land of the evening,
the occident, that region of the earth where the sun sets.

It is known that Ferenczi thought the word Untergang was
too strong and that he assumed that Freud was alarmed by
"Rank's tendency to replace the Oedipus complex by the birth
trauma as the essential etiological factor in the neuroses and
elsewhere" (Jones 1957, p. 108). We also learn from Jones that the
paper "contained at first a slight criticism of Rank's theory about
birth trauma (later omitted)," and that Freud (in a letter to
Ferenczi) "admitted that the word in the title might have been
emotionally influenced by his feelings about Rank's new ideas."
It seems clear that Freud was concerned about this challenge to
the genetic centrality of the Oedipus complex.

Freud states in his paper that the phallic phase, being that of
the Oedipus complex, does not directly proceed on to the definitive genital organization but submerges (versinkt) and is replaced by the latency period. In the conflict between "narcissistic"
interest in the penis and libidinal cathexis of parental objects the
first is victorious: the child's ego turns away from the Oedipus
complex (this account refers to the boy). He stresses the importance of castration and of the ego's defenses against castration
anxiety. He speaks of the relinquishment of oedipal object
cathexes and their substitution by identification with parental
authority which forms the nucleus of the superego; of desexualization and sublimation of the libidinal strivings of the complex,
and of aim inhibition and transformation of these strivings into
tender impulses. He emphasizes that this process of the ego's
turning away (Abwendung) from the complex is "more than a
repression," that it amounts, when ideally carried out, to a
destruction and abolition of it. He implies that the ideal norm,
never attained, would be such destruction as contrasted with
repression. Insofar as it is repressed, the complex persists unconsciously in the id and will later show its pathogenic effects.

The title of this chapter is meant to call to mind two different problem areas. First, no matter how resolutely the ego turns away from it and what the relative proportions of repression, sublimation, and "destruction" might be, in adolescence the Oedipus complex rears its head again, and so it does during later periods in life, in normal people as well as in neurotics. It repeatedly requires repression, internalization, transformation, sublimation, in short some forms of mastery, in the course of life— granted that the foundations for such repeated mastery are established during latency and that the forms and levels of mastery are likely to vary with changing levels of experience and maturity. Seen in this light, there is no definitive destruction of the Oedipus complex, even when it is more than repressed; but we can speak of its waning and the various forms in which this occurs.

Secondly, "waning of the Oedipus complex" suggests the contemporary decline of psychoanalytic interest in the oedipal phase and oedipal conflicts and the predominance of interest and research in pre-oedipal development, in the infant–mother dyad and issues of separation–individuation and of the self and narcissism (in the recently elaborated sense of these terms). What Ernest Jones tells us about Freud's paper and the exchange between Freud and Ferenczi in regard to it constitutes a significant precedent. Even in contemporary so-called object-relations theory there is great emphasis on early stages of self–object differentiation, on separation–individuation, on the primitive origins of object relations. Instead of referring to the "passing" of the Oedipus complex in the course of further development, to the paramount influence its resolution or lack of it has on later development, waning in this second sense then, points to the diminished interest in the complex itself and its resolution. To a significant extent psychoanalytic interest has shifted away from this nuclear conflict of the transference neuroses and on to the narcissistic neuroses (I am using Freud's nosological classification here), in which oedipal conflicts are held not to be central, and to narcissistic aspects of classical and character neuroses.

In what follows I shall consider certain facets of the content of the Oedipus complex and of its resolution, and then some aspects of the decrease of interest in the complex. I hope to show that increased understanding of pre-oedipal issues, far from devaluating oedipal ones, may in the end help to gain deeper insight into them.

PARRICIDE, GUILT, RESPONSIBILITY, ATONEMENT

The active words, destruction and demolition, which Freud has used in referring to the dissolution of the Oedipus complex, may be heard as reverberations of that dominant feature of the oedipal conflict, parricide, the destruction of the parent by the child.[1]

A parricide, that is, one who commits an act of parricide, is defined as follows: "One who murders a person to whom he stands in a specially sacred relation, as a father, mother, or other near relative, or (in a wider sense) a ruler. Sometimes, one guilty of treason" (Webster, International Dictionary, 2d ed.). The meaning of the word, as distinguished from patricide, thus is not limited to the murder of the father (Freud's essay, translated as "Dostoevski and Parricide," published in 1928 uses the word patricide, *Vatertötung,* in the title). Parricide, strictly, is the murder of a parent or near relative; it includes the murder of one who represents or symbolizes a parent, mother or father, and even the serious betrayal of an entity or group standing for parental authority. It is a parental authority that is murdered; by that, whatever is sacred about the bond between child and parent is violated. If we take etymology as a guide, it is the bringing forth, nourishing, providing for, and protecting of the child by the parents that constitute their parenthood, authority (authorship), and render sacred the child's ties with the parents.[2] Parricide is a crime against the sanctity of such a bond. The bond is most clearly exemplified for us by the relationship to biological parents. In a patriarchal society the murder of the father, patri-

1. I am aware that Freud's main thesis is that the "demolition" of the Oedipus complex is the result of the castration threat. The destruction wrought by parricide, however, is but the complement to the threat of destruction of the child by castration. Moreover, as will be seen later, the distinction between repression and "destruction" of the complex involves far more than the distinction between two different forms of defense against the castration threat. The problem here is the inadequate psychoanalytic theory of internalization and sublimation and of the maturing of object relations.

2. The word "parent" derives from the Latin verb *parere,* to bring forth, and is related to Latin *parare,* to prepare, procure, as well as to the English "parturition."

cide, is the prototype of the crime of parricide. For Freud the father was the foremost provider and protector, as well as the castrator if his authority and predominance were challenged.

A brief clinical illustration will help to set the stage for the discussion to follow. A student, working for a degree in the same field as his father's, had trouble in completing his thesis. He was brilliant; the thesis so far had progressed well. His father had died about a year earlier. The patient began to procrastinate; he felt strongly that he needed support and advice from his thesis advisor. But he knew quite well that he was perfectly capable of finishing the work on his thesis without help. He chided himself for his delaying techniques. In part, these took the form of paralyzing doubts about the originality of his work, regarding which at other times and for good reasons he had no doubts. He also wanted encouragement and support from me, but he kept telling me that it was wholly his responsibility, not the advisor's or mine. Becoming independent, taking responsibility for the conduct of his own life, was one of the themes that had come up repeatedly during the analysis. As he continued, over several hours, to insist that completing the thesis was his and no one else's responsibility, but that he could not bring himself to work on it, it dawned on me that he might be speaking of responsibility also in a sense not consciously intended by him. In addition to or underneath the meaning of responsibility as accountability to himself, as self-autonomy, perhaps he was talking about being responsible for a crime. It would be a crime he wished to delay, avoid, or undo. An interpretation along these lines led to further work on his relationship with his father, his murderous impulses and fantasies regarding him, his ambitions and fears of outdistancing him, and on his guilt about these ambitions (in part already fulfilled) and about his father's death. In this case, as in so many others, pre-oedipal currents and those belonging to the positive and negative Oedipus complex were inextricably blended.

The clinical example puts in bold relief the ambiguity of adult responsibility and autonomy as considered in the light of the Oedipus complex and its vicissitudes in the course of life. In the process of becoming and being an adult significant emotional ties with parents are severed. They are not simply renounced by force of circumstances, castration threats, etc.—although these play an important instrumental role—but they are also actively rejected, fought against, and destroyed to varying degrees. Perhaps this active rejection represents a "change of function," a form of taking over actively what had to be endured passively in the beginning. Be that as it may, in the course of what we consider as healthy development this active urge for emancipation comes to the fore (already in early phases of the separation–individuation process).

In the oedipal struggle between the generations, the descendant's assuming or asserting responsibility and authority that belonged to the ascendants arouses guilt in the descendant (although not only guilt). It looks as if opponents are required with whom the drama of gaining power, authority, autonomy, and the distribution of guilt can be played out. In analytic work, and particularly as revived in the transference, we see this in magnified form.

I focus here on that aspect of the mastering of the Oedipus complex that leads to the constitution of the superego and is more than repression or, as I would say, different from repression. In considering this from the particular angle I wish to emphasize, it is no exaggeration to say that the assumption of responsibility for one's own life and its conduct is in psychic reality tantamount to the murder of the parents, to the crime of parricide, and involves dealing with the guilt incurred thereby. Not only is parental authority destroyed by wresting authority from the parents and taking it over, but the parents, if the process were thoroughly carried out, are being destroyed as libidinal objects as well (all this, as I have already mentioned, *pro tempore*).

I spoke of dealing with the guilt for the crime of parricide. The organization of the superego, as internalization or narcissistic transformation of oedipal object relations, documents parricide and at the same time is its atonement and metamorphosis: atonement insofar as the superego makes up for and is a restitution of oedipal relationships; metamorphosis insofar as in this restitution oedipal object relations are transmuted into internal, intrapsychic structural relations. To the extent to which patients and others insist on cruel, inflexible standards and demands and persist in unconsciously dealing with love objects as incestuous objects, they fight against bearing and mastering the guilt of parricide by internalizing atonement. Need for punishment tends to become inexhaustible if atonement or reconciliation is not eventually brought about by mourning, which leads to a mature superego and to the possibility of non-incestuous object relations (the word "atone," literally and in many contexts, means to become or cause to become *at one,* to reconcile, to bring to concord or harmony).

In an important sense, by evolving our own autonomy, our own superego, and by engaging in non-incestuous object relations, we are killing our parents. We are usurping their power, their competence, their responsibility for us, and we are abnegating, rejecting them as libidinal objects. In short, we destroy them in regard to some of their qualities hitherto most vital to us. Parents resist as well as promote such destruction no less ambivalently than children carry it out. What will be left if things go well, is tenderness, mutual trust, and respect, the signs of equality. This depends, more than on anything else, on the predominant form of mastery of the Oedipus complex.

The Oedipus complex wanes as a crucial pathogenic focus to the exent to which its resolution—never achieved once and for all—is "more than a repression," something other than a retreat from and exclusion by what Freud called the coherent ego. Seen from the perspective of parricide, guilt, and responsibility, repression of the complex is an unconscious evasion of the emancipatory murder of the parents, and a way of preserving infantile libidinal-dependent ties with them. Parricide is carried out, instead of being sidestepped, in that dual activity in which aspects of oedipal relations are transformed into ego–superego relations (internalization), and other aspects are, *qua* relations with external objects, restructured in such a way that the incestuous character of object relations gives way to novel forms of object choice. These novel object choices are under the influence of those internalizations. Insofar as human beings strive for emancipation and individuation as well as for object love, parricide on the plane of psychic action is a developmental necessity.

We take for granted that this murder renders us guilty and calls for atonement. But when Freud equates the sense of guilt with need for punishment, he takes too superficial a view on the matter and appears to ignore his own deeper insight that more than repression is involved in superego development. Punishment is sought to evade or undo guilt. It is hoped that punishment will extinguish guilt, but it does not work for any length of time and more punishment is needed. Punishment, whether inflicted by others or by oneself, is too much in the service of repression of the sense of guilt (although it may serve other purposes). Guilt, in other words, may and often does lead to a need for punishment. Similarly, anxiety often leads to defense against it in various forms, but anxiety is not therefore to be equated with a need for assuaging or eliminating it. Nor is anxiety, in its primary function, a signal to induce flight or repression, but a sign of internal conflict and danger that may be dealt with in a number of ways. Guilt, whether conscious or not, is a sign of internal discord (more specific than anxiety), which may lead to a variety of internal and external actions, only one of which (a short circuit) is punishment (with its strong masochistic components). For action that is not compulsive to take place, the affect is to be borne for a time (it is here where the "holding environment" is of help). Thought and feeling (affect) are "delayed action," that is, activity that lingers, is "long," instead of being a short circuit (it should be kept in mind that seeing any action or process that does not short-circuit as a delay, takes reflex action and direct "energy discharge" as the standard).

Bearing the burden of guilt makes it possible to master guilt, not in the hasty form of repression and punishment, but by achieving a reconciliation of conflicting strivings. Completing his thesis was for my patient, to a significant degree, the outcome of reconciling parricide with love for his father, and of reconciling his quest for emancipation and self-responsibility with his desire for identification and becoming one with his father. I understand his eventual ability to complete the thesis in time (as well as other positive developments) as a confluence and integration of conflicting needs rather than mainly as evidence of defense against one or the other of these currents. By the same token, I disagree with the characterization and classification of sublimation as a form of successful defense (Fenichel, 1945, p. 141). It is hard to come by sure, unambiguous signs to show that such confluence occurred. In this case I relied on the patient's more even mood, a certain unpressured resolve, and his balanced awareness, manifest only at significant moments, of the different elements. Their convergence is an inference drawn by me, no less and no more than repression is an inference we draw from given signs.

By acting responsibly, by completing his thesis on his own, the patient is guilty of parricide. At the same time, he submits to his father whose strong interest in the patient's career choice had acted as a command. A submissive, "castrated" attitude toward the father is an element in the oedipal conflict; but so is that direct, pre-oedipal father identification, which, according to Freud, helps to prepare the oedipal constellation and is reinforced and modified in the direction of submission by the castration threat. While submission bespeaks a passive-homosexual position vis-à-vis the father, it also shows the retreat from and rejection of an active libidinal position vis-à-vis the mother, and often a simultaneous identification with mother's passive-receptive attitude toward father. If we add to this the less-well explored intricacies of the feminine oedipal conflict, the complexities of the Oedipus complex tend to become overwhelming. To master all of these currents permanently and without the aid of degrees and waves of repression appears to be beyond human capacity. In neurotic illness, however, repression and other defenses have become the mainstay of the attempt at mastery.

Responsibility to oneself, within the context of authoritative norms consciously and unconsciously accepted or assimilated from parental and societal sources, is the essence of superego as internal agency. I will stress here only certain relevant aspects of self-responsibility. It involves appropriating or owning up to one's needs and impulses as one's own, impulses and desires we appear to have been born with or that seem to have taken shape in interaction with parents during infancy. Such appropriation (notice that I use the same word as when I spoke of appropriating parental authority), in the course of which we begin to develop a sense of self-identity, means to experience ourselves as agents, notwithstanding the fact that we were born without our informed consent and did not pick our parents. To begin with we were more or less fortunate victims, and it may be claimed that in some sense this remains true as long as we live, victims of our instincts and of those of others, not to mention other forces of nature and social life.

When I speak of appropriating our desires and impulses,

active forces themselves, I do not mean repressing or overpowering them. I mean allowing or granting them actively that existence
that they have in any event, with or without our permission. Following the lead of the word responsibility, one may say that
appropriation consists in being responsive to their urgings,
acknowledging that they are ours. A harsh, unyielding superego
is unresponsive and in that sense irresponsible. Unless modified
it leads to self-destruction or to its having to be bribed and cor-
rupted. Self-inflicted or "arranged" punishment is one form of
such corruption; it merely assuages guilt for a while.

Responsibility to oneself, in the sense of being responsive to
one's urgings in the manner I described, involves facing and
bearing the guilt for those acts we consider as criminal. Prototypical, in oedipal context, are parricide and incest. From the
standpoint of psychic reality it matters little if these acts are,
from the viewpoint of objective reality, merely fantasies or symbolic acts. (Parricide and incest, themselves strongly interwoven,
stand for the basic aggressive and sexual instincts in their trans-
gressive, "evil" aspects.) If parricide and incest are not carried
out in factual reality, they nevertheless partake of psychic
reality. I spoke earlier of the implications of internal, intrapsychic atonement. Atonement for these crimes — which I defined
as reconciliation, being again at one — consists in a reconstitution
of child–parent relations on the internal scene of action (internalization). As mentioned before, this transposition or transmutation, at once destruction and restitution, in metapsychological
language is a transformation of object cathexis into narcissistic
cathexis.

We are faced with a double paradox. Self-responsibility,
involving parricide in psychic reality and in symbolic form (we
shall see later how it is more than symbolic), is, from the viewpoint of received morality, a crime. But it is not only a crime of
which humans inevitably become guilty in the process of emancipating individuation (cf. the expulsion from the Garden of Eden
and original sin); self-responsibility at the same time is the restitutive atonement for that crime. Without the guilty deed of
parricide there is no autonomous self. And further, also from the
viewpoint of received morality, individuality and its maturity—
I am not speaking of unbridled individualism—is a virtue, a
summum bonum, at any rate in modern Western civilizations.

To live among these paradoxes appears to be our fate for the time being.

If without the guilty deed of parricide there is no individual self worthy of that name, no advanced internal organization of psychic life, then guilt and atonement are crucial motivational elements of the self. Guilt then is not a troublesome affect that we might hope to eliminate in some fashion, but one of the driving forces in the organization of the self. The self, in its autonomy, is an atonement structure, a structure of reconciliation, and as such a supreme achievement. In the abstract, as the organization of this structure proceeds, the Oedipus complex would be destroyed as a constellation of object relations or their fantasy representations. But, in the words of Ariel in Shakespeare's Tempest, nothing fades, "but doth suffer a sea-change into something rich and strange."

In mature object relations, ideally the self engages in a return movement with objects that are differently organized and experienced by the self thanks to its own richer organization. It is this richer self-organization that can lead to novel ways of relating to objects while being enriched by their novelty. In some sense that novel way of relating with objects—most obvious in mature love relations—creatively destroys and reconstitutes, in a sea-change on the plane of object love, the old oedipal relations. It also constitutes an atonement.

Summarizing, I may list the various forms of the Oedipus complex's waning that I discussed: (1) repression; (2) "destruction" (transmutation) by internalization, involving parricide, guilt, and atonement. If I were to go deeper into these matters, issues such as mourning, remorse, repentance, would have to be considered. (3) "Destruction" on the plane of object love, by relinquishing incestuous ties and recreating the murdered and mourned oedipal ties through novel love relations. I am condensing here psychic events that repeat themselves on different levels of development throughout life. In that sense, there is no such thing as definitive destruction of the Oedipus complex.

I now return briefly to parricide from a somewhat different angle. Parricide is symbolically carried out and atoned for by the severance of oedipal object ties, or aspects of them, and the establishment of new love relations, as in adolescence. However, if we look at the adolescent dependence–emancipation struggles from the standpoint of how they are experienced by adolescents (as well as by patients in the transference neurosis) and by parents, something more than symbolic action is apparent. In magnified and extended form our present age experiences or witnesses in various parts of the world something approaching a life-and-death struggle between generations. The structure of society at large and of the family are in jeopardy, although certainly not for the first time. Perhaps the crisis is less ominous than we often tend to think. Nevertheless, what we almost daily hear and see in this larger arena is alarming. As I said, it may be viewed as portraying in magnified and more complex forms the generational conflict and love–hate struggle represented by the Oedipus complex in individual and family life. I hope I will not be misunderstood to be suggesting that the social problems alluded to are simply to be explained as or reduced to oedipal problems.

The generational struggles, most manifest in adolescence but often prolonged far beyond and later resumed in reversed form when children become parents, are palpable factual experiences that may and in the end do diminish one or the other side. Parents or children tend to be rendered relatively impotent, at least as far as the generational engagement itself is concerned. Parricide, if the child convincingly develops as an individual, is more than symbolic or on the plane of intrapsychic reorganization. If we do not shrink from blunt language, in our role as children of our parents, by genuine emancipation we do kill something vital in them—not all in one blow and not in all respects, but contributing to their dying. As parents of our children we undergo the same fate, unless we diminish them. If eventually some sort of balance, equality, or transcending conciliation is achieved, children and parents are fortunate. It is a balance or harmony that in the external no less than in the internal arena remains vulnerable. The good outcome of an analysis, in terms of the resolution of the transference neurosis, shows itself in the increasing but fragile establishment of such equality. It is not established once and for all, but requires continued internal activity, and it is not necessarily obvious at the point of actual termination.

INCEST

Incest may be seen as the other side of parricide, the side where love appears dominant. In parricide, however, underneath or mingled with destructive aggression, there also is a more or less violent, passionate appropriation of what is experienced as lovable and admirable in parents. Similarly, incest does not merely spell love or the urge of Eros to bind together and unite. Incest also contains the exclusion and destruction of the third in the triangle, and often a hateful vengeance perpetrated on the incestuous object that wanted, or allowed and responded to, the rival. Would the rival be a rival if he or she were not an incestuous love object in disguise? I include in incest here homosexual trends or acts between children and parents or siblings.

Incestuous object relations are evil, according to received morality, in that they interfere with or destroy that sacred family bond of which I spoke earlier, and not simply in the sense of rivalrous exclusion of or triumph over the third party. What is felt to be sacred about this bond? I assume that it is the original oneness, most obvious in the mother–infant dual unity, which shines through or is sensed as remaining the innermost core in later family relations. The identities and identifications that precede object cathexis and prepare the ground for the first object relations in the oedipal stage reveal an original intimate unity that is anterior to what is commonly called sexuality. Perhaps this accounts for the blindness to infantile sexuality, including, at least in Freud's time, blindness to "phallic," oedipal sexuality. The "sacred" innocence of primary narcissistic unity and its derivatives, anterior to individuation and its inherent guilt and atonement, while resulting from sexual union of the parents, precedes and is the undifferentiated source of the child's emerging sexuality. Our vision tends to be blurred by a nostalgic longing for such a state; there is an investment in preserving or prolonging that state of innocence in one's children, and in recapturing some of it for ourselves in our identifying and protecting relations with children. Implicit in the modern objective, scientific world view, on the other hand, is an investment in the opposite direction that tends to negate the validity, however compromised and complicated by subsequent development, of the primacy of that unitary source.

My thesis is that the pre-oedipal identificatory bonds within the family, as direct derivatives of narcissistic unity, are felt to be sacred, to belong to a state of innocence, and that incestuous fantasies and acts are felt to violate that sacred innocence. The reason is that object-libidinal fantasies or acts are entertained with a person with whom strong pre-objectal, identificatory bonds not only exist (this may be the case also in non-incestuous object relations), but that in incest the other *qua* libidinal object is emerging or has emerged directly and without substitutive change of person from an identificatory bond or unity. The very same person with whom there has been a pre-objectal bond prior to and continuing into the oedipal phase now becomes an object of sexual desire. Insofar as the oedipal *objectum* is consubstantial with the pre-oedipal *identificatum*, is the same body as that with whom the identificatory bond existed and still persists, the pre-oedipal bond is violated (I use the Latin expressions *objectum* and *identificatum* for greater clarity of meaning). The incest barrier, which seen in this light is a barrier between identification and object cathexis, is overturned.

Applied to the oedipal boy and his sexual desire for his mother: the maternal libidinal object is gradually and directly evolving from a stage where she was not an object (*objectum*) for the boy but where there was (and still is) a symbiotic bond uniting them. The pre-oedipal stage of primary lack of subject–object differentiation is evolving into the object stage (with the enabling person of the mother as vehicle), an object stage that can be characterized as incestuous. The incestuous object thus is an intermediate, ambiguous entity, neither a full-fledged libidinal *objectum* nor an unequivocal *identificatum*. The fact that the incestuous object, insofar as it is libidinal object, is the very same person that originally has been and continues to be also an *identificatum*, renders incest evil in our eyes. The identificatory intimacy of child and parent (or close relative) is both exploited and defied in incest.

Adult relations with a partner who in actuality is not an incestuous object are, as we know, influenced by oedipal currents. The less prominent the novel aspects of the relationship are, or the more they become overshadowed by old oedipal problems (for example, through the arrival of a baby), the more we consider the relationship to be neurotic. In actual incest the sexual act, which seems designed to overcome temporarily and consciously the established individuality of the partners, appears perverted in that the partners enact, live out oedipal relations. The Oedipus complex, then, is neither repressed nor "waning" by transforma-

tions that destroy its original form, but it is carried out, reproduced in action. Incest is in this sense a regressive, back-sliding
repetition of an intermediate stage in the process of individuation, and not a creative repetition achieving novel resolutions.

The oedipal stage itself is still so enmeshed in and pervaded
by identificatory processes—as manifested by the actual sameness of *identificatum* and *objectum*—that incestuous oedipal
fantasies dominating sexual life in adulthood represent non-
resolution of the Oedipus complex.

Identification processes develop, on a new plane of organization established in the oedipal phase, into secondary identifications of superego development. If in the interactions between
children and parents incestuous trends are fostered by parents
to predominate, that development is interfered with. The older,
primary identifications, inherent in the incestuous trends, are
then not allowed to become partially transformed into superego
identifications, as the oedipal relationship is not relinquished
but perpetuated. When one says that the relinquishment of
oedipal-incestuous ties and the emancipatory-restitutive identification with aspects of oedipal objects leads to superego formation, it is implied that to a significant degree primary identifications give way to secondary or superego identifications. Therefore,
lack of resolution of the Oedipus complex does not only mean
that antiquated object relations are not given up and replaced by
more mature object relations. It also means that primary identifications, those direct derivatives of primary narcissism, have
not been sufficiently transformed into and replaced by superego
identifications, because the latter come into being by way of
relinquishing oedipal object choices and by narcissistic transformation (internalization).

THE WANING INTEREST IN THE OEDIPUS COMPLEX

Perhaps I have succeeded in showing that the Oedipus complex is no less crucial and interesting today than it was. Its
interest and significance may be enhanced if one focuses on the
ambiguous and intermediate nature of incestuous object relations.

For years many of us have been concerned with the less
explored reaches of earliest, pre-oedipal development; with problems of the so-called symbiotic phase (Mahler) and the self-

object stage (Kohut) and their derivatives, as well as with their direct (I am tempted to say non-oedipal) continuations and permutations in the adult life of patients with psychotic, borderline, and narcissistic personality disorders. Problems of primal transference in analysis, complexities of transference–countertransference phenomena, and of direct communication between the unconscious of different persons are related to such issues. We find parallels and similarities in the mental life of primitive peoples. Some of these problems, in my opinion, raise the important but largely unexplored and for the present unanswerable question whether we are justified in simply equating, as we do, psychic life with the intrapsychic.

To be fully alive to the fact that the oedipal stage itself contains—more than was realized by Freud although he acknowledged the fact long ago—in its very core features of primary identification and symbiosis, may give new luster to the Oedipus complex in the present psychoanalytic climate.

In this concluding section I shall consider this problem area from a somewhat different angle. It is not unusual, I believe, for those who attempt to do analytic work with certain gifted and articulate patients showing psychotic or psychotic-like traits, to experience something like the following (the experience is not easy to describe): They often give one the feeling that they are struggling with basic, primary dilemmas of human life in forms and contents that seem less diluted and tempered, less qualified and overshadowed by the ordinary, familiar vicissitudes of life, than is generally true of neurotic patients. Oedipal and post-oedipal conflicts are not absent, but they seem to pale in comparison with issues that appear to lay the groundwork for and to go deeper than the conflicts of everyday interpersonal problems and their intrapyschic counterparts. To put it quite pointedly, life itself, and especially individual life and separateness, are not taken for granted. The objectivity of the object and the subjectivity of self don't seem to be common ground shared by such patients and ourselves, although they may use language that presupposes these distinctions. But bizarre features, over-concreteness and the like, may indicate that their language itself is affected by the problematic status of these distinctions.

It is as though, in comparison, the neurotic conflicts commonly encountered are, as viewed from this uncommon ground, blurred reflections, garbled echoes of a basic quest those patients desperately pursue in pure culture. They seem unable or unwilling to let go of it, to be less single-minded and turn to matters less intractable, or to come to terms with it step by step, by allowing the unfolding of more complex developments and temporary solutions, with detours, failures, accommodations, and renunciations along the way. Such people seem too serious or unyielding, from our point of view, about the ultimate antinomies and dilemmas of human life, and too cynical or judgmental about our faltering and faulty steps, attempts at conciliation, and compromises. They have an unwavering eye for the pitfalls of getting embroiled in what many of us experience as the troubling but rewarding richness of life.

For the present, in the light of our growing understanding of the separation–individuation process, of the development of subject–object differentiation from primary narcissism during the early, pre-oedipal stages, it is reasonable to assume that the fundamental issues by which such patients are transfixed have to do with problems of this genetic depth and antiquity. Unquestionably there is something archaic about their mentality; it is archaic in the sense of antiquated, but also in the sense of belonging to the origins of human life and thereby to its essence or core. Just as the Oedipus complex, the neurotic core, wanes but is never actually or definitively destroyed, and rises again at different periods in life and in different shapes, so, too, that more archaic, psychotic core tends to wane but remains with us. Indeed the Oedipus complex and its sequelae, viewed prospectively rather than retrospectively from adult life, are later versions of archaic yet enduring, indestructible life issues. In normality the psychotic core is harder to find than the Oedipus complex; in the classical neuroses it may not need specific analytic work.

Normality, however, is a standard far less clearcut and immutable than even our psychoanalytic forefathers, who saw its relativity, were wont to think. Norms of conduct, behavior, convention, thought, of what is rational, realistic, and "ego-syntonic" are interdependent with the stability of a civilization. This stability does not only include the general acceptance of ethical or religious precepts or of the valuation of scientific rationality, but also the comparative lack of change of living conditions within a given cultural area and of life on this planet. To mention only the last, is it possible to doubt that the revolutionary changes, manifested and promoted by the discovery of atomic fission and fusion and the invention of space travel, would be paralleled and reflected by profound changes in the norms of human thought and life? But we need not go outside our own field. Psychoanalysis itself is a sign of and at the same time promoting far-reaching changes in the sensibility of our age. As much as we value the dominance of secondary-process rational thought and action, the released influence of primary-process thinking on many spheres of life, for good and ill, is undeniable, unsettling our notions of normality and changing our concept, experience, and organization of reality itself. As a new psychology psychoanalysis does not only change our knowledge of the human mind, it changes the human mind by that new knowledge.

Psychoanalysis certainly has contributed, wittingly and unwittingly, to a change in sexual mores and in family life, to the loosening of the family structure and of the structure of society, as well as giving less exalted value and prominence to rationality and its norms. For this it should not be condemned any more than modern physics and biology can be condemned for the unsettling changes they bring about. But like physicists and biologists we must be aware of our responsibility to stem the tides of precipitous action and to guide novel potentials into channels that make for a viable mental and societal life.

With reference to the problem of individuation and the status and valuation of the individual, psychoanalysis appears to be in an awkward position. On the one hand, it seems to stand and fall with the proposition that the emergence of a relatively autonomous individual is the culmination of human development. How this may come about and what interferes with such an outcome, resulting in psychopathology, is a most important aspect of psychoanalytic research, reconstruction, and treatment. Also, psychoanalysis is individual treatment; it takes place between two individuals. The idea of the resolution of the transference neurosis, for example, makes little sense if individual autonomy is not envisioned.

On the other hand, owing in part to analytic research, there is a growing awareness of the force and validity of another striving, that for unity, symbiosis, fusion, merging, or identification—whatever name we wish to give to this sense of and longing for nonseparateness and undifferentiation. I pointed out that oedipal, incestuous object relations are characterized by hovering between the poles of identification and object cathexis, between merging and individuality. The more we understand about primitive mentality, which constitutes a deep layer of advanced mentality, the harder it becomes to escape the idea that its implicit sense of and quest for irrational nondifferentiation of subject and object contains a truth of its own, granted that this other truth fits badly with our rational world view and quest for objectivity. Even a schizophrenic's sense of a continuum or an uncanny, cherished or dreaded affinity and sameness of himself and another person, as if both merely pose as two distinct individuals, begins to make sense if viewed in the light of deep unconscious levels.

But psychoanalysis has always been in an awkward position, even when only the Oedipus complex was the center of its attention. While it has been its intent to penetrate unconscious mentality with the light of rational understanding, it also has been and is its intent to uncover the irrational unconscious sources and forces motivating and organizing conscious and rational mental processes. In the course of these explorations unconscious processes became accessible to rational understanding, and at the same time rational thought itself and our rational experience of the world as an "object world" became problematic. In the conceptualization and investigation of the Oedipus complex and of transference it became apparent that not only the neurotic's libidinal object is "unrealistic" in that its objectivity is contaminated and distorted by transferences. In normality as well, object relations as established in the oedipal period contribute to the constitution of the contemporary libidinal object. In other words, the contemporary libidinal object, even if freed of the gross transference distortions seen in neurosis (which helped us to see the ubiquitous phenomenon of transference), is "unrealistic" or contains "irrational" elements. If this is so, objectivity, rationality, and reality themselves are not what we thought them to be, not absolute states of mind and the world that would be independent of and unaffected by the generative process-structures of mind and world.

Research into psychic life antecedent to the oedipal phase

only has led us more deeply into the thicket of such problems. Awareness of forms of reality in which there is no definite distinction between a subject or self and objects, while not new, has been newly recovered by psychoanalysis (and certain branches of developmental psychology and of anthropology). Once seen, we can detect the relevance of nonobjective forms of reality organization for the understanding of narcissistic disorders and of normal mental life. If we exclude the whole realm of identification and empathy from normality, for example, we arrive at a normality that has little resemblance to actual life. Identification and empathy, where subject–object boundaries are temporarily suspended or inoperative, play a significant part in everyday interpersonal relations, not to mention the psychoanalyst's and psychotherapist's daily working life.

In the psychosexual and social life of the present day "archaic" currents are more in evidence, less repressed, I believe. They consequently make for different troubles, often closer to "perversion" than to "neurosis." Our own views on what is to be considered as perversion are changing, for example, in regard to homosexuality. Modern life, partly moved by and partly moving psychoanalysis, is redrawing the outlines of normality, of what is archaic in mental life and what is advanced, mature mentality.

The Oedipus complex is a constituent of normal psychic life of the adult, and as such is active again and again. A psychotic core, related to the earliest vicissitudes of the ambivalent search for primary narcissistic unity and individuation, also is an active constituent of normal psychic life. Its activity has become more apparent through a variety of investigations into archaic mental life and, partly in their wake, more prominent in the pathology of patients and in modern life in general. These deeper unconscious currents, having been uncovered and re-entering modern sensibility, influence the organization of mind, experience, and action.

Our hitherto normal form of organizing reality, aiming at a strict distinction and separation between an internal, subjective, and an external, objective world, is in question. Our psychotic core, as it comes increasingly into view, prevents us from being as much at home and at ease with this solution as our scientific forefathers were. I believe that our quest for individuation and individuality, and for an objective world view, is being modulated by insights we are gaining from the "psychic reality" of pre-oedipal life stages. We even need to reexamine Freud's distinction between psychic reality and factual, objective reality, not that this distinction might be invalid. But its validity appears to be more circumscribed and limited than we assumed, analogous to Newtonian physics: the new theories and discoveries of modern physics do not invalidate Newtonian physics, but they limit their applicability.

Interest in the Oedipus complex has been on the wane because of these developments. But it is also true that perspectives on the Oedipus complex are changing, that the different modes of its waning and waxing during life stages give it renewed significance and weight, and that the intermediate nature of incestuous relations, intermediate between identification and object cathexis, throws additional light on its centrality. I pointed out that the superego as the heir of the Oedipus complex is the structure resulting from parricide, representing both guilt and atonement for the usurpation of authority. We are reminded that the oedipal attachments, struggles, and conflicts must also be understood as new versions of the basic union–individuation dilemma. The superego, as the culmination of individual psychic structure formation, represents something ultimate in the basic separation–individuation process.

I am aware that, perhaps confusingly, I have shifted perspectives several times in my presentation. I hope that the composite picture I have tried to sketch in this fashion has not become too blurred by my approach.

REFERENCES

Fenichel, O. (1945): *The Psychoanalytic Theory of Neurosis.* New York: W. W. Norton.
Freud, S. (1893–95): Studies on hysteria. S.E. 2:3–305. .
_____. (1921): Group psychology and the analysis of the ego. S.E. 18:67–143.
_____. (1923): The ego and the id. S.E. 19:3–66.
_____. (1924): The dissolution of the oedipus complex. S.E. 19: 172–79.
_____. (1925): Some psychical consequences of the anatomical distinction between the sexes. S.E. 19:243–58.
_____. (1928): Dostoevski and parricide. S.E. 21:175–94.
Jones, E. (1957): *The Life and Work of Sigmund Freud.* vol. 3. New York: Basic Books.

24

BOOK REVIEW ESSAY ON *THE FREUD/JUNG LETTERS*

By necessity, my discussion of the correspondence between Freud and Jung is one-sided: I am incomparably more familiar with Freud's work and personality than with Jung's. In particular, I have not read Jung's later writings, with the exception of *Memories, Dreams, Reflections*,[1] put off, in part, by what Freud has called Jung's hiding behind a "religious-libidinal cloud" (298F, p. 485).[2]

Toward the end of his life Jung wrote about Freud as follows: "Freud was the first man of real importance I had encountered; in my experience up to that time, no one else could compare with him. There was nothing the least trivial in his attitude. I found him extremely intelligent, shrewd, and altogether remarkable. And yet my first impressions of him remained tangled; I could not make him out" (*Memories*, p. 149). "He remained the victim of the one aspect he could recognize ["mere sexuality" or "psychosexuality"], and for that reason I see him as a tragic figure; for he was a great man, and what is more, a man in the grip of his daimon" (p. 153).

The correspondence started in 1906 with a letter by Freud in which he thanked Jung for sending him the first volume of *Diagnostische Assoziationsstudien*, a work that acknowledges the importance of Freud's writings and Freud's influence on Jung.

William McGuire, editor, *The Freud/Jung Letters: The Correspondence between Sigmund Freud and C. G. Jung.* Translated by Ralph Mannheim and R. F. C. Hull. Princeton, N.J.: Princeton University Press, 1974, 650 pp. (German edition: *Sigmund Freud C. G. Jung. Briefwechsel*, edited by William McGuire and Wolfgang Sauerländer. Frankfurt am Main: S. Fischer Verlag, 1974. 722 pp.).

1. C. G. Jung, *Memories, Dreams, Reflections.* Recorded and edited by Aniela Jaffé. Translated from the German by Richard and Clara Winston. New York: Pantheon Books, 1963. Cited hereafter as *Memories*.

2. In both the American and German editions, the letters are numbered consecutively; F behind the number indicates that the letter was written by Freud, J that it was written by Jung. Except in special instances, I cite only the page of the American edition.

Freud was almost fifty and Jung close to thirty-one. They met for the first time less than a year later when Jung, invited by Freud, came to visit him in Vienna, accompanied by his wife Emma and a young colleague, Ludwig Binswanger. Their last meeting took place at the Psychoanalytic Convention in Munich in September, 1913. The correspondence ended with Jung's resignation from his post as President of The International Psychoanalytic Association in 1914, except for a brief letter of 1923 in which Jung referred a patient to Freud. The actual break in their relationship, proposed by Freud and accepted by Jung, came in an exchange of letters in January, 1913 (*Correspondence*, pp. 539, 540); Freud was fifty-six, Jung thirty-seven.

Both had been conscious of the intensity and, in some respects, intimacy of their friendship, of the emotional and intellectual demands they made on each other—demands that in the long run neither of them could tolerate, so that passionate mutual rejection became inevitable. There was nothing lukewarm about them. For Freud the rupture followed his break with Adler and Stekel; for Jung it came in the wake of his disillusionment with and estrangement from Bleuler. But Adler and Stekel never were as personally close and important to Freud as Jung was, and Bleuler apparently was a man too reserved and remote to engage in the kind of friendship with Jung that existed for some years between Jung and Freud.

The years between 1906 and 1913 were of singular importance for the organization and growth of psychoanalysis as a worldwide intellectual movement, as a new psychological science, and as a revolutionary approach to neurotic and psychotic illness. To a considerable extent, Jung's enthusiastic efforts and verve and his close contacts with academic psychiatry were responsible during those years for psychoanalysis becoming known in academic circles as a force to reckon with and for its being organized in the forms of local societies, in The International Association and through the publication of periodicals. This could hardly have been accomplished at that time by the diffident Freud and his Viennese followers alone. Considering the prejudices and parochialism then prevailing in the academic life of Austria and Germany, Bleuler's prestige as professor of psychiatry at the Zurich Medical School and as director of the famous Burghölzli was most valuable to the young psychoanalytic movement. In the academic atmosphere of those times in Austria and Germany, Freud was well aware of the meaning of the fact that neither Bleuler nor Jung was Jewish.

Furthermore, in those years both Freud and Jung widened their horizons, grew intellectually, developed their ideas at an accelerated pace, in part by virtue of the influence they exerted on each other and the resulting elaboration and crystallization of their respective positions. If one considers the revolutionary changes occurring during that period in other sciences, especially physics, and in the arts, these were altogether remarkable years, ushering in the world of today. All this ferment—all the changes in values, ideas, perspectives, and sensibilities—was followed by the outbreak of the first World War in 1914.

After 1913 Freud and Jung went their separate ways without, as far as is known, ever meeting again, although both reached ripe old age. (Freud died in 1939, Jung in 1961.) Their intellectual and personal differences had become irreconcilable. Each followed his own path with single-minded devotion and persistence, apparently paying no further attention to the other.

It takes no psychoanalytic acumen to recognize that the relationship, seen in its most personal dimension, foundered on the rock of the "father complex." Both men, from the beginning to the end of their friendship, were intensely aware of that tie, which brought them emotionally so close and which they were at last compelled to tear to shreds, although they tried to find resolutions or accommodations before the final break. The initial youthful straightforwardness and vigor, the enthusiastic—although not unqualified—support, the respect, admiration, and tenderness, coming from a younger man whom he loved for the qualities of his mind and character, were immensely attractive to Freud. In Freud's letters it comes through again and again that he almost desperately tried to see in Jung the spiritual son and heir who would put his life's work on a firm footing and carry it forward— a son who seemed freer, more radiant, less somber and diffident than himself and who would be faithful to him and to the common work. Such hopes seldom come true: the demands implicit in such expectations and idealizations too often carry their own death sentence within them.

Jung never was and never saw himself as that kind of son. He was, when he met Freud, already his own man and had, it seems to me, a rather inflamed sense of his own destiny, as much as he loved and admired Freud. It also appears that he was a far more troubled spirit than Freud thought in the beginning and than Freud himself was. If Jung was in search of a father, he was looking for an older man to admire, from whom he could seek wise counsel but who would let him go his own way.

Jung had a religious-mystical bent that he cultivated. In contrast, if Freud had such inclinations he fought against them, in himself and others, with all the vehemence of an heir of the Enlightenment, of a man who had to subdue such tendencies in himself for the sake of his work as he saw it, for the sake of lucid rationality. Jung might have been right in believing that Freud was driven by forces that in a deep and nontechnical sense could be called religious. We must think here also of the still unfathomed subterranean links and affinities between religion and sexuality, which both men explored in their different ways. But Freud, in my view, was right in profoundly distrusting the undisciplined mystical-visionary inclinations that led Jung into nebulous regions of alchemy, astrology, and the occult, regions from which it is hard to return with a clear mind. To Freud, this smacked too much of obscurantism and of an evasion and hypocritical embellishment of the "exigencies of life," man's troubled existence—an attitude that Freud abhorred. The emerging marked differences between the psychoanalytic and the Jungian approach to therapy—Freud's concentration on the unconscious of the individual, Jung's focus on the collective unconscious, archetypes, and the imaginative life of the race—show the gulf between their deepest motivations and convictions.

Freud was engaged in what Max Weber has called the disenchantment of the world (*die Entzauberung der Welt*). He saw it as a necessary step, for the individual and for humanity as a whole, in the development toward greater maturity and sanity, although he did not proclaim it as the end of all wisdom. He repudiated any mystical claims for the unconscious, or any claims that psychoanalysis was a consoling *Weltanschauung*. In fact, he rejected consolation. Jung, on his part, was in search of enchantment, a Holy Grail, a healing vision which could undo or compensate for the ills of the world, for all the ugliness, misery, and triviality of human life and human weakness.

Both men come alive in their letters as passionate and very

moving human beings. They loved each other for a time, although never without reservations. They could at times be direct and uncompromising in the exchanges of their feelings and views. At other times they were somewhat devious and politely accommodating in the interests of their own privacy and of maintaining their precariously balanced friendship, as well as for the sake of the common cause. In the end, the balance was utterly destroyed; pent-up feelings of mutual distrust and disillusionment erupted into open hostility and bitter accusations on both sides. Freud's coldly detached rage and carefully measured words were no less wounding than Jung's more direct and defiant, often vicious attacks and recriminations. In their late letters, both were in a fury, "hitting below the belt" in their analytic interpretations of each other's behavior, telling each other truths that ceased to be true as all caution was thrown to the winds and all proportion lost. As astute analytic observers they all too easily recognized each other's weaknesses, unconscious motives, defensive rationalizations—in the manner in which analyst-friends (or foes) may come to know each other, and sometimes analyst and patient if the analytic process goes deep enough. In such moments it may no longer be clear who is the patient and who the analyst.

Jung's merciless frankness in his last personal letters to Freud became cruel and disingenuous; his intention was not to enlighten Freud by the interpretations he offered, but to hurt and humiliate him. Jung's pride was hurt, and his self-esteem—apparently far more vulnerable than Freud's—was endangered and shaken by Freud's increasing disapproval of his views and of the direction of his interests and research. As Jung saw it, Freud's repeated protestations of fatherly concern were masking his growing withdrawal and disaffection. Jung came to see these expressions of Freud's continued interest in him as efforts similar to the attitude of a physician who has given up on his patient but wishes to be "kind." He chided Freud for treating his pupils like patients, that is, continuing to analyze them. At this distance it is difficult to assess that accusation. Freud denied it, but it stands to reason that Freud, as the father of psychoanalysis and for a time the only analyst, could hardly have been altogether immune to that temptation.

Jung, as the younger of the two, less experienced and less emotionally secure, understandably felt the need to insist on his independence, rather than remain the analysand or faithful son.

I also believe that as a man of a different generation, he was less fenced in by the particular scientific tradition of radical rationalism in which Freud had grown up. He had intimations of the positive, nonstupefying, creative side of religion that Freud did not have or did not wish to explore—whatever one may think of the ways in which Jung pursued and used them therapeutically. Freud, on the other hand, not only felt deeply hurt by what to him was his chosen son's and successor's disloyalty and betrayal. More objectively, he considered Jung's deviating theories and orientation—with much justification as the future would prove —as challenging and negating many of his own most profound and original discoveries and insights.

The correspondence, taken as a whole, has qualities of a poignant drama, at first joyful and in the end deeply disturbing, displaying some of the grandeur and the pettiness of human affairs and human passions. Two dedicated men, endowed with exceptional gifts, devoting their lives to the understanding of the unconscious, to the higher development of the mind and of their own and their patients' and students' emotional-intellectual life, came to a love–hate impasse that they could not resolve other than by complete and final disruption of their friendship. But—as the editor of the correspondence points out—neither was shattered by the experience, and "each derived creative values from the inevitable break."

Freud and Jung—Ferenczi should be included here—were the early explorers of transference. Did they know too much, and yet still too little, about transference? They could not leave each other alone at the right moment. They could not maintain a proper balance of closeness and distance—sustain the critical temperature, so to speak—that seems essential for preserving love and friendship. As originators of the exploration of transference and under the spell of its powerful forces, at the time of their relationship they appeared not yet able to distinguish clearly enough between an analytic and nonanalytic relationship, and between the requirements and proprieties of analysis and those of a teacher–student relationship in analytic training. Jung, in one of his last letters (338J, p. 534) accused Freud of just that, only to turn the tables by playing the analyst–father to Freud, with motivations no less suspect than those he blamed Freud for.

To this day there remains some blurring of the roles of psychoanalytic patient, apprentice of the art of psychoanalysis, and student of psychoanalytic science. This is not altogether to be ascribed to human error and inexperience, nor to neurotic tendencies in analyst, student, or patient. The vital originality and ambiguity of a new venture of the human spirit, such as psychoanalysis was and still is, defies a strict confinement within precise categories and compartments—be they science versus religion or art, education versus therapy, sanity versus madness. Despite Freud's strong disclaimer, I dare say that even the dividing line between priest or shaman and physician or investigator is less than neatly fixed in the case of psychoanalysis. This is not to deny the need for or the importance of such distinctions and the dangers of disregarding them and of fostering ambiguity. In the early days of psychoanalysis the division of labor between training analyst and psychoanalytic instructor or supervisor was not yet possible. Some of the early pioneers may have derived some benefit from that fact, but there is little doubt that few, if any, escaped its troublesome consequences.

Freud's "splendid isolation" came to an end with the growing recognition he found at the Burghölzli where Bleuler, Jung, Abraham, Binswanger, and some others, later well known in the psychoanalytic movement, worked in the early years of the century. From 1905 on Jung "took up the cudgels" for Freud in his writings and in presentations and discussions at psychiatric congresses. This is the brief and apt characterization that the editor of the *Correspondence*, William McGuire, gives of the course of their relationship:

the gradual warming of mutual regard, confidence, and affection, the continual interchange of professional information and opinions, the rapidly elaborating business of the psychoanalytic movement, the intimate give-and-take of family news, the often acerb and witty observations on colleagues and adversaries, and at length the emergence of differences, disagreements, misunderstandings, injured feelings, and finally disruption and separation (p. xix).

Only in one respect should this description be amended: Differences, if not disagreements, in theoretical views were already apparent in the very first letters they exchanged in October, 1906

(2J and 3F, p. 4). They refer to crucial matters—"delicate theoretical questions" as Jung put it—as the future was to show. It is the
centrality of sexuality in the genesis of neurosis and in the therapeutic transference that Jung, in his very first letter to Freud,
singled out as not easy for him to accept without reservations.
And Freud replied: "Your writings have long led me to suspect
that your appreciation of my psychology does not extend to all
my views on hysteria and the problem of sexuality, but I venture
to hope that in the course of the years you will come much closer
to me than you now think possible. . . . I continue to hope that this
aspect of my investigations will prove to be the most significant."
Speaking then of Aschaffenburg, an early critic, Freud continued:
"Like so many of our pundits, he is motivated chiefly by an in-
clination to repress sexuality, that troublesome factor so unwelcome in good society. Here we have two warring worlds and
soon it will be obvious to all[3] which is on the decline and which
on the ascendant" (p. 5n). He hoped "that all those who are able
to overcome their own inner resistance to the truth will wish to
count themselves among my followers and will cast off the last
vestiges of pusillanimity in their thinking" (p. 6)—a clear challenge to Jung. In subsequent letters each made some concessions
to the other's point of view but in essence maintained his own. At
the same time both were aware of the complexities of the issue of
sexuality as well as other issues related to it, such as the con-
fluences and differences of certain cases of hysteria and schizophrenia and the question of the psychogenesis of the latter.

One can detect Jung's influence as Freud broadened his concept of sexuality, especially in regard to the problems of psychosis
and "autoerotism." The latter term, during the time of their correspondence, still encompassed what Freud eventually called
narcissism. The concept of narcissistic libido (versus object
libido)—although the term was not yet used—was taking shape
in Freud's thinking. In a letter of May, 1907 (25F), correcting a
misunderstanding of Jung's, Freud made it very clear that in
dementia praecox, according to his view, the libido does not

3. The American translation omits the clause "*wer im Leben steht*," following
"obvious to all" in the German text. It might be translated as: "who live in the real world."
See German edition, p. 6.

withdraw from the real object to throw itself on a substitute fantasy object. This, he explained, would not be truly autoerotic (today we would say "not truly narcissistic") libido, since in that case the libido still has an object, albeit a fantasy object. Instead, in dementia praecox the libido withdraws from the object representation altogether; thus freed, it "would somehow manifest itself autoerotically as in childhood" (p. 46); i.e., it becomes narcissistic libido. The fundamental status of sexuality was saved (against the objections of Jung and Bleuler) by giving up the equation, sexuality = object libido, and Freud adumbrated the concept of primary narcissism. In a letter of the same period (April, 1907) entitled "A Few Theoretical Remarks on Paranoia," Freud explicitly stated: "The sexual instinct is originally auto-erotic, later on it lends affective cathexis, object love, to memory images."[4]

The two letters from which I quoted (22F, 25F) contain a remarkable discussion of projection. They also discuss the difference between perceptions of external reality, characterized mainly by "quality," and experiences from within (sensations, Empfindungen), which are instinct manifestations characterized mainly by "quantity" (affective cathexis), and finally the various vicissitudes of these exogenous and endogenous experiences under the influence of repression in neurosis and psychosis.

The crucial importance to Freud of sexuality and therefore of the libido theory has some aspects that are not sufficiently appreciated today. Here I shall single out only that aspect which is especially relevant to his controversy with Jung. Freud's insist-

---

4. The sentence reads as follows in German: "*Der Sexualtrieb ist ursprünglich auto-erotisch, später erteilt er den Erinnerungsvorstellungen von Objekten Affektbesetzung, Objektliebe.*" The translation omits "*von Objekten*" and should read: ". . . to memory images of objects." "*Vorstellung*" is here translated as "image." The usual translation is idea, presentation, or representation. It should be noted that the two sentences following the above quotation contain an error—due to erroneous transcription from the German manuscript—that was discovered too late to be corrected in the American edition (see, German edition, p. 42, n.2a). In the American edition the sentences read: "A wish fantasy such as that presupposed above is to be regarded as a libidinal object-cathexis, because it must be subjected to repression before it becomes conscious. This can occur in various ways . . ." (American edition, p. 39). This clearly does not make sense. The text should read: "A wish fantasy such as that presupposed above is to be regarded as a libidinal object-cathexis; *if it can be subjected to repression before it becomes conscious,* this may occur in various ways . . ."

ence on the centrality of sexuality vis-à-vis Jung was in good part a fight against the religiously and theologically tinged, moralistic separation of and opposition between the sacred and the profane, between earthly body and sexual lust versus heavenly spirit and divine love or, in more secularized terms, between instinctual life and spiritual life. It was a fight against what Freud saw as a religious or philosophical escapism in the face of the human condition. In terms of the development of civilization, especially in the form of the Judeo-Christian tradition, this dichotomy was seen by him as the expression of a defensive-repressive movement against the bodily-instinctual nature of man, which in its excesses had led to the hypocritical cultural norms and to the neurotic misery he saw in his consulting room and elsewhere. Jung quoted Freud as saying to him: "My dear Jung, promise me never to abandon the sexual theory. That is the most essential thing of all. You see, we must make a dogma of it, an unshakable bulwark." The bulwark was to be erected "against the black tide of mud . . . of occultism." What Freud, according to Jung, meant by occultism was "virtually everything that philosophy and religion, including the rising contemporary science of parapsychology, had learned about the psyche" (*Memories*, p. 150).

In Jung's view, sexuality for Freud "took over the role of a *deus absconditus,* a hidden or concealed god." "The lost god had now to be sought below, not above." (Compare this with Freud's motto for *The Interpretation of Dreams: Flectere si nequeo superos, Acheronta movebo.*) Jung continued: "The problem still remains: how to overcome or escape our anxiety, bad conscience, guilt, compulsion, unconsciousness, and instinctuality" (*Memories*, pp. 151–52). Later, in the same chapter on Freud, Jung speaks of his own quest for the Holy Grail, "of the world of the Knights of the Grail and their quest—for that was, in the deepest sense, my own world, which had scarcely anything to do with Freud's. My whole being was seeking something still unknown which might confer meaning upon the banality of life" (p. 165). It is precisely this quest, this wish to escape instinctuality by seeking something unknown to confer meaning upon the banality of life, that Freud was compelled to combat.

In reflecting later on Freud's quest, Jung came to feel that Freud basically "wanted to teach . . . that, regarded from within, sexuality included spirituality or had an intrinsic meaning.[5] But his concretistic terminology was too narrow to express this idea. He gave me the impression that at bottom he was working against his own goal and against himself . . ." (p. 152). Jung was strongly impressed by "the fact that Freud was emotionally involved in his sexual theory to an extraordinary degree. When he spoke of it, his tone became urgent, almost anxious, and all signs of his normally critical and skeptical manner vanished. A strange, deeply moved expression came over his face, the cause of which I was at a loss to understand. I had a strong intuition that for him sexuality was a sort of *numinosum*"[6] (p. 150).

I have quoted rather extensively from Jung's memoirs here because these sentences vividly illustrate the different ideological attitudes and commitments of the two men. But one cannot simply dismiss Jung's impressions and "intuitions" in regard to Freud's deep concern with sexuality as nothing more than expressions of Jung's own preoccupations and inclinations, granted that they colored his perceptions.

Freud *did* attempt to develop, as it were, spirituality out of the biological-archaic roots of man's existence. And he went much further in this direction in the years after the break with Jung. How else can we truly understand his increasing concern with primary narcissism and primary masochism, with the problem of internalization, and with death, guilt, conscience, and cultural development? How else can we account for the emergence of the superego concept, for the structural theory, for his conception of ego development ("where id was, there ego shall be") and the concept of sublimation; finally, for the last instinct theory in which Eros and Thanatos become, in Jung's terminology, numinous powers? It is precisely for that reason that the majority of psychoanalysts part company with Freud when it comes to his "unscientific" conception of the life and death instincts, uncomfortably aware that with these concepts

5. The German text reads: ". . . dass . . . *Sexualität auch Geistigkeit umfasse, oder Sinn enthalte.*" A more correct translation would be: "sexuality encompassed spirituality or contains meaning."

6. *Numinosum*: term "for the inexpressible, mysterious, terrifying, directly experienced, and pertaining only to the divinity" (*Memories*, p. 385). It contains the idea of the sacred, including its awe-inspiring quality. Jung borrowed the term from Rudolf Otto, a German scholar of the philosophy of religion who wrote a book titled *The Idea of the Holy* in the twenties.

he explicitly oversteps the boundaries of positivistic or rationalistic biology and psychology and postulates powers that are
both overreaching and immanent in man as finite being.

Jung, a man of a younger generation, was less confined by the
positivist philosophy that constricted the idea of science and its
very scope during the period of Freud's scientific training. He
found it easier to recognize that by the very fact of positing the
unconscious as a subject for scientific research, psychoanalysis
as a new science implicitly eroded the boundaries of positivist
science. He also did not share Freud's rationalistic prejudice
against religion.

Still, what Jung labeled Freud's concretistic terminology and
personalistic view of the unconscious manifests Freud's awareness that authentic transcendental experiences and insights
("spirituality") are anchored in the individual's personal life
history and its instinctual roots. Psychoanalysis, I believe, shares
with modern existentialism the tenet that superpersonal and
transcendental aspects of human existence and of unconscious
and instinctual life (so much stressed by Jung) can be experienced and integrated convincingly—without escapist embellish-
ments, otherworldly consolations and going off into the clouds—
only in the concreteness of one's own personal life, including the
ugliness, trivialities, and sham that go with it. It would seem that
Jungian psychology and psychotherapy jump all too readily
from the here-and-now of individual life, from concrete personal
experience, to the collective unconscious, myth, archetypes, re-
ligiosity, and "spirituality"—as refuge and healing visions to
cling to, leading easily to evasions and hypocrisy instead of to
genuine transcendence or, in psychoanalytic terminology, to
sublimation and true ego expansion.

Included in the volume are seven letters from Jung's wife to
Freud, four of which, written in the fall of 1911, are among the
most moving letters in this collection (pp. 452–53, 455–57, 462–
63, 467). In them Emma Jung gave voice to her growing concern
about the beginning estrangement between the two men. Unfor-
tunately, Freud's replies are not available. Mrs. Jung showed
herself to be a most perceptive and sympathetic observer of their
conflicts. As a woman—wife, mother, in a daughter relation to
Freud, and troubled by her own feminine conflicts—and as one

not directly involved in the men's struggles, she had a perspective on the situation, inspired by her love for both of them, which was not granted to the men themselves. She also had the courage to overcome much timidity and self-doubt, in order to confront Freud with some of his own defenses and countertransference problems in a manner much in contrast to Jung's later defiant attacks and accusations. Judging from the allusions to Freud's replies in her letters and from some brief quotes from the replies, Freud apparently was more eager to analyze her motives for writing what she did and to reject observations she made than he was to take them to heart, or at least to let her know if he did so. A few remarks of hers concerning his family life—in response to things he had told her in a personal conversation—have the ring of truth. One can read between the lines that Freud had difficulty in hearing such truths from her. He clearly misinterpreted, out of anger, some of her comments about the father–son relationship (see letter of November 14, 1911, pp. 462–63). However, in a few letters to Jung himself during that period, there are indications that Freud kept some of her ideas in mind. But it seems to me that he adhered to the letter rather than to the spirit of what she had written.

The translation is probably as good as any translation can be when personal style of the original counts for so much. A certain stiffness of expression, absent to an admirable degree in both letter writers, unavoidably creeps in. Something of the spontaneity and personal flavor, the wit, the warmth mixed with reserve, the sharp or overly formal tone in the late letters, gets lost in translation. Occasionally there are inaccuracies that could have been avoided. For example, there are two in Emma Jung's letters: the German *erfreut* should have been translated as *pleased*, not *overjoyed* (German edition, p. 504, next to last paragraph; American edition, p. 456, last paragraph). Mrs. Jung was not given to hyperbole. *Verkappte Huldigung* is not a "*blessing in disguise*"; *Huldigung* means *homage* (German edition, p. 512, end of letter; American edition, p. 463). I have mentioned earlier the translation of *Vorstellung* as *image*. This is not necessarily inaccurate, but it is at variance with the standard translation as *idea, presentation,* or *representation,* and tends to be confusing for that reason. These, however, are minor points that do not detract from the general excellence of the American edition which in many ways is a model of thoughtful and meticulous editorship. The same goes for the German edition. William McGuire's introduction, printed in both editions, is a superb, balanced account of the complex vicissitudes and negotiations that made this invaluable document available at this time rather than many years hence.

In my opinion, all of us who care about psychoanalysis and the history of the psychoanalytic movement are greatly indebted to Freud's and Jung's surviving children for permitting and encouraging the publication of the *Correspondence* at the present time, despite Jung's own misgivings and vacillations about it before his death. It is safe to assume that Freud would not have approved its publication, reticent as he was about his own personal life and his personal relations with others. To him, what belonged in the public domain was his work, and that is as it should be. For those coming after him and living in a world so greatly influenced by his work, it is a different matter.

INDEX

Day residue, 44, 144, 247, 249

Deaggressivization, 51, 272

Death, 260

Death instinct, 60, 61, 62, 63, 65, 66, 68, 72, 79, 122, 123–24, 141, 265; motivating power of, 80; origin of, 322; prevalence of, in psychic life, 316–17, 320, 324; rejected by psychoanalysts, 415–16

Dedifferentiation, 48, 167, 293, 379

Defense, 16, 21, 33, 34, 113, 143, 266, 307, 363, 377; basis of, 23–24; concept, 106, 107, 176–77; defined, 176; ego-organization and, 174–77; and motivation, 108–10; and neurotic interpretation of reality, 21–32; organization of psychic apparatus understood in terms of, 27–28; presupposes possibility of psychological response to traumatic experience, 34; and primary-process mentation, 184; regression in, 24–25, 26–27; repression as, 73–80; as resistance, 312; against stimuli, 28n6; sublimation as, 391; successful, 305–06; synthetic function of ego as, 3, 4, 8

Defense mechanisms, 24–25, 26–27, 175, 177, 253

Deferred action (concept), 35n1

Déjà vu, 139

Dementia praecox, 412–13

Dependency, prolonged, 23, 27

Depersonalization, 142

Depression, 263, 317, 321

Deprivation, 160–63, 263–64, 274

Derealization, 142

Derepression, 36, 170

Descendant, 389

Desexualization, 51, 78, 258, 272, 331, 335, 385

Destiny, 91–92

Desublimation, 335, 339

Determinism, 140

Development, 25, 80–82, 89, 139, 273, 306–07; early, 25–26, 44, 210, 237–44, 293, 357, 359, 398–404. *See also* Psychic development

Differential, 239, 240, 253

Differentiation, 16, 17, 152–53, 164, 168, 187–88, 191, 211, 236; ego/object, 213–15, 216, 246, 258; id/ego, 209; of instincts and objects, 129, 131, 136; in mother-child unit, 208; of object and narcissistic

cathexes, 153, 154, 157, 164, 175, 212; past/present, 359; between patient and analyst, 283–84; progressive, of ego, 272; self/object, 174, 175, 376, 377, 378, 379, 386; subject/object, 160, 164, 166, 209, 211–12, 235, 291, 342, 343–44, 350; of undifferentiated state, 266; of word-from thing-presentations, 190–91

Discharge, 79, 80, 292

Discrepancies, 23, 24, 27, 29

Disillusionment, 269

Displacement, 168, 184, 190, 248

"Diver, The" (Schiller) (poem), 9n5

Drama, psychoanalysis as, 353–60, 361–63

Dreams, 44, 66, 140, 144, 184, 247, 248, 249

Dream thought, latent, 170

Dual instinct theory, 123, 126, 315, 317–18, 322. *See also* Eros; Thanatos

Duality of secondary process, 168, 196, 275

Ecstatic states, 68, 81, 141–42, 168

Ego, 19, 122, 135–36, 167, 209, 212, 214–15, 223, 236; danger to, 14, 23, 213–14, 215; defense and, 8, 12, 74–75, 78; defined, 171, 210; differentiation of, 152–53, 272, 274; disintegration of, 223; global, 349, 351; and external reality, 232; Freud's conception of, 3–4; future, 45–46, 47, 50, 51, 52; genesis of, 4–5, 6–8, 12, 16–18, 19–20, 209, 211–12; healthy, 336, 340, 363; id becomes, through transference, 250; immature, 37, 42, 348; intact, 342; libido in, 244, 245; loss of, 16–17; masochistic surrender of, to id, 67–68; mature, 3, 6, 20, 37, 38, 67; observing, of patient, 96, 228, 279, 354; as organization, 12, 44, 48, 90, 92, 93, 169, 171, 175; post-oedipal, 8, 16; pre-oedipal, 321, 324; primary, 6, 9; primary autonomy of, 81, 110, 209; primitive, 18; as psychic structure, 110–12; psychodynamics of, 231; in re-creative repetition, 94–95; regression in service of, 82, 293; regression of, 26, 112–13, 224–25; related to psychic present, 45; relation of the repressed to, 78; relation with reality, 3–20, 194; relation with superego, 48, 49–50, 51–52, 271–73, 275; relevance of reality principle to, 59–60; secondary autonomy of, 264; and secondary process, 168, 178; strong, 241; syn-

Memorial systems, 166–69, 170
Memories, 88, 92, 99, 159, 166, 169
Memories, Dreams, Reflections (Jung), 405, 414–15
Memory, 35–36, 37, 41, 94, 138, 145–46, 368; defined, 149; as ego function, 209–10; of experience of satisfaction, 63–64; genesis of, 154, 163–64; and mourning, 170–71; and perception, 154–56, 157–59, 164, 166; perspectives on, 148–73; as recollection, 44, 364
Memory development, 160–63
Memory images, 201–02
Memory theory, 157–59
Memory traces, 44, 94, 145, 151, 156–57, 181–82, 185; and repression, 34, 36, 37, 38
Mental acts, 197–98, 248
Mental functioning, 58–68, 188–89
Mental life, 84, 138, 145–46, 252, 253, 377–78
Mental processes, 115–19, 150–51, 164, 168, 199. *See also* Primary process; Secondary process; Unconscious mental processes
Mental representations, 351, 364
Mentality, primitive, 402
Mentation, 169, 215, 216, 217–18, 380–81
Merging, 402
Metapsychology, 79, 148n, 166, 191–99, 299, 376
Mind, 57, 119–20, 121, 123, 149–50, 293, 351, 401; "connection with the body," 118
Mirror, analyst as, 223, 225, 227, 232, 239
Mirror transference, 344, 345–46, 350, 351
Mirroring, parent/child, 168
Mnemic images, 130, 131, 151, 156–57
Monotheism, 104
Morality, 320, 393, 396
Moral standards, 29, 95
Mother, 9, 13–14, 15–16, 131, 134
Mother-child unit, 6, 7, 11, 17, 134n20, 164, 167, 290, 378, 386; archaic mental functioning in, 215; differentiation in, 208, 211; disturbances in, 212; and early psychic development, 321–22, 324; empathic quality of, 19; instinctual drives are processes within, 291–92; interaction in, 237; language in, 180, 185, 187, 197, 203; as model for analysis, 239; and origin of

instincts, 128, 129, 152; similarities of, to psychoanalytic situation, 283, 284; tension system between, 12–14, 15–16
Motivation, 102–37, 140, 152–54, 162–63, 210, 319; becomes personalized, 112
Motivational forces, hierarchy of, 320–21
Motives, 131
Motor images, 130, 159
Mourning, 51, 148, 150, 160, 170–71, 257–76, 329, 390; work of, 77, 83, 95, 266, 274, 329–30, 331–32, 333–34, 335–36, 337
Mystics, 100, 141
"Mystic Writing Pad," 150, 151, 186
Myth, 146

Nadir (concept), 142n2
Names, 190, 202
Narcissism, 57, 69, 109, 128–29, 289, 299, 334n3, 343, 349–50, 386, 412; Hartmann on, 196n11; Freud's essay on, 5; Kohut's concept, 346–47, 349; mature, 350; in moral masochists, 319; in object relationships, 82
Narcissism, primary. *See* Primary narcissism
Narcissistic cathexis, 71, 76–77, 153, 154, 157, 163–64, 194, 195, 257–58, 343; differentiation of, from object cathexis, 153, 154, 157, 164, 175, 212; and genesis of memory, 154, 163–64; founded on primary narcissism, 264–65; transformation of object cathexis into, 244, 245–46, 247, 248, 250, 252, 254, 266, 267, 331, 334, 393
Narcissistic libido (concept), 154, 164, 412–13
Narcissistic neuroses, 21, 244, 245–46, 386
Narcissistic perfection, 268–69, 270
Narcissistic personality disorders, 176, 212–13, 214, 215, 342–51, 377, 399, 403
Narcissistic recathexis, 267, 329
Narcissistic transference, 217, 343, 344, 348, 379
Narrative (history), 364–66, 368
Need, 116, 129n15, 237, 263–64
"Negation," 186
Negative therapeutic reaction, 315–25
Neonate, 5, 130–32, 133–34. *See also* Infant
Nervous system, 27–28n6, 28, 62n3, 116, 118, 233–34, 236
Neurone system, 28n6

Neurosis, 25n4, 26, 44, 89, 184, 224, 247,
402, 403; cause of, 22, 23, 24, 26–27, 29;
classical, 231; concept, 304–08; experi-
ential meaning of word, 311–12; Oedi-
pus complex, nucleus of, 378. See also
Character neurosis; Infantile neurosis
Neutralization, 51, 78, 331, 339, 340
Nietzsche, Friedrich W., 71–72, 264n1, 318;
The Genealogy of Morals, 71, 318
Nirvana principle, 27, 62–63, 74, 79, 80
Normality, 400–01, 403
Normal mechanisms, 40
Norms, 29, 414
Nostalgia, 140
Nunc stans, 141, 142

Object, 5, 81, 128, 153–54, 212, 214–15, 344,
350, 351
Object boundaries, 246, 270
Object cathexis, 76–77, 181, 194, 195, 257–
58, 343, 350, 376; differentiation of, from
narcissistic, 153, 154, 157, 164, 175, 212;
transformation of infantile, 244, 245–46,
247, 248, 250, 252, 254, 266, 267, 331, 334,
393
Object choice, 199, 212, 390
Object constancy, 139, 144
Object libido, 10, 329
Object love, 349, 350
Object presentation, 44, 76
Object relations, 51, 65, 69, 70, 140, 175,
349, 350; defined, 296; dissolution of,
167; early, 81–83; and ego formation,
221; elements of libidinal-aggressive
cathexes in, 82–83; fantasy, 337; incestuous, 396, 402; infantile, 76–77; internalization of, 83–84, 335–36; mature,
230, 372, 394; new, 225, 226, 227, 229;
non-incestuous, 390; oedipal, 76–77; and
psychic structure formation, 207–18;
and psychoanalytic method, 284–85; in
psychoanalytic theory, 236; role of, 57,
80; term, 212, 214–15; transference and,
244, 245–46, 247, 248, 250, 252, 254
Object relations theory, 126–27, 386
Object representation, 44, 351
Object structuralization, 24
Object-ties, 80, 175, 299, 321, 350
Object withdrawal, 160–63
Objectivity, 16, 130, 146, 277, 279, 402; of

analyst, 223, 225, 226–27, 228, 229, 287,
309, 360–61, 373
Objects, 6, 11, 127, 167, 257–58, 267, 270,
343, 345; instinctual drives and, 232–37;
relation of instincts to, 115, 124–36
Obscene words, 201, 202
"Observing ego" (of patient), 96, 228, 279,
354
Obsessional neurosis, 26
Obsessions, 248
Obsessive character, 26
Obsessive character neurosis, 30
Obsessive-compulsive character, 144,
355–56
"Oceanic" feeling, 7, 142, 168
Occultism, 408, 414
Oedipal identifications, 264, 265
Oedipal introjects, 48
Oedipal objects, 266
Oedipal phase, 311
Oedipus complex, 7, 12, 14, 48, 259; and
analysis of ego, 216, 217; changing perspectives on, 404; components in, 15–16;
consolidation of ego organization in,
224; destruction of, 75–78, 176, 374, 384–
85, 387n1; dissolution of, 90; failure to
resolve, 262; formation of, 15; incest
and, 397–98; nucleus of neurosis, 25,
357, 378; primary identification contained in, 399; prototype of universal
conflict, 25; reactivated in termination
phase of analysis, 328–30, 334–36, 340–
41, 376–77; as re-enactment of early
psychic development, 358–59; repeated in
puberty, 89; repeated throughout life, 90,
386; repression of, 25, 75–76, 176; resolution of, 47, 49, 51, 83, 84, 160, 266–68, 274,
326–27, 328, 329, 332, 333–34, 335–36,
337, 339, 340, 386, 390, 392; superego
heir of, 257, 270, 274; waning of, 384–404
Oedipus Rex, 358
Oedipus situation, 6, 28, 263, 290–91, 369–
71
Olinick, S. L., 321
Omnipotence, 18n13, 19, 66, 168, 319
Oneness, 196. See also Unity
On Human Symbiosis and the Vicissitudes of Individuation (Mahler), 213
"On Obscene Words" (Ferenczi), 201
Oral aggression, 263